AGRICULTURE
AND STRUCTURAL TRANSFORMATION

ECONOMIC DEVELOPMENT SERIES

General Editor
Gerald M. Meier, Professor of International Economics,
Stanford University

Published
FINANCIAL DEEPENING IN ECONOMIC DEVELOPMENT
   Edward S. Shaw

HUMAN RESOURCES AS THE WEALTH OF NATIONS
   Frederick H. Harbison

ECONOMIC THEORY AND THE UNDERDEVELOPED WORLD
   H. Myint

AGRICULTURE AND STRUCTURAL TRANSFORMATION

Economic Strategies in Late-Developing Countries

BRUCE F. JOHNSTON
Food Research Institute
Stanford University

and

PETER KILBY
Wesleyan University

New York
OXFORD UNIVERSITY PRESS
London   1975   Toronto

Copyright © 1975 by Oxford University Press, Inc.
Library of Congress Catalogue Card Number: 74-22880
Printed in the United States of America

To Rosamond H. Peirce

Introduction to the Economic Development Series

Two centuries ago it all began with *The Wealth of Nations;* today it is called the Poverty of Nations. If economics has always been asked to propose means of social betterment, and if economists are, as Lord Keynes suggested, the trustees of the possibility of civilization —then the problems of world poverty will persistently challenge each generation of economists. But what is new for this generation is the concentrated effort by so many countries to undertake conscious programs of economic development. With the heightened awareness of world inequalities, development policies have been deliberately adopted on a national basis and supported by international institutions.

The time has come for a reappraisal of this experience. This Economic Development Series has therefore been designed to take a hard look at the central problems and strategic policy issues that have emerged to the forefront of development efforts. Recognizing that it has become impossible and undesirable for any one author to attempt to cover the entire subject of economic development, this series concentrates on a set of special problems analyzed by authors who are widely recognized authorities in their respective fields and who have had extensive experience in the developing countries. Each volume offers an incisive study of a specific problem area that now requires more understanding by students and practitioners of development alike. The treatment emphasizes both experience and theory.

Taken together, the volumes in this Series formulate a number of policies that may be better designed to cope with some of the most troublesome problems of development.

G. M. MEIER

Acknowledgements

This book is the final product of an enterprise that has stretched over some five years. During this period we have accumulated many debts, both intellectual and financial.

The authors have benefited from generous material support from a number of sources. The initial exploratory trip to Asia in the autumn of 1969 was made possible by a Director's Grant from the Rockefeller Foundation. Since 1970 a major project grant by the Ford Foundation for the study of rural development and structural transformation has funded summer salaries, travel, and other expenses for ourselves and our collaborator, William J. Chancellor. Not only has the Ford Foundation been our principal financial benefactor, but its field offices in India and Pakistan supplied us with invaluable administrative and logistical support for field investigations in those countries. In Taiwan extensive assistance in field research was given to us by the Joint Commission on Rural Reconstruction. Supplementary support for various periods of "writing up" has been extended by the OECD Development Center in Paris, the Social Science Research Committee of Wesleyan University, and the Technology and Development Institute of the East-West Center in Honolulu. To all these institutions we express our deepest gratitude.

Our intellectual debts are no less numerous. Whatever success we have had in obtaining a greater purchase on the subject of farm equipment—its precise relationship to technical change in agriculture, the scope for adaptive research, linkages on the supply side with factor proportions, and technological advance in the capital goods industry—much of it is owed to the third partner and our fellow traveler in the Ford Foundation project, Professor William J. Chancellor of the Department of Agricultural Engineering of the University of California at Davis. His technical knowledge and powers of observation were a resource the likes of which few economists are privileged to exploit. Other agricultural engineers who assisted in our education were Roy Harrington, John Balis, T. S. Peng, Roland Heath, and M. L. Taneja.

The second technical area outside of our discipline we felt compelled to explore was fertilizer technology, including the construction and operation of nitrogen plants in Asia. Here we acknowledge, without implicating, the aid and counsel of Raymond Ewell, Clark Kingery, David Woody, Victor Henny, David Bell, Chauncey Dewey, James Lee, and N. A. Perwaze.

Many individuals in Taiwan, India, and Pakistan freely gave of their extensive knowledge of agricultural matters and in other ways contributed to the success of our research. Among these we would like to single out for special thanks T. H. Shen, T. H. Lee, W. C. Lai, Charles Kao, Bob Edwards, Jerry Eckert, Muhammad Naseem, James Boulware, Wolf Ladejinsky, Martin Billings, Arjan Singh, Wayne Freeman, P. D. Malgavkar, S. S. Johl and P. Subba Rao.

This book and an earlier OECD monograph have been much improved as the result of critical manuscript reading by our colleagues. Parts of the manuscript were read by John Cownie, Guy Hunter, William O. Jones, Carl Gotsch, Scott Pearson, Clark Reynolds, Vernon Ruttan, Raj Krishna, and Stanley Lebergott. The entire manuscript was read by Walter Falcon, Kazushi Ohkawa, G. M. Meier, and Tony Killick. We also received significant help from a number of Food Research Institute graduate students. Erik van Lent, Yoshimi Kuroda, Peter Warr, Bernard Pillet, Victor Horcasitas, and Bill Kinsey assembled data, edited and criticized our exposition.

At Wesleyan, Joan Halberg and Linda Kazimir typed numerous drafts of those chapters produced in Connecticut.

We owe a special debt to Minnie Jurow who assisted us in count-

ACKNOWLEDGEMENTS

less ways throughout this joint effort. Mrs. Jurow not only typed many drafts of the text and prepared the name index, she also cheerfully and competently attended to all the administrative details of this project over its five year life.

Rosamond H. Peirce along with Catherine Whittemore developed many of the tables that appear in this book and verified the correspondence between assertion and datum. As in the past, she has saved us from error and, by her skillful work, has improved the quality of our product. It gives us much pleasure to dedicate this book to Miss Peirce, on the occasion of her retirement, as an indication of our gratitude for her many years of extraordinarily competent and selfless work as the Food Research Institute's Associate Statistician.

Contents

	Prologue	xv
1	Agriculture in a Traditional Economy	3
2	Structural Transformation	34
3	On Being Late: The Technology Backlog	76
4	The Design of an Agricultural Strategy	127
5	Historical Patterns: England, The United States, and Japan	182
6	Agriculture's Role in Three Latecomers: Taiwan, Mexico, and the Soviet Union	240
7	Agriculture–Industry Interactions	299
8	Backward Linkages: Fertilizer and Farm Equipment	328
9	The Catching-Up Process	389
10	Intercountry Variations and the Choice of Strategy	437
	Appendices	455
	Subject Index	463
	Name Index	469

Prologue

This book goes to press as the World Food Conference in Rome is adjourning. Soaring food prices, bad weather, and shortfalls in farm output hold the attention of citizens of every country. For underdeveloped nations the immediate issue is whether existing world food supplies can be directed to those localities where starvation is imminent. Concern has shifted for the moment from that of raising per capita farm output in low-income countries to simply maintaining an even balance between increases in food production and population growth. While some of the discussion in later chapters bears on this immediate issue, our analysis is directed at those longer-term alterations in economic structure which will, among their other consequences, transform the relationship between agricultural productivity and population increase so as to permanently banish the Malthusian spectre.

The most distinctive feature of this joint effort by an agricultural economist and an industrial economist is its focus on the reciprocal interactions between agricultural development and the expansion of manufacturing and other nonfarm sectors. There is now widespread recognition that poverty is a distressingly persistent problem in the world's less-developed countries and that in large measure it is a problem of rural poverty. Earlier views that rapid industrialization would soon transform the structure of these countries and provide alternative employment so as to reduce the size of the agricultural work force have been discredited by the events of the past twenty-five years. Perhaps as much as two-thirds of the world's population are citizens of countries that are characterized by acute and pervasive poverty and also by an economic structure in which agriculture still provides some 50 to 80 per cent of the labor force with work and income.

We have attempted to explore systematically the ramifications of three conditioning factors which we believe are fundamental to an understanding of the process of structural transformation in these late-developing countries. The first of these conditioning factors is the simple fact of being late. The principal consequence of being late is the enormous technological backlog that a developing country can draw upon. Freed of the necessity to invest the time and resources that are required to produce useful knowledge, very rapid economic growth becomes a possibility. But technology is a double-edged sword. The dramatic lowering of the death rate that has followed the instigation of modern public health measures has led to a rapid expansion of the population which in many countries threatens to undermine gains in per capita output. Moreover, the large number of choices that exist for raising productivity in agriculture and industry is a mixed blessing because of the strong possibility that the particular technology that is borrowed will prove ill-suited to the resource endowment of low-income countries. The likelihood of inappropriate technology transfer is heightened, on the one hand, by the capital-intensive form in which new techniques are embodied in the technology-exporting countries and, on the other, by the distorted price signals that guide decision-makers in the borrowing countries. To draw maximum advantage from the technology backlog while avoiding its pitfalls is one of the most demanding tasks that a successful development strategy must fulfill.

Our second theme is that the development of agriculture can only be fully understood in the context of the interdependence between agriculture and the other sectors of the economy. The two facets of this interdependence which have received most attention are the need (i) to transfer investible resources from agriculture to the faster growing nonfarm sectors and (ii) to maintain a rate of farm productivity advance consistent with constant or falling urban consumer food prices. There are, however, other aspects of sectoral interdependence which are no less vital for the achievement of sustained economic growth. We emphasize three additional aspects: rates of labor transfer between sectors, the level of commodity flows, and the composition of those commodity flows.

It is now fifteen years since Folke Dovring pointed out that the size of agriculture relative to the rest of the economy imposes a ceiling on the rate at which workers can be shifted to nonfarm occupations. This effect of the sheer weight of agriculture is reinforced by the rapid rate of growth of the population of working age which compounds the difficulty of altering the occupational composition of the labor force and other structural characteristics of a late-developing country. Thus, in a predominantly agrarian economy, even with very rapid growth in the industrial and service sectors, the proportionate size of the agricultural labor force will fall only slowly; and for many years—in some cases many decades—the absolute size of the farm labor force will grow. These structural-demographic characteristics obviously have powerful implications for the design of an efficient agricultural strategy.

A second and unnoticed corollary of the relatively small size of the nonfarm sectors is that the volume of intersectoral commodity flows is also subject to a ceiling that can only be raised as the weight of the agricultural population in the total is reduced. This constraint on the volume of intersectoral commodity flows, which is examined in some detail in Chapter 2, arises because the urban population dependent on purchased food is so small relative to the number of farm households. With agricultural sales thus limited, the farm sector's demand for manufactured consumer goods and purchased inputs such as fertilizer and farm equipment is subject to a purchasing-power constraint of equal magnitude. (This sales-purchase limitation is less binding for small countries with buoyant export markets.) The existence of this farm purchasing-power constraint has far-reaching implications. In particular, it means that the nature and time sequence of innovations will determine the proportion of farm producers who are able to participate in the process of agricultural modernization.

The final conditioning factor that we emphasize concerns the effects of the size distribution of operational holdings and the type of agricultural technologies adopted on the pattern of rural development. Although the *average* farm unit in an underdeveloped economy is inevitably small, there is great variation in the dispersion of farm size around the mean as is shown by the comparative data presented in Chapter 1. The more unequal the size distribution the more concentrated are commercial farm sales in a subsector of atypically large and capital-intensive farm units. The degree to which a farmer participates in commercial sales is a critical factor determining the extent to which he is able to transform his traditional technology by purchasing modern inputs. By shaping the pattern of agricultural modernization and the distribution of rural income, the farm size distribution is the principal determinant of the composition of intersectoral commodity flows. The type of farm inputs and consumer goods purchased by a large-scale mechanized farm household is very different from that purchased by a small commercial peasant farmer and his family. Hence, as analyzed at length in Chapter 7, differences in farm size distribution have a significant impact on the pattern of industrial development.

Much of our analysis is concerned directly and indirectly with those policy variables that determine the pattern of operational holdings. Is agricultural research oriented toward the development of divisible innovations—innovations that can be used efficiently by small-scale units so as to complement rather than displace the nation's relatively abundant resources of labor? Are farmer-training programs directed toward fostering widespread adoption of innovations? Does the design of public irrigation facilities and the layout of the road network tend to favor large-scale farmers over peasant cultivators? Is research and development activity in agricultural engineering concentrated on tractor-related equipment or on improved bullock-powered equipment and other items that are suited to the needs of small-scale farmers subject to a severe purchasing power constraint? Is the rationing of scarce inputs handled by means of market-clearing prices which give all producers equal access, or are

PROLOGUE   xix

they rationed out administratively in such a way that individuals with influence and wealth have privileged access? Do land rental ceilings, designed to aid the tenant, have the effect of encouraging the landlord to evict his tenants and engage in direct cultivation of a large operational unit on a mechanized basis?

The progressive modernization of millions of small-scale farmers is clearly a formidable task. The task is often rendered more difficult because of the strength of political forces that favor a dualistic pattern of development. Furthermore, the issues are often confused by emphasis on the frequently misleading dichotomy between "efficiency" and "equity." On the one hand, proponents of a dualistic pattern of agricultural development often claim that only large farm units can achieve the efficiency required for rapid expansion of output. Such a view ignores the structural-demographic characteristics of a late-developing country that constrain the *sectorwide* expansion in the use of "external inputs," that is, fertilizers, farm machinery, and other items produced by firms outside the agricultural sector. It is our contention that a choice and sequence of innovations that is compatible with the progressive modernization of a large and increasing fraction of a country's small farmers has important economic as well as social advantages. A "unimodal" strategy designed to raise the productivity of a large and increasing fraction of a nation's farm units is an effective means of fostering rapid economic growth and structural transformation while simultaneously contributing to the social goals of expanding employment opportunities and reducing inequalities in income distribution.

On the other hand, it is often asserted that a "bimodal" pattern of agricultural development, where a subsector of large farm units accounts for a major part of a country's agricultural production, is inevitable in the absence of land reform that drastically modifies the distribution of land ownership.[1] Although redistributive land reform

---

[1] As explained in Chapters 1 and 4, we use the terms "unimodal" and "bimodal" as shorthand expressions to describe contrasting strategies of agricultural development according to the pattern of rural development that they promote.

is likely to make a positive contribution to both the economic and social goals of development, we reject the view that it represents an indispensable prerequisite for a "unimodal" strategy aimed at the progressive modernization of the entire agricultural sector. There may be special circumstances, especially in parts of Latin America, which justify that view. But basically it is the size distribution of *operational* units that is of decisive importance. Consequently, the analysis of factors that determine the pattern of agricultural development presented in Chapter 4 includes a careful examination of the advantages and disadvantages of rental arrangements that permit a "unimodal" pattern of operational units even though the ownership of agricultural land is highly skewed. More generally, we suggest that it is essential to consider the complex interactions between a country's agrarian structure and institutions, the nature of the new technologies that become available and are adopted, and the growth of new economic opportunities outside agriculture. These interlinked changes are of critical importance in determining whether the growth of demand for labor, including improved income-earning opportunities for owner-cultivators and tenants, expands rapidly enough to ensure a healthy rate of increase in the return to labor as rising productivity leads to increased output in agriculture and in other sectors.

These propositions raise issues that are both complex and controversial. They cannot be resolved on the basis of a priori reasoning alone. Our conclusions have in fact been influenced by historical evidence concerning agriculture's role in the development process. In Chapters 5 and 6 we review the experience of six countries that represent a variety of patterns of agricultural development, ranging from the slow, evolutionary process of agricultural change in eighteenth and nineteenth century England to the whirlwind collectivization of agriculture in the Soviet Union. Although the Soviet approach to agricultural development is examined as an important historical case study, the emphasis in this book is on the problems of agricultural development and economic growth in countries characterized by a mixed economy with a substantial private sector. The similarities and even more the contrasts between experience in the United

States and Japan and in Mexico and Taiwan are especially illuminating.

In considering the problems faced by the contemporary late-developing countries, we attempt to bring together the general principles that should guide the choice of measures to accelerate agricultural progress that are suggested by the lessons of past experience as well as the analytical framework presented in Chapter 4. Major attention is given in Chapter 9 to examining those issues in the context of recent experience in India and Pakistan which serves to clarify some of the problems and opportunities associated with the Green Revolution. The elements of diversity that condition the design and implementation of strategies for agricultural development are reviewed in Chapter 10 as a backdrop for some general conclusions that are believed to be of wide applicability notwithstanding the importance of the particular circumstances that need to be considered in individual countries.

The starting point of the development process is, of course, the traditional farmer in a traditional economy. Chapter 1 delineates the principal economic, technical, environmental, and social characteristics of agriculture in a late-developing economy. In seeking to focus attention on the most significant features, many variations are ignored. Here as elsewhere our aim has been to identify the major forces at work in order to shed light on a highly complex process that is subject to many variations.

AGRICULTURE AND STRUCTURAL TRANSFORMATION

1 | Agriculture in a Traditional Economy

In the low-income countries of Africa, Asia, and Latin America the bulk of the population lives on the farm. Because the level of production of goods and services on these farms is modest, economic welfare in terms of nutrition, clothing, housing, education, and health is of a low standard not only for those in the countryside but for most urban dwellers as well.

Low agricultural productivity and low income, which characterize these countries, are inevitable given the high degree of self-sufficiency and the technologies employed in the village communities which predominate in traditional economies. In these semi-isolated village economies, not only is there a large share of self-produced consumption goods, but the tools of production and intermediate inputs such as feed, seed, and fertilizer also originate on the farmstead or in the village. The technical knowledge applied in farming and crafts is largely the result of local experience accumulated over many generations. And the social institutions which define the scope of cooperative efforts in production and the extent of economic horizons center around local kinship networks. By way of contrast, when productivity and income are high, consumption of self-produced commodities is slight, reliance on local knowledge is limited to adaptive practices, and the use of locally made inputs is negligible.

The process by which meager self-sufficiency is transformed into prosperous interdependence as producers are integrated into a national network of markets, information flows, and social institutions is described in Chapter 2. The special significance of the backlog of technology that is available to countries beginning structural transformation in the latter decades of the twentieth century is analyzed in Chapter 3. Later chapters examine, from various perspectives, the choices that are open to policy-makers for accelerating or retarding the developmental process.

SOME COMMON ELEMENTS

The number of people who live and work in low-income rural economies is large: indeed it amounts to about half the world's population. The size of the rural economy is commonly measured by the proportion of economically active persons engaged in agriculture. We shall be using this statistic frequently. It is comprised of those people whose primary occupation is reported in the census as farming, fishing, forestry, or hunting. On the one hand, this grouping overstates the proportion of productive time devoted to the growing of food and fiber because these individuals are also producing a wide range of nonagricultural goods and services consumed within their own households. On the other hand, this figure excludes the considerable fraction of the labor force that is engaged in rural nonfarm occupations—craftsmen, traders, transporters, teachers, ecclesiastics, and moneylenders.

Table 1.1 presents the agricultural labor force statistic for selected underdeveloped countries. For most of these countries, as for most less-developed countries, some 50 to 70 per cent of the working population is engaged in agriculture. By way of contrast, in Sweden, the United States, and England the share of the working population engaged in agriculture in 1965 was only 11 per cent, 6 per cent, and 4 per cent, respectively. African countries with the least-developed economies have the highest proportion of their population in the rural economy, averaging 75 per cent or more. North African and Asian countries have a somewhat lower proportion of their work force in agriculture, but it is still well above 50 per cent for all but a few. In Latin America the range toward the lower end of the

Table 1.1. Population in agriculture, average output, and nutrition levels

Country	Labor force in agriculture, 1965 (per cent)	In economic wheat equivalents per person		
		Agricultural output (kilograms)	Food consumption (kilograms)	Calories per gram of consumption
Tanzania	95	426	334	2.38
Kenya	88	463	366	2.23
Nigeria	80	507	435	2.25
Togo	79	466	344	2.81
Zaire (Congo)	69	412	363	2.66
Ghana	56	637	477	1.99
Libya	60	265	398	2.0
Egypt	55	529	480	1.78
Syria	50	474	502	1.65
Pakistan	74	432	383	1.93
India	70	346	354	2.11
Indonesia	66	504	471	1.65
Burma	62	600	485	1.62
Malaysia	55	953	528	1.58
South Korea	54	535	488	1.66
Ceylon	54	646	514	1.46
Taiwan	47	736	551	1.55
Haiti	79	414	377	1.81
El Salvador	59	671	400	1.80
Mexico	52	799	573	1.74
Ecuador	52	745	444	1.59
Colombia	47	849	657	1.23
Brazil	48	973	657	1.57
Peru	47	615	527	1.41
Chile	26	809	823	1.16

SOURCE: Labor force in agriculture from Food and Agriculture Organization of the United Nations, *Production Yearbook 1970* (Rome, 1971), Table 5. All other data are for the late 1950s from Colin Clark and Margaret Haswell, *The Economics of Subsistence Agriculture* (London, 1970), 4th ed., pp. 76-82.

distribution is greater. In Chile and Argentina (not shown in the table) only about a quarter of the labor force is in agriculture; although both countries have difficult economic problems, they are not the distinctive problems of late-developing countries.

The figures in the second column of Table 1.1 are agricultural output per head of the whole population. Countries with large agricultural sectors exhibit low farm productivity. Because per capita output is calculated on the basis of the entire population, the pattern of rising output indicated by this table actually understates the rate at which farm labor productivity increases as one moves to countries with larger shares of nonagricultural population. This observed inverse relationship between agricultural output and the relative size of the rural economy is a central phenomenon of the development process.

In poor countries food constitutes the principal item of consumption. Its quantity and quality are a major determinant of the nation's economic welfare and of the health and productivity of its people. Agricultural product cannot be translated directly into food consumption. From it must be subtracted all food exports and nonfood items (cotton, tobacco, animal feed, etc.); the resultant figure must be adjusted for food imports and changes in stocks. This is the figure that is reported in the third column of Table 1.1.[1]

Judgments differ concerning the extent of hunger and malnutrition in the underdeveloped world. Estimates of food supplies available for human consumption in those countries are no better than rough approximations, although in some countries survey data provide fairly reliable figures for limited population groups. Moreover, serious problems arise in establishing reasonably satisfactory standards for determining the nutritional adequacy of a particular level of food intake, especially in the case of minimum requirements for protein and certain essential vitamins and minerals. Protein deficiency, for example, is related to the quality as well as the quantity of protein in the diet; and it also may be a consequence of an insufficiency of calories so that protein is used by the body to meet its calorie needs rather than performing its distinctive functions. Assessing the nutritional status of a population is also complicated by regional and income-related variations in food intake and by interactions between nutritional status and other health problems resulting from disease or parasites. In spite of these difficulties, however, it is clear that malnutrition is more prevalent than inadequate intake of calories.

The evidence at hand indicates that in even the poorest countries *average* food supplies are appreciably above bare subsistence standards. According to rough estimates by Colin Clark and Margaret Haswell, calorie and protein requirements for a normal level of activity will be met by a diet that provides from 245 to 290 kilograms of wheat equivalent per annum, depending upon average body size, the age composition of the population, and climate. Even though average food supplies are adequate, there may be considerable malnutrition and undernutrition among the poorer segments of the population. Limited evidence from surveys that have been designed to study the diets of different income groups suggest that such is often the case. Diet deficiencies may also be of considerable importance among certain vulnerable groups such as lactating mothers and small children who need additional protein for body growth. Some localities characterized by a long dry season experience seasonal hunger in the preharvest period. Drought or other natural calamity may bring more prolonged and acute deficiency in years when food production falls below a normal level, as in the successive years of severe drought that hit the Indian subcontinent in the mid-1960s. Thus out-and-out shortages of food may be a chronic problem for some groups and an occasional problem for wider segments of society. In general, however, problems of distribution and of nutritional education are largely responsible for the nutritional problems that exist.

While all of the countries shown have consumption levels above subsistence, the value of food intake tends to rise with higher levels of agricultural productivity. This is mainly a result of the shift from starchy staples to more expensive, preferred foods such as meat, dairy products, fish, poultry, vegetables, and fruit. Animal products are inherently inefficient, and therefore expensive, sources of human energy since only a fraction of the primary calories ingested by the animal are converted into edible material. Even within the starchy staple category itself there is a movement away from roots or tubers, such as cassava or sweet potatoes, and from coarse grains such as millet, sorghum, and maize, to rice and wheat, the cereal crops that are universally preferred by consumers. This movement from economical to more expensive but preferred foods as the level of consumption rises is seen in the final column of Table 1.1. In Togo, a country with relatively low productivity in agriculture, consumers arrange their diet so as to obtain 2.8 calories per gram of consumption (measured in wheat equivalents); this contrasts with only 1.2 calories per gram for Chile, a country where agricultural product per capita is nearly twice that of Togo.

So far we have identified three characteristics common to all traditional economies. First, the percentage of the population engaged in farming and the rural economy is high. Second, the productivity of this large rural labor force is low. Third, although average consumption levels are above the subsistence threshold, diets are heavily weighted toward less-preferred starchy staples. There are a number of other regularities seldom absent from low-income agrarian economies which are a consequence of limited farm cash sales and the need to minimize risk, these latter factors themselves being derivative from the first and second items listed above. However, before proceeding it is necessary to review a number of differences between these economies—differences in natural resource endowments, in farm size, in climate and soil conditions, and in agricultural regimes that are practiced.

NATURAL RESOURCES

Labor and natural resources constitute the original factors of production. In the early stages of economic development when the supply of the "produced factor," capital, is modest and the level of technology is rudimentary, a country's natural resource endowment

AGRICULTURE IN A TRADITIONAL ECONOMY 9

looms large in determining the volume of agricultural output and the possibilities for high rates of savings. Advances in technology, capital accumulation, and international trade that come with economic growth progressively free the production process from a one-to-one relationship between output and specific resource inputs. Hence for developed economies, for a Holland or a Japan, a meager natural resource endowment is no longer a serious handicap to increases in per capita output.

The economic usefulness of a particular natural resource is defined by the state of the arts. Flint was initially a valuable commodity which provided the material for weapons and tools; later, because it damaged tillage implements and impeded cultivation, flint became a nuisance and had to be removed from farmers' fields at considerable cost. Prior to atomic energy, uranium was of little practical use, as was the case for bauxite and petroleum in an earlier period. Modern transportation technology has only marginally reduced the economic value of navigable waterways, a flat terrain, and a coastline with natural harbors.

To be of economic value, the existence of a natural resource must be known, in limited supply relative to demand, and access to it must not be so costly as to offset the benefit. Perhaps the most dramatic recent example of the former is the additional geological knowledge that transformed Libya from one of the poorest to one of the richest countries in the world. The Libyan case also illustrates the need for investment as a prerequisite for exploiting the "free" gifts of nature and the ease of attracting such investment from abroad when the resource commands a high world price relative to the costs of extraction. Less valuable mineral resources that are not easily tapped for export, such as inland reserves of iron ore or bauxite, may not justify the investment needed to make their utilization possible. Developed countries as a group exhibit a more diversified natural resource base, at least in part because of a greater capacity for surveying their physical environment and low cost of access resulting from the existing stock of infrastructure and technical know how.

In comparing differences in natural resource endowments between

Table 1.2. Differences in natural resource endowment around 1965

Country	Mining as a per cent of GDP	Cubic meters of roundwood per capita	Fish catch per capita (*kilograms*)	Agricultural land per capita (*hectares*)
Tanzania	2.5	1.00	8.0	4.87
Kenya	0.4	0.83	3.0	0.69
Nigeria	4.8	0.55	1.0	0.92
Togo	6.3	0.65	3.8	1.48
Zaire (Congo)	6.4	0.12	0.9	5.16
Ghana	...	1.28	10.5	0.33
Libya	54.2	0.20	...	1.92
Egypt	...	0.01	3.2	0.09[a]
Syria	...	0.02	...	2.47
Pakistan	0.3	0.03	3.3	0.25
India	1.1	0.03	2.7	0.36
Indonesia	3.3	0.81	9.1	0.12
Burma	0.8	0.14	1.5	0.66
Malaysia	7.7	1.11	26.9	0.61[a]
South Korea	2.0	0.07	22.5	0.08
Ceylon	0.6	0.03	8.4	0.17
Taiwan	1.9	0.11	30.8	0.07
Haiti	1.0	1.87	...	0.18
El Salvador	0.2	1.02	2.9	0.50
Mexico	4.5	0.14	6.0	2.86
Ecuador	2.0	0.50	10.3	3.83
Colombia	2.7	1.39	2.9	1.31
Brazil	0.3	1.78	4.6	1.70
Peru	6.2	0.25	637.8[b]	2.56
Chile	10.5	0.80	81.4	1.90

[a] Too low; excludes data for permanent meadows and pastures.
[b] Including 620.6 used in manufacture of animal feed and other nonfoods.
SOURCE: Data from International Bank for Reconstruction and Development, *World Tables* (Washington, D.C., 1971), Table 4; Food and Agriculture Organization of the United Nations, *Production Yearbook* (Rome, various years), Table 1; idem, *Yearbook of Forest Products Statistics* (Rome, 1965), Table P1; and idem, *Yearbook of Fishery Statistics Vol. 22, 1966* (Rome, 1967), Tables A1-1, A1-2, A1-3, A1-4.

underdeveloped countries, published data limit us to the four categories reported in Table 1.2. In the case of the first three—minerals, timber, fish—the measure is not of natural resources but the rate of their commercial exploitation. In the case of the fourth category, agricultural land, we do have a measure of the quantity of the resource; on the other hand, wide variations in natural fertility qualify the usefulness of hectares per capita as an index of the farm lands' potential economic value. Nevertheless, the four measures provide meaningful evidence as to the uneven distribution of nature's benefactions.

Countries in which mining constitutes more than 2 per cent of GDP are typically exporters of minerals. Because mineral extraction is usually very capital-intensive and requires a large input of imported equipment and technical services, it does not generate much labor income or demand for inputs from local industries. Aside from some contribution to the development of nonspecialized land transportation and harbor facilities, the primary benefits of valuable mineral resources are net foreign exchange earnings and a sizable element of economic rent which can be captured by the government in the form of lease rents, royalties, profit taxes, and the like. Liberal foreign exchange earnings go a long way to ease the import constraint on introducing modern technology embodied in intermediate goods and capital equipment; additional public revenues, whether channeled through development lending, public investment, or expanded current expenditures on health and education, make it possible to expand the nation's productive capacity. Thus the natural resources of countries like Libya, Zaire, Chile, and Peru provide them with a distinct advantage in sustaining the process of economic development.

Because they are less scarce than oil, copper, and the like, marine and timber resources command little economic rent. On the other hand, their exploitation does save or earn foreign exchange and is often undertaken by domestic entrepreneurs rather than foreign firms. Moreover, their production processes are such that extensive use is made of domestic factors of production and inputs from local industries. From Table 1.2 it can be seen that timber resources are important in a number of African and Latin American countries, with Malaysia and Indonesia being the only significant producers in Asia and North Africa. Six of the 24 countries boast a fish catch of over 10 kilograms per capita. In the case of Peru, which also has extensive deposits of copper and iron ore, the Humbolt current provides a catch (equivalent to 638 kilograms per capita) that has become a leading source of foreign exchange.

A thorough study of the Peruvian case by Michael Roemer forcefully illustrates a number of the points discussed earlier about the relativity of natural resources and the economic benefits that can flow from nonmineral resource endowments.[2] In 1950 there were no commercially exploited iron ore deposits; fishing and copper contributed 1.4 per cent of national output. By 1966 anchovies and tuna, iron ore, and copper accounted for over 9 per cent of a national output that was some 2.3 times larger than it had been in 1950. The exploitation of Toquepala copper and the iron ore deposits was made possible by investments totaling several hundred million dollars. In the case of anchovies, displacement of cotton fishing nets in 1956 by stronger, lighter, more durable nylon nets and the introduction of sonar "fish-finders" transformed a 59,000 ton catch in 1955 to 8.5 million tons in 1966. In contrast to large royalties from copper, fishing has contributed less than 3 per cent of public revenue. On the other hand, the fish meal industry employed 2 per cent of the nonagricultural labor force in the mid-1960s and was responsible for another 0.8 per cent in supplier industries. The industry earned a quarter of the country's foreign exchange, gave rise to four new industries (boats, fish nets, processing equipment, jute sacks), and had brought about the enlargement of five seaports.

The final set of differences in resource endowment among underdeveloped countries is agricultural space. Like other natural resources, the economic value of arable land can only be fixed in a wider context which takes into account soil fertility, climate, location, manmade improvements, and the agricultural methods employed. We will consider these additional factors presently. At this

AGRICULTURE IN A TRADITIONAL ECONOMY

point we need only note that in the face of high rates of population growth the tasks of agricultural development—mobilizing savings, adapting high-productivity technologies, shaping new organizations—are very much more difficult in the land-scarce Asian and Caribbean economies than in the countries of Africa and Latin America where 10 to 50 times more land per capita provides a good deal more spatial and temporal room for experimentation.

FARM SIZE

Closely related to the amount of a country's arable land relative to its inhabitants is the manner in which this land is allocated among farms. The size distribution of operational units is a structural characteristic that bears heavily on the course of agricultural development. Illustrative data from Japan, Senegal, and six countries from Table 1.2 are set forth in Table 1.3.

Average farm size is closely linked to agricultural land per capita (see Tables 1.2 and 1.3). The relationship between the two varies somewhat between countries owing to differences in the share of the farm work force in the total labor force. The more developed a country, the larger the nonagricultural labor force relative to the total labor force (L_n/L_t) and, hence, the larger is average farm size relative to agricultural land per capita. The number of workers per farm is also affected by this economic factor, but even more powerfully by differences in the technical requirements for animal and crop production and by social factors, particularly inheritance practices. The statistics on average farm size reveal the same vast differences between countries as the earlier index of per capita agricultural land. The figures for Kerala and Punjab in India point up the importance of regional disparities in many countries.

A good indicator of the relative scarcity of land as a factor of production is the percentage of the "average size farm" devoted to crop land. The far more densely populated countries in Asia devote at least three-quarters of land in farm holdings to the production of crops while farms in East Africa and the Americas generally crop less than one-quarter of their total area (Table 1.3). The difference is reflected in the large areas in the latter group used as pastures for grazing livestock. The differences across countries in crop land per holding then do not vary so radically and can be explained in large measure by variations in the intensity of cultivation. Since pasturing livestock is by most standards the most extensive form of

Table 1.3. Farm size in nine countries

Country	L_n/L_t [a] (per cent)	Average size farm			Top one percentile	
		Total area (hectares)	Area in crop land (hectares)	Crop land to total area (per cent)	Farm size (hectares)	Share of all farm land (per cent)
Japan	67	1.2	1.0	84.7	13.6	11.6
Taiwan	44	1.3	1.0	76.9	15.8	14.4
W. Pakistan	41	3.5	2.6	76.1	96.9	25.0
India	30	2.7	2.5	91.2	30.7	11.4
Kerala	62	0.8	...	...	20.8	26.3
Punjab	36	4.5	...	...	27.9	6.2
Brazil	46	74.9	8.6	11.5	2,587.7	34.6
Colombia	43	22.6	4.2	18.5	1,038.9	46.0
Mexico [b]	46	92.5	9.4	14.1	6,891.6	74.4
Kenya	12	8.3	1.9	27.3	611.1	51.4
Senegal	26	3.6	3.6	100.0	20.7	5.7

[a] Share of nonfarm labor force in total labor force.
[b] Data in this table exclude *ejidos* and therefore differs from the land distribution shown in Figure 1.2 which includes *ejidal* land.
SOURCE: Data for Japan, Taiwan, Colombia, Kenya, and Senegal from FAO, *Report on the 1960 World Census of Agriculture* (Rome, 1966), Vol. 1a; ibid. (Rome, 1967), Vol. 1b; ibid. (Rome, 1971), Vol. 5; for Brazil from Brazil, Instituto Brasileiro de Estatística (IBGE), *Anuário Estatístico do Brasil—1970* (Rio de Janeiro, 1970); for India from Government of India, Cabinet Secretariat, *The National Sample Survey, Sixteenth Round: July 1960-Jun 1961, No. 113, Tables with Notes on Agricultural Holdings in Rural India* (Delhi, 1967); for Mexico from Mexico, Direccion General de Estadistics, *IV Censo Agricola-Ganadero Ejidal, 1960: Resumen General* (Mexico, D.F., 1965), Table 3; for Pakistan from Sir Alexander Gibb & Partners, *Land Tenure*, Vol. 8, International Bank for Reconstruction and Development, *Programme for Development of Irrigation and Agriculture in West Pakistan* (London, May 1966), Table 1.2. Labor statistics are from FAO, *Production Yearbook* (Rome, various years) and ILO, *Year Book of Labour Statistics* (Geneva, various years).

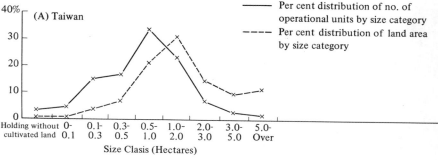
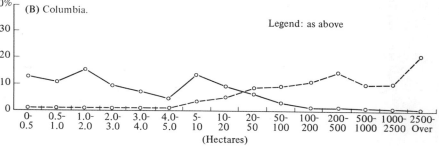

Figure 1.1 Farm size distribution by number of operational units and by area cultivated, Taiwan and Columbia.

SOURCE: Data from FAO, *Report on the 1960 World Census of Agriculture*, Vol. 1a (Rome, 1966), pp. 50, 64, 65.

agricultural production, these particular statistics draw into focus the relative scarcity of land in Asia vis-à-vis those countries in South and Central America.

The last two columns in Table 1.3 and Figures 1.1 and 1.2 provide measures of the distribution of farm size within each country. Figure 1.1 presents the distribution of both farms and farm land by size of operational holding for Taiwan and Colombia. This is a more graphic, although less economical, measure of the relative inequality of farm holdings than that provided by the Lorenz curves plotted in Figure 1.2. The Lorenz curves are frequency distributions, in this instance based on decile averages, relating any given cumulative pro-

AGRICULTURE AND STRUCTURAL TRANSFORMATION

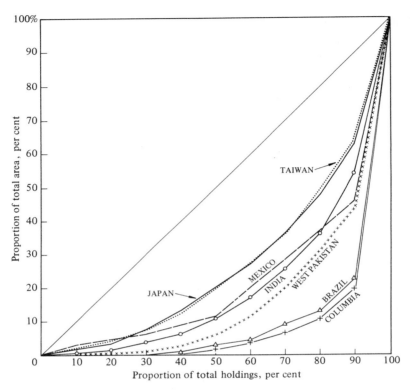

Figure 1.2 Lorenz curves of agricultural land distribution by operational holdings.

SOURCE: Data for Japan, Taiwan, West Pakistan, and Colombia from FAO, *Report on the 1960 World Census of Agriculture* (Rome, 1966); for Brazil from Brazil, Instituto Brasileiro de Estatística (IBGE), *Anuário Estatístico do Brasil—1970* (Rio de Janeiro, 1970); for Mexico from R. D. Hansen, *The Politics of Mexican Development* (Baltimore, 1971), p. 79; for India from Government of India, Cabinet Secretariat, *The National Sample Survey, Sixteenth Round: July 1960-June 1961, No. 113, Tables with Notes on Agricultural Holdings in Rural India* (Delhi, 1967).

portion of the population of farm households (horizontal axis, from the left) to its share in the total amount of agricultural land (vertical axis, upward). The share of any percentile grouping, for example, the second top decile category, is given by the slope of the curve over that particular interval. Finally, the last two columns in Table 1.3 focus on the farm size and share of total farm land held by the largest 1 per cent of operational units.

Looking at the most comprehensive measure first, the Lorenz curves show that the degree of inequality in the distribution of farm size varies greatly between countries. The curves for Japan and Taiwan lie closest to the 45° line of complete equality, while that of Colombia lies farthest away. Not only is the area between the Lorenz curves and the 45° line (which is the measure of the degree of inequality in land distribution) approximately twice as great for Brazil and Colombia, but their curves are bowed to the right, indicating greater skew in the proportion of land going to the largest size farms. The disproportionately large share of the land cultivated by the biggest farms, which can be seen most clearly in Figure 1.1, gives rise to a dualistic or "bimodal" farm size structure in Colombia as contrasted to a "unimodal" structure in Taiwan.[3] This difference in size distribution not only indicates differences in the distribution of income in the traditional economy, but it has a profound effect on the pattern of agricultural modernization to which we will turn in Chapter 4. A sizable fraction of the farms in Latin America and Asia rent their land from landlords; however our concern here is only with operational units, that is, units managed by an individual farm operator irrespective of whether the land is owned or rented. Tenure arrangements are taken up in Chapters 2 and 4.

In panels (A) and (B) of Figure 1.1 the solid lines plot the distribution of farms by size of holdings. Four-fifths of Taiwanese farms are within *one acre* of the average size farm and the top 1 per cent are 11.6 times the mean farm size of three acres (*1.2* hectares). In contrast, in Colombia only one-tenth of the farmsteads are within *five acres* of the average and the top 1 per cent are 46 times the mean farm size of 56 acres. The dotted lines plot the share of farm land commanded by the various farm size categories. In the case of Taiwan the bulk of the land is cultivated by the bulk of the farmers; in Colombia the bulk of the land is cultivated by but one-fifth of the farmers.

The other countries in Table 1.3 fall at various places on a spectrum between the two cases just discussed. West Pakistan tends toward a bimodal structure while India is closer to the unimodal pole, but as the statistics for Kerala and Punjab reveal, there is considerable regional variation. The dualistic situation depicted for Kenya in 1960 reflected colonial land policies which reserved over half the farm land for European or Asian controlled estates that accounted for 0.5 per cent of the farm units. African farmers operated holdings that averaged slightly over 4 hectares, and these were fairly equally distributed. Since independence in 1963, much of the land held by the estates has been purchased by the government and allocated to African farmers under settlement schemes so that the size distribution of operational units is now considerably less skewed. Senegal is more typical of tropical Africa where communal land ownership has produced a relatively egalitarian distribution of farm holdings.

The significance of the degree of skewness of farm size goes beyond its direct effects on rural income distribution and its indirect effects on economic and political power. The size distribution of operational farms is the principal determinant of participation in commercial sales of farm products; and the ability of a farmer to purchase modern inputs, to transform traditional technology, is of course dependent upon earnings from commercial sales. In Colombia, for instance, the four-fifths of the farm households which cultivate 12 per cent of agricultural land must perforce devote all but a small fraction of their land to supply their own subsistence needs; conversely the lion's share of commercial sales for both domestic and export markets comes from the top two deciles. The one partial exception to be noted is coffee which constitutes the only significant source of cash income for Colombia's smallholder. Over half of the country's coffee farms are less than 5 hectares, although their share in total production is obviously much less. We shall return to this question of the "distribution" of commercial sales in later chapters. In the meantime we turn to the salient features of the natural environment which impinge directly upon the conduct of traditional agriculture.

CLIMATE AND AGRICULTURAL ZONES

The underdeveloped countries are to a striking degree concentrated in tropical or subtropical regions. In these regions the sun's rays strike the earth more directly giving rise to minimal variation in length of day, relatively high average temperatures, and lack of marked seasonal change. These solar effects, along with distinctive rainfall patterns, are key factors in defining both the possibilities and the limits of agricultural endeavor in the developing economies.

In principle the tropics possess several advantages over temperate climes in terms of their sheer agricultural potential. The longer duration and greater intensity of sunlight through the year means that there is more photosynthetic energy available for plant production. The absence of frost and of marked seasonal variation creates the possibility of continuous cropping. In practice, however, the interaction of solar radiation with the physical environment frequently creates conditions which more than offset this advantage.

Let us look at the interaction of sunlight regime and rainfall. High temperatures produce high rates of evaporation and plant transpiration so that the agricultural "efficiency" of a given level of rainfall is much less than in the temperate regions. It has been calculated, for example, that although Manchester, England, and Accra in Ghana receive about the same annual rainfall, Accra receives only one-third to one-half the amount required to balance evaporation, whereas Manchester receives about twice the amount required to achieve balance.[4] High temperatures also produce a high moisture-carrying capacity of the air so that rainfall and cloud cover tend to be greatest in coastal regions and near other bodies of water, giving rise to forested areas and heavy vegetation. Far inland, where neither lakes, elevation, nor wind streams intervene, one encounters semi-arid savanna and desert. Not only is rainfall extreme in its abundance or paucity, but it is often concentrated in one or two rainy seasons usually characterized by intense downpours. Because the soil can retain only so much moisture, water runoff is high and fields are parched in the dry season; because of intense downpours top soil is in many places eroded. The action of high temperatures and high rainfall leads to the rapid loss of organic matter in tropical soils, which reduces not only their nutrient level but their capacity to retain moisture as well.

These climatic influences in conjunction with other factors have produced three broad agricultural zones. The distinguishing features of *rain forest* are continuously warm-to-hot temperatures and ample moisture supplies for vegetative growth throughout the year. Tree crops—cocoa, rubber, coconut, oil palms—and such perennials as yams, cassava, and banana-plantain grow well in this environment. Tree crops, with their deep root-given capacity to mobilize water and nutrient materials for the greater part of the year, are perhaps the best example of advantageous use of the tropics' more abundant photosynthetic energy. Because of leaching from heavy rains, once cleared for cultivation these soils quickly lose the fertility that had been maintained by organic litter from the tree cover. The response to this situation is usually shifting cultivation. The root and tuber crops mentioned above have high calorie yields per acre and per man-hour, but are low in proteins and other nutrients.

The *savanna* zone, receiving less moisture than the rain forest, usually exhibits a vegetation cover of grass, scattered trees, and shrubs. This zone displays enormous diversity. Much of present savanna is man-made, having once been under forest. Maize and yams are commonly grown as staple food crops in the more humid areas; millets and sorghums, with their short growing season, low moisture requirements, and ability to withstand drought by going into a period of dormancy when moisture is lacking, are found in the semi-arid parts. In extensive areas in Asia the savanna vegetation has long since given way to continuous cultivation by dense and settled farm populations, while in much of Africa it is still cropped on the basis of shifting cultivation. Although leaching is less of a problem in savanna zones, the smaller amount of plant debris means that natural fallow is less effective in restoring soil fertility.

A large part of the population of the tropics and subtropics is concentrated in the *riverine areas of alluvial soil* of Asia where relatively good soils and annual flooding permit continuous cultivation of wet rice. As Pierre Gourou has noted, "the flooded rice field offers mankind in the tropics the best chance of a yearly production of a sufficiency of carbohydrates with a minimum of manure and without fallow periods or risk of erosion or exhaustion of the soil."[5] The rice economy of monsoon Asia reflects not only nature's contribution of river valleys and flood plains but also man-made irrigation systems, leveling and bunding of fields, and sometimes elaborate terracing of otherwise unpromising terrain. Other cereal crops generally do not yield as well as rice in a humid tropical environment, and the higher calorie yields of manioc and other root crops are associated with a much longer growing season. The chief problems with these lowlying soils are drainage and water control, the leaching of nutrients, and the prevention of excess acidity.[6]

We have mentioned that the greater availability of sunlight in the tropics and the absence of frost creates the possibility of continuous cropping, a possibility that is realized in the case of some tree crops and in some wet rice locations. These same factors make possible the continuous reproduction and growth of pests and parasites which attack crops, animals, and man. And in this case the possibility is realized in abundance in virtually every region of the tropics.

In the absence of a season when all plant and insect life ceases, the tropics spawn not only most of the predators of the temperate zone, but a further multiplicity of birds, weeds, viruses, worms, insects, and mites. The high temperatures and humidities favor rapid multiplication and spread of pests and diseases which often cause severe crop losses. The introduction of a new crop or plant variety will frequently call forth a new antagonist, sometimes an antagonist fatal to the enterprise. In many cases research can provide an antidote. But resources are limited and the number of natural enemies is great; and many pests develop immunities to insecticides and the resistance bred into new varieties often loses its effectiveness as mutant forms of rust or other diseases evolve.

What is the quantitative impact of these tropical predators? A recent collation of available evidence suggests that 20 to 50 per cent of most planted crops are lost to weeds, insects, and storage pests.[7] Intestinal parasites are well nigh universal in domestic animals, causing increased mortality, reduced yields of milk and meat, and impaired capacity of draft animals. The incidence of major human diseases, causing varying degrees of debilitation, as estimated by the World Health Organization and reported by Andrew Kamarck are: intestinal worms (1 billion), malaria (700 million), filariasis (250 million), bilharzia (200 million), and river-blindness (20 million). In addition, the tropics have the full set of diseases still prevalent in the temperate zone, among which tuberculosis is probably the most important.

The above estimates are extremely rough and the extent to which some of these diseases diminish energy and well-being is not yet fully determined. Nevertheless, it seems reasonable to conclude that the tropics, particularly the humid climates, do impose certain handicaps relative to the temperate regions in the matter of natural wastage in agricultural produce and in somewhat diminished levels of energy and mental concentration in certain segments of the larbor force.

AGRICULTURAL METHODS

Within the bounds imposed by the natural environment and available resources, the traditional farmer has practiced his art with remarkable ingenuity. Let us consider the case of the Indian farmer operating in a savanna region. He grows rice in the wet season and wheat, pulses, and peanuts in the dry season. His stock of tools consists of a desi plow, a leveling plank, a hoe, a spade, and a sickle; other items of equipment may include an ox cart and a water-pumping Persian wheel. The farmer's power sources are a pair of bullocks, his own muscle, and the muscle of his family. The principal tillage implement, the desi plow, is extremely simple. It consists of two wooden elements, the plow itself, large at the sole and tapering down to a handle at the far end, and a beam connecting the plow to the oxen's yoke. There may or may not be a metal tip affixed to the point of the plow.

Within the context of low-income traditional agriculture, the desi plow provides a good example of a tool well adapted to the farmers' needs. It is very inexpensive, costing between one and two dollars. It fulfills a range of functions—plowing, harrowing, puddling, intercultivation—which in other farming regimes calls for a number of implements. In the realm of technical efficiency, where the priority of turning under weeds is low and that of conserving moisture is high, the desi plow may be superior to far more sophisticated soil-inverting instruments such as the moldboard plow. Although requiring a relatively large number of passes, the desi plow is well adapted to the strength of poorly fed bullocks and to the rudimentary techniques for controlling them. It has been estimated that some 40 million desi plows are in use in India.[8]

A similar tendency toward optimization within existing technological parameters can be seen in the case of seed selection. *Indica* rice varieties are dominant in most tropical climates. Through a long process of natural and human selection a type has evolved which is well suited to prevailing physical and economic conditions. The important environmental circumstances within which the farmer operates are soils with low average nutrient levels and a marked wet-dry seasonal dichotomy with considerable cloud cover during the wet season. The vital economic constraint is the community's limited ability to sustain marked down-side variation in crop yields. The plant type that has evolved to meet these needs is tall, profuse in its leaf growth, delayed in flowering, and of long duration to maturity. The height provides protection against heavy rains and flood conditions. Large drooping leaves cut off weeds which would compete for the limited nutrients and sunlight. Late flowering and late maturing permits grain formation, the period when greatest photosynthetic activity occurs, to take place after the rains when strong sunlight is available. Beyond a certain minimum threshold, grain yields of *indica* varieties are relatively insensitive to variations in the level of nutrients.

In the rain forest of West Africa, farming regimes give the appearance of being even more rudimentary than that described for the Indian savanna. Here the farmer grows assorted food crops including cassava, yams, maize, cocoyams, and plantain, and frequently a tree crop as his principal source of cash income. If soil and climatic conditions are suitable, cocoa is likely to be the "cash crop." The tools for such cocoa farmers are confined to a number of short-handled hoes, cutlasses, cocoa knives, and baskets, the cost of the total stock not exceeding $15. The tsetse fly (and trypanosomiasis) rules out draft animals, and since the food crops are interplanted with cocoa or in small forest clearings, the presence of extensive tree roots interferes with the use of tillage implements other than the hoe. All farming operations must thus be powered by the human arm. The irregular parcels of crop land cut out of the bush are only imperfectly cleared before burning. In the first few years before the cocoa plant matures sufficiently to cut off sunlight, food crops are planted among the young trees; on plots where no cocoa trees are planted the field will be abandoned after three or four years to natural growth for a decade or more. Cultivated only by the hoe, mixed food crops are planted in apparent disorder and fields are typically not well weeded.

Appearances to the contrary, African farming methods are quite successful in protecting the fragile fertility of rain forest soils. The constant vegetative cover provided by mixed and sequential cropping prevents erosion and excessive leaching of nutrients that unimpeded heavy rainfall would bring; the cover also slows down oxidation of humus content from the heat of the sun. Total crop failure is insured against by a mixture of plants with different moisture and soil requirements and with differing tolerances for drought, wind, and pests. Incomplete clearing and poor weeding, although not unrelated to the limited range of African farm tools, serves to provide shade and protection to the soil and to assist in re-establishing natural forest. Small isolated fields are more easily recaptured by the natural vegetation than larger ones; at the same time spread of plant disease is much slower.

From these examples of farming methods it can be seen that most implements and agricultural practices are part of a well-integrated farming system. For this reason, the introduction of one or two modern inputs is seldom successful. Because it fulfills so many functions at so low a cost, the desi plow is not easily replaced. Adequate substitution calls for several specialized implements, and the substantially higher equipment cost associated with improved land preparation is not likely to be justified without complementary changes in seed variety, fertilization, and water supply. In our rice example, modern farming inputs have limited impact if traditional *indica* varieties are not replaced by new fertilizer-responsive plants. With traditional varieties increased nutrients result in excessive stalk and leaf growth which often causes the plant to topple over in the wind; losses due to this "lodging" may more than offset the yield effect of applying modern inputs.

While the farming regimes of traditional agriculture are in most instances well adapted to their environment, it remains true that the underlying technology everywhere provides but modest returns to human effort. This, of course, is reflected in the low levels of agricultural output per head shown in Table 1.1. Closely associated with rudimentary technologies are limited markets and limited specialization. Let us consider the market limitations first.

LIMITED MARKETS AND THE DIVISION OF LABOR

The fact that a very high proportion of the population resides within the farming sector means that the possibilities for earning money income are rather severely constrained. Taking Nigeria as an example, with only 20 per cent of the population living off the farm, the effective domestic market demand is held to about one-fifth of the food produced apart from transactions within the rural sector itself. The other component of cash farm sales is receipts from sale of export crops; this averages about $10 per capita of farm population per annum. Limited money income means limited expenditures on production inputs as well as on consumer goods and services. This in turn implies that despite its very large size, the agricultural sector makes only modest purchases from other sectors and they in consequence tend to remain small. Farm households, not having the means to purchase all the commodities they desire from specialized producers, engage in the "manufacture" of a wide range of goods—houses, household furnishings, farm tools, utensils, clothing, and so on.

The fact that farm households are involved in the production of a large number of goods necessarily entails limited specialization and, within the productive process for any given good, restricted division of labor. This same phenomenon is present in the monetized sectors of the economy. The combining of retail trade with other occupations is well known and is certainly the most ubiquitous example in urban areas. In the countryside the most common joint occupation is housekeeping and farming for the women and farming and a craft for the men. Of 163 Ghanaian cocoa farmers surveyed in Akokoaso in 1938 by W. H. Beckett, just under one-third earned a significant portion of their money income from a second occupation: palm wine tapper (11), armadillo hunter (8), mason (5), sawyer (2), shoemaker (3), native doctor (3), blacksmith (2), carpenter (1), petty trader (5), and cocoa buyer (1).[9] In the early 1950s an even higher proportion of Nigerian cocoa farmers were engaged in secondary income-earning occupations.[10] According to a more recent survey of 60 farmers in Katsina Province in the savanna area of northern Nigeria, just over half of the farmers interviewed reported supplementary income from trading, weaving, tailoring, blacksmithing, and 10 other pursuits.[11]

Limited division of labor concomitant with limited markets brings in its wake a certain organization of work. Productive units are small, usually based upon the family. (For occasional tasks requiring a larger work force, community labor is supplied on the basis of reciprocity rather than monetary payment.) Capital equipment is limited to simple tools powered by men or animals. Work in the traditional economy is sequential with no division of labor for individual commodities, the individual producer carrying the product through every stage of production. This lack of specialization means that neither coordinating activities nor organizational hierarchy are required, characteristics that are particularly pertinent to the introduction of modern manufacturing methods. In addition, production techniques rest upon a fairly confined range of physical principles, and skills are simple. Technical knowledge and work competencies are transmitted by observation and learning by doing. In traditional farming the precise seasonal requirements impose a pattern on the timing of work, and organic growth provides a rough standardization of product. Neither of those built-in controls are present in primitive manufacture: raw material and labor inputs are variable, as are product specifications and product quality. As we shall see in the next chapter, the absence of any coordinating and controlling functions in primitive manufacture is one of the antecedents of low levels of efficiency in modern industrial undertakings.

SOCIAL STRUCTURE

Concomitant with low productivity and limited markets is the presence of a large number of social institutions and technical practices which have as one of their functions insurance against the loss of income. Old age, sickness, crop failure, and injury to livestock represent the principal causes of loss of income. Because of the lack of scientific knowledge these risks are greater in traditional agriculture than in developed economies. At the same time, the hardship imposed by a loss in production is also greater. Because the traditional farmer's margin above subsistence is relatively modest, a partial loss of output could easily put him and his family below the survival minimum. In the case of total crop failure, compared to a farmer in a high-income economy the traditional farmer has little or no accumulated wealth from which to provide sustenance until circumstances improve; hence, the wide range of mechanisms for averting risk and for spreading the cost of insurance.

Several risk-averting devices have already been identified within farming practices. Seed varieties, such as *indica* rice, have been selected not for maximum average yields but for minimum variation in yield. Mixed and sequential planting makes labor operations more difficult but reduces the likelihood that all crops will be lost to drought, disease, or pests. One of the main motives for large families is to insure that enough hands will be available to tend the fields when the household is visited by sickness or death and that there will be surviving sons and daughters to support parents in their old age.

In addition to the measures for averting risk, there are many arrangements for spreading their cost. Rental of farm land for a share of the final produce reduces the possible loss to the cultivator by shifting a portion of the risk to the landlord. Kinship obligations to provide support for relatives in need operates in the same way of spreading loss so that it does not impose a crushing burden on any single individual.

Kinship reciprocity is a central organizing principle in the social structure of small-scale village communities. The virtues of the kinship network in providing security to even the poorest members of the village are, it must be pointed out, closely linked to its disposition to inhibit change, including beneficial change:

> Potentially, people are either reciprocators or exploiters; and which of these potentialities is actually realized evidently turns in great measure on the numbers of persons which given social structures link to each other in mutually servicing activities. When the structures limit the size of collective units of action mainly to the extended family, clan, or tribe, total helplessness of the individual to meet even his simplest needs without the helping hands of others induces a depth and richness and power of kinship bonds which is well-nigh incomprehensible to Western societies.[12]

If patience, endurance and the highest sense of family and social obligation are among the great virtues of traditional village life, suspicion, faction and fear are on the reverse of the coin. Village societies are levelling societies, in which attempts by equals to gain individual advantage are constantly suspected and bitterly resented. No doubt this springs from fear that the fundamental security of the village will slowly be lost if one individual after another can reach a platform of prosperity from which he might not need the help of the community and could therefore excuse himself from helping them. There are terrible weapons against this offence—social ostracism, and witchcraft of various forms. To be a "model farmer," by currying favour with the officials, men will say, or to set yourself up as superior in any way is to risk unleashing this social attack; and thereafter if a cow dies or a crop is trampled by wild animals, the thought of malice and even witchcraft will quickly be aroused. Those who have traditional status, by lineage or caste or long-established wealth, can escape this; and these are the men who will chiefly appear as "traditional leaders," because they can be seen to lead without attracting this penalty.[13]

Innovation is inhibited not only by the negative leveling tendencies described by Guy Hunter. The positive incentive of material gain to the individual who shoulders the expense and uncertainty of a would-be innovation is weakened by the imperative of communal sharing; when new arrangements entail an absolute loss to any one claimant, innovation may be blocked altogether. An instance of the latter is successful resistance by demonstrating women in the early 1950s to the introduction of mechanical palm oil extraction in eastern Nigeria and Senegal. The diversion of palm fruit from cottage processors to the new oil mills increased household income but it deprived the housewife of her personal income from the sale of the residual palm kernel. Beyond incentives there is the question of capacity to innovate: the small scale of traditional social networks necessary means (a) limited exposure to new technical knowledge and limited ability to evaluate its possible uses and (b) inability to absorb innovations involving substantial interdependencies extending beyond the communal boundaries of trust, for example, participation in large-scale irrigation schemes or agricultural cooperatives.

However, to fault traditional social structures as unreceptive to contemporary forces of change is to point to needs different from those to which they were the response. The survival of kinship societies over the centuries attests to their success in meeting the basic social needs when technology is rudimentary and enduring large-scale political organization is absent.

THE URBAN SECTOR

A final aspect of the traditional economy which deserves our attention is the urban sector. Culture and history place their distinctive mark on the appearance, style, and organization of city life from one underdeveloped economy to the next. Even in a single country like Nigeria one encounters such diverse urban communities as the large Muslim entrepot city of Kano; the wholly modern administrative center of Enugu; and the ocean port, manufacturing center, and capital city of Lagos. Nevertheless, the economic structure of urban communities is characterized by the same low productivity, limited division of labor, and narrow markets that produce rough uniformity among the rural sectors of low-income countries. In particular, cities and towns in traditional economies are alike in that they do not represent an interconnected set of specialist firms, subject to economies of scale and of agglomeration, whose principal activity is the production of goods and services for exchange with other sectors of the economy.

Large urban communities in poor countries are comparatively few in number and tend to be based on governmental administration, foreign trade-related activities, or a combination of the two functions. The weight of the former is reflected in the large fraction of urban population that is made up of public employees and their dependents. Foreign trade is based on the main item of farm cash sales, namely primary exports. Governmental administration and external trade are closely linked. Most of the revenue which supports the public sector is derived from taxes on exports and the imports which they make possible. In turn the public sector provides the transportation system, storage, and port facilities without which international trade could not be carried on. Manufacturing is typically limited in extent and located in the port cities, with a large part of the items it consumes—raw materials, intermediate goods, capital equipment, skilled services—purchased from abroad. Thus the greater portion of manufacturing can accurately be described as either an import-processing or an export-processing activity.

There is a third element in the urban economy beyond governmental administration/public services and activities related to the export-import trade. This is the small-scale service sector which caters to the consumer demand of the first two groups—personal services, retail distribution, and artisan production of the simpler household goods. This segment of the urban economy, the most populated, contrasts in a number of ways with the distribution and manufacturing activities in the foreign trade-related sector. In the latter, foreign enterprises are frequently prominent; with high barriers to entry markets are monopolistic, wages are high relative to average per capital income, and returns to capital are generous. In the small-scale service sector self-employment and family units are dominant; extremely low investment and skill requirements for entry produce atomistic competition and meager returns to capital and labor.

To what extent does the urban sector interact with the surrounding agrarian economy? Most of the goods and services consumed in the urban economy are either imported or produced in that sector. On the other hand, the urban sector, or rather its foreign trade-related segment in conjunction with the road and rail network, supplies the marketing and transportation services necessary for selling agricultural produce to world markets. The food requirements of the urban population provide an additional outlet for farm cash sales. However, this intersectoral exchange is limited in the traditional economy by the low ratio of urban to farm population and modest levels of per capita expenditure on food. When 70 per cent of the population is in agriculture, an "average" farm family of five has a market of 1.25 persons in the nonfarm sectors; when the agricultural population has fallen to 10 per cent the size of this market rises to 40 persons. Thus the lack of exchange and intersectoral specialization in a traditional economy is not only a result of foreign enclaves and low average productivity, it is also a consequence of the economy's predominantly agrarian structure. How this structure is transformed during the course of economic development is the subject of the next chapter.

NOTES

1. These data and that in the final column were developed by Colin Clark and Margaret Haswell for the years 1957-60 and are thus not strictly com-

parable to the labor force and output statistics. However, comparison of FAO net food supply tables for 1965 with the calorie data given by Clark and Haswell indicates that their figures are, with the exceptions of Ghana (down) and Taiwan (up), within 10 per cent of those for the later period. Colin Clark and Margaret Haswell, *The Economics of Subsistence Agriculture* (London, 1970), 4th ed.

2. Michael Roemer, *Fishing for Growth: Export-Led Development in Peru 1950-1967* (Cambridge, Massachusetts, 1970). Shifts in ocean currents led to a sharp reduction in anchovy production in 1972 and 1973, but according to Peru's Sea Institute water temperatures and other conditions have again become favorable, and it is expected that anchovy concentrations will return to normal in two years. Thus 1974 production may reach 7 to 8 million tons compared to the 1973 catch of about 3 million tons and a normal level of some 10 million tons. Paul Ferree, "Peru Again Bans Anchovy Fishing, Fishmeal Supplies Tighten," *Foreign Agriculture* Vol. 11, No. 32 (August 6, 1973).

3. From a strictly statistical point of view "bimodal" is correct only in the sense that the modes of the frequency distributions pertaining to the number of operational units and to the area cultivated are at polar ends of the distribution whereas in the unimodal case the two modes tend to overlap. In later chapters we shall be using the term "bimodal structure of farm size" in a generic sense to depict a situation where a small subsector of large farm units cultivates a large part of the farm land, while the greater part of the farm population is confined to very small, semi-subsistence holdings. The term was first used by Theodore W. Schultz to characterize Soviet collective farms with their small private plots coexisting with a large mechanized unit. Theodore W. Schultz, *Transforming Traditional Agriculture* (New Haven, Connecticut, 1964), p. 123. We also refer to agricultural strategies as "bimodal" or "unimodal" according to the type of pattern of rural development that they promote.

4. H. O. Walker, "Evaporation," *Journal of the West African Science Association* Vol. 2, No. 2 (August 1956), p. 108.

5. Pierre Gourou, *The Tropical World* (London, 1953), pp. 93-94.

6. We have omitted a fourth agricultural region because of the far smaller population involved. *Highlands* exhibit great variation in temperature and moisture conditions depending upon altitude and the direction of the prevailing winds. The uneven topography of the highland regions is often an obstacle to agricultural production, especially when the hoe is replaced by animal or mechanical draft power. Offsetting advantages frequently include young volcanic soils of high fertility, a relatively high and reliable rainfall, and lower risk of disease. Cooler temperatures suit the highland areas for wheat, Arabica coffee, tea, pyrethrum, and livestock.

7. Andrew Kamarck, "Climate and Economic Development," International Bank for Reconstruction and Development, Economic Development Institute Seminar Paper No. 2 (Washington, D.C., November 1972).

8. National Productivity Council, *Survey of Agricultural Machinery and Implements in India* (New Delhi, 1968), p. 45.

9. W. H. Beckett, *Akokoaso: A Survey of a Gold Coast Village* (London, 1944), p. 16.
10. R. Galletti, K. D. S. Baldwin, and I. O. Dina, *Nigerian Cocoa Farmers* (Oxford, 1956), p. 655.
11. Kenneth R. M. Anthony and Bruce F. Johnston, "Field Study of Agricultural Change: Northern Katsina, Nigeria," Food Research Institute Study of Economic, Cultural, and Technical Determinants of Agricultural Change in Tropical Africa, Preliminary Report No. 6 (Stanford, California, 1968).
12. John M. Brewster, "Traditional Social Structures as Barriers to Change," in *Agricultural Development and Economic Growth,* edited by Herman M. Southworth and Bruce F. Johnston (Ithaca, New York, 1967), pp. 78-79.
13. Guy Hunter, *Modernizing Peasant Societies* (New York and London, 1969), p. 40.

2 | Structural Transformation

The mechanism of economic progress in farming is the same one that operates in every other sector of the economy. The mechanism is *specialization*. Not only is there specialization along specific crop lines among farmers, but a host of functions formerly carried out by the household is transferred to specialist producers. Increasing division of labor in all economic activity brings with it the opportunity for using machinery whose power, speed, and precision multiplies the yield of human effort. Specialization not only makes possible the introduction of capital equipment, it facilitates changes to better organization and more productive technologies. The result is to raise the productivity of land and capital as well as that of labor. As these processes get under way, individual productive units shift from self-sufficiency to dependence upon markets, both for disposal of their production and for purchase of their raw materials and factor services.

A corollary of the movement toward specialization and market dependence at the producer level is increased differentiation at the sectoral level. New manufacturing and service activities emerge. Formerly small sectors—education, medicine, financial services—are greatly enlarged. The most dominant change, however, is the proportionate decline in the agricultural sector, both in its contribution to national output and to total employment, and the rise of the manufacturing sector. Although a substantial part of the diminution in the importance of agriculture can be attributed to the relatively greater demand for nonagricultural goods with rising incomes, the more fundamental cause is the transfer of function from generalist producers in the countryside to specialist firms in the towns. Such is the case for the making of clothing, utensils, furniture, weapons, jewelry, the processing of crops into food, the construction of buildings, boats, and so on. Nor is the transfer of these tasks out of the farm household limited to the production of hard goods: "fetching water, gathering fuel, educating, litigating, adjudicating, healing, regulating individual conduct, propitiating the Deity, waging war, and governing are increasingly turned over to public utilities and oil companies, and to teachers, lawyers, judges, doctors, policemen, priests, soldiers, and congressmen."[1] In this way the functions of agriculture are gradually pared down to the single activity of growing raw materials.

The fundamental point that economic development necessarily implies structural transformation is best illustrated by examining wealthy agricultural economies which cater to external markets. Examples might be Denmark, New Zealand, or, within a country, the state of Iowa. What is the proportion of total output in these economies that originates in farming? The figures are as follows: Denmark: 12 per cent, New Zealand: 13 per cent, and Iowa: 11 per cent.[2] Farm productivity is high in these economies precisely because of the abundant use of high-productivity inputs obtained from outside the agricultural sector: farm machinery, chemicals, financial credit, transportation facilities, and professional services ranging from those of agronomist to tax consultant. Taking the United States in 1967, the value added by these externally supplied inputs to farm output was $30.7 billion as against $12.3 billion contributed by the land, labor, and capital of the farmer.[3] High-productivity agriculture entrains industrialization directly; it also fosters it indirectly since the specialized factor services, differentiated market networks, financial institutions, and so on, that serve farming simultaneously lead to increased efficiency in various manufacturing and service activities.

PATTERNS OF STRUCTURAL CHANGE

Table 2.1 presents data for a cross section of countries on certain aspects of these sectoral changes in output and employment as per

Table 2.1. Selected measures of structural transformation, 1965
(*Per cent except as indicated*)

Country	Per cent of labor force in		Per cent of GDP in		Per capita GNP (*U.S. 1964 dollars per head*)
	Agriculture	Manufacturing	Agriculture	Manufacturing	
Tanzania	95	...	54.1	4.8	66
Kenya	88	...	34.9	11.3	98
Nigeria	80	...	54.9	6.3	75
Togo	79	...	49.8	6.0	87
Zaire (Congo)	69	...	21.5	15.9	68
Ghana	56	...	35.7	19.6	157
Libya	60	7	5.0	2.6	694
Egypt	55	11	29.5	21.4[a]	147
Syria	50	12	28.0	11.7[a]	165
Pakistan	74	10	48.1	11.1	83
India	70	...	46.1	15.3	84
Indonesia	66	6	47.3	11.6	91
Burma	62	...	31.8	9.5	65
Malaysia	55	...	31.0	10.1	258
South Korea	54	11	41.3	17.2	123
Ceylon	54	9[b]	39.4	9.3	135
Taiwan	47	...	25.9	20.7	201
Haiti	79	...	49.6[c]	12.1[c]	85
El Salvador	59	...	29.8	16.3	240
Mexico	52	16[b]	14.5	22.0	419
Ecuador	52	15[b]	33.9	17.3	191
Colombia	50	13	31.1	18.3	226
Brazil	48	...	22.3	20.9	208
Peru	47	13	20.3	15.9	290
Chile	26	...	10.4	26.1	419

[a] Includes mining, and for Syria also includes utilities.
[b] For Ceylon 1963, Mexico 1968, and Ecuador 1962.
[c] 1960.
SOURCE: Data for labor force in agriculture from Food and Agriculture Organization of the United Nations, *Production Yearbook 1970* (Rome, 1971), Table 5; for labor force in manufacturing from International Bank for Reconstruction and Development, *World Tables* (Washington, D.C., 1971), Table 2; all other data from ibid., Table 4.

capita incomes rise. The general pattern is that countries with high incomes have proportionately smaller agricultural sectors and larger manufacturing sectors. As we saw in Table 1.1, the countries with a smaller fraction of their labor force engaged in farming also have, despite the reduced manpower input, higher absolute levels of national per capita agricultural output. In addition to manufacturing, as development proceeds, the shares of transportation and educational, governmental, and professional services are also enlarged.

There is, of course, considerable variation in the general pattern of change in sectoral shares with rising per capita income caused by differences in natural resource endowment, size of country, and economic policies. With reference to natural resource differences, as described in Table 1.2, the effect of mineral wealth in Libya and Chile is to raise per capita income and to reduce the share of agriculture in GDP (although not in employment in the case of Libya). The influence of size of country (measured by population) derives from the larger ratio of foreign trade to national output for smaller countries and the ability of larger countries to take advantage of economies of scale in manufacturing. The consequence of these effects at any given level of income is to produce a bias toward primary exports for smaller countries and toward industrial import substitution for larger countries, for example, Togo versus India.

Because our sample of countries is limited to underdeveloped economies, the full force of structural transformation is not observed. This can be remedied by looking at the historical pattern of developed countries as their income levels rose from $100 to $200 per head to $1500 to $3000 per head over a period of 100 years. Changing sectoral shares are shown for eight such countries in Figure 2.1. "Primary" includes mining as well as agriculture, forestry, and fishing; "industry" consists of manufacturing, utilities, and construction. Over the income range mentioned, the share of primary production fell from 50 to 60 per cent of GNP to 5 to 10 per cent, while that of industry rose from 15 to 40 per cent. In both cases the historical experience is similar to the relationship derived from a 1960 cross section of high-, low-, and medium-income countries with population above 15 million, as shown by the line marked "large country pat-

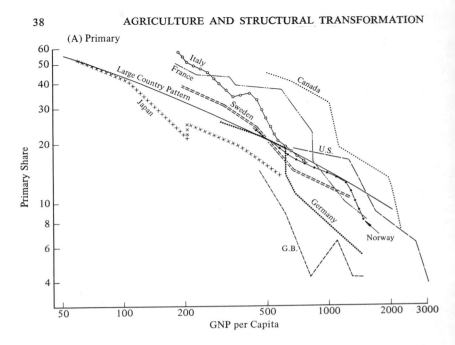

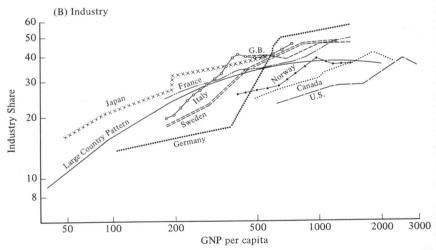

Figure 2.1 Sectoral output shares in eight countries, 1860-1960 *(1960 prices)*.

tern." The one deviation of the cross-section regressions from the historical experience is that the share of primary output tends to fall lower than would be predicted by the cross-section estimate. This results from a mild trend factor reflecting long-term technological changes which have been operating over the last century to diminish agriculture's share in GNP for any given level of per capita income. More specifically, the direction of economic innovation has been to substitute man-made products for those of nature. Thus detergents, electricity, synthetic textiles, plastics, and so on all meet consumer wants which were served by agricultural commodities 50 or 100 years ago.

Under the influence of changing demand and production relationships that accompany structural transformation there are systematic alterations within the manufacturing sector itself. Table 2.2 summarizes data for a cross section of 55 countries, divided at the 10 million population mark into small and large countries. The top row shows the aggregate share of manufacturing as per capita income rises from $92 to $1020. For the reasons noted earlier, large countries enjoy a higher rate of sectoral change, particularly in the early stages of development over the $100 to $300 range in per capita income. Looking at the individual groupings, food processing, tobacco, and textile products constitute over half of manufacturing output for large and small countries alike below per capita income levels of $150. While these industries continue to maintain the share in national output that they attained at the $300 level, indicating an income elasticity of demand of about one, their share in manufacturing output falls. The fastest growing subsector is fabricated metal products, which has an income elasticity of almost two over the entire range. It is in this category and the two above it where small countries lag most behind the large countries; not surprisingly they are the industries where economies of scale are most pronounced.

SOURCE: Data from Hollis B. Chenery and Lance Taylor, "Development Patterns: Among Countries and Over Time," *Review of Economics and Statistics* Vol. 50, No. 4 (November 1968), p. 401.

Table 2.2. Percentage share of manufacturing industries in GDP at different levels of per capita income in large and small countries, 1958

Manufacturing industries	Benchmark values of per capita GDP (*1958 dollars*)				
	92	153	306	510	1,020
	(*per cent share in GDP*)				
Total manufacturing					
Large	12	16	22	26	31
Small	12	14	17	21	27
Food, beverages, and tobacco					
Large	3.8	4.7	5.1	5.1	4.6
Small	4.1	5.5	6.3	6.6	5.5
Textiles and clothing					
Large	2.6	3.4	4.1	4.2	4.1
Small	2.6	2.9	3.2	3.6	3.5
Wood, paper, printing, and leather					
Large	1.2	1.8	2.5	3.0	4.0
Small	1.3	1.5	2.0	2.8	4.6
Rubber, chemicals, and petroleum products					
Large	1.5	2.0	3.0	3.5	3.9
Small	1.2	1.3	1.6	1.9	2.4
Industrial raw materials					
Large	1.2	1.5	2.4	3.0	3.5
Small	1.3	1.3	1.5	1.9	2.5
Fabricated metal products					
Large	1.7	2.6	4.9	7.2	10.9
Small	1.5	1.5	2.4	4.2	8.5

SOURCE: Data from Simon Kuznets, *Economic Growth of Nations: Total Output and Production Structure* (Cambridge, Massachusetts, 1971), pp. 124-25. All figures are averages of cross-section shares for 1953 and 1963 for 22 large countries and 33 small countries (i.e., population less than 10 million).

SPECIALIZATION AND THE DEVELOPMENT OF MARKETS

The pattern of change in the structure of production we have just described is but one aspect of the central development process of specialization. Division of labor among producers cannot go ahead without a concomitant expansion and evolution of markets to integrate their activities. Markets for consumer goods and services, for tools and machinery, for processed materials and components, for labor services, for land, for capital funds, for financial services multiply in number and in size, and in all dimensions there is a proliferation in the services provided to buyers and sellers.

Commodity Markets

Markets for agricultural commodities and simple consumer goods can usually be found at the earliest stage of development; such markets are typically the consequence of the first instance of occupational specialization which comes with the establishment of a central political administration. As communication with other countries develops, foreign trade evolves from a limited traffic in firearms and exotic luxuries to sizable imports of more basic consumer items which are superior substitutes for some local products which they displace; machine-made cotton textiles are perhaps the most notable example. Traded in exchange for imports are one or more primary products, which initially may be produced with the aid of underutilized land and labor. Export production is later augmented by the resources dislodged from their previous employment as a result of the new imports.

As the volume of commodity trade rises, its organization becomes more complex and generally more efficient. A common pattern is the following. Initially distribution consists of a two-stage system based on coastal towns, itinerant traders, and periodic markets. As economic development proceeds the system evolves into a highly articulated network, continuous in space and time, which encompasses large importing and exporting houses, commission agents, several tiers of wholesalers, and a spectrum of retail channels ranging from department stores to petty hawkers. These merchanting activities are themselves supported by a network of specialists providing warehousing, transport, processing, credit, insurance, and so on. The volume of market exchange rises more rapidly than the production of final goods and services owing to (a) the gradual but uninterrupted transfer of function from the household to the market and (b) rising trade in intermediate goods and services that is associated with advancing producer specialization. The efficiency with which markets operate at any given point constitutes in itself a significant stimulant or deterrent to further structural transformation.

The Labor Market

The development of the labor market accommodates differentiation in two directions, specialization by commodity and by skill. At the subsistence stage, household labor is employed in the production of many items to meet family consumption needs. As more and more goods are purchased on the market, the range of cultivated crops and household crafts is gradually narrowed. For a while there may be a partially offsetting diversification of labor time toward marketing activities and part-time employment in plantations, mines, and various seasonal processing jobs in cotton ginneries, rice mills, canneries, and so forth. However, as average productivity in the economy rises, greater occupational specialization in the distribution network, improved storage for agricultural commodities, and the emergence of a permanent urban labor force tend to reduce such opportunities for short-term commercial employment; at the same time the returns to full-time modern farming make such opportunities less attractive. Within the farming sector itself the extent to which a permanent wage labor force develops is determined by the pattern of land ownership and tenure arrangements. The availability of long-distance transportation, urban housing, and widely diffused job information, along with the horizon-widening effects of a certain amount of schooling, all contribute to the success with which the labor market allocates workers to the new nonfarm activities.

The labor market does more than reallocate manpower geographically and between productive sectors. Wage and salary differentials play a central role in facilitating the formation of specialized human competencies. Without such human capital to bind together more complex technology and organization, the process of structural transformation cannot be sustained. Even more so than in the case of commodity markets, the development of the appropriate set of labor skills is heavily dependent upon other inputs besides pecuniary incentives. The principal nonmarket inputs are the extent and quality of education, both general and technical, employer policies, and inherited traditions. Given reasonable education and training initiatives by public authorities and private firms, the supplies of purely technical skills of the many varieties of artisans, craftsmen, technicians, and scientists are responsive to market generated wage premiums. On the other hand, supervisory and managerial skills, which appear to be more influenced by sociological factors, tend to develop at a much slower pace.

Financial Intermediation

The capital market is the principal institution for specialization between savers and investors. By increasing the incentive to save and the profitability of investment, money markets are a major contributor to raising the level of physical capital formation. They make it possible to shift investable resources from one sector to another, from areas of limited growth potential to those where rapid expansion is possible. In addition to promoting fixed investment, well-functioning capital markets augment national product and consumer welfare by financing a higher level of current business transactions and by enabling households to have more freedom in the timing of large expenditures.

In the subsistence economy, capital formation consists of applying labor to land improvement and the making of tools and buildings. Investment by the individual producer is limited to his own ability and willingness to save, that is, the amount of household labor time that can be diverted from production for current consumption and from noneconomic activities. Saving and investment are thus combined in the same mutually constraining act. Capital projects for the village face a similar limit of labor availability. As monetization advances and a market for debt emerges, savings and investment are gradually separated and the geographic boundaries within which investable resources can be mobilized are greatly extended.

Initially, in most traditional communities, risks are great and competition among lenders is slight. The result is that interest rates are extremely high and borrowing is confined to distress situations. However, as the economy advances, developments on a number of fronts work to lower the real cost of lending and to increase competition. Consider the case of agriculture. With the introduction on the farm of such new inputs as improved seed varieties and chemical fertilizers, the absolute level of output begins to climb, thereby raising the margin above subsistence that is available for debt servicing. While an increase in purchased inputs taken by itself necessarily raises the risk to the cultivator of sustaining a monetary loss, other innovations such as better control of water and more effective plant protection have the effect of reducing output variation from one season to the next. These innovations reduce the probability of default and hence the size of the risk premium that the lender must charge. With cadastral and soil surveys dispelling uncertainty about property boundaries and agronomic value, the amount of land given as surety can be lowered and the costs of contract enforcement are reduced. Finally, as demand for agricultural borrowing expands in response to the growing availability of profitable farm inputs, and as lender costs fall, there is an enlargement of the scale of lending which permits spreading of risk among different productive activities and increases the number of lenders competing for clients in any given market.

Now let us consider the supply of savings. When the volume of borrowing is limited, the savings lent are those of the landlord, shopowner, or moneylender. As the real costs of lending diminish (for the reasons set forth in the paragraph above) and the demand for loanable funds expands, individual lenders are progressively displaced by commercial banks, savings banks, and cooperative societies. On the cost side, these financial intermediaries can take advantage of powerful economies of scale in risk spreading, information gathering, and loan administration. While the individual lender is limited to his own resources, financial intermediaries mobilize the savings of countless asset holders. By offering secure return to depositors, hoardings of cash and precious metals can now be tapped. Households that previously did not save at all, because their potential saving capacity fell below the threshold for making a primary loan, are now enticed to do so. These new savers are induced to come forward not only by the secure return on their savings no matter how small, but also by security of principal that is provided by diversification in lending and by the right of immediate withdrawal in case of emergency needs. Just as better information, reduction in risk, and lower transactions cost lower the interest paid by the borrower, these same forces tend to result in a higher net interest being received by the saver.

Governmental Influences on Markets

In the preceding paragraphs we have sketched the central tendency of market evolution that accompanies economic development, but this is a simplified description that abstracts from many significant details. In painting a more realistic picture of contemporary low-income countries we would want to include important nonindigenous elements—international corporations, skilled expatriate personnel, foreign aid—and governmental development efforts in such areas as state enterprise and publicly financed credit programs. A major amendment to our description would be the extent of involuntary saving (taxation and inflation) as a supplement and/or substitute for private capital markets as the channel for mobilizing investment resources. However, if we are interested in the success or failure of market coordination in promoting specialization and advances in per capita income, particular attention must be given to the effects of government measures on the allocation of resources.

Under most conditions well-functioning markets draw forth maximum supplies of labor, capital, and entrepreneurial endeavor and direct these resources to their most productive uses. For a wide variety of reasons, governments in less-developed countries have become involved in the pricing and allocation of certain strategic resources. Because capital markets are frequently slow to develop, public lending programs using tax funds are established with lending rates fixed at a low level. In the face of foreign exchange shortages, rather than allow the cost of foreign currencies to rise sufficiently to equate supply and demand, governments typically ration this scarce commodity by means of import licenses. Insofar as such underpricing prevails and rationing takes place on the basis of the claimant's sociopolitical influence, there is a tendency both in manufacturing and farming to create an artificial partition between favored larger concerns, which receive the lion's share of government-controlled resources, and the bulk of producers. Government taxation policies—import tariffs, export duties, excise taxes—differentially alter the profitability of industries with the potential of directing resources into less-productive lines. Artificially high wage rates for privileged groups of workers and the establishment of rental ceilings on agricultural land are other factors which can lead to inefficient allocation. Monetary policies if excessively inflationary will erode the value of financial assets and lower the real rate of interest and, as a consequence, undermine incentives to save. The effects of financial policies which fix lending rates at a low level and impose ceilings on deposit rates receive further attention in Chapter 3.

The observation that governments in late-developing countries have tended to intervene in product, factor, and money markets in ways that impede healthy development should not be taken to imply that laissez-faire is the best policy. Quite the contrary. Factor immobilities and a paucity of information about prices, product specifications, and choice of production techniques are inherent characteristics of an underdeveloped economy. The need for government action thus extends far beyond performance of its role as tax collector and provider of social overhead capital; it has an equally important role in perfecting the working of markets. Such mundane but difficult tasks as the collection of statistics in all lines of organized productive activity, dissemination on an industry basis of pertinent statistical and technical information, enforcement of engineering standards, weights and measures—these are public functions that are of the utmost importance. Likewise government has a central coordinating, facilitating, research-sponsoring role to play in the transfer of technology. With specific reference to agriculture, public bodies must shoulder the responsibility for farmer training, crop research, agricultural engineering research, and such infrastructural items as feeder roads, irrigation projects, and so on.

The spatial location of economic activities is another area where governmental action influences the effectiveness with which markets draw forth resources for use in production. Government decisions with regard to the transportation system and the location of public facilities help to determine the number and dispersion of urban centers that service and are supported by the agrarian economy. A pattern of development where nonagricultural activities are located in a number of regional towns, rather than being concentrated in one or two extremely large cities, provides greater stimulus to the rural-urban interactions which lie at the heart of structural transformation. Incentives to farmers to increase output are improved by easier access to competitive produce markets in centers where inputs, services, and consumer goods are also available. On the other side of the market, closer proximity to their clientele operates in a number of ways to enhance the efficiency of public administration, educational institutions, manufacturers, processors, and so on. In short, an appropriate degree of urban decentralization, which increases the flow of information between producers and strengthens economic incentives, is another element in creating a well-articulated national economy based on comprehensive market networks.

PRODUCTIVITY GROWTH

From the foregoing discussion of the evolution of the market network we can summarize three principal contributions to the raising of per capita national product. First, markets draw into productive use land, labor, and entrepreneurship that might otherwise go untapped. Second, since competitive pricing creates incentives for all participants to allocate resources to those areas where their marginal return is highest, output per worker tends to increase as a result of efficient resource allocation. Third, the operation of financial markets results in a more rapid increase in the stock of capital available to assist the individual laborer, thereby augmenting his or her productivity.

There are, however, additional sources of growth in per capita product intermeshed with the process of specialization which depend upon activities carried out by individuals and institutions that are related only loosely to market incentives. Simon Kuznets, on the basis of long-term input and product data from some 15 advanced economies, concludes that the growth of all inputs as measured in conventional economic accounting explains only 20 to 25 per cent of the growth in per capita output.[4] Hence it is the growth in factor productivity—the increase in output per unit of total inputs—that has been the major engine of structural transformation. Of the interconnected elements that have resulted in this continuous increase in output from a given quantity of inputs, advances in applied technology have played the single most important role. Technological progress is in turn related to the growth of the natural sciences, itself an instance of specialization in the systematic production of knowledge. Other sources of productivity growth frequently but not always linked to the introduction of technological innovation are improvements in managerial efficiency, changes in industrial organization, and the upgrading of labor skills. Allocational gains in output flowing from a shift in inputs from one use to another, as described in the paragraph above, also belong in this category.

It is possible to delineate in a general way how technological progress and the other sources of productivity growth interact to affect the organization of the economy and raise per capita income. As a general rule, more productive technologies are more complex, refining the production process into a larger number of specialized operations. Thus when a new technology is introduced the firm, as an organization, must attain a higher level of knowledge and have command over a wider range of specialized skills. Individual production units grow in scale, employing a larger capital stock and more capital per employee. Cost being but the reciprocal of productivity, superior technology means that cost per unit of output falls, usually both the cost of capital services and unit labor cost.

As division of labor proceeds within the production unit under the influence of newer techniques, those processes that are subject to increasing returns to scale are taken over by specialist companies which, by obtaining a scale of production that permits full-cost minimization, can then sell this input to a number of producers cheaper than they can supply it to themselves. In addition to specialist firms making standardized components or providing wholesaling, purchasing, or maintenance services, the producer network is further expanded by supervised subcontracting with smaller workshops that realize lower costs by virtue of lower overheads and less well-paid labor. Thus for the individual firm the proportion of value added to gross output falls and new vertically linked firms emerge as the specialization and market interdependence progress. This pattern of rising productivity, the shedding of functions, and increased reliance upon purchased inputs holds for agriculture no less than for industry. Economic growth may, however, be slowed or brought to a halt by scarcity of inputs, limitations of final demand, or the exhaustion of economies of specialization.

For sustained productivity growth the motive force is the flow of improvements in applied technology. At the most general level these improvements stem from application of scientific knowledge to the problems of production. For those countries that are technological leaders, outward shifts in the production function to a large degree must await new discoveries in the pure and applied sciences. Once the process of research and development has been institutionalized, increases in factor productivity result in large measure from applied research that translates new theoretical possibilities into specific products or production techniques which fit prevailing factor prices, technical conditions, and consumer tastes. In earlier periods, however, technical progress was slower and more evolutionary, relying on the accidental or intuitively inspired experiments of a multitude of small producers and the occasional inventor. Agricultural change in eighteenth century England and nineteenth century America and Japan, discussed in Chapter 5, was of this type.

The sources of technical progress are very different in late-developing countries. In this case the flow of more productive techniques is little affected by capabilities in the higher reaches of science. Rather advances come from drawing upon the existing body of knowledge in high-income countries. Not only are the mechanisms for tapping the most appropriate kinds of knowledge important, but in many cases local institutions are needed to carry out adaptive research, adjusting product specifications, and input requirements to better meet local conditions. Beyond technology transfer and technology adaptation, technical progress depends upon effective channels for disseminating the appropriate bundles of knowledge to large numbers of producers.

The effective transfer of knowledge and adjustment of product and technique to local circumstances in late-developing countries entails actions at many levels and depends upon the workings of markets, administrative organizations, and individual ingenuity. Applied technology is embodied in people and in products: its transfer is easiest when the improvement is wholly embodied in the product—such as a sharper tool or more durable tire—and becomes more difficult when the improvement also depends upon new skills, restructured organization, and altered relationships with other economic agents, such as suppliers and customers. New technology is obtained through the importing of capital equipment and intermediate goods, licensing of patented processes, hiring of experts, foreign investment, and education. The rate of diffusion of new technology once it has been introduced, varies greatly. Where the techniques are only moderately different from activities already mastered, the diffusion is likely to be fairly rapid. When local personnel are fully experienced with all the processes of the new industry, some of them leave to join a locally sponsored rival project, and the process of spreading via imitative competition is under way. Where the scale and complexity of the new technology is vastly greater than existing activities, the transplant remains an enclave with limited impact on the level of productivity.

The spread of new technology requires the services of various public organizations. Supervised uniform weights and measures, engineering standards, soil surveys and similar provision of exact knowledge about products and factors of production is an essential prerequisite for the application of more advanced techniques as well as for improvement in the functioning of markets. Because private resources are inadequate, adaptive research—on industrial processing of local materials, on manufacturing techniques, on agricultural equipment, on plant varieties—must be carried out by governmental bodies. It is not only that there are sizable economies of scale. More often than not the end product of development research is easily copied by competitors; since firms cannot capture the full returns to their efforts in this area, private investment falls far short of the level that is socially profitable. Collective action by farmers to operate more efficient systems for irrigation, marketing, seed distribution, and the like will in most circumstances entail administrative structures. And, most pervasive, the educational system imparts general knowledge, forms specific skills, and nourishes the analytical powers of the participants in all sectors of the economy. The success with which these publicly operated institutions carry out their functions is a critical determinant of the flow of improvements in applied technology.

ELEMENTS OF SOCIAL CHANGE

As the previous discussion would suggest, the evolution of marketing relationships, the proliferation of firms and public institutions, and the associated changes in individual behavior cannot take place without considerable alteration in the traditional social structure. While every country evolves its own unique blend of indigenous and modern elements, the functional requirements of technoeconomic advance do tend to impose a certain directional influence on the evolution of all traditional societies as they progress to higher levels of per capita income.

The general direction of social change as the economy undergoes structural transformation is toward ever greater differentiation of social roles and institutions on the one hand, and the emergence of new mechanisms of social integration on the other.[5] To take one example of role differentiation, the functions of the village elders in a traditional society are gradually taken over by lawyers, judges, legislators, and family counselors, or in terms of institutions, by the court system, the legislature, and social welfare agencies. These particular examples of differentiation parallel occupational specialization. Examples of integrative mechanisms in this same area which transmit information and supply control are electoral campaigns, elections, political parties, professional associations, and consumer organizations.

Just as the successful development of markets and finer division of labor in production calls for more exact specification of products and processes, the increasing complexity of the social structure and the diminished importance of primary relationships requires formalization of role behavior by written charter and law. Thus in a modern factory a worker's behavior is regulated by his employment contract, the union-management agreement, and managerial directives. With the decentralization of decision making and greater role differentiation, there is a necessity to collect and transmit an increasing volume of information. This task is carried out by private organizations and public bureaucracies; the latter through administrative action also exercise social control.

The evolution in social structure, whereby the individual's activities and loyalties are progressively shifted from the primary grouping of kin and village to societywide interest groups, is a difficult and uneven process. Old relationships are disrupted and new ones must be forged; imported institutions (e.g., trade unions, parliamentary government) fit poorly and sometimes not at all. Of the many aspects of social behavior that are undergoing differentiation and reintegration, it is political development where breakdown is perhaps most frequent.

Integrating thousands of local and regional communities—often differing in language, culture, and religion—into a functioning voluntary collective is itself an extraordinarily arduous task. As the individuals from the various parochial groupings of caste, tribe, and religion enter into the modernization process, competing for jobs, wealth, and status in the country's cities and towns, the search for competitive advantage and shelter from urban insecurities frequently leads to intensification of a reconstituted communal particularism and of communal conflict. Needless to say, these conflicts and other dislocations caused by economic change soon find expression in political form. Not only must the political system be capable of eliciting acceptance of the overriding authority of national political decisions, it also must be capable of organizing and staffing an effective public bureaucracy to collect taxes, provide services, and implement government policies.

What types of change does rising personal income and integration into large-scale market networks bring to the social life of the village? The most basic change is the weakening of the central axis of reciprocity. There are two reasons why this happens. On the one hand, continuing advances in output above minimum subsistence provide the household with monetary savings and other liquid assets which can be used to secure the basic consumption needs in case of local crop failure. In like manner for other types of emergencies, these same resources plus current cash farm income can purchase the needed services previously extended on a nonmonetary basis. Not only do national markets and transport systems allow a food-deficit community to draw on the surplus of distant areas, modern storage facilities mean that an inventory of staple foodstuffs, accumulated in years of abundance, can be carried over to supplement reliance on international markets in the event of widespread calamity. Since rural market networks are far from perfect and take time to adjust to large shifts in supply or demand, total emancipation from communal reciprocity occurs only in the very late stages of structural transformation.

As the security basis of reciprocity weakens, the incentives for ignoring its commands grow stronger. In a community with no substantial external outlet for the produce of the land, the rewards for expanding output above a certain level are usually very slight. Once a community enters the market economy, unlimited production for sale becomes a possibility. The individual who is prepared to spurn, or at least substantially evade, those ancient canons which apply to the heirs of good fortune—expanded obligation to kin and neighbor, to communal celebration, to village improvement, to charity—can now raise his material standard of living and the wealth he will bequeath to his children to heretofore unimagined levels.

The transformation of traditional reciprocal labor arrangements is related to this kind of change. In smallholder communities those farmsteads which expand their output relative to the majority of producers have greater need for outside labor to perform certain tasks. Yet increased exertion on their own farms means that they have even less time to reciprocate in the prescribed manner. Fortunately, the consequence of this expansion supplies its own remedy: enlarged cash sales make possible the payment of money wages. A system of one-to-one labor exchange gradually gives way to a wage system. There is a gain in specialization as some individuals can devote themselves more fully to managerial functions. On the other hand, traditional communal solidarity is necessarily weakened as diffuse, personalistic ties are displaced by specific and sharply delimited contractual obligations.

In communities where farm land is rented rather than owned the disruptive effects of new technology and market opportunities are more pronounced. The share of crop paid in rent, relatively undisturbed by changes in technology or relative prices for several generations, becomes thought of as uniquely fixed by custom and tradition. The size of the rental share is but one important element in the landlord-tenant relationship, a relationship of paternalism and deference wherein the landlord is accorded the moral right to exercise authority in return for accepting the responsibility to provide security for his tenants. When new seeds, fertilizers, and irrigation dramatically raise farm yields, the old equilibrium, already under strain, is further disrupted. More and more conditioned by market opportunities, landlords see these gains as accruing to the scarce resources which they own. For their part tenants strongly resist the enlargement of the rental share, regarding it as a violation of customary norms of distributive justice. Conflict with tenants or government-imposed rental ceilings may lead the landlord to evict his tenants and undertake direct cultivation. Land tenure and taxation policies best designed to deal with this situation are examined in Chapter 4.

With reduced natural risks and new ways for insuring against their occurrence, large families no longer yield the same economic benefit. And on the other side of the balance, rising standards of nutrition, clothing, health, and education greatly augment the cost of having children. The maximum monetary returns, albeit involving a delay in time, are now obtained by having a few children and investing heavily in their education. More knowledge about contraception and concern for the mother and the children's welfare are among the noneconomic factors that operate in the same direction. Thus, as economic calculation becomes a more powerful influence and the balance of costs and benefits change, there is a gradual reduction in family size.

Related to individualistic enterprise is the growth of economic inequality, in the rural economy no less than in the city. While the real income of almost all members of the community is rising, wholly arbitrary factors dictate that some individuals (and some communities and regions) will pull ahead of others. Unequal gains flow from unearned advantages which include the happenstance of being first, good fortune in ownership of specific resources (soil, water, location), or the genetic "luck of the draw" in terms of personal energy and ability. Unless government policies are specifically tailored to the contrary, initial wealth is more often than not transformed into permanent economic advantage. Beyond the inherent advantages of having the lead and educational superiority in the second generation, participation in politics that money makes possible and the cultivation of informal contact networks tend to create privileged access to scarce resources and to raise barriers through statutes, administrative practices, and the like, against would-be competitors. Examples of the latter would include price supports cum output restrictions and concentration of public investment in the fastest growing areas to the neglect of exploiting similar or even greater opportunities in other areas. As emphasized in Chapter 3, impediments to the diffusion of economic gains are noticeably more prominent where administrative rather than market mechanisms are employed for distributing inputs that are in shortest supply.

We have mentioned a number of areas where social change in the countryside is the same as in city or town. Most of these can be interpreted as responses to a common set of pushing and pulling market forces. The divergences in rural-urban social change—specifically the much less radical break with traditional social organization in the farm sector—are to be explained by differences in technology. The common elements of change in new production techniques in farm and factory include the increased use of capital equipment, of purchased inputs, of technical knowledge. Only the last element has an impact upon social structure and even this only indirectly through the diffused influence of education. By contrast the differences between agriculture and industry in the organization of production and in the technologies employed have profound implications for social change.

The shift from craft production to modern manufacturing entails migration to a new place, to a new society, and to a new mode of work. Spending most of the daylight hours away from home, far less time is available to working members of the household for social intercourse with kin and neighbors. New ideas and new activities undermine traditional modes of behavior. Not only do the scale of factories and their needs for diverse inputs require an urban location, the nature of modern production techniques imposes a fundamentally different organization of work. Working among strangers in a largely impersonal setting, the individual performs but a few of the many operations that constitute the production process. Thus he no longer has control over the pace of work, nor can he identify with the finished product, nor take much pride in his craftsmanship.

The shift from the sequential operations that characterize craft production and farming to specialized industrial tasks creates the necessity for a wide range of coordinating, supervising, and controlling functions that had no place in the earlier technology: even where farming or craft work is carried out in large cooperative groups most of the individuals are doing the same operation and are not subject to direct controls. As mentioned in the discussion of labor markets, it is in this area of supervision and management that skill development has proved so difficult. These are, of course, the skills that most involve social relationships and human interaction. In traditional society work organization derived from already existing social units having functions other than work, and maximum productive efficiency was seldom an overriding goal. The behavioral demands on participants are quite different when the organization is structured solely according to technological task requirements: authority must be delegated to persons of lower status, sanctions must be applied to kin and strangers alike, supervisors must take a continuing interest in their subordinate's tasks, and so on. Supervisory and management roles thus have few antecedents in traditional technology and make demands that are often incongruent with traditional behavior.

By contrast, the shift to higher technologies in agriculture entrains far fewer disruptions in existing social relationships. This is so because the unalterable character of biological growth, however it may be augmented, provides a basic continuity for farm organization and work patterns. The locus of modern farming remains as before in the village setting. The family laboring unit continues as an important if not central institution in the organization of production. Thus dealings with strangers, novel activities, depersonalized relationships, and new norms of behavior are at the periphery rather than the center of the social milieu. The absence of sharp breaks with what went before also holds for work skills. The productive operations of plowing, harrowing, planting, applying water and nutrients, weeding, harvesting, and threshing are unchanged. Because the agricultural operations remain consecutive even with the highest degree of mechanization, the farm worker partakes in each stage of production and can identify with the fruit of his labor. And most important from the point of view of technical efficiency, the sequential nature of farming operations bypasses the need for the greater part of the coordinating, controlling, and supervising functions which are so critical in manufacturing.

STRUCTURAL TRANSFORMATION AND THE DISTRIBUTION OF THE LABOR FORCE

Having sketched out the nature of the changes in technology, markets, and social patterns which underly the process of structural transformation, we are ready to return to our examination of its macroeconomic manifestations. In the beginning of this chapter systematic shifts in the composition of national output were shown to be related to rising per capita output. We now look at the accompanying trends in the distribution of employment. Table 2.3 presents cross-sectional figures developed by Kuznets on the changing intersectoral distribution of output and labor force at successively higher levels of per capita income.

Our attention at the beginning of the chapter was focused on two sectors, agriculture and manufacturing. The statistics in Table 2.3 reveal the relative growth of other sectors besides manufacturing. The rising share in national product of construction, transportation, commerce, finance, and a large spectrum of services as per capita income rises is related to both shifts in consumer demand at higher levels of real income and to changes in the organization of production. Cross-section household expenditure surveys in many countries have revealed an apparently invariant pattern of income-related demand preferences: at higher levels of per capita income proportionally less expenditure is devoted to agricultural products and proportionately more to industrial processing of food, to manufactured consumer goods, to education, and to medical care.

However, as Kuznets has frequently noted, a substantial portion of the shift in sectoral shares would occur as a result of technological change even apart from the operation of Engel's Law. Economies of scale associated with modern industrial methods (leading to a shift from small-scale to large-scale production units) and the need for factories to locate in the vicinity of their supplier and customer industries, work to concentrate the growing nonagricultural population in a comparatively few urban centers. Movement from the rural villages and towns to the new cities necessarily imposes novel patterns of working and living. Urban residents now require goods and services that were not needed in the village setting; among these are food processing and storage, transportation, construction of urban dwellings, and a range of services for regulating and maintaining urban life (police, judicial, utilities, etc.). Moreover, changes in opportunity costs and the availability of new manufactured products (construction materials, vitamins, synthetics, etc.) would also contribute to changing sectoral shares even if consumer tastes were identical at all levels of income.

A number of significant relationships are clearly seen in the above

Table 2.3. Distribution of product (P) and labor force (L) by sector at different levels of per capita income for 59 countries, 1958

Sector	$70 P	$70 L	$150 P	$150 L	$300 P	$300 L	$500 P	$500 L	$1,000 P	$1,000 L
Agriculture	48.4	80.3	36.8	63.7	26.4	46.0	18.7	31.4	11.7	17.0
Manufacturing	9.3	6.7	13.6	10.3	18.2	16.5	23.4	21.4	29.6	27.9
Construction	4.1	1.3	4.2	3.2	5.0	5.4	6.1	7.1	6.6	8.4
Utilities, transport, and commerce	6.1	1.6	6.9	3.5	7.8	4.9	9.4	6.4	10.4	8.2
Trade	12.7	4.7	13.8	7.2	14.6	10.0	13.6	12.2	13.4	15.2
Finance, public administration, and other services	18.2	5.8	23.1	12.2	26.0	17.1	26.9	20.2	26.5	21.8

SOURCE: Data from Simon Kuznets, *Economic Growth of Nations: Total Output and Production Structure* (Cambridge, Massachusetts, 1971), pp. 111 and 203. P and L represent percentage share of sectoral product and labor force, respectively. The labor figures may not add exactly to 100 per cent because rows 2 to 5 are for the year 1960.

table. First, the agricultural sector employs over half the labor force until per capita income nears the $300 mark. Second, the share of the farm sector in the national labor force is at every stage very much greater than its share in the national output; the opposite holds true for the eight nonagricultural sectors. These two facts—the sheer bulk of human resources in agriculture in the early stage of development and their low productivity relative to all other sectors—explain the frequent reference to the proportionate size of the agricultural labor force as a key index of structural transformation.

Among the nonagricultural sectors, manufacturing exhibits the largest expansion in employment, rising some 21 percentage points from 6.7 per cent of the labor force at $70 per head to 27.9 per cent at $1000 per head. This is one of the reasons why economic development is commonly equated with industrialization. But here it is important to note that although their share in product only rises 15 percentage points (from 42 to 58 per cent) the nonagricultural sectors other than manufacturing in aggregate account for a far higher increase in employment, going from 13 to 55 per cent of the total labor force or a rise of 42 percentage points.

While the 1958 cross section of low- and middle-income countries faithfully mirrors the general experience of individual countries as they undergo structural transformation, differences in technology, economic policies, and demographic factors have produced variations in the margin by which agriculture's share in the labor force exceeds its share in national product. Kuznets's estimates suggest that between 1910 and 1950 there was a trend for this margin to narrow; that is, for a given product share the proportionate size of the farm work force was less in 1950 than it had been in 1910, and conversely the labor shares of the other sectors were somewhat higher than they had been in 1910. Since 1950, however, this trend has been reversed so that for any given level of per capita income below $500 the share of the labor force in agriculture is now increasing while its proportionate contribution to national product, as noted at the beginning of the chapter, has been diminishing.[6] The causes for this post-World War II trend—most conspicuously the higher rates of

Table 2.4 Sectoral product per worker as a ratio of national product per worker for 59 countries, 1958

Sector	$70	$150	$300	$500	$1000	Percentage change relative to national average		
						$70-$300	$300-$1000	$70-$1000
Agriculture	0.63	0.63	0.63	0.65	0.75	...	+12	+12
Manufacturing	1.75	1.58	1.28	1.20	1.15	−47	−13	−60
Construction	3.23	1.42	1.04	0.95	0.85	−219	−19	−238
Utilities, transport, and commerce	4.18	2.15	1.75	1.60	1.38	−243	−37	−280
Trade	2.97	1.96	1.55	1.19	0.94	−142	−61	−203
Public administration and other services	2.65	1.39	1.13	0.99	0.92	−152	−21	−173

SOURCE: Data from Simon Kuznets, *Economic Growth of Nations: Total Output and Production Structure* (Cambridge, Massachusetts, 1971), p. 209.

population growth in the rural sector and a lessening of employment opportunities in the nonagricultural sectors—are explored in the next chapter.

Since questions of labor absorption and labor productivity are one of the central concerns in this study, it is worthwhile clarifying the structural connections between a given sector's changing share in national output, the level of average labor productivity in that sector, and the amount of labor it absorbs or releases. Let us begin with the intersectoral differences in average labor productivity. As the dissimilar ratios of product share to employment share in Table 2.3 indicate, these differences are considerable. By dividing the product share by the employment share, productivity differentials can be made explicit; this Kuznets has done, obtaining average product per worker for individual sectors expressed as a ratio to national product per worker. These productivity ratios are presented in Table 2.4.

The statistics in Table 2.4 suggest several generalizations. First, intersectoral productivity differentials are greatest at the beginning of the development process and narrow as per capita income rises. Second, labor productivity is lowest in agriculture, being well below the national average over the entire range. However, starting from its very low level, productivity in agriculture grows at a faster rate than that of any other sector. (This follows from the fact that its productivity ratio is the only one to converge upward on the national average.) Third, all the nonagricultural sectors commence with labor productivity levels far above the national average and show much faster rates of convergence (downward) toward the national average. It should be remembered in discussing downward convergence that these ratios are relative to a rising average output per worker: even in the steepest fall of relative productivity from 4.18 to 2.15 for utilities, transport, and commerce, given that the value of average product (1.0) more than doubled over the same interval, absolute output per worker was rising. When assessing these trends it is helpful to recall that in the early stages of development many nonfarm activities are performed by the subsistence household—cottage crafts, construction, transport, various services, and barter trade. Thus it is likely that some part of the initially very large productivity differentials for the nonagricultural sectors and their subsequent decline is attributable to the transfer of the low productivity segments of transport, services, and so on, from the farm household to specialist market suppliers.

The labor absorbed by a particular sector follows directly from its productivity ratio (i.e., its average product per worker relative to national product per worker) and the sector's share of national output. If we assume that the latter is approximately fixed by the level of per capita income, then the amount of employment is inversely related to average labor productivity in that sector. Of the nonfarm sectors, manufacturing initially has the lowest productivity ratio and hence provides proportionately the most employment (first column Table 2.3). However, as shown in Table 2.4, it also exhibits the highest rate of productivity advance as one moves to countries with successively higher incomes: in contrast to a 60 per cent decline in its productivity relative, the decline of the other six sectors range between 173 and 280 per cent. This very high rate of productivity advance, which means that manufacturing has a very low-employment elasticity, is primarily the result of growing capital-intensity. The latter is a function of a changing mix of industrial products and greater mechanization in existing lines. As we shall discover in Chapter 3, during the period to which these cross-sectional relationships pertain (the 1950s), government policies in underdeveloped countries were such as to subsidize the price of capital and to remove the discipline of comparative advantage in the choice of new industry. A different set of policies would have resulted in considerably more employment generation.

What about employment in the other nonfarm sectors? In these sectors labor absorption grows at a faster rate than in manufacturing. This results from the fact that, in contrast to the manufacturing situation, the growth in demand is biased toward those segments of trade, construction, transport, and so on, in which productivity is below the sector average. For example, in construction there is a compositional shift in favor of urban dwellings (relatively labor-intensive) over heavy civil engineering projects such as ports, bridges, and roads. In trade there is a shift in favor of retail services over the less labor-using activities of wholesaling and storage. As the extended family declines and more women enter the labor force, there is a shift from home-supplied to market-supplied personal services—restaurants, lodging, beauty care, domestic services, household repair, and the like.[7]

The recent migrant from agriculture does not possess the qualifications or experience to find employment in financial institutions, the professions, public administration, or even in most areas of manufacturing. It is construction, retail trade, and personal services—labor-intensive, low-skill sectors—where he is most likely to be able to find a job. Having obtained on-the-job training, he may later be able to fill a semiskilled position in manufacturing, communications, or transport.

What is the effect of high rates of population growth on this pattern of sectoral employment? The areas with the lowest skill and capital requirements are agriculture, trade, and personal services. It is these sectors, particularly agriculture (owing to its much larger size) that tend to be the residual employers. To the extent that farming, trade, and personal services cannot productively absorb additional increments in the labor force, disguised and open unemployment are the result.

STRUCTURAL TRANSFORMATION AND THE DEVELOPMENT OF AGRICULTURE

Structural transformation is not only a useful vantage point for analyzing the growth of the economy at large, it also illuminates some of the key factors that govern the speed and direction of agricultural development. When the primary sector bulks so large in the economy, say when it accounts for 50 per cent or more of the labor force, there is a limit on the volume of commodity flows from agriculture to other sectors which sets a ceiling on the rate at which farm output can be expanded. (As will be noted shortly, the possibility of exporting farm products eases that constraint to some extent but does not eliminate it.) Equally, the constrained purchasing power of farmers is a brake on the overall rate of expansion for nonagricultural sectors. Finally, the disbursement pattern of farm income influences the differential growth of particular industry and service subsectors.

The process of specialization depends upon the expansion of markets: to the extent farmers are held back in the amount of food and fiber they can sell, they are prevented from purchasing the externally supplied, high-technology inputs—seed, fertilizers, tools, transport equipment, and so forth—that will raise their productivity. What are the factors that determine the level of cash farm income? Especially in large countries, the main determinant is the demand for food by the nonfarm work force and their dependents. For a country such as India where 70 per cent of the population is in agriculture, an "average" farm family of five has a market of just over two persons.

When the farm population has dropped to 40 per cent, commercial sales by an "average" farm unit will be made to 7.5 people; when the farm population is but a fifth of the total, the number is 20 persons. This simple arithmetic, even after all the appropriate refinements are taken into account, dramatically illustrates that for large countries the farm sector, as a whole, is subject to a severe purchasing power constraint in the early stages of structural transformation. This fact, as we shall see in Chapter 4, constitutes one of the key starting points in drawing up an efficient agricultural strategy.

There are two refinements that need to be made to this simple arithmetical model. The first is to introduce several elements that slightly raise the gradient at which average cash farm income expands as sectoral shares are altered. Although less than unity, the income elasticity of demand for food (valued at farm gate) is positive so that average expenditure per individual is increasing at the same time that the share of the nonfarm population is being enlarged. This same pattern holds for the growth in demand for nonfood primary products that are consumed as inputs in the relatively fast-growing manufacturing sector. Another source of enlarged monetary income that accrues to members of farm households is the growth of off-farm employment which typically becomes more significant when the nonagricultural sectors have grown to considerable size. Wage earnings from farm labor, like intrasectoral sales between specialized farmers, help to raise productivity and welfare in the agricultural sector but do not directly augment the aggregate amount of purchasing power vis à vis the nonagricultural sectors.

The second and more important qualification is the possibility of cash sales to the export market. For small countries agricultural exports can greatly ease the purchasing power constraint; for large countries the contribution is more limited. This can be seen from the comparison of large and small countries in Table 2.5. Even a small country may encounter difficulty in expanding foreign exchange earnings from a traditional export crop if it accounts for a sizable share of world exports. Ghana's cocoa industry is a case in point. Furthermore, the almost universal attractiveness of expanding existing pri-

Table 2.5. Per capita GNP and agricultural exports in large and small countries, 1969
(*In dollars except population figures in parenthesis in millions*)

Large countries	GNP	Agricultural exports	Small countries	GNP	Agricultural exports
Nigeria (64)	80	7	Tanzania (13)	70	15
India (537)	90	1	Malagasy (7)	92	14
Pakistan (126)	91	2	Uganda (8)	110	22
Brazil (91)	231	20	Dominican Republic (4)	234	36
Mexico (49)	476	14	Costa Rica (2)	423	90[a]
Indonesia (116)	95	(2-4)[b]	Averages for 27 other small countries (population less than 15 million)	188[c]	28[c]

[a] For 1968.
[b] No satisfactory conversion to U.S. dollars is available. Comparing the computed value of exports of coffee and rubber, the two major agricultural exports, based on quantity figures and world prices in dollars indicates that a $2 per capita figure, as implied by direct conversion of rupiah values for agricultural exports given in the UN source, is a substantial underestimate. But that comparison also suggests that the correct figure is probably less than $4 per capita.
[c] Partially 1968.
SOURCE: Per capita GNP estimates expressed in 1964 dollar prices are based on International Bank for Reconstruction and Development, *World Tables* (Washington, D. C., 1971), Table 4. Population estimates are from Table 2. Agricultural export data are from FAO, *Trade Yearbook 1971* (Rome, 1972), Table 132.

mary commodity exports is the root cause of the persistent tendency of world supply to outrun demand for certain of these products. Cocoa, coffee, tea, rubber, jute, cotton, and vegetable oils fall into this category. Because so many developing countries attempt to enlarge farm incomes and foreign exchange earnings in this way, producing countries frequently experience deterioration in terms of trade. (The currently favorable terms of trade for primary products represent, in our view, another one of the periodic deviations from this trend rather than the beginning of a new era.) However, as we shall see in

Chapter 7, for the country that can alter the composition of its cash crops, buoyant foreign markets for some farm products can usually be found.[8]

The major determinants of the rate of growth of farm cash receipts (R'_a) can be summarized in the following expression:

$$R'_a = w_1 (P'_n + \eta g'_n) - w_2 M'_a + w_3 X'_a,$$

where P is population, η is the per capita income elasticity of demand for agricultural products, g is per capita income, and M and X represent the value of agricultural imports and exports. The primes indicate annual percentage rates of change, the subscripts a and n denote agriculture and nonagriculture, and the w's are weights which reflect each component's relative contribution to total farm receipts. This formulation requires the simplifying assumption that the terms of trade between agriculture and nonagriculture remain unchanged. In reality, the rate of change of the domestic component may be either more or less rapid than $P'_n + \eta g'_n$. But if sharp increases in food prices result from failure of food production to keep pace with the growth of demand, structural transformation will be impeded so this is not a sustainable means of enlarging farm cash income. The M' and X' terms refer to changes in farm receipts associated with changes in agricultural imports or exports. It is noted in Chapter 9 that the dramatic impact of the seed-fertilizer revolution in India and Pakistan was related to the large scope that existed for import substitution. Changes affecting earnings from agricultural exports may of course be related to either the volume of exports or prices received.

As we have noted, under the dual influence of a rising marketed share of farm output and rising per capita consumption of food, the absolute volume of cash farm receipts, and hence purchases from other sectors, rises. However, the value of these purchases as a per cent of NNP falls owing to the dominant effect of the declining share of primary products in national output. Because the manufacturing sector is very small in the early stages of development, less than 10 per cent of NNP, agriculture's purchases have their maximum quantitative impact on industrial development during this period. Finally, under the influence of the modernization of agriculture and the emergence of a technically mature manufacturing sector, average cash expenditures by the individual farm rise sharply, and changes occur in the types of farm equipment and consumer goods that are demanded.

The impact of agriculture's purchases on other sectors of the economy, as well as the changing input configuration in the farm production function, can be brought into sharper focus by examining the pattern of farm cash disbursements. For this purpose it is useful to distinguish five components:

1. taxes
2. acquisition of financial assets
3. payments to factors of production (wages, interest, rent)
4. current inputs and capital goods employed in production
5. final consumer goods and services

Categories 1 and 2 represent agriculture's "monetary savings" from which most of the capital transfers to other sectors derive. Taxes, if not spent on current services, are either directly invested by the public sector or, through financial intermediation, made available to private investors. Acquisition of financial assets includes not only cash accumulation, savings accounts, and bond purchases, but also any equity investments made in enterprises outside of the household farming operations. One other type of intersectoral resource transfer, a change in agriculture's terms of trade (which can be either positive or negative), is not picked up in this analytical framework.

Of the factor payments, category 3, the bulk of wages and rent are typically intrasectoral payments, whereas interest on borrowed funds accrues to financial asset owners both within and outside of the farm sector.

By far the largest of the components in the disposition of farm income are categories 4 and 5; these are the categories which involve commodity flows. Agriculture's backward linkages to manufacturing, along with payments for distribution services, are contained in 4 and are comprised for the most part of fertilizer and other agricultural chemicals, farm equipment, irrigation pumpsets, vehicles, and construction materials. The "final demand" linkages associated with agriculture's demands for manufactured consumer goods are contained in category 5. In addition to the intersectoral commodity flows, these last two categories also contain commodity purchases from within agriculture such as unprocessed feed and seed, livestock, and foodstuffs.

There is one further, and very important intersectoral commodity flow involving agricultural produce which is not picked up by either farm cash receipts or expenditures. This is the value added to the farmer's food and fiber after he has sold it and before it reaches the final consumer. In addition to marketing proper, these services include processing, storage, transport, and distribution; their value is the difference between farm receipts and farm produce at retail or f.o.b. prices. On the basis of historical data from Japan, the United States, and five European countries, A. Simantov has estimated that for economies at a per capita income level of about $200 and upward (in terms of our earlier 1958 prices) the aggregate value of these "marketing services" constitutes a remarkably stable 8 to 9 per cent of NNP. Over the same range of income levels, purchased inputs from other sectors—our category 4—constitutes 2.5 to 3 per cent of NNP, or one-third the value of marketing services.[9]

By contrast, marketing services are much less important at the earliest stages of structural transformation when most households produce their own food. This means that over the per capita income range of $75 to $200 when the size of the nonagricultural population grows from about 20 per cent to about 45 per cent, marketed farm produce expands at an enormously rapid rate. Using the earlier construct of the number of individuals outside of agriculture fed by an average farm, the number rises from 1.25 to 9, a more than sevenfold expansion. A much more gradual growth—a twofold increase—occurs as the nonfarm population increases another 25 percentage points and reaches 70 per cent of the total.

The level of farm receipts is more or less predetermined by the degree of structural transformation. However, the special significance of farm cash disbursements is that their pattern can be substantially influenced by conscious policies and programs. The share of taxes and acquisition of financial assets can be raised or lowered by changes in tax- and interest-rate policies. The portion of farm receipts going to wages and rent are affected by land tenure and other policies that are major determinants of the size distribution of operational units. And it is this size distribution of farm units and their participation in the expansion of commercial sales, along with agricultural research and agricultural engineering policies, that largely determine what kind of manufactured inputs are purchased by the farm sector. This pattern of farm demand in turn has differential impacts on the various producer goods industries in the manufacturing sector with respect to value added, employment, and foreign exchange requirements. Finally, the whole collection of policies and programs shapes the distribution of income within the agricultural sector which, among its other effects, plays back upon the development of consumer goods industries.

Having established the usefulness of the farm cash disbursement pattern as a device for studying structural transformation, can we find numbers to put into the theoretical boxes we have drawn? The data most suited for this purpose come from farm household surveys. While the expenditure classifications in these studies are not in every case clearly assignable to a single analytical category and do not partition payments within the agricultural sector from intersectoral payments (likewise for sales), they nevertheless provide a rough picture of the composition of commodity and financial flows. In Table 2.6 we present farm survey data for three countries at very different levels of structural transformation. In 1967 per capita income in Ethiopia was about $60 as compared to $240 in Taiwan; approximately 85 per cent of the Ethiopian labor force was in agriculture as compared to just over 50 per cent in Taiwan. In the case of the United States in 1961, with the process of structural transformation all but completed, per capita income was $2750 with 7 per cent of the labor force in agriculture.

The first item to note in Table 2.6 is the extreme difference in cash receipts per farm. The figure for Taiwan is 10 times that of Ethiopia, and the figure for the United States is nine times that of Taiwan (or

STRUCTURAL TRANSFORMATION 71

more than 10 times if 1967 prices were applied).[10] The share of taxes in gross receipts is lowest in Ethiopia (2.7 per cent) and highest in the United States (6.5 per cent). The small share of wage payments testifies to the predominance of family labor in all three countries. There are, however, large differences in the land-man ratios, particularly evident in the contrast between Taiwan and the United States. On the other hand, income per acre and fertilizer expenditure per acre are considerably higher in Taiwan. With more than 30 times the area cultivated, the American farmer relies on land-extensive, mechanized techniques. The Repair and Depreciation categories account for nearly 40 per cent of total production expenses, whereas in Taiwan fertilizers alone represented 36 per cent of all production expenses, and outlays for other agricultural chemicals were nearly as large as for buildings and equipment combined.

In all three countries the intersectoral commodity flows, contained in categories 4 and 5, account for more than three-quarters of all disbursements. It is the absolute size of these two magnitudes and their composition which reveal the central workings of structural transformation. The absolute level of production expenditures, agriculture's backward linkages, is a measure of the degree to which farmers are using high-technology inputs supplied by specialist producers outside of agriculture. The volume of consumer expenditures is, of course, an index to the farm family's level of economic welfare. This moves upward with marketed output, but at a somewhat slower pace. Consumption expenditures as a proportion of farm sales falls from 62 per cent for Ethiopia, to 48 per cent for Taiwan, and to 32 per cent for the United States. This falling proportion is but the other side of the rising degree of specialization wherein the farmer's contribution to the value of food and fiber he sells declines and that of industrial farm inputs rises. Thus in Ethiopia the ratio of consumption to production expenditures is 2.45, in Taiwan 1.59, and in the United States, .71.

What about the influence of farm purchases on the development of manufacturing? As mentioned earlier, although the value of agriculture's purchases rises with economic development, the value of

Table 2.6. Average cash farm expenditures on production and consumption in Ethiopia and Taiwan, 1967 and the United States, 1961 (*U.S. dollars per farm*)

A. Ethiopia (*farm size 3.7 to 18.3 acres*)

Total all categories	*129.74*	4. Production expenses	*32.76*	Other food	19.1:
		Animal pur-		Drinks and	
1. Taxes	*3.48*	chases	23.64	tobacco	9.0!
		Feed and veteri-		Clothing	18.0:
2. Financial assets	*3.43*	nary services	.76	Furniture	1.5:
		Tools and		Utensils	1.4!
3. Factor payments	*9.95*	equipment	2.36	Transport	2.7!
Wages	.20	Construction	6.00	Education	0.5!
Rent	9.75			Medical	1.8"
		5. Consumption		Other	4.4:
		expenses	*80.12*		
		Cereals	21.26		

B. Taiwan (*mean farm size 2.5 acres*)

Total all cate-		4. Production		5. Consumer goods	
gories	*1,329.98*	expenses	*402.27*	and services	*639.0*
		Fertilizer	142.98[a]	Food	228.6:
1. Taxes	*62.15*	Agricultural		Clothing	56.2:
		chemicals	37.15	Furniture	7.8!
2. Financial assets	*80.48*	Seed	18.68	Electricity	28.6
		Feed	93.15	Medical	61.5:
3. Factor payments	*146.00*	Livestock	25.50	Education	50.0
Interest	28.40	Irrigation fee	31.15	Ceremonies[b]	83.0:
Rent	12.30	Buildings and		Social	41.2!
Wages	105.30	equipment	46.05	Transport	14.2:
		Other	7.62	House main-	
				tenance	8.4!
				Other	59.2

C. United States (*mean farm size 302 acres*)[c]

Total all categories	*11,939*	4. Production expenses	*5,432*	5. Consumption expenses	*3,849*
1. Taxes	*771*	Feed and livestock	2,055	Food, drink tobacco	958
2. Financial assets[d]	*519*	Seed	136	Clothing	427
		Fertilizer and lime	359	Shelter[e]	751
3. Factor payments	*1,369*			Transportation	612
Interest	210	Repairs etc.	1,010	Medical and personal care	416
Rent	380	Miscellaneous	768		
Wages	779	Depreciation	1,103	Recreation	123
				Other	562

[a] An additional U.S. $44.38 of rice was exchanged for fertilizer under the compulsory barter program of the Provincial Food Bureau.
[b] Weddings, funerals, festivals.
[c] Since pasture and grazing are relatively unimportant in Taiwan, the more directly comparable "farm size" figure for the U.S. is crop land harvested per farm. According to the 1959 census of agriculture this is 94 acres.
[d] Net change in assets and liabilities including purchase, improvement, and sale of farm homes.
[e] Furniture and equipment, fuel and light, household operation, repair, and maintenance.

SOURCE: Excludes all consumption in-kind and family-supplied labor. Data for Ethiopia based on Teketel Haile-Mariam, "The Production, Marketing, and Economic Impact of Coffee in Ethiopia" (Ph.D. dissertation, Stanford University, 1973), Chap. 9, pp. 174-77, as compiled from Ethiopia, Central Statistical Office, "Draft Report on Rural Household and Consumption Survey: December 1966-June 1968," unpublished (Addis Ababa, January 1971). These figures are population weighted averages of Provincial data. Data for Taiwan from Joint Commission on Rural Reconstruction, *Taiwan Farm Income Survey of 1967* (Taipei, 1970), p. 25 and appendix Tables 18 and 23 converted to U.S. dollars at 40 NT dollars per U.S. dollar. Data for the United States from U.S. Department of Agriculture, *Agricultural Statistics 1972* (Washington, D. C., 1972), pp. 504, 566-67, for expenditures per family from idem, *Consumer Expenditures and Income: Rural Farm Population, United States, 1961*, Agricultural Research Service, Consumer Expenditure Survey Report no. 35 (Washington, D. C., 1966), pp. 2-15.

these expenditures as a per cent of NNP falls. Hence, it is in the early stages of structural transformation that agriculture has its major impact on manufacturing; and during this early period farm demand will have its greatest effect on industries producing consumer goods rather than producer goods.

In summary, we would stress that structural transformation is both a consequence and a cause of economic growth. The movement toward specialization and market dependence at the producer level and the growth of interindustry specialization lead to increases in the productivity of all factors. This in turn facilitates further progress in specialization and in the capacity to utilize more productive technologies. And it will be argued in later chapters that an important consideration in assessing the efficiency of alternative economic strategies is their influence on this process of structural change. Even though the close links between agricultural and industrial development need to be emphasized, it is equally important to recognize that pursuit of industrialization as a goal in itself can be counterproductive. This is especially likely if it leads to policies that foster the adoption of inappropriate technologies, encourage inefficiency, and distort the pattern of investment, issues to which we turn in the next chapter.

NOTES

1. William O. Jones, "Measuring the Effectiveness of Agricultural Marketing in Contributing to Economic Development: Some African Examples," *Food Research Institute Studies* Vol. 9, No. 3 (1970), p. 178.
2. The data are for 1970; U.S., Bureau of the Census, *Statistical Abstract of the United States 1972* (Washington, D.C., 1972), p. 320; and International Bank for Reconstruction and Development, *World Tables* (Washington, D.C., 1972), Table 4.
3. H. B. Arthur, R. A. Goldberg, and K. M. Bird, *The United States Food and Fiber System in a Changing World Environment,* Vol 4, Technical Papers, National Advisory Commission on Food and Fiber (Washington, D.C., August 1967), p. 31.
4. Simon Kuznets, *Economic Growth of Nations: Total Output and Production Structure* (Cambridge, Massachusetts, 1971), Chap. 2.

5. This conceptualization is based on William H. Friedland, "A Sociological Approach to Modernization," in *Modernization by Design,* edited by Chandler Morse et al. (Ithaca, New York, 1969); and Neil J. Smelser, "Mechanisms of Change and Adjustment to Changes," in *Industrialization and Society,* edited by Bert F. Hoselitz and Wilbert E. Moore (The Hague, 1963).
6. Kuznets, *Economic Growth of Nations,* pp. 275-88.
7. We owe this point to Anna Luiza Ozoria de Almeida. Her doctoral research in Brazil and that of Arthur Gibb in the Philippines documents the extremely high-income elasticity of demand for personal services, including retail trade and personal transportation. By contrast, in developed countries these same needs are now being met to a considerable extent by goods rather than services, for example, convenience foods instead of restaurant service, wash and wear clothes instead of commercial laundering, household appliances instead of domestic services.
8. For a review of the evidence on these points during the 1960s, see Daniel G. Sisler, "The Demise of Comparative Advantage: The Impact of Trade," in *Food, Population, and Employment: The Impact of the Green Revolution,* edited by Thomas T. Poleman and Donald K. Freebairn (New York, 1973).
9. A. Simantov, "The Dynamics of Growth of Agriculture," *Zeitschrift für Nationalökonomie* Vol. 27, No. 3 (1967).
10. Cash receipts for the average Ethiopian farm are biased upward since the sample was drawn from the coffee-growing provinces. The U.S. and Taiwanese data are derived from very large, carefully drawn random samples.

3 | On Being Late: The Technology Backlog

The most fundamental factor conditioning structural transformation in contemporary underdeveloped countries is the existence of a large stock of proven technical innovations in the more-developed countries. The existence of this technology backlog, much of which is transferable, creates the possibility for late-developing countries to bypass the vast investment of time and resources that the accumulation of this knowledge involved. This opens the way for far more rapid rates of economic growth than those witnessed, say, prior to World War I.

Differences in per capita income, which range from $100 to $4500 are, of course, the most general index of the technological backlog. One illustration of the very much greater size of this backlog for contemporary low-income countries in contrast to their nineteenth century counterparts can be found in agriculture. Recalling from Chapter 1 the link between the farm labor force ratio[1] and the level of agricultural productivity (see Table 1.1), we can compare the technology gap facing Japan in 1880 to that of India in 1960. In 1880 output per male worker in Japan, with 79 per cent of its labor force in agriculture, was the equivalent of 2.7 tons of wheat; in England, the world's most-developed country with only 16 per cent of its labor force in farming, the same productivity figure was 15.7 tons. India in 1960 had a somewhat lower farm labor force ratio than 1880 Japan, 69 per cent, but output per worker was a little lower at 2.1 tons; in Sweden, whose 1960 farm labor force ratio at 18 per cent is the closest to 1880 England, output per male worker was the equivalent of 44.3 tons of wheat.[2] Thus, the productivity gap has expanded nearly threefold. That this enlarged inventory of technical innovations can be effectively drawn upon is suggested by more rapid rates of structural transformation: starting in 1930 Taiwan was able to reduce its farm labor force ratio from 70 to 40 per cent in a matter of four decades, whereas the United States, starting in 1830, required seven decades to accomplish the same task.[3]

While the success of a Taiwan or a Mexico demonstrates that the potential of the technology backlog is real, the lack of significant progress by a far larger number of countries bears witness to the special problems concomitant with the technological gap, difficulties not faced by early-developing countries and faced to a much lesser degree (owing to a smaller disparity) by Japan in the late nineteenth century. We shall be concerned with three of these problem areas. The first and most far reaching is the extremely high rates of population growth that are in large part the result of modern public health technology. The second problem is the imperfect fit between the requirements of imported technology and the quantity and quality of the local factors of production; these difficulties are most frequently encountered in manufacturing, leading to high costs and low levels of technical efficiency. Finally, affecting both import-substituting industrialization and the modernization of agriculture, there are problems as well as advantages in being in a position to choose from the broad array of possibilities that are available. This means that the costs of search and of reaching a consensus are likely to be substantial; but more important, there is the danger of adopting products or techniques that jump ahead of the sequence of innovations warranted by existing circumstances.

This chapter explores some of the technical innovations that are being transferred to late-developing countries. We shall look at some specific instances that are particularly germane to agricultural development—public health, seed varieties, fertilizer, and various mechanical innovations—and attempt to trace through their several economic consequenecs. The difficulties created by the new manufacturing technologies and their relationship to agriculture-industry interactions will be examined. Finally, we will take up policy biases in selected areas (import substitution, farm mechanization, monetary policy) that external influences on late-developing countries have created or accentuated. In Chapter 4 all of these elements are brought into sharp focus as they bear on the problem of designing an agricultural strategy.

MEDICAL TECHNOLOGY AND THE DEMOGRAPHIC REVOLUTION

In the western world prior to the industrial revolution, as in nonwestern societies before they came into contact with the West, the rate of population growth was low, in the neighborhood of 0.2 to 0.4 per cent per annum. Population growth was low because both birth and death rates were high. With the onset of the industrial revolution death rates fell slowly as incomes rose and medical knowledge advanced. Birthrates did not begin to decline until some 60 to 100 years later; however, since the death rate dropped gradually, and with the help of emigration to newly settled regions overseas, net additions to the population seldom surpassed 1 per cent. The exceptions were, of course, precisely the "empty lands" of North America, Australia, and New Zealand which received the outflow from Europe; here population growth ranged between 2 and 3 per cent before tapering off after 1920.

In the underdeveloped countries of Asia, Latin America, and Africa the pattern has been quite different. As can be seen in Table 3.1 both birth and death rates remained high until after the turn of the century. The 1910 mortality figures for Asia suggest that the rate of population growth was about 1 per cent at that time. Reduction in the death rate prior to 1940 was limited to 3 or 4 per thousand for most countries, with Chile, Malaysia, Taiwan, and Ceylon being notable exceptions, boasting declines of 10 to 13 per thousand. For most countries the greater part of the mortality decline came in the decade following World War II. If 1940 figures were available, this decrease would be seen to have been most dramatic in Africa where death rates prior to the control of malaria are thought to have been

Table 3.1. Vital statistics for selected countries, 1920-1970

Country	Crude death rates[a]				Crude birthrates[a]			
	1910	1940	1960	1970	1927	1950	1960	1970
United Kingdom	14.6	12.5	11.5	11.7	17.6	15.9	17.5	16.2
Sweden	14.1	10.8	10.0	9.9	16.3	15.5	13.7	13.7
Japan	20.2	16.3	7.6	6.9	34.0	23.7	17.2	18.8
United States	...	10.6	9.5	9.4	20.1	24.5	23.7	18.2
Tanzania	...	...	24.5	22.0	...	44.0	46.0	47.0
Kenya	...	...	...	17.5	...	...	...	47.8
Zambia	...	...	19.6	20.7	...	56.0	51.4	49.8
Nigeria	...	...	...	24.9	...	55.0	49.2	49.6
Togo	...	...	29.0	25.5	...	...	55.0	50.9
Zaire (Congo)	...	...	12.3	20.7	...	30.3	38.1	44.4
Ghana	...	...	24.0	17.8	...	51.0	49.5	46.6
Libya	...	...	4.1	15.8	...	38.5	25.1	45.9
Egypt	25.7[b]	26.8	16.9	15.0	43.9	43.8	36.1	34.9
Syria	...	7.9	6.0	15.3	...	24.2	32.4	47.5
Pakistan	...	13.2	16.2	18.4	...	...	55.0	50.9
India	36.3[b]	27.4	15.1	16.7	...	41.7	38.4	42.8
Indonesia	...	20.0	21.4	19.4	...	52.0	43.0	48.3
Burma	25.4	22.0	35.0	17.4	24.3	43.0	42.3	40.3
Malaysia	36.9	19.8	9.5	10.8	37.0	44.1	40.9	37.9
Korea, South	22.0[b]	19.2	16.0	11.0	34.4	45.0	36.3	35.6
Ceylon	31.8	19.7	8.6	7.5	40.6	38.5	36.6	29.4
Taiwan	31.0	18.3	6.9	5.3	44.0	45.9	39.5	25.6
Haiti	...	5.4	22.0	19.7	...	...	47.5	43.9
El Salvador	24.3[b]	20.6	13.0	9.9	44.7	49.0	48.0	40.0
Mexico	25.1[b]	22.0	11.2	9.9	33.3	44.1	44.5	27.4
Ecuador	28.9[b]	20.9	14.0	11.4	50.5	45.3	48.5	44.9
Brazil	...	20.6	11.0	9.5	...	...	42.0	37.8
Colombia	14.2[b]	16.0	13.0	10.6	30.0	36.9	42.5	44.6
Chile	30.2[b]	19.8	11.5	8.8	41.9	35.9	35.0	25.0

[a] Rates per 1000. Many of the figures represent a five-year average, sometimes but not always centered on the year shown.
[b] 1920.

SOURCE: Data from United Nations, *Demographic Yearbook 1971* (New York, 1972), Tables 23 and 30; ibid., *1969* (New York, 1970), Table 12; ibid., *1966* (New York, 1967), Table 17.

in the high 40s per thousand. In sum, unlike the earlier experience where a gradually diminishing death rate was associated with rising income and education, urbanization, and the like, in this case a comparatively swift fall in mortality occurred in low-income, agrarian societies largely as a result of the application of scientific knowledge which originated in the developed countries. With no commensurate drop in fertility, the result is the much talked of "population explosion."

While the crude death rate, taken with the corresponding natality rate, has the advantage of showing the natural rate of population increase (e.g., Tanzania 47.0 − 22.0 = 25 per thousand or 2.5 per cent), it does not fully reflect the decline in mortality. A more refined, although less available statistic is life expectancy at birth. The following figures for six countries show that life expectancy has approximately doubled since 1910[4]:

	Life expectancy (*years*)					
	Ceylon	India	Taiwan	Mexico	Chile	Brazil
1910	36.5	23.0	30.5	27.6	30.2	30.6
1967	66.0	41.0[a]	67.5	61.2	62.7	55.5

[a] For the year 1960.

What are the causes for the sharp drop in mortality? Four stages can be distinguished. The first stage is the elimination of local famine, and perhaps internecine feuding, as the extension of the transportation network and rule by a central government bring about market integration and law and order. The next phase in mortality reduction comes from the control—or at least partial control—of the major epidemic and endemic diseases that strike at all segments of the population: malaria, cholera, yellow fever, typhus, typhoid, and tuberculosis. The World Health Organization and the United States Public Health Service played important roles in organizing the campaigns of vaccination, spraying, and drainage used to combat the diseases. The chemicals used to control the malaria mosquito also kill other germ carriers such as lice and fleas. The third major stage in the lowering of the death rate is sharp reduction in infant mortality from rates which sometimes run as high as 50 per cent. Gastroenteritis, which kills through dehydration and general weakening, has been the principal cause of infant death. Preventive measures in this case have included control over human waste disposal, avoiding the use of contaminated water supplies (e.g., by use of underground water from tubewells or boiled water instead of ponds or streams), and the widespread establishment of maternity clinics to instruct mothers in hygienic baby care and child feeding. Waste control and pure water also help to eliminate hookworm, schistosomiasis, cholera, and dysentery. The fourth stage, requiring the most resources and having the smallest quantitative effect, is the lessening in mortality brought about by widespread availability of curative medicine —doctors, hospitals, laboratories.

Does modern technology have any effect on the birthrate? Although not as potent as in the case of mortality reduction, there are at least one direct and one indirect channel through which medical knowledge operates to lower natality rates. The direct channel is the provision of the means—abortion, sterilization, pills, IUDs, conventional contraceptives—to prevent undesired births. Owing to religious and political reservations, sizable family planning programs were not launched until the early 1960s, and even in the mid-1970s the coverage of these programs is still limited.[5] The leading role in organizing family planning programs in developing countries was played by American voluntary agencies including the Ford Foundation, the Population Council, and the International Federation of Planned Parenthood.

The indirect channel is the sharp fall in the death rate. Since more children survive into adulthood, the number of "replacement births" to sustain a given family size falls. Conditioned by countless generations of high mortality rates and the traditions generated by this experience, only after considerable time is it realized that something more than good luck is at work. Perhaps as much as two or even three generations are required before socially defined norms for number of pregnancies are adjusted downward. It is tempting to invoke such changed expectations, perhaps aided by more knowledge of birth control techniques, to explain the decline in fertility that seems to have been occurring since the late 1960s in so many low-income countries irrespective of their progress in economic development.

In the long run it is factors associated with economic development that lead to the natality transition. As described in the preceding chapter, the reduction in extreme risks in farming and the alternative means of insurance against those risks that remain diminish the utility of having a large family as a source of security. For the increasing share of the population living in urban areas, rising standards of nutrition, clothing, health, and education greatly augment the cost per child. There are other factors beside the absolute cost of large urban families that lead to a reduction in the desired number of births. Prospective employment for children with primary education or less promises extremely low returns, in contrast to the now much expanded returns on investment in postprimary and higher education. For the housewife, not only is a rising standard of education likely to change her preferences on quantity versus quality, but the possibility of wage employment outside the home raises the opportunity cost of child rearing. The outcome of these changes is a parental choice of fewer, better educated children.[6] All the above factors, along with a somewhat later age of marriage and greater knowledge of birth control procedures, operate to reduce the birthrate and complete the demographic transition.

For those latecomers where the natality rate is still 20 per thousand or more above the death rate the impact of public health technology is very much of a mixed blessing. The benefits are great. Reduction in malaria, dysentery, hookworms, and the like means that people feel better. Increased absorption of calories and nutrients results from a diminished incidence of gastro-enteritis and internal parasites: there is more energy to work and to enjoy life. The tragedy of infant mortality is played out less frequently. Longer life expectancy undermines fatalism and raises self-reliance; people are more inclined to work harder today for improvement tomorrow. Thus public health measures contribute directly to human happiness and to creating greater productive capacity.

If the benefits are great, so too is the cost. The resultant rates of population growth, ranging from 2 to 3.5 per cent, are perhaps the single greatest handicap that latecomers face in their efforts to achieve economic modernization. The problems of expanding food supplies, educational facilities, housing, and other goods and services are obviously much more severe when a country's population is doubling every 23 years rather than every 70 years. This difference in the natural rate of increase between 1 and 3 per cent actually understates the latecomer's handicap since the higher rate of population growth imposes an additional burden in the form of a higher dependency ratio. High birthrates mean a young population: in Africa 44 per cent of the population is under the age of 15, in Latin America 42 per cent, and in Asia 40 per cent; in contrast, for Europe and America the figures are 25 and 29, respectively.[7] Savings that otherwise could have been directed toward raising the human and material capital stock at the disposal of a given sized labor force must instead be expended to combat decreasing returns in agriculture and to provide for the consumption needs of additional children. Nathaniel Leff's finding for 47 underdeveloped countries that the dependency ratio explains more variation in the savings ratio than does per capita income is a measure of the "drag" imposed by high birthrates.[8]

A rise in the natural rate of population increase is translated with about a 15 year lag into a similar augmented expansion of the labor force.[9] This will tend to slow down the change in the occupational composition of the labor force. More exactly, the time it takes to transfer the bulk of the labor force from agriculture to higher productivity sectors depends upon three magnitudes: the initial weight of nonagricultural sectors in the total labor force (L_n/L_t), the rate of growth of the total labor force (L'_t), and the rate of growth of nonfarm employment (L'_n). This assumes that agriculture is the residual employer, a not unrealistic assumption as long as agriculture remains the largest sector. The rate of structural transformation may then be defined as the absolute increase per year in the nonfarm labor force ratio[10]:

$$RST = L_n/L_t \ (L'_n - L'_t).$$

The rate of structural transformation so defined is simply the nonfarm labor force ratio multiplied by Folke Dovring's "coefficient of differential growth." In the early stage of economic development L_n/L_t is by definition low, so even assuming a very high value for $(L'_n - L'_t)$ RST cannot be much larger than .005. If the high rates of L'_n can be maintained as L_n/L_t rises, RST accelerates during the middle and latter stage of economic development, reaching .025 and above. As an illustration, if $(L'_n - L'_t) = .015$, that is, nonfarm employment is increasing at an annual rate which exceeds the growth rate of the total labor force by 1.5 per cent, it requires approximately 28 years to reduce agriculture's share in the labor force from 80 to 70 per cent, but only about 11 years to reduce it from 40 to 30 per cent.

The impact of a high rate of population growth (L'_t) is, of course, to diminish the value of $(L'_n - L'_t)$. In Ceylon, Egypt, and Indonesia, high rates of population growth equalled or surpassed L'_n in recent decades so that structural transformation ceased or was reversed.[11] Before we examine the beneficial consequences of lowering the birthrate, let us briefly consider the other variable that codetermines the coefficient of differential growth, the growth rate of nonfarm employment (L'_n). In his 1959 paper Dovring reviewed average values of L'_n for 30 year periods in eight European countries during 1800-1940. These values ranged from a minimum of 1.3 to a maximum of 2.7 per cent per annum.[12] Table 3.2 presents similar long-period nonfarm employment growth rates for the United States, Japan, Mexico, and Taiwan, and the performance over the last two decades for a larger number of currently underdeveloped countries.

The statistics in Table 3.2 reveal nonfarm employment growth rates ranging from 0.3 to 6.5 per cent. With the exception of the United States during the three decades ending in 1850, the rate has never exceeded 4 per cent for prolonged periods. Taiwan is a good example: as the fastest growing economy in the world during the 1960s with NNP climbing at 9.3 per cent per year,[13] nonfarm employment grew at a rate of 6.5 per cent; nevertheless over the longer period of 1920-70, which witnessed the shift of one-quarter of the

Table 3.2. Annual rate of growth of nonagricultural labor force

Country	1820–1850	1890–1920	1920–1970	Country	Decade ending about 1960	1970
Japan	...	2.9	2.9	Brazil	3.7	4.6
Mexico	...	0.3	3.9	Ceylon	2.3	1.2
Taiwan	...	1.2	3.8	Egypt	2.9	2.0
United States	5.9	3.3	2.0	Ghana	...	3.0
				Haiti		3.6
				India	3.6	3.8
				Indonesia	...	0.9
				Mexico	4.0	3.9
				Pakistan	3.3	...
				South Korea	...	4.4
				Taiwan	3.2	6.5

SOURCE: Data from Food and Agriculture Organization of the United Nations, *Production Yearbook 1971* (Rome, 1972); ibid., *1965* (Rome, 1966); ibid., *1958* (Rome, 1959) and International Labour Office, *Yearbook of Labour Statistics 1968* (Geneva, 1968); ibid., *1959* (Geneva, 1959). For the long-term data see appendix tables. For Taiwan 1967-71 see Republic of China, Council for International Economic Cooperation and Development, *Taiwan Statistical Data Book 1972* (Taipei, 1972), p. 9.
For the decade ending in 1960, in the case of Colombia and Egypt the rate pertains to a 13 year period. For 1970 the averages pertain to nine years for India and Indonesia, seven years for Ceylon, and six years for Colombia.

labor out of agriculture, nonfarm employment grew at only 3.8 per cent. Some of the factors responsible for the exceptionally rapid growth of nonfarm employment during the 1960s are examined in Chapter 7.

Clearly those factors which control the value of L'_n play a central role in the process of economic development, and we shall be looking at some of them later in this chapter. For the moment, however, let us employ historical values of L'_n to estimate the benefit that would accrue by a lowering of the birthrate by 15 per thousand, a feat achieved by Taiwan between 1960 and 1970. In the case of

India ($L'_n = 3.8$ per cent) the time required to reduce the agricultural labor force ratio from 70 to 50 per cent would be cut from 44 years to 19 years, abstracting from the lag that would occur before a reduced birthrate is reflected in the rate of growth of the labor force.

In addition to the time required to obtain a certain stage of structural transformation, the relationship between L'_t and L'_n also fixes the point at which the absolute size of the farm labor force reaches its maximum.[14] Employing various assumptions about growth in population and nonfarm employment, we have calculated the number of years that will elapse before this turning point occurs. The calculations have been made for two types of economies: "Earlyphasia" where 80 per cent of the labor force is still in agriculture (e.g., Haiti, most of tropical Africa) and "Middlephasia" where, with only half of the labor force still in farming, the most difficult part of the labor transfer has already been effected (e.g., Taiwan, Mexico).

Years required to reach turning point when absolute size of farm labor force begins to decline

Earlyphasia ($L_n/L_t = .2$)				Middlephasia ($L_n/L_t = .5$)			
L'_t (*per cent*):	3	2	1	L'_t (*per cent*):	3	2	1
		(years required)				(years required)	
$L'_n = 3$ per cent	∞	123	26	$L'_n = 3$ per cent	∞	29	1
$L'_n = 4.5$ per cent	83	33	3	$L'_n = 4.5$ per cent	20	a	a

a Turning point is already reached.

The turning-point calculations compel us to the same conclusions that flow from the structural transformation analysis. First, under any reasonable set of assumptions about growth in nonfarm employment, countries with 60, 70, or 80 per cent of their labor force in farming must absorb additional manpower in agriculture for many years. If agriculture cannot productively utilize these population increments, a rapid expansion in unemployment or underemployment and a worsening of the distribution of income will result. Second, a reduction in the birthrate is a potent lever for compressing by 20 to

ON BEING LATE: THE TECHNOLOGY BACKLOG 87

50 years (or even more) the interval required by these countries to transfer at least half of their labor force into nonfarming pursuits. Attention to factors that bear most directly on family limitation—new birth control technology, financial incentive programs, information dissemination—should thus command first place in the development effort. Third, more rapid growth of nonfarm employment can have as powerful an influence on accelerating structural transformation as a reduction in population increase (indeed, even more powerful since a change in L'_n is not necessarily limited to 2 or 3 percentage points). While the growth of nonfarm employment is subject to a much broader range of determinants—almost as many as economic development itself—there are several areas that are of particular importance and easily identified.

The balance of this chapter will examine two such determinants of nonfarm employment, determinants that are also closely connected to the existence of the technology backlog and of being "late." The first of these is the *range* of choice from the technology inventory that is actually accessible to the latecomer. The second determinant is external policy influences which guide decision-makers in making their selection within the feasible set of options.

THE FACTOR PROPORTIONS PROBLEM

The constraints upon late-industrializing countries in their choice of products and manufacturing techniques are alluded to by a wide variety of labels. Three of the more common "problem" labels are transfer of technology, intermediate technology, and fixed factor proportions. While each of these approaches to choice of technique in underdeveloped countries differ in their stress on peripheral issues, their central concern is the same.

Choice of Technology

At the most general level the factor proportions problem can be explained with the aid of three simple diagrams. On the basis of existing scientific knowledge and machine-building know-how, at

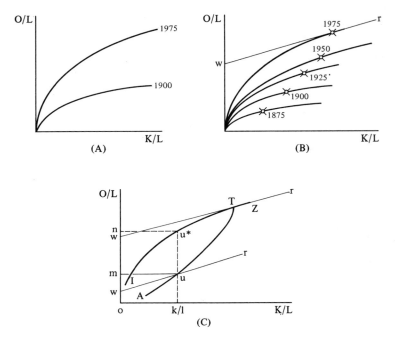

Figure 3.1 The choice of technique in technology-borrowing countries.

any point in time a society has the capability of constructing a wide range of equipment packages with differing levels of capital intensity (K/L) to produce a given commodity. In Figure 3.1 panel (A) depicts two such hypothetical *ex-ante* production functions, one for 1900 and one for 1975.[15] For any particular amount of capital stock per worker (or more exactly, capital services per worker hour) output of the product in question is in every case higher in the later years: advances in technical knowledge continually raise the productivity of all inputs and thereby shift the production function upward.

In the real world of scarce resources, not all the factory design possibilities mapped out in the *ex-ante* production function are brought to the blueprint stage or are even investigated. Given the relative prices of capital and labor there is only one technique which will minimize production costs (or several, if we allow for regional variation). Thus, only a relatively small number of commercially feasible production techniques, representing a narrow range of factor proportions, are actually embodied by the capital goods industry in equipment that is available to investors. Moreover, as one moves forward in time, the available production processes become progressively more capital-intensive. This situation is depicted in panel (B), where only a single technique (large dot) is developed from the menu of technological possibilities in each period, and the embodied capital-labor ratio rises with each newer vintage.

The secular trend of a rising capital-intensity in production techniques available to investors in developed and underdeveloped countries alike is a result of technical progress itself and systematic changes in factor prices that occur as a by-product of economic growth in the technology-initiating countries. Specifically, capital is cheapened relative to labor as (a) higher levels of per capita income and growth of financial intermediation lead to increased savings and lower interest rates, (b) technical advances in the production of capital goods lower the cost of capital equipment, and (c) widespread increases in labor productivity lead to higher wages. The price of labor and capital are introduced into the analysis by the line wr (shown only for the most recent year). The wage rate is given by the point of intersection on the O/L axis, while the price of capital is given by the slope of the line.[16] If product and factor markets are competitive and free of externally imposed distortions, the tangency point between the factor price line and the production function will identify the least-cost production technique and it will be this production technique which will become embodied in capital equipment.

Panel (C) illustrates the situation faced by the technology-borrowing country. The lower its degree of economic development, the smaller will be the capital endowment per worker, that is the distance of k/l from the origin. The schedule ITZ represents the range of capital-labor proportions that are theoretically available to produce the commodity in question using the latest technological knowledge. In fact, without a capital goods industry that possesses an extensive research and development capability only the relatively capital-intensive technique T is available to the borrowing country. The range of effective choice lies along AT, the embodied technology from the previous periods.[17] The line AT thus represents the "technology shelf" from which developing countries can actually borrow. If the equipment embodying all the older designs are available and known to investors the price line will intersect AT at u. To the extent that older equipment is not available or unknown to the investor, the actual choice will lie closer to T. Similarly, to the extent that the wage rate exceeds the scarcity value of labor or the interest rate undervalues the opportunity cost of capital, the profit-maximizing capital-labor ratio will lie to the right of k/l, the only factor combination which fully utilizes all available supplies of both capital and labor. This means that a sizable proportion of the labor available to the manufacturing sector at the going wage rate cannot be absorbed and is either left unemployed or shunted into other sectors where it lowers the returns to labor and contributes a smaller marginal product. In terms of the analysis in the preceding section, the transfer of inappropriate modern industrial technology contributes to a slower growth in nonfarm employment and hence in delayed structural transformation.

An obvious response to the factor proportions problem stated in these terms is to have some public agency or, if commercial incentives can be suitably manipulated, the capital goods industry in the private sector, direct its energies to the development of embodied techniques from that segment of the production function in the neighborhood of u^*. This would lead to a sharp gain in the productivity of capital, nm/mo, and to the employment of a much larger portion of the available labor supply in activities that are as productive as possible given the availability of capital and the existing scientific knowledge.

The foregoing exposition of choice of production techniques with two homogeneous factor inputs catches only one facet, albeit an important one, of the technology transfer problem. In the real world technology input requirements are both numerous and highly specific. A given production process calls for a very particular set of labor skills, raw materials of certain uniform specifications, and some minimum (perhaps very large) scale of output. Even electricity voltage, water impurities, and climate are inputs into the production process. One example of many where the unnoticed climatic input proved inimical is the case of chocolate: owing to temperature and humidity factors the cocoa butter produced by existing technologies is a "different" product (i.e., lower quality) when undertaken in the tropics, the home of the cocoa bean. Technology attributes such as these mean that in both borrowing production techniques from advanced economies and in undertaking research to develop new embodied techniques in the region of u^*, a much broader range of environmental circumstances than just the interest rate and the unskilled wage rate must be taken into account.

Before proceeding to discuss the possibilities for developing new techniques which embody a more appropriate input combination and scale of plant output, let us briefly indicate the consequences of direct technology borrowing for the industrial structure of the low-wage economy. In the advanced countries where new technologies are evolved there is wide variation in capital-labor ratios and scale of production between the various branches of manufacturing. Although capital goods are designed to match the economy's factor scarcities, the technological characteristics associated with different products generate a spectrum of capital-labor ratios. In the technology-borrowing country where many of the embodied techniques are far more capital-intensive than need be,[18] the range in factor intensities is far greater and exhibits a discontinuous bimodal distribution. Toward the upper end of the scale there is a distribution of capital-labor ratios much the same as in the developed economies; at the lower end of the scale there is a second clustering of small-scale manufacturing activities with very low capital-labor ratios. This second group of labor-intensive producers is sometimes referred to as the semitraditional sector. Production functions in this sector are of a very old vintage and/or are characterized by a high degree of substitutability between capital and labor. In some instances the products of this sector (e.g., shoes, textiles) are in competition with similar although not identical products of the large-scale mechanized producers in the modern sector. Various price distortions and rationing of scarce inputs reinforce this dualistic structure. However, before we turn to the influence of these economic policy factors we shall review the technical possibilities for lowering capital-intensities and altering other input requirements in an appropriate direction.

Genetic Engineering in Rice and Wheat

Perhaps the most dramatic example of development research which achieved a new embodiment of existing scientific knowledge in a uniquely appropriate form for underdeveloped countries is to be found in the domain of agriculture. The case of developing high-yielding cereal crops for the tropics is especially interesting because of the large number of input alterations that were required. In this instance the adapted technology raised the productivity of land, as well as that of labor and capital.

It was observed in Chapter 1 that *indica* rice varieties in the tropics had evolved to meet the technical and economic conditions of the traditional economy. Similar hardy but low-yielding varieties of wheat were selected in response to much the same kind of circumstances in subtropical regions. With the continuing fall in the price of fertilizers, during the 1950s and 1960s, raising the fertility of tropical soils on a fairly wide scale increasingly became an economic possibility. However, existing cereal varieties, selected for their capacity to produce a mediocre yield in spite of a low level of soil fertility were not well suited to benefit from fertilizer applications. In the case of both traditional rice and wheat, additional nutrients result in excessive stalk and leaf growth, causing the plant to topple over in the wind. Losses to such lodging, increased incidence of disease in the case of rice, and modest grain-yield response sharply limited the commercial feasibility of intensive fertilizer applications.

Drawing on the same body of biological knowledge that had been utilized in developing high-yielding varieties for the temperate climates of Europe, Japan, and America in the first half of the twentieth century, agricultural scientists in Mexico, Taiwan, and the Philippines have recently bred new fertilizer-responsive plant types that are well adapted to tropical and subtropical environments. The landmark names and dates in what has become known as the "Green Revolution" are Taichung Native 1 (Taiwan 1956) and IR-8 (Philippines 1966) for rice and Pitic 62 and Penjamo 62 (Mexico 1962) for wheat.[19] Since these initial breakthroughs there has been a continuous stream of new dwarf wheat and rice varieties which yield up to three or four times more grain than the traditional varieties. The "revolutionary" significance of this biological innovation derives from the fact that wheat and rice supply over half of the food calories consumed in the underdeveloped world.

The upward shift of the rice farmer's production function from u to u^* entailed crossbreeding not only for high-fertilizer responsiveness but for a new plant architecture. The dwarf varieties are short in stature, with sturdy straw and narrow erect leaves; the plants have a high capacity for tillering (stems per plant) and are insensitive to the length of day. The short sturdy straw means that the plants are resistant to lodging, despite a doubling of the grain-to-straw ratio. The leaf configuration minimizes the shaded area and thus permits greater density of plants per acre. With uninterrupted photosynthesis the crop matures at a fixed interval after planting; early maturity lays open the way for double or triple cropping.

Figure 3.2 presents data from the 1950s assembled by Robert Herdt and John Mellor for 55 experiment stations in the United States and India.[20] The United States rice varieties are scientific crosses between *indica* types from the Philippines and Taiwan; the Indian trials used some of the better yielding traditional *indica* varieties. Although the dwarf plants of 1970 yielded some 30 to 50 per cent more than the United States improved varieties of the 1950s, the basic differences between the improved and the traditional plant varieties are clearly evident in Figure 3.2.[21] In this instance the improved variety has a 50 per cent greater yield with no fertilization, although often new varieties with high-yield potential have no yield

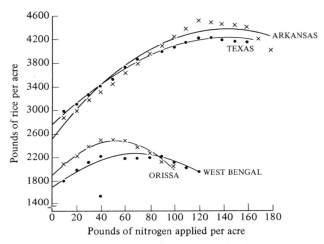

Figure 3.2 Rice production functions for four states.

SOURCE: Data from Robert W. Herdt and John W. Mellor, "The Contrasting Response of Rice to Nitrogen: India and the United States," *Journal of Farm Economics* Vol. 46, No. 1 (February 1964), p. 152.

advantage at low-fertilitity levels. For Orissa, maximum yield is obtained at about 40 pounds of nitrogen applied and only an additional 600 pounds of rice is obtained. In Arkansas, yield continued to increase up to about 120 pounds of nitrogen, for an additional 1600 pounds of rice or almost three times that of the traditional variety.

The new technology is not totally embodied in the seed and fertilizer; it does require changes in labor inputs and in farm management. Higher soil fertility and narrow leaves improve conditions for weed growth: substantially more labor must be expended to hold weeds to a given level. For better control over all operations, including weeding, planting is best done by transplanting seedlings in straight rows at even intervals. Although the returns in higher yields to these practices are great, the labor requirements far exceed those of simple seed broadcasting which prevails in many areas. (Indeed, it is the opportunity to productively employ more labor services per crop and to raise the number of crops per year that makes the new technology so appropriate to the demographic conditions of the latecomers.) Greater precision in farming operations is also called for if the full benefits of the new varieties are to be reaped: higher plant population, control of the depth at which seed is planted, deeper plowing, the use of checkrow markers, more careful placement and timing of fertilizer application, and more exact water control. And the shorter growth period of the new plants often requires adjustments in the seasonal organization of farm activities.

The Case of Inorganic Fertilizers

The development of dwarf plant varieties was the Third Act of the dramatic seed-fertilizer revolution. The First Act was a slow-moving affair which opened with Liebig's discoveries in the mid-nineteenth century and provided the basis for scientific understanding of plant nutrition. The pace quickened in the Second Act with the advances in chemistry and chemical engineering which led to the remarkable changes in production of inorganic fertilizers which are the subject of this section. The impact of these advances was to greatly raise the productivity of capital and labor and thereby reduce costs correspondingly to the farmer. Figure 3.3 below traces the extent of this fall in price for the period 1910-72, a fall of nearly 60 per cent. Even more significant than this decline in price is the fact that the supply of fertilizers, which was of necessity extremely inelastic as long as farmers depended on organic fertilizers and nitrate deposits, has now become highly elastic so that huge increases in production have been associated with an almost uninterrupted decline in real price. The recent worldwide surge in demand for fertilizer, with its dramatic short-term effects on prices, is examined in Chapter 8.

As technical change in the production of chemical fertilizers was laying the basis for the seed-fertilizer revolution, it was at the same

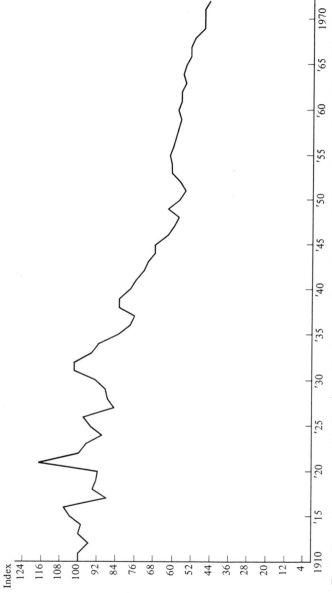

Figure 3.3 Long term trend in the price of fertilizer relative to the price of all farm inputs, United States 1910-72.

SOURCE: Data from U.S. Department of Agriculture, Crop Reporting Board, *Agricultural Prices* (November 1970), p. 30; ibid., *Annual Summary for 1971*, p. 10; ibid., supplement No. 1 (May 1973), p. 20.

time rendering the manufacture of that product increasingly inappropriate for most low-income countries. As with various forms of mineral refining (including oil) and some other petrochemical industries, the input of labor, and hence its relative price, is inconsequential. Capital, power, and raw material constitute over 95 per cent of production cost. Not only is the capital a high-priced factor in low-income countries, but more of it is required to build a given amount of capacity in the absence of a sophisticated domestic heavy engineering industry. Just as new dwarf seed varieties represent one polar case of a near-perfect re-embodiment of known scientific principles to fit the circumstances of labor-abundant tropical economies, this group of chemical-process industries would seem to represent the other polar case where technical coefficients are indeed rigidly set. The unique set of conditions needed for optimum chemical reactions tend to fix both the scale of production and input proportions within a very narrow range. That is, threshold requirements or powerful economies of scale associated with the chemical process do not provide much room for an appropriate re-embodiment in small-scale, less-capital-intensive techniques. As we shall see, the advances in knowledge in applied chemistry and engineering have all worked to raise the scale of productive units and to make them more vulnerable to any interruption in the flow of raw materials, of electricity, of spare parts, and so on.

In calculating the price of fertilizer relative to the price of all farm inputs from 1910 to 1972 that is summarized in Figure 3.3, fertilizer was defined in terms of the nitrogen, phosphate, and potassium content of the fertilizer materials purchased by the farmer. The price of all farm inputs, as shown in Gian Sahota's careful study of United States fertilizer production during the period 1936-60, moves in step with the national price level as measured by the GNP price deflator.[22] Over the six decades plotted in this figure, the relative price of inorganic plant nutrients has dropped by just over 55 per cent. Although changes in fertilizer production technology have been the most important source of cost reduction, other factors have also been at work. Between 1936 and 1958 the relative price of electricity, a major input, was cut by two-thirds.[23] A shift to higher-concentrate fertilizer materials (e.g., from ammonium sulfate with 21 per cent nitrogen content to urea with 46 per cent) has reduced the cost of distribution. Finally, a more competitive market structure since 1945 has probably contributed to a lower price to the American farmer.

In terms of volume of production and consumption, potash (K_2O) is the smallest of the three major fertilizer nutrients. Its production is markedly different from nitrogen and phosphate in that (a) it is more of a mining than a chemical industry, (b) all processing of potash salts takes place near the mining area, and (c) there are no overriding economies of scale. Save for the lucky handful with commercially exploitable deposits, underdeveloped countries will continue to import their potash fertilizer. In short, the choice of technology for the production of potash is not a problem of general concern.

While phosphate fertilizers have historically been location specific, the occurrence of phosphate deposits is much more widespread than potash. And recent processing developments to produce enriched rock and concentrated phosphoric acid for export suggest that the industry is becoming even less location specific. We shall briefly review technological developments in this industry, concentrating on superphosphate, before examining the technological advances in the production of nitrogen fertilizers.[24]

Phosphorous is found in natural form as the principal element in bone and phosphate rock. Prior to the mid-nineteenth century crude use of this element was made by direct application of ground rock or bone; however, the availability to the plant of P_2O_5 was limited by the ability of the acids in the soil to break the apatite bond between fluorine and phosphorous. Following Liebig's famous report in 1840, John Lawes patented a sulfuric acid process and began commercial production of superphosphate in 1854.

The original process was extremely simple and highly labor intensive.[25] Open boxes of wood or brick were filled with a weighed quantity of crushed phosphate rock. Sulfuric acid was added and the two were manually mixed. Later the mass was transferred by wheelbarrow to cure in a storage building for several months. Finally it was screened by hand prior to delivery. Lawes's basic process is still discernible despite successive refinements in the chemical process, mechanization of virtually every operation, and greatly enlarged scale. About 1900 mechanical means for mixing the phosphate rock with sulfuric acid were introduced, and later batch production gave way to continuous production. Automatically metered materials now flow by gravity and conveyor belt from feeding devices through the mixers and eventually to curing piles. The economic result of cumulative advances over the period 1872 to 1950 has been to sharply reduce the unit cost of superphosphate, to raise capital intensity, and to vastly expand the scale of operation.

Phosphoric acid is the basic intermediate for all phosphate fertilizers other than superphosphate. Its production involves a similar but somewhat more complex process than superphosphate.[26] Because the demand in developed countries for the more concentrated fertilizers has grown so much more rapidly, it is this segment of the industry that has been the subject of most research and development in the past two decades. Technical advances include simplification of rock dissolution, larger and more efficient filters, higher P_2O_5 recovery rates, and more efficient purification methods.[27] While the capacity of an optimum-sized superphosphate plant remained relatively unchanged between 1955 and 1970 (about 175 tons per day), it has risen from 200 tons per day to 1110 tons per day in the case of phosphoric acid.[28]

We now turn to developments in the production of nitrogen fertilizers, the largest fertilizer group and the one requiring the most capital-intensive manufacturing methods. During the nineteenth century the principal commercial sources of nitrogen were sodium nitrate from the mines of Chile and organic materials including Peruvian guano, bone meal, fish meal, soybean cake, dried blood, packing house waste, and the like. Following the discovery that ammonium sulfate could be produced as a by-product from coal gas, this industry grew to rival Chilean nitrate as a source of inorganic nitrogen. Because of the importance of the iron and steel industry (and hence the coking of coal) in the United States, the output of by-product nitrogen was particularly important in the United States, running ahead of synthetic ammonia until 1950. On a worldwide basis it had lost its primacy by 1924.

Improvements in the process for recovering nitrogen from coal contributed to the lowering of fertilizer prices. Initially ammonia was recovered by cooling the coal gas and bubbling it through water. The original process has been improved by a number of innovations including the "direct method" introduced after World War II; in this process the oven gases pass through coolers, a tar extractor, and then to a saturator containing dilute sulfuric acid. These technological improvements not only improved the quality of the fertilizers, they lowered the cost per unit of throughput and raised the recovery rate from 13 pounds of ammonium sulfate per ton of coal coked in 1900 to 25 pounds by the 1930s.

Comprising some three-quarters of the atmosphere, nitrogen gas is one of the most common elements in nature.[29] It is, however, chemically inert and under ordinary conditions does not react with other elements. The "fixing" of free nitrogen in the soil occurs naturally through the action of certain types of bacteria and by electrical discharge in the atmosphere (the resultant nitric oxide being conveyed to the soil by rain). With the advent of high explosives and rapidly growing industrial and agricultural applications of nitrogen, it became evident that the supply of Chilean nitrates and by-product nitrogen were not sufficiently expandable to meet future demand. As a result major efforts were made in Europe and America from 1890 onward to develop a commercial process for fixing atmospheric nitrogen. A number of scientific discoveries were achieved in the first years of the present century, and three fixation methods were subsequently embodied in commercial scale plants: the electric arc method (Norway 1904), the cyanamide method (Germany 1905), and direct ammonia synthesis (Germany 1913).

The direct synthesis of ammonia from elemental nitrogen and hydrogen quickly proved the most economical method and now represents one of the basic processes in the chemical industry. During the years 1905 to 1908 Professor Fritz Haber and his associates determined the exact conditions of temperature and pressure in the presence of a catalyst for the following chemical reaction:

$$3H_2 + N_2 \rightleftarrows 2NH_3 + 24{,}000 \text{ calories.}$$

As this ammonia-producing reaction results in a reduction in volume with a liberation of heat, it follows that the higher the pressure and the lower the temperature the larger will be the proportion of ammonia formed at the equilibrium. However, high temperatures are required to trigger the reaction; depending upon the effectiveness of the catalyst (which reduces the reaction temperature) the "compromise" conversion temperature falls in the range of 450 to 600 degrees centigrade. The technical difficulties of the Haber process—that of handling a flammable gas at elevated temperatures and pressures—were overcome by Dr. Carl Bosch. It is upon the Haber-Bosch process that the present nitrogen industry is based.

The production of ammonia can be divided into four steps. The first is the production of hydrogen from superheated steam and some form of carbon feedstock. The carbon combines with the oxygen of the water, thus freeing the hydrogen ($H_2O + C = CO + H_2$). In the second step, shift conversion, the resultant mixture is compressed and, with the aid of a catalyst, freed of carbon monoxide and other impurities, leaving a mixture of nitrogen and hydrogen in the correct proportion for the ammonia synthesis. The third step, undertaken at elevated temperature and pressure, is the catalytic conversion into ammonia. In the fourth step, the ammonia is either removed in a water solution or reacted with sulfuric acid, nitric acid, or carbon dioxide (itself an ammonia by-product) to produce a fertilizer compound, ammonium sulfate, ammonium nitrate, or urea, respectively.

Each of the processes just described has been subject to a continuing stream of major technical advances.[30] In the production of hydrogen there have been changes to more economical feedstocks and to more efficient processes. In the case of the former, coal was displaced by the oil distillates of naphtha or kerosene in the 1940s and they in turn by natural gas in the late 1950s. Paralleling the change

Table 3.3. Comparative data on the post-1963 nitrogen fertilizer technology

(*U.S. dollars at 1970 prices*)

Anhydrous ammonia	Unit	Post-1963: centrifugal compressor	Pre-1963: piston compressor
Natural gas[a]	cubic feet	34,200	38,000
Electricity[a]	KWH	5	760
Labor[a]	man-hours	.15	.24
Fixed investment	dollars	18,000,000	9,220,000
Capacity	tons/day	1,000	300
Expected life	years	15	12
Investment/ton	dollars	53	88
Depreciation[a]	dollars	3.53	7.32
Working capital[a]	dollars	3.50	20.48

Urea	Unit	Post-1963: carbamate oil recycle	Pre-1963: gas separation
Anhydrous ammonia[a]	tons	.58	.58
Carbon dioxide[a]	tons	.77	.75
Electricity[a]	KWH	73	173
Labor[a]	man-hours	.78	1.10
Fixed investment	dollars	7,550,000	5,714,000
Capacity	tons/days	1,000	320
Expected life	years	15	15
Investment/ton	dollars	22.88	54.11
Depreciation[a]	dollars	1.52	3.61
Working capital[a]	dollars	6.06	8.12

[a] Input requirement per ton of output.
SOURCE: Data from D. R. Henderson, G. R. Perkins, and D. M. Bell, *Simulating the Fertilizer Industry: Data* (East Lansing, 1972), pp. 23, 30. These technical and cost data were assembled by the authors in collaboration with 17 fertilizer producing companies located in the mid-western United States.

in feedstocks has been a change from the original water-gas process to partial oxidization to steam reforming. In shift conversion, the second stage of production, catalyst improvements—first the introduction of chromium and more recently a second-stage low-temperature copper-zinc catalyst—have raised the efficiency of carbon monoxide removal and hence the yield of hydrogen. Each of these process changes has resulted in operational economies and also in a lower capital cost per unit of output.

Probably the most dramatic cost-reducing developments have occurred since 1963 when the centrifugal compressor was introduced. The centrifugal unit, which replaced a very much larger piston compressor which required more maintenance, depends for its feasibility upon changes in other parts of the plant—among them an increase in overall plant size, a 50 per cent improvement in heat recovery, and lower pressures in the synthesis loop. The impact of these advances, both to lower the cost of production and to extend the scale of an optimum sized unit, is clearly seen in Table 3.3.

Looking first at ammonia production, the new process utilizes 10 per cent less natural gas and 99 per cent less electricity! Working capital and labor requirements also fall, but the most important saving occurs in the halving of the principal cost item, capital consumption. Advances in the production of urea from ammonia follow the same pattern, but are not quite as dramatic. In both cases more advanced technology entails a larger scale of production and a greater capital investment. While the new processes reduce the capital input per unit of output more than that of labor, fertilizer production remains an extraordinarily capital-intensive process.

Figure 3.4 summarizes the basic chemical interactions and product interrelationships of nitrogen and phosphate fertilizers. The pivotal position of ammonia production is clearly seen. Many of these products are used in other industries. Ammonium nitrate is a common explosive. Urea is used as an animal feed and as a base for the plastics industry. Phosphates are used in pesticides, detergents, and cleaning compounds. Nitric, sulfuric, and phosphoric acid are important industrial chemicals. Given raw material availability, the

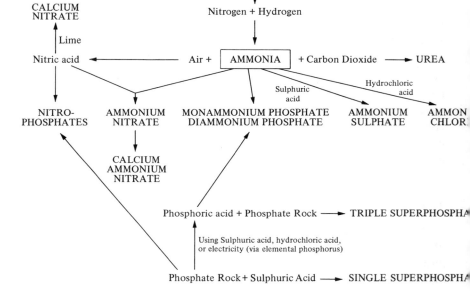

Figure 3.4 Product interrelationships of nitrogen and phosphate fertilizers.

[a] Hydrocarbon feedstock can be natural gas, ethane, liquefied petroleum gases (LPG), or light naphtha for the reforming process. With heavier hydrocarbon feedstocks, partial oxidation processes would have to be used, which require higher capital costs than the reforming process.
CAPITALS indicate products used as fertilizer materials.
SOURCE: Data from The White House, *The World Food Problem*. Report of the President's Science Advisory Committee, Vol. 2 (Washington, D.C., May 1967), pp. 385-86.

level of demand in a developing economy for these products in their nonfertilizer uses can have an important bearing on the economic viability of producing rather than importing the capital-intensive intermediates of ammonia and phosphoric acid.

We have now examined what appears to be two polar cases of technology transfer. In the instance of cereal plant varieties, adaptive research was able to restructure plant architecture to meet essential environmental conditions in the tropics, including the possibility for greater labor absorption. In the case of chemical fertilizers, efforts at embodying known scientific principles in new equipment or processes better suited to underdeveloped countries—lower capital-intensity, smaller scale, simpler factory construction, different feedstocks, reduced vulnerability to shutdown—have as yet provided no counterweight to the continuing trend toward larger scale, more complex technologies.[31] In such cases where technical coefficients are fixed, and fixed in a way that leaves low-income economies at a pronounced comparative disadvantage, the best solution will usually be to import.

The Spectrum of Intermediate Cases

In the continuous process chemical industries such as oil refining and synthetic nitrogen every aspect of production—scheduling of inputs, production processes, materials handling, packaging—is fully automated. The human intrusion upon the manufacturing process is limited to instrument reading, valve setting, and maintenance. Most other industries differ in three respects: (a) economies of scale are exhausted at a much earlier stage, (b) the integration between successive production phases is less rigidly determined, and (c) the human input is quantitatively more important. Earlier exhaustion of economies of scale means that the establishment of such industries is less likely to be thwarted by high investment cost or inadequate market size. The second and third characteristics open the way for some degree of technical substitution in response to local conditions.

In examining the production process of these industries it is useful to make the distinction between the primary or core manufacturing transformations and ancillary activities such as the receiving, preparation, and moving of materials and packaging operations. These latter activities frequently account for a considerable proportion of factory space and of the labor force. They also offer considerable possibilities for substituting semiskilled labor for capital. The variability of factor proportions in auxiliary activities is in part explained by their comparatively limited effect on product quality (hence, less need for precision) and by the fact that many of these activities were originally manual operations. Not only will the substitution of semiskilled labor in various auxiliary production processes in low-wage countries provide more employment and reduce costs, it may also reduce minimum plant size.

A recent field study in Kenya by Howard Pack provides a good deal of illustrative data on the flexibility of technical coefficients in these auxiliary operations.[32] For a wide variety of food processing and other light industries, he found that British firms had substituted manual operations for the conveyor belts, fork-lift trucks, and filling-labelling-capping machines that they employed in their home factories.[33] Where mechanized processes were retained in these peripheral activities, for example, unloading pineapple, the decision was related to quality control. In a majority of the industries surveyed, well over half of the factory labor force was engaged in such operations. These labor substitutions were in response to low wages and the desirability of introducing more factor divisibility; for example, replacing a single high-volume machine, not fully utilized, by a group of workers whose number can be varied according to the desired level of output. Pack notes that such labor-using adaptations of imported technology usually occur when the manager comes from a technical background; managers from a sales or finance background, not having the ability to envisage various technical routes for achieving a given production goal, tend to duplicate the home country process in toto.

The substitution of labor for capital in the primary production process is generally more difficult than in the case of ancillary activities and requires greater entrepreneurial capacity. In chemical processes there may be no substitution possibilities at all, or at least not without effecting a drastic alteration in product quality or unit cost. In mechanical processes two types of adaptation may be distinguished. We shall term these two types of adaptation despecialization and labor-addition.

Despecialization consists of choosing an earlier, more labor-using method of production, such as employing a standard loom in place of an automatic loom. This is the same kind of modification as described for ancillary activities and it is closely related to the subject of second-hand machinery. The economics of this type of substitution—whether the lower wage rate is sufficient to offset the disadvantage of a less-specialized operation—depends upon the effect on productivity of the additional technical knowledge embodied in the more recent equipment—or, in terms of Figure 3.1 (C), the curvature of the line AT. Labor-addition consists of adding more labor to work with the latest equipment in such a way as to increase the latter's rate of output. Both of these adaptations of imported technology lower the capital-labor ratio, the first by uitilizing less-expensive capital goods and the second by raising the amount of labor that can be productively combined with up-to-date machinery.[34]

Despecialization. Despecialization, both in auxiliary operations and in primary mechanical manufacturing processes, is the most widely observed form of factor substitution in late-developing countries. In the core manufacturing process it takes two forms: the use of earlier vintage capital goods to produce an identical product and the use of more labor-intensive methods (embodying less scientific knowledge) to produce a somewhat different product to meet the same needs.

The spinning, weaving, bleaching, and printing of cotton textiles are areas where older vintage equipment has frequently been used. Around the turn of the century manually operated weaving looms in low-wage countries (e.g., Japan, India) were frequently competitive with power looms; in sharp contrast cottage industry techniques were quickly crushed in competition with mechanized spinning. Different rates of technical progress in the following half-century reversed this situation: in the 1950s and 1960s relatively labor-using 1930 vintage spinning and printing equipment was compatible in low-wage countries with reasonably low-cost production, whereas only automatic looms of the most recent design could similarly qualify. Machine tools represent a more dramatic case: in the context of the types of products that are demanded in low-income countries, earlier vintage equipment is competitively superior as well as being more labor-using.[35]

Equipment of the older design has a number of advantages for late-developing countries in addition to labor intensity. First, such equipment nearly always permits a lower scale of output than equipment of more recent design. Second, although used equipment generally needs more maintenance attention, the skill levels required for such servicing are lower. Third, older equipment is less demanding with respect to such complementary inputs as raw material uniformity, temperature and humidity tolerance, voltage constancy. Finally, the introduction of new and improved movable parts (most used machinery is reconditioned prior to its export to underdeveloped countries) can sometimes greatly enhance productivity relative to the original design.

Not surprisingly, secondhand equipment also has its drawbacks. The matching of equipment between processes often requires considerable technical ingenuity. Standardized spare parts are no longer available and must be made to order. Being less automated, such equipment calls for more supervision on the factory floor. Finally, price determination for second-hand equipment occurs in a highly imperfect market; sellers typically possess much greater knowledge about the value of the equipment to the buyer than the latter does about its cost to the seller. These potential drawbacks mean that only fairly advanced underdeveloped countries—possessing a well-developed light engineering industry, adequate supplies of supervisory personnel, and an ability to search in a number of overseas markets—are in a position to benefit from extensive use of second-hand machinery.[36]

As noted above, the second form of despecialization which can mold factor proportions to make them more labor-intensive involves the production of a somewhat different product to meet the same needs. This type of product variation covers a broad spectrum, from minor qualitative differences (e.g., wrapped versus unwrapped bread) to essentially different products (e.g., fashion leather shoes versus tire-rubber sandals). Such product variation can be observed in every underdeveloped country and with it is associated differences in scale of operation, capital intensity, and other input requirements. Some Nigerian examples illustrate the point. An armchair made in a small-scale workshop sold in 1964 for 40 shillings while the same model chair—but constructed from seasoned wood, squarely joined and perfectly flush on the floor—sold for over 120 shillings from any one of the country's major furniture manufacturers. In the case of sandals there is a wide range of possibilities, going from the tire sandal at 2 shillings (cut from discarded automobile tires with a plastic thong tacked on) up to the 55 shilling English "cross sandal." Household utensils range from the tinker's products, beaten out of scrap metals, to the light steel "Hong Kong" enamelware to durable polished aluminum goods. The soap market is supplied by black wood-ash soap from cottage producers, cold process caustic soda soap from modern small-scale Nigerian firms at a price about 80 per cent above that of black soap, and finally hot process emulsion soap from large-scale expatriate-run factories at double the cost of cold process soap.

As the description of these product groups suggests, the production characteristics of the lower-quality goods are far better suited to the resource endowments of underdeveloped economies than those of the higher-quality goods: lesser use of imported raw materials or equipment, smaller scale, lower capital-intensity (including human capital), and lower price to the consumer. Choice of product within a product group generally offers more scope for varying factor proportions than does choice of technique narrowly construed.

Two interpretations of the observed pattern of market segmentation have been advanced. The first accepts consumer preferences as reflecting objective differences in durability and quality.[37] With severely limited purchasing power the poorer members of the community choose inexpensive, low-quality products. As incomes rise and consumer time preferences for present over future goods diminish, the value placed on durability and quality increases and the market share of inferior goods falls. The second interpretation, put forward by Frances Stewart, emphasizes external institutional factors which shape consumer tastes.[38] The effects of advertising the standardized products of international corporations developed for high-income consumers, and the desire of indigenous elites to imitate western consumption standards create preferences which are not always strictly related to functional needs. Mrs. Stewart questions many of the attributes that are equated with higher quality:

> Just as little research and development takes place with reference to the special labour-intensive modern methods of production, so little research goes to *appropriate products*. Products developed *for* developed countries tend in many cases to have characteristics unnecessary to developing countries, as well as requiring complex and capital intensive methods of production. Nylon shirts, for example, are not essential for adequate clothing in a very poor country, and indeed are uncomfortable in the heat. Bricks designed to support the Empire State Building are certainly excessively strong for a single storey accommodation. Modern methods of maize grinding involving complex automated roller mills, while removing much of the nutritious content of the maize, are less appropriate than the hammer mills which they replace.[39]

Whether observed consumption expenditures are rooted in (a) rational assessment of functional needs and differing disposable incomes or (b) institutionally distorted consumer preferences (or some combination of the two) is not of great importance as far as the imperatives of policy are concerned. The remedies for shifting the product mix in a more favorable direction are more or less the same under either diagnosis. These policy issues—getting price signals right, disseminating knowledge about the range of intermediate production techniques, lessening the inequality in the distribution of income—are discussed at length in the concluding section of the chapter.

So far we have examined only the extreme case of product variation. Relatively minor changes in product quality—for instance, the somewhat greater variation in crust coloration of bread baked in a wood-fired peel oven as against the perfectly homogenous product from an automated electric reel oven—can be associated with radically different capital-labor ratios. In the case of baking, careful investigation in Nigeria revealed that in addition to a choice between ovens, there are options with respect to dough-brake, bread pans, wrapping methods, and financial control techniques. Producers competing in the same market segment exhibited a range of capital-labor ratios from $390 per worker to $900 per worker.[40]

While it is technically a subcase of product variation, technological adaptations associated with minor variations in product quality are of sufficient quantitative importance to distinguish them from the latter. We shall term this category of despecialization process simplification. Process simplification usually comes about when an inventive local mechanic or technician successfully copies an imported machine, but does so in a way that permits the use of cheaper local materials, fewer quality-control procedures, and less skilled labor. While there is almost always a diminution in the efficiency of the machine relative to its original design, the imitation becomes a successful innovation because the efficiency loss is confined to performance characteristics (e.g., specification tolerances, speed of operation) which are not essential in the environment of the less-advanced economy.

We shall consider two examples of process simplification. The first is an already mentioned piece of equipment that is used in making bread in West Africa, the dough-brake. Designed in Europe for milling pastry dough, this machine was first used for kneading bread dough by a West Indian baker in Lagos in the 1920s. Consumer response to the resultant fine textured bread quickly made the $1800 dough-brake a required tool of the trade. In 1954 a Nigerian entrepreneur, one of whose sidelines was copying imported equipment used by farmers and food processors, began marketing a $345 dough-brake constructed from reconditioned scrap sheet metal and used pipe.[41] Somewhat more cumbersome to operate than an imported machine and requiring more maintenance, this locally made dough-brake nevertheless supplied a fully satisfactory kneading action to the bread dough. This instance of process simplification sharply reduced capital requirements for establishing a bakery; as a result the number of firms tripled within four years, greatly accelerating the rate of growth of employment and output.

Our second example of process simplification is the slow-speed diesel engine produced in India and Pakistan. As a principal energy source for tubewells and low-lift canal water pumps in areas where electricity is not available, this engine has been an essential ingredient in the seed-fertilizer revolution. Over half a million of these 10- to-30 h.p. stationary prime movers have been produced since 1965. The engine is based on the English Ruston and Blackstone horizontal single-cylinder engines which were designed about 1890. Portable high-speed engines of the Lister type, produced by some of the more sophisticated larger firms, have been unable to compete with the earlier vintage horizontal engines as a power source for irrigation because the latter uses cheaper crude fuel and has a longer life and fewer breakdowns.

The horizontal engine was first imitated in India by three large-scale engineering firms during the 1930s.[42] From the mid-1950s onward, a second round of imitation has occurred as small-scale workshops have entered the market and captured an increasing share of total sales. It is these small producers, under the spur of competition, who have effected various process simplifications that have cheapened the machine without impairing its essential functions. The major changes have been at the foundry stage, substituting scrap for pig iron for as much as 50 per cent of the charge, and in lowering skill requirements. Minor design adaptations have been made with respect to the fuel pump, the lubrication system, the governor, and the atomizer.

Labor-addition. Labor-addition takes two principal forms. The first is the altering of a particular machine or production process so that additional labor inputs can be applied and additional output can be obtained. Gustav Ranis has assembled a number of examples of this type of technological adaptation from Japan, Korea, and Taiwan.[43] In the Meiji Japanese case the latest British and American spinning equipment was run at faster-than-designed speeds while the number of attendants was increased to handle the larger number of broken threads. A variant of this practice was to spin the breakage-prone short-staple Indian cotton rather than the more expensive American cotton. In both spinning and weaving the Japanese employed about four times the number of machine attendants as identical plants in America. Similarly, in silk reeling the Japanese employed more than double the number of operatives as the Italians, with the same result of greatly enhanced capital productivity. In contemporary Korean plywood factories not only are machines run at a higher speed in combination with a larger repair and maintenance staff, but defective sections of lumber, rather than being discarded, are cut out and plugged by hand. The employment effect of the speed-up and raw material upgrading is to raise the labor complement per production line from 72 (in Japan) to 123. Alterations in United States electronics technology when transferred to Taiwan involve similar accelerated operation and manual repair of defective pieces, with more workers engaged in inspection and maintenance activities.

The second form of labor-addition is multiple shift operation. Since the useful life of buildings, stationary structures, and many nonmoving machinery parts is a function of time rather than use, an increase in the number of hours of operation does not lead to a proportionate increase in capital consumption. A reduction in idleness of production facilities is also a reduction in the capital-labor ratio: the same stock of capital equipment can provide employment for double or triple the labor force as under a regime of single shift operation.

Despite the much greater scarcity of capital in underdeveloped countries, all available evidence indicates that capital stock is less-intensively utilized than in a capital-abundant economy such as the

United States.[44] For the countries where there is reasonably comprehensive information—India, Mexico, West Pakistan, Argentina—capital utilization, exclusive of continuous process industries, ranges between seven and nine hours.[45] The potential for achieving more favorable capital-labor ratios by means of multiple shift operation would seem considerable. Many things impinge upon the entrepreneur's ability and willingness to more fully employ his capital investment. Economic policies which encourage or discourage higher rates of utilization are reviewed in the next section. Social preferences are also an important factor. With substantial urban unemployment, a labor force for the second and third shift is easily recruited. More difficult is the requisite supervisory and managerial personnel: these individuals are generally not in excess supply and social status factors may dampen their enthusiasm for shift work.[46] Clearly, differences in cultural orientation and the intensity of the entrepreneurial drive come to bear at this point. On the basis of a number of plant visits, Ranis suggests that multiple shifts are a good deal more prevalent in Taiwan and South Korea than in other Asian countries.[47] Evidence that more nearly isolates the entrepreneurial factor per se is the considerably longer hours of factory operation among Lebanese and Greek firms in West Africa in comparison with their European and African counterparts in the same industries.

PRICING POLICIES AND PUBLIC RESEARCH

In this chapter we are concerned with the special circumstances which condition the growth path of late-developing countries. We have argued that the large technological backlog opens the way for backward economies to achieve structural transformation in a shorter interval than was previously possible. At the same time the technological backlog creates hazards in the form of accelerated population growth and production methods biased against the low-income countries' principal economic resource—hazards which if not properly dealt with can undermine the development process. In the preceding section we examined the technical possibilities for altering borrowed technology with the objective of lowering capital-labor ratios. We have seen that there are in fact many avenues for enlarging the complement of productive labor employed by a given quantum of capital. These range from multiple-shift operation, machine speedup, and raw material conservation to process simplification, product variation, and the use of second-hand equipment and nonmechanized material handling procedures. The principal task of this final section is to examine government pricing policies which guide investors as they make their choice from the set of all possible production methods.

From the end of World War II to the mid-1960s the majority of less-developed countries have shared the common goal of promoting import-substituting industrialization. The establishment of industry as an objective was pursued with little consideration given to the effects of these promotional policies on factor proportions, industrial efficiency, or relationships between manufacturing and other sectors of the economy.

The genesis of what economists now recognize to have been an indiscriminate pursuit of industrialization was the experience of these countries during the 1930s and World War II. In the 1920s underdeveloped countries were dependent upon the export of primary products for their foreign exchange earnings. With the onset of the great depression foreign exchange earnings dropped precipitously: during the period 1929-32 foreign exchange receipts fell by over 60 per cent.[48] The price of imported manufactured goods fell, but to a lesser degree. To make matters worse, these countries had been importers of capital and had accumulated considerable foreign debt. Meeting fixed debt-servicing obligations out of foreign exchange during a period of falling export prices meant that imports had to be cut back even further. This experience created a resolve in the underdeveloped countries to reduce their dependence on the world economy. This resolve was strengthened by World War II; the demand for primary products was buoyant, but industrial imports were unavailable at any price.

Thus, after World War II the governments of most Latin American and Asian countries embarked on an aggressive policy of import substitution. In Africa where the deflationary hardships had been no less punishing, colonial trade policies and monetary systems initially impeded such efforts; however, by the late 1950s the new African states were launched on a similar course.[49] The principal instrument of industrial promotion was import control, initially by protective tariffs and later by quantitative restrictions.

Import restrictions raise the domestic price of the imported product and thereby the profitability of local production. The protective subsidy, ranging from 50 to 200 per cent of the value added at world prices, was made good by permitting domestic producers to import needed capital equipment and raw materials free of duty. Generous protection not only removed the necessity for investors to seek out cost-minimizing factor proportions, it also attracted additional entrants in these small markets. The result has often been too many firms, each with too small a share of the market to fully utilize their productive capacity. "In other words, high profits in manufacturing secured by import restrictions, whether or not they are curbed or eliminated by domestic competition, encourage high costs of production and the wasteful use of capital, one of whose most striking and most tangible manifestations is the under-utilization of productive capacity."[50]

High capital-labor ratios were further encouraged by public policies which had the effect of distorting factor prices. Associated with more general policies to hold down the interest rate as a stimulus to investment, debenture capital from public lending agencies was provided at low interest rates. Income tax incentives (accelerated depreciation and tax holidays graduated upward with size of investment) also had the effect of artificially cheapening capital. The price of unskilled labor, on the other hand, was raised above its market level. Government efforts to promote private collective bargaining have had the result of strengthening the political power of trade unions to influence wages in the public sector and large-scale undertakings, thus opening up a large differential between wages of workers in those enterprises and incomes of the bulk of the labor force. Moreover, setting those wages so much higher than alternative earnings in agriculture not only discourages maximum use of this abundant re-

ON BEING LATE: THE TECHNOLOGY BACKLOG

source in manufacturing, it also attracts migration from the rural areas in excess of employment opportunities in the towns, thereby generating unemployment.

These policies which encouraged the early wave of import substitution have had unfavorable ramifications, both for further industrial advance and for the growth of output in other sectors of the economy. Since the second stage of equally high-cost, vertically linked industries cuts into the protective subsidy of existing producers, tariff protection is further increased. This pyramiding of high-cost manufacture through successive stages of production constricts final markets and chokes off industrial expansion. No less important, more costly manufactured goods purchased by the farmer turn the terms of trade against agriculture, reducing incentives to expand marketed food supplies and primary exports. Reduced exports mean less foreign exchange, and consequently necessitate stricter rationing of imports. This cycle of restriction, distortion, and further restriction is aggravated by inflationary monetary policies.

Some of the effects of nonequilibrium factor pricing are illustrated in Figure 3.5. In Figure 3.5 (A) the price of foreign exchange (the

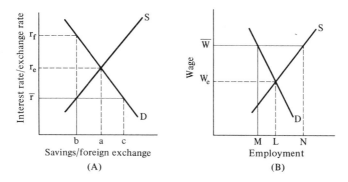

Figure 3.5 Disequilibrium factor pricing and its consequences.

rate of exchange between the domestic currency and foreign currencies) and the price of loan capital (the interest rate) are represented by r on the vertical axis; the amount of foreign exchange and loanable savings are shown on the horizontal axis. The market-clearing price is

r_e. On the supply side, fixing r below the equilibrium price reduces the incentives to produce for export and to save, so that the amount supplied falls from a to b. At r there is excess demand equal to bc, and administrative rationing becomes necessary. With less foreign exchange and capital now available their market value increases to r_f, so that the fortunate recipients of rationed supplies benefit from a subsidy equivalent to (r_f-r).

The effects of fixing the unskilled wage rate above a market-clearing price are depicted in panel (B). Here, those workers who are employed receive a wage subsidy equal to w_eW. The higher wage W attracts additional applicants into the labor market. However, at the higher wage employers will tend to substitute capital for labor so that the demand for labor is reduced from L to M. Not only is less labor now employed, but unemployment in the amount of MN has been created. In the case of overpricing, domestic inflationary policies tend to lessen the wage rate distortion, at least between the periodic upward adjustments of W.

If there are privileged firms, there are a far larger number of deprived firms. With no access to the rationed inputs except at elevated "grey market" prices (approximately r_f), these producers are forced to employ excessively unspecialized, labor-intensive production methods. Because barriers to entry are low, competition is intense and profits are slight or nonexistent. Atomistic competition combined with low-productivity technology also dictates that the returns to labor are meager in this sector. Whereas among the protected firms entrepreneurial striving for greater efficiency and technological betterment is undermined for lack of compelling incentive, in the deprived sector the barrier is the severely limited capacity to command the carriers of more advanced technology—modern capital and intermediate goods, skilled labor, and managerial talent. Firms in this sector do not frequently escape, they tend to remain small and unproductive.

The consequences of moving from administrative rationing to a regime of market-clearing prices are beneficial and thoroughgoing. At much reduced levels of protection the principle of comparative cost comes to the fore, signaling investors away from industries that are capital-intensive (save where capital-intensity is offset by high ocean transport costs or cheap raw materials). In addition to a lowered capital-labor ratio as a result of a more appropriate composition of industrial output, high-priced capital induces entrepreneurs to operate their physical plants more hours per day. Gordon Winston estimated that in prewar West Pakistan realistic factor pricing would have resulted in approximately 75 per cent more labor employed in the manufacturing sector following from multiple-shift operation.[51] Most directly, of course, expensive capital equipment and imported materials force investors to search diligently for ways of organizing production, as outlined in the previous sections, to allow for maximum substitution of labor and local intermediate goods. Purchase of components from low-cost, supervised ancillaries and specialist firms helps to transmit new design and quality control capabilities to the small-scale sector. The main facilitator of technological progress for these formerly deprived producers is easier access to the scarce, technology-carrying inputs.

Not only does the freeing of factor prices have favorable allocational results, but, as indicated in our discussion of Figure 3.4, total supplies of savings and foreign exchange are expanded. A higher rate of capital formation becomes possible, and with it more nonfarm employment. Furthermore, a reduction in protection and a wider dispersion of modern inputs means a far larger number of producers share in the gains from growth. The pattern of consumption expenditure associated with a less unequal income distribution shifts demand in favor of simpler, more labor-intensive commodities. Thus the consumption effect of "getting prices right" reinforces the factor proportions effect.

It is clear that correct pricing policies are of fundamental importance for fostering the adoption of labor-using technologies. Nevertheless, the functioning of the market must be supplemented by public agencies in at least two areas. The first is the collection and dissemination of knowledge on appropriate products and techniques not widely in use in the domestic economy. Assemblying data on performance, specifications, and cost of various items of second-hand equipment would be one such instance. Simple testing of promising product adaptations and new labor-intensive manufacturing procedures from other countries carries the process one step further. Gains from international cooperation are particularly great in this field.

The second area where the public sector has a role to play is research and development (R&D). Here we are referring to the new embodiment of existing scientific knowledge in a form appropriate to the conditions of low-income, labor-rich economies. The development of dwarf wheat and rice varieties is an instance of this type of research. Certain kinds of innovations are generated in the private sector. Process simplification described earlier—the cheapening of an imported prototype by altering certain of its attributes (diesel engine, dough-brake)—occurs in the small-scale sector in response to competitive pressures. Although subsidiaries of multinational corporations command both the resources and the trained personnel to undertake more fundamental R&D, they have rarely done so. Research has been confined to quality control and minor modifications of their existing "differentiated" products where they enjoy a good measure of monopoly. Development of "appropriate products" or intermediate technology equipment, difficult to patent and easy to copy and manufacture, holds no promise of enduring profitability. While scale requirements and uncertain success may add to its unattractiveness for large private firms, the problem of capturing the benefits of R&D is the pivotal factor which points to publicly sponsored organizations as the principal vehicle for this activity.

As in the case of assembling information, economies of scale mean that international cooperation in R&D is highly advantageous. The success of the International Maize and Wheat Improvement Center (CIMMYT) in Mexico and the International Rice Research Institute (IRRI) in the Philippines in developing biological technology for the "Green Revolution" has led to the establishment of other international research institutes in Nigeria, Colombia, Peru, and India to work on high-yielding varieties of root crops, legumes, and rainfed cereals.[52] Similar activities in the field of mechanical and industrial engineering also offer the promise of large social returns. The agricultural engineering program at IRRI has already achieved some success in developing appropriate equipment and in overcoming the problems involved in taking the step from producing a prototype to the launching of commercial manufacture. The program at IRRI has not been concerned with equipment for upland cultivation or for use with animal draft power. It seems clear that considerably more needs to be done to increase the availability to farmers of simple, inexpensive equipment of good design by making available prototypes, blueprints, and photographs, and disseminating information based on testing and farm experience under a variety of soil and climatic conditions.

Much of the analysis in this chapter and the one before it has been concerned with the ways in which the rate of structural transformation can be accelerated. Because of the special difficulties posed by the rapid labor force expansion, we have taken as our focus those factors affecting the rate of growth of nonfarm employment. It is already apparent that the pattern of agricultural development has many indirect effects on the speed with which nonfarm jobs can be created, not to mention its direct influence upon the expansion of income-earning opportunities within the agricultural sector itself. The exact nature of these effects will depend upon the strategy of agricultural development that is pursued, a topic to which we now turn.

NOTES

1. This term is a shorthand form of the phrase "the farm labor force as a percent of the total labor force."
2. Maximum output in 1960 was 142 tons per man in New Zealand. These data are from Yujiro Hayami and Vernon W. Ruttan, *Agricultural Development: An International Perspective* (Baltimore, 1971), Tables 4-1 and A-5. Note that Hayami and Ruttan employ a definition of the labor force different from the one we are using; theirs is restricted to men only.
3. See Appendix Tables I and III.
4. Data supplied by Robert Gardner, Population Institute, East-West Center, Honolulu, Hawaii.
5. Many governments have yet to approve even in principle the desirability of family planning. Religious beliefs are an important factor, but so too is na-

tionalism which sees strength in numbers. Internal political divisions along communal lines, by itself or in combination with population-based electoral arrangements, also operates to prevent some governments from taking any meaningful initiatives.

6. For a complete microeconomic modeling of household behavior with respect to number of children, see the special supplement, "New Economic Approaches to Fertility," *Journal of Political Economy* Vol. 81, No. 2, Pt. 2 (March/April 1973). The article by T. Paul Schultz on Taiwan included in the *Journal of Political Economy* special supplement and an unpublished paper by Professor Eva Mueller, "Agricultural Change and Fertility Change: The Case of Taiwan," mimeographed (Ann Arbor: University of Michigan, 1971), document how quickly these factors and improved information on birth control techniques can reduce birthrates in rural as well as urban areas. According to the 1969 survey analyzed by Mueller, 71 per cent of the farmers in the sample had knowledge of at least one contraceptive method and 37 per cent were practicing contraception; and this was only five years after a national family planning program was launched. Her analysis of the influence of strong aspirations—to save and to invest (in the education of children as well as in the farm enterprise) and to raise consumption standards—on variations in fertility among farm households suggests that the rapidity of the spread of family planning in rural Taiwan was almost certainly related to the widespread participation of the farm population in the process of agricultural modernization.

7. For the year 1972. See Population Reference Bureau, *1972 World Population Data Sheet* (Washington, D.C., 1973).

8. Nathaniel Leff, "Dependency Rates and Savings Rates," *American Economic Review* Vol 59, No. 5 (December 1969).

9. The dependency ratio will increase during the lag period, after which time it will remain constant. A fall in the birthrate will lower the dependency ratio in a symmetrical fashion.

10. We owe this definition of the rate of structural transformation to John Cownie, "Agriculture, Domestic Manufacturing, and Structural Transformation: Assessing Economic Development," *African Studies Review* Vol. 17, No. 1 (April 1974). It is easily derived by differentiating (L_n/L_t) with respect to time.

The difference between the growth rates of nonfarm employment and of the total labor force $(L_n'-L_t')$ has been termed the "coefficient of differential growth." It indicates the *rate* at which the percentage share of the nonagricultural labor force will increase. A coefficient of differential growth of 1 percent, for example, would mean an increase from, say, 20.0 to 20.2 per cent or perhaps from 50.0 to 50.5, depending on the initial nonfarm labor force ratio. The RST would obviously be much larger in the second instance than in the first—.5 as a per cent or .005 as a change in the ratio compared to .2 or .002.

11. See Tables 3.1 and 3.2.

12. The corresponding values for L'_t were also low, ranging from 0.5 to 1.5 per cent. Folke Dovring, "The Share of Agriculture in a Growing Population," *FAO Monthly Bulletin of Agricultural Economics and Statistics* Vol. 8, No. 8/9 (August/September 1959), p. 8.
13. Excepting oil-producing Libya, whose NNP grew at a rate of 20 per cent per annum.
14. For the algebraic expressions used to calculate this turning point as well as the results of the preceding paragraph, see John Cownie, "Appendix Note" to Kazushi Ohkawa and Bruce F. Johnston, "The Transferability of the Japanese Pattern of Modernizing Traditional Agriculture," in *The Role of Agriculture in Economic Development*, edited by Erik Thorbecke (New York, 1969), p. 301. Cownie shows that if L'_n is less than double L'_t the turning point will occur after the nonfarm labor force ratio reaches the 50 per cent mark; if L'_n is more than double L'_t, then the turning point occurs before the 50 per cent mark.
15. Our analysis assumes constant returns to scale and neutral or labor-saving technical progress.
16. The equation of the line is $O/L = w + r (K/L)$, where w is the marginal product of labor and r is the marginal product of capital.
17. The line AT intersects the tangency points of each historical period. It links rather than envelopes the tangency points so that the profit-maximizing point of this quasiproduction function is at the right-hand intersection of the output-capital price line with AT. AT may be either concave or convex relative to IT depending upon changes in the rate of scientific progress in the past. As derived from panel (B) its shape implies a more rapid rate of progress in recent decades.
18. That is, with respect to what is scientifically possible. In terms of isoquant analysis, the marginal rate of technical substitution of capital for labor exceeds the labor/capital price ratio.
19. For a comprehensive history of the evolution of dwarf rice and wheat, as well as a review of the current status of research, see D. S. Athwal, "Semidwarf Rice and Wheat in Global Food Needs," *Quarterly Review of Biology* Vol. 46, No. 1 (March 1971).

Owing to its extremely limited supply of land, the search for plant varieties responsive to the application of nitrogen was first pursued intensively in Japan. One report indicates that Japanese farmers grew dwarf wheat as early as 1873. Scientific breeding efforts were begun during the second decade of this century, eventually culminating in the Norin wheats of the 1930s. Japanese dwarfs were being used in breeding programs in Italy in the late 1920s. It was Norin 10 (1935), crossed with an American spring wheat, that was the male parent in developing the Mexican dwarf wheat, the first important dwarf variety suitable for the tropics and subtropics (provided that temperatures and humidity are not too high for successful wheat production).

20. Robert W. Herdt and John W. Mellor, "The Contrasting Response of **Rice** to Nitrogen: India and the United States," *Journal of Farm Economics* **Vol.**

46, No. 1 (February 1964), p. 152.
21. Athwal, "Global Food Needs."
22. G. S. Sahota, *Fertilizer in Economic Development: An Econometric Analysis* (New York, 1968), p. 2.
23. Ibid. p. 96.
24. The amount of P_2O_5 in normal superphosphate is 16 to 20 per cent, in basic slag 16 per cent, in triple superphosphate 32 to 46 per cent, in phosphoric acid 54 per cent, in superphosphoric acid 70 per cent. The phosphoric acids are used in complex fertilizers which incorporate ammonia and nitrogen; for example, ammonium phosphate and nitrophosphate. Basic slag, obtained as a by-product from the manufacture of steel from high-phosphorus iron ores, is an important phosphate fertilizer in the acidic soils of Europe, but little used elsewhere.
25. For a detailed discussion of the evolution of the technology, see Vincent Suachelli, editor, *Chemistry and Technology of Fertilizers* (New York, 1960), Chap. 5.
26. We confine our attention to the dominant wet process method.
27. S. V. Slack, *Fertilizer Developments and Trends* (Park Ridge, New Jersey, 1968), Chap. 8.
28. United Nations Industrial Development Organization, *Fertilizer Industry* (New York, 1969), p. 29; and D. R. Henderson, G. R. Perkins, and D. M. Bell, *Simulating the Fertilizer Industry: Data* (East Lansing, 1972), pp. 32, 37.
29. The material in this paragraph is based on G. H. Collings, *Commercial Fertilizers* (New York, 1955), 5th ed., Chap. 3; and K. D. Jacobs, editor, *Fertilizer Technology and Resources in the United States* (New York, 1953), Chap. 2.
30. Much of the material in this and the following paragraphs is drawn from Slack, *Fertilizer Development and Trends,* Chap. 3.
31. Considerable adaptive research efforts in the areas enumerated are being made by a state corporation in India and by the major fertilizer equipment producers in Europe, the United States, and Japan. See Slack, *Fertilizer Development and Trends,* passim.
32. Howard Pack, "The Use of Labor-Intensive Techniques in Kenya Industry," in *Technology and Economics in International Development,* Agency for International Development, Office of Science and Technology (Washington, D.C., 1972).
33. Other light industries include soap, paint, metal and plastic containers, shoes, textiles, and toletries.
34. The two can also occur together, such as adapting older vintage equipment to utilize a larger complement of labor than called for by the original design. Despecialization can also be associated with a reduction in plant scale and a widening of input specification tolerances.
35. For the evidence pertaining to spinning, weaving, and printing, see Peter Kilby, *Industrialization in an Open Economy: Nigeria 1945-1966* (Cambridge, 1969), pp. 116-18. The point relating to the advantages of early vintage ma-

chine tools and much of the following two paragraphs is drawn from United Nations, *Group on Second-Hand Equipment for Developing Countries* (New York, 1966).

36. Foreign investors with access to obsolescent equipment (obsolescent at high-wage rates) in their own home-country plants have special advantages in utilizing such equipment. However, their motivation for doing so is frequently related to financial manipulations that overvalued second-hand machinery makes possible (e.g., inflated share in equity capital, tax avoidance). Where such manipulations occur they may offset the benefit from increased employment. For a full discussion, see Kilby, *Industrialization in an Open Economy*, pp. 119 ff., 360.

37. Peter Kilby, "Investment Criteria, Productivity and Economic Development: A Reinterpretation," *Quarterly Journal of Economics* Vol. 78, No. 3 (August 1964).

38. Frances Stewart, "Choice of Technique in Developing Countries," *Journal of Development Studies* Vol. 9, No. 1 (October 1972).

39. Ibid. p. 113.

40. Peter Kilby, *African Enterprise: The Nigerian Bread Industry* (Stanford, 1965), pp. 46-51. The submarket referred to is for wrapped, high-quality bread. The largest producer had the lowest capital-labor ratio.

41. As in our next case, the innovator lacked any formal technical training. He was a retired Treasury clerk whose businesses included baking, metalworking, brewing, and chalk-making—all on a small scale.

42. See Government of India, Development Commissioner (Small Scale Industry), *Diesel Engines* (New Delhi, 1961); and, for West Pakistan, Edward Smith, "The Diesel Engine Industry in Pakistan's Punjab," mimeographed (Islamabad: AID, August 1970).

43. Gustav Ranis, "Some Observations on the Economic Framework for Optimum LDC Utilization of Technology," in *Technology and Economics in International Development,* Agency for International Development, Office of Science and Technology (Washington, D.C., 1972).

44. Gordon Winston, "Capital Utilisation in Economic Development," *Economic Journal* Vol. 81, No. 321 (March 1971).

45. Ian Little, Tibor Scitovsky, and Maurice Scott, *Industry and Trade in Some Developing Countries* (Oxford, 1970), pp. 93-98.

46. The studies summarized by Gordon Winston show that in developed countries reluctance among employed persons to switch to shift work is greatest among the more educated. "One suspects that this is due largely to social status and expectations which are likely to be even more pronounced in hierarchical traditional societies and especially ones with a colonial background in which social status and shift work rarely went hand in hand." "Capital Utilization: Physiological Costs and Preferences for Shift Work," mimeographed (Williamstown, Massachusetts: Williams College, Center for Development Economics, Research Memorandum No. 42, October 1971), p. 19.

47. Ranis, "LDC Utilization of Technology," pp. 22-24.

48. Little, Scitovsky, and Scott, *Industry and Trade,* p. 31.
49. For a discussion of events in Africa, see Peter Kilby, "Manufacturing in Colonial Africa," in *Colonialism in Africa,* Vol. IV, edited by Peter J. Duignan and Lewis H. Gann (Cambridge, 1975).
50. Little, Scitovsky, and Scott, *Industry and Trade,* pp. 98-99.
51. Gordon Winston, "Capital Utilization, Investment and Employment: A Neoclassical Model of Optimal Shift Work," mimeographed (Karachi: Pakistan Institute of Development Economics, 1971).
52. IRRI was established in 1960. CIMMYT was organized as an international institute in 1966, but it was essentially an expansion on an international scale of the research program launched on a national scale in 1944 by the Rockefeller Foundation and the Mexican government. (See Chapter 6.) The other centers in this international network were established as follows: International Institute for Tropical Agriculture (IITA) at Ibadan, Nigeria, in 1967; the International Center for Tropical Agriculture (CIAT) at Cali, Colombia, in 1968; International Potato Center (IPC) in Peru in 1972, and the International Crop Research Institute for the Semi-Arid Tropics (ICRISAT) near Hyderabad, India, in 1972. Although these international centers were initially financed by the Ford and Rockefeller Foundations, a number of national and international aid agencies are now providing significant budget support.

4 The Design of An Agricultural Strategy

In this chapter we address the thorny problems involved in designing an efficient agricultural strategy. But what do we mean by agricultural strategy—and an "efficient" one at that? Webster defines *strategy* as "the science and art of employing the political, economic, psychological, and military forces of a nation . . . to afford the maximum support to adopted policies in peace or war." In orthodox economic terms an *efficient* strategy is one that "maximizes output for a given input." We will, however, argue that alternative agricultural strategies should be assessed in relation to outcomes that encompass more than the efficient expansion of agricultural production.

Because of their structural and demographic characteristics, late-developing countries face a fundamental choice between a strategy aimed at the progressive modernization of the entire agricultural sector and a crash modernization strategy that concentrates resources in a highly commercialized subsector. We refer to the first alternative, well illustrated by the patterns of agricultural development in Japan and Taiwan, as a "unimodal strategy." The second alternative, which results in a development pattern based on a dualistic size structure of farm units, as in Mexico or Colombia, is labeled a "bimodal strategy."

We will be arguing that a unimodal strategy has significant advantages because it is consistent with maximum mobilization of a late-developing country's resources of labor and land. Because the nonagricultural sectors are so small in relation to the number of farm households, agriculture is subject to the severe demand constraint examined in Chapter 2. The resulting purchasing power constraint limits the extent to which expansion of the agricultural sector's output can be based on increased use of purchased inputs, whether imported or manufactured domestically. These considerations underscore the importance of the dynamic forces that determine the rate and character of technical change, especially the process of generating a sequence of divisible innovations that leads to widespread increases in the productivity of land and labor. The success of individual farm units in allocating resources so as to minimize costs is clearly an essential ingredient of an efficient agricultural strategy. It is, however, the nature of technical innovations and their diffusion among farmers that are decisive in minimizing the cost of the sector-wide expansion of farm output and in determining the pattern of development. It will be suggested that the patterns of agricultural development associated with the unimodal and bimodal alternatives differ a great deal in the contributions that they make to achieving three major objectives of an agricultural strategy: advancing structural transformation, raising the welfare of the farm population, and fostering changes in rural attitudes and behavior that will have beneficial effects on the process of modernization.

After considering the elements that comprise an agricultural strategy, we examine the three basic objectives mentioned above, giving particular attention to the extent to which alternative strategies influence the competitiveness and complementarity among those objectives. In sections on pp. 140 and 153 we consider the economic constraints that influence the choice of means for promoting agricultural progress and the political and administrative constraints that condition the governmental decision making that determines a country's agricultural strategy and its implementation. A final section (p. 161) focuses on some of the factors that are of critical importance in shaping the pattern of agricultural development.

ELEMENTS OF AN AGRICULTURAL STRATEGY

Although the concept of "strategy" has become fashionable in development economics, few attempts have been made to define it. A useful general definition is that a strategy is a mix of policies and programs that influences the pattern as well as the rate of growth. Particular attention is given here to the differential effects of the patterns of agricultural development associated with a unimodal as contrasted with a bimodal strategy. Any strategy for agricultural development will embrace some combination of (a) programs of institution building related to such activities as agricultural research and rural education and farmer training, (b) programs of investment in infrastructure, including irrigation and drainage facilities and rural roads, (c) programs to improve product marketing and the distribution of inputs, and (d) policies related to prices, taxation, and land tenure. Its "efficiency" will depend in part on promoting optimal use of available resources, and still more on modifying existing constraints.

In brief, the emphasis is on action to change the production possibilities available to farmers by modifying their institutional, technical, and economic environment. An underlying premise is that decentralized decision making by individual producers has especially significant advantages in agriculture. The price mechanism performs a critical function in harmonizing decentralized decisions and in harnessing the powerful motive of profit. Although the role of market mechanisms in resource allocation is emphasized, we also stress the interactions between the activities of individual producers and government programs and policies. Of special significance is the role of government in undertaking research and farmer training programs to favorably alter input-output relations while public investments in infrastructure enlarge the scope for applying profitable innovations. In addition, governments may find it desirable to adopt policies to make prices reflect more adequately the social costs and benefits of using resources in different types of productive activities.

Our stress on strategy differs sharply from the conventional approach of agricultural planning which has emphasized the setting of production targets for individual commodities.[1] Demand projections can, of course, serve a number of useful purposes. But there is a tendency for target-setting exercises to divert attention from more basic issues and to absorb scarce resources of manpower that could be better employed in the design and implementation of an efficient agricultural strategy.

The present orientation also may be contrasted with the approach, often emphasized by the World Bank and bilateral aid-giving agencies, which concentrates on decisions related to individual projects. Strictly speaking, this should not be regarded as an alternative approach. Logically, the choice of an agricultural strategy and a clear definition of its major objectives should be a prior stage in decision making; and the identification, preparation, and evaluation of individual projects should be carried out within the framework of a carefully designed development strategy.[2] But in fact a project-oriented approach has often been a substitute for serious concern with the design of a strategy for the agricultural sector. And a primary focus on individual projects involving costs and returns that are easy to quantify encourages a partial view of the options available. The result is undue reliance on a narrow concept of efficiency, a tendency to exaggerate the returns to be realized from concentrating resources in "bankable projects," and neglect of the measures needed to achieve an efficient expansion path for the agricultural sector.

A number of attempts are being made to overcome the limitations of a project-oriented approach by use of sector models employing the techniques of linear programming, recursive linear programming, or simulation systems. On the basis of a review of a number of the sector models that have been evolved, Erik Thorbecke has concluded that "there is still a large gap between what the models can deliver and what the users need and desire for policy-formulation purposes" and that sector analysis applied to agriculture is still "more of an art than a science."[3]

All three alternative approaches—target setting, project evaluation, and construction of sector models—confront a common problem. Many variables of fundamental importance to the design and implementation of an agricultural strategy are difficult to measure and model because they "are almost invariably surrounded by a host of indeterminate and imponderable elements."[4] In addition to the problems of quantification, the number of variables and the complex interrelations between institutions, behavioral characteristics, technical possibilities, and economic factors make it impossible to consider all possible alternatives and to identify *the* optimum set of policies and programs. The inevitable and considerable margin of uncertainty in predicting the results forthcoming from agricultural research and from efforts to diffuse innovations are examples of a pervasive problem. And because the essence of the problem is to promote efficient, evolutionary change of a complex, dynamic system, an attempt to apply rigorous optimization techniques to a subset of variables is likely to be worse than decision making that is guided by a more comprehensive attempt to take account of all of the significant variables, including a number of factors that are exceedingly difficult to quantify but too important to ignore. There is an inherently difficult problem in extracting from the mass of information that is in some degree pertinent to the design of an agricultural strategy only that information which is essential to rational decision making and which can be handled by the communication channels that are available— or capable of being created without undue cost. It is, of course, an important virtue of a price system that it is a very economical mechanism for transmitting information that influences the decisions of individual producers and consumers. But many of the key decisions in the design of an agricultural strategy involve the provision of "public goods"—research, irrigation systems, training programs—or policy decisions that must be made by governmental organizations. Hence, there is a need for an analytical framework to serve as a guide for extracting essential information and for determining the critical questions that should find a place on the government's decision-making agenda.[5]

Formal analytical techniques obviously have an important role to play. But they need to be supplemented by "reasoned methods of explanation and prediction" that take account of many types of evidence.[6] Past experience, familiarity with agricultural science and the technological possibilities that are available or in prospect, and intimate knowledge of the specific problems and potentialities of a particular country and its agricultural regions are thus essential. Because the elements that should be included in an agricultural strategy depend so much on factors that are specific to a particular location and point in time, it is essential to achieve a proper balance between centralized and decentralized decision making in the formulation and implementation of programs of research, extension, and infrastructure. The difficult questions involved in devising an efficient management system and procedures for plan formulation and the implementation and monitoring of agricultural programs have not received the attention that they deserve.[7] Some recent attempts to consider these problems of agricultural administration and implementation are examined briefly in Chapter 10.

In more general terms we would emphasize that a fundamental requirement of a suitable analytical approach is simultaneous consideration of the *objectives* to be furthered by an agricultural strategy and the *means* (policies and programs) by which those objectives are to be attained. It is also essential for the choice of objectives and of means to be guided by explicit recognition of certain *constraints* that can only be gradually eliminated, especially those imposed by the structural and demographic situation in a late-developing country. The critical factors limiting agricultural development and the pace of structural transformation are technological capabilities, availability of investable funds and foreign exchange, and the level of farm purchasing power. It is our argument that a unimodal agricultural strategy aimed at the progressive modernization of the bulk of a nation's cultivators, as contrasted to a bimodal crash modernization effort concentrated upon a small subsector of large-scale mechanized farms, minimizes the extent to which the above constraints impede the development of agriculture and the process of transformation. It does so through its effects on: (a) the disbursement pattern of farm cash receipts, (b) the allocation of investment resources, (c) the kinds of new technological knowledge that are produced, and (d) the proportion of the nation's producers that has access to the new modes of production.

It is clearly an oversimplification to concentrate on the polar extremes represented by unimodal and bimodal alternatives. There are

THE DESIGN OF AN AGRICULTURAL STRATEGY

good reasons, however, for focusing initially on the choice between those two extreme alternatives. Governments, like most bureaucratic organizations, are disposed to concentrate on coping with the agenda of pressing problems rather than on developing long-run strategies. Consequently, the "choice" of an agricultural strategy will often be made by default. Moreover, for reasons examined in the section on p. 153, there are often strong political pressures that tend to bias the outcome toward a bimodal strategy. For both reasons, it is especially important to arrive at a clear understanding of the nature of the alternatives and of their differential effects on the pattern of agricultural development and on overall economic growth.

CHOICE CRITERIA: THE MULTIPLE OBJECTIVES OF
AN AGRICULTURAL STRATEGY

What criteria should guide this choice between a unimodal and bimodal strategy? We propose that the efficiency of alternative strategies should be assessed in terms of their contributions to attaining three major objectives: first, facilitating the process of structural transformation and growth in national product; second, enhancing the welfare of the farm population; and third, promoting changes in attitudes and behavior in rural communities that have a favorable impact on the process of social modernization.

Objectives of an Agricultural Strategy

Because agriculture and its interrelations with other sectors bulk so large in late-developing countries, it is essential to assess alternative agricultural strategies in terms of their intersectoral effects as well as their direct effects on the expansion of farm output and incomes. Hence, the *first objective* of an agricultural strategy focuses on the need to achieve a rate and pattern of output expansion in the agricultural sector that will promote overall economic growth and structural transformation and take full advantage of positive interactions between agriculture and other sectors. This objective encompasses what has often been referred to as agriculture's "contributions" to development: (a) providing increased supplies of food and raw materials to meet the needs of the expanding nonfarm sectors, (b) earning foreign exchange through production for export, and (c) providing a net flow of capital to finance a considerable part of the investment requirements for infrastructure and industrial growth.

The problems involved in achieving a net flow of resources from agriculture clearly represent the most difficult area of competitiveness between this first objective of fostering structural transformation and the second objective of improving the well being of the rural population. We give considerable attention to those problems in our review of the historical experience of Japan, Taiwan, and Mexico and in the discussion of agriculture-industry interactions in Chapter 7.

The expansion in the absolute and relative importance of commercial production in agriculture is, of course, an aspect of the structural transformation and increasing sectoral interdependence that were examined in Chapter 2. The growth of a marketable surplus of farm products, expansion of foreign exchange earnings, and increased availability of resources for capital formation are necessary conditions for the development of a diversified modern economy. At the same time the growth of farm cash income associated with structural transformation means increased rural demand for inputs and consumer goods that can provide an important stimulus to domestic industry. The strength of that stimulus and the associated feedback effects will be strongly influenced, however, by the composition of rural demand.

A broadly based expansion of farm cash income generating demand for low-cost and relatively simple inputs and consumer goods can be expected to foster efficient, evolutionary growth of domestic manufacturing that is characterized by relatively low import content and which leads to the strengthening and diffusion of entrepreneurial and technical competence. Basic to all of these interrelations between agricultural development and overall economic growth is the creation of an integrated national economy characterized by increased specialization and growing interdependence among sectors. This requires the development of flexible and sensitive market networks and continuing improvement in transportation and other types of infrastructure.

The *second objective,* achieving broadly based improvement of the welfare of the rural population, is important simply because such a large fraction of the population of developing countries is destined to live and die in farming communities. Achievement of that objective depends in the long run on altering the predominantly agrarian structure of these economies. The possibility of enlarging the income of the agricultural sector, and still more the *average* income of farm households, is determined mainly by the rate and character of structural transformation, particularly as manifested in the decline of the relative and, eventually, absolute size of the farm work force and the associated growth of commercial demand for agricultural products.

Inequality in income distribution is a conspicuous feature of most less-developed countries and a matter for particular concern because the poverty of the low-income groups is so extreme. The extent to which such inequality in income distribution will be either reduced or exacerbated will be determined mainly by whether the demand for labor increases more or less rapidly than the country's work force. At issue is the growth of demand for labor in all sectors; but the increase in demand for labor in agriculture, including the employment opportunities available to family members working on their own or rented land, is of special significance. And the extent to which the expansion of farm output will lead to widespread increases in income-earning opportunities will, for reasons considered shortly, hinge on the development and diffusion of divisible innovations.

Certain dimensions of welfare can be furthered most effectively by direct action through government programs, notably public health and related activities. The cost effectiveness of such programs can be very high if they are oriented toward preventive measures and make maximum use of subprofessional staff trained to deal competently with a limited but carefully selected set of objectives. Prime examples are programs aimed at environmental sanitation, health education, and infectious disease control, for example, stamping out malaria and innoculation against smallpox and measles. Experience has been uneven, but "delivery systems" for attaining those objectives have often been quite successful. Nutrition programs also offer promise of significant gains in health at moderate cost, but accomplishments in that field have been limited. Typically, the greatest need is to improve diets of the most vulnerable groups—children between six months and three or four years of age and pregnant and lactating mothers. This requires nutrition education geared to the foods locally available; and in many instances there is also a need to promote the manufacture and distribution of inexpensive mixtures based on local oilseed proteins, legumes, and cereals that provide high-quality protein and other nutrients needed during the post-weaning period. Genetic manipulation of cereals to improve their protein quality also offers promise of being a low-cost, practical approach. New varieties of maize with a high lysine content are especially promising, although problems related to the storability and consumer acceptance of "floury" or "opaque" varieties have not yet been overcome.[8]

Rural works programs can provide supplementary employment and income for some of the most disadvantaged elements of the rural population. But the indirect contribution of such programs to the expansion of farm output and income, through the construction of roads, irrigation works, and other useful infrastructure, is likely to be more important. Considerable planning and technical supervision is required, however, to insure the usefulness of employment-oriented projects of that nature. Because of those organizational problems and the fiscal constraints which limit their magnitude, such programs apparently have not had a very large effect on under- and unemployment in rural areas. For the rural works program in Bangladesh (then East Pakistan), which was one of the more ambitious undertakings of this type and one that was financed to a large extent by P. L. 480 grain imports, Walter Falcon reports an annual reduction of agricultural unemployment of only about 3.5 per cent.[9]

Judgments will differ concerning the importance of the *third objective*, that is, fostering a pattern of agricultural development that will have a favorable impact on social modernization as a result of inducing changes in rural attitudes, behavior, and institutions. The evolutionary development of a variety of social institutions is clearly a significant feature of structural transformation. Salient examples pertaining to agriculture include the creation and strengthening of agricultural experiment stations; expansion of educational facilities and programs for training farmers; establishing irrigation associations or other groups that enable farmers to concert their behavior when group action is advantageous; and strengthening the organizations—private, public, or cooperative—that distribute credit and inputs and market farm products.

The need for "institutional progress" is especially significant in countries undertaking a unimodal strategy of agricultural development. Hence, the interactions between technical and economic change at the farm level and institutional, attitudinal, and behavioral change merit attention in assessing the differential effects of alternative strategies. Broader participation in the modernization of agriculture implies a more widespread familiarity with calculations of costs and returns and with the evaluation and selective adoption of innovations. Such opportunities for "learning by doing" foster the development and spread of managerial competence that facilitates the recruitment and training of the entrepreneurs and skilled workers required in a modernizing economy.

It also is to be expected that broad participation of the farm population in improved income-earning opportunities will influence the rural power structure and political institutions. This has obvious implications with respect to political and financial support for rural schools and other institutions to serve farming communities. There are, of course, reciprocal interactions between the effects of the pattern of rural development on the distribution of political power and the influence of the power structure on the choice of strategy for agricultural development, but we defer those questions until a later section.

There is one other area in which the interrelations between the pattern of agricultural development and changes in rural attitudes and behavior is potentially of very great significance. Many years ago John Stuart Mill asserted that an agricultural system based on peasant proprietorship would have a beneficial effect on the "prudence" as well as the "industry" of the rural population and would therefore "discourage an improvident increase in their numbers. . . ."[10]

The key question concerns the way in which the modernization of agriculture will affect the spread of the knowledge, incentives, and motivation essential to the practice of family planning. It is certainly a reasonable hypothesis that conscious action to limit family size will take hold more readily if rural households are actively involved in a process of economic and technical change, whether as owner cultivators or as tenants, rather than being relegated to a "surplus population-supporting sector" with slight opportunity to better their condition. The analysis of the relationships between various economic factors and fertility change in Taiwan reported in Chapter 3 seems to provide considerable support for that hypothesis. In her concluding comments, Eva Mueller declares that:

Where agricultural improvement is confined to a minority of cultivators . . . the expansion of economic horizons will be more limited than in Taiwan. Only a minority will then experience the rising aspirations that in Taiwan seem to be contributing so importantly to acceptance of family planning in rural areas. The majority of farmers will have no experience with progress and no reason to raise their sights. They will continue to feel that yield-raising farm investments, a better education for their children, and modern consumer goods and services are not 'for them.' The transformation of household preferences which we observed in Taiwan will be much less extensive.[11]

Clearly, there is a marked contrast between the rapid reduction in birthrates during the past two decades in Taiwan, and also South Korea, and the slight changes that have taken place in other developing countries.[12] This can probably be attributed in part to relatively well-organized family planning programs in those two countries. But the changes in rural attitudes and motivation resulting from broad participation in development and the widespread influence of education and other modernizing institutions and of the mass media undoubtedly strengthened the direct effects of family planning programs. There are also indications that those factors and the rising aspirations which they have engendered have also contributed to more spontaneous reductions in fertility. One fact is beyond dispute. Given the structural-demographic characteristics of late-developing countries, there is no hope of bringing birthrates into tolerable balance with the sharply reduced death rates that now prevail unless conscious limitation of family size becomes widespread in rural areas.

Competitiveness and Complementarity Among Objectives

To argue, as we have done in this section, that the choice of agricultural strategy should be guided by explicit attention to their effects on a set of objectives is a somewhat unorthodox approach—but one that is now receiving much attention. Richard Musgrave sums up the orthodox approach, which is in accord with the compensation principle of welfare economics, with the statement that policy makers should opt for "the efficient choice" and then supplement that decision with "the necessary distribution adjustment through a tax-transfer mechanism."[13] But where poverty is widespread and tax revenues are severely limited, distributional adjustments through a tax transfer mechanism cannot be carried out on a significant scale even if the political climate is favorable.

It has become a common practice to admonish policy makers in low-income countries to make development decisions by assigning appropriate weights to (a) growth of output, (b) employment expansion, and (c) income distribution goals. This is in accord with the predilection of economists to assume that there are invariably trade-offs between output and equity goals. This is, of course, true at the margin. Additional funds allocated to a program of nutritional improvement will, at least indirectly, be at the expense of reduced allocations for some other program such as agricultural research, farmer training, or investments in infrastructure.

Although it is necessary to consider trade-offs in making decisions with respect to particular policies or programs, the trade-offs that arise in connection with the set of policies required to implement a unimodal strategy will be small compared to the situation under the bimodal alternative. In the latter case, for example, a truly massive (and usually politically infeasible) program of rural public works would be required for unemployment relief to offset the labor-displacing effects of a capital-intensive expansion path. But within the framework of a unimodal strategy, the need to generate additional employment via a works program would be much less. Moreover, the prospects for planning and financing rural public works projects that will have favorable effects on output are better in the context of a unimodal pattern of development; and in that context it is legitimate to give greater weight to output effects than employment creation.

The crux of our argument is that it is wrong to assume that the choice between unimodal and bimodal strategies necessarily involves a sacrifice with respect to the economic objective of increasing output in order to further the social objectives of expanding employment opportunities and reducing inequalities in income distribution. Given the economic constraints that condition the choice of means for promoting agricultural development, progressive modernization of the rural sector is, in general, the most efficient means of attaining the threefold objectives of an agricultural strategy. The principal qualification applies to situations in which large farm enterprises are able to achieve export expansion that would not be feasible for small units because of the importance of scale economies, quality control requirements, or contacts with overseas markets. Even in those instances, smallholders may have an important role to play as satellite producers. And Kenya's success in expanding smallholder tea production demonstrates that an institutional innovation—the Kenya Tea Development Authority in this instance—can provide the necessary coordination of transportation and processing to permit efficient smallholder production of a crop that was traditionally regarded as a plantation crop par excellence.

ECONOMIC CONSTRAINTS AND THE CHOICE OF MEANS

We turn now to the reasons why late comers face a choice between a unimodal or bimodal strategy, a choice that will largely determine

THE DESIGN OF AN AGRICULTURAL STRATEGY

the portion of a nation's farmers that is able to exploit new modes of production and new income opportunities. The orientation of a country's agricultural research and the nature of its educational and farmer training programs will clearly have differential effects on farms of different size and resource endowments. In the light of experience in the United States, Earl Heady summarizes the distributional implications of technical change in these terms:

> The structure of the farm firms and the resource restraints under which different groups of them operate creates the possibility for contrasting outcomes for producers of different scales and capital availability. As indicated in numerous studies of farm economics, the revolution in technology has provided important scale or cost economies for the farms which shift to the new forms of capital equipment and extend to large volume operations. . . . Farms unable to make the fairly discrete and large jumps from old to new capital technologies suffer reduced incomes [because of lower prices resulting from the increases in total output] and thus pay part of the costs of progress.[14]

In the agricultural sector of an economically advanced country such as the United States, it is inevitable that the new technologies will include large investments in tractors and related forms of capital equipment that are labor saving and characterized by economies of scale. Emphasis on new capital technologies of that nature in a late-developing country will make "the possibility of contrasting outcomes" a certainty.

Because of the structural and demographic characteristics emphasized in preceding chapters, the growth of domestic commercial demand (an increasingly important component of the farm sector's cash receipts) is a gradual process governed by the transformation of the predominantly agrarian structure of a late-developing country. Hence, the sectorwide expansion in the use of external inputs (i.e., purchased from nonfarm sectors or imported) is subject to a purchasing power constraint that derives from the limited size of the commercial market for farm products relative to the number of farm households. Given that the demand for farm products is price inelastic, expansion of production for market at a faster rate than the secular increase in commercial demand would mean a reduction in farm cash receipts. Once a "structural transformation turning point" has been reached, cash receipts per farm unit can grow more rapidly than the total cash income accruing to the sector. But for the reasons set out in Chapter 3, the farm labor force in late-developing countries will continue to grow in absolute numbers for several decades because of the rapid growth of the economically active population and the weight of agriculture in the total labor force.

Farm Labor Productivity and the Sequence of Innovations

A major thesis of this book is that sequences of innovations *can* be generated and diffused that will foster the widespread increases in productivity that characterize a unimodal strategy and thus avoid the polarization of agriculture into subsectors using drastically different technologies. It is convenient, in considering the choice of innovations, to partition increases in agricultural output per worker (Y/L) into changes in the number of acres cultivated per worker (A/L) and in the average yield per acre (Y/A). It is apparent that at any point in time, output per worker will be given by the identity:

$$\frac{Y}{L} \equiv \frac{A}{L} \cdot \frac{Y}{A}$$

The rate of change over time in output per worker will, to a close approximation, be equal to the sum of the rates of change in the right-hand terms, that is, the percentage changes in acreage cultivated per worker and in yield per acre. Considering only factors influencing the supply of agricultural products, this partitioning of the factors affecting output per worker gives no indication whether mechanical innovations that enlarge the cultivated area per worker or yield-increasing innovations should be emphasized. In fact, in countries beyond the "structural transformation turning point" so that the size of the farm labor force is declining, the two components will both make major contributions.

In Table 4.1 we bring together estimates of the rates of change in output per worker, cultivated acreage per worker, and yield per acre

Table 4.1. Rates of change in output per worker, acreage per worker, and yield per acre in Japan, Taiwan, Mexico, and the U.S., selected periods between 1876-1968

(*Per cent*)

Period	Y/L	A/L	Y/A
Japan			
1876-1920	1.82	0.72	1.10
1920-40	0.71[a]	0.19[a]	0.52
1952-67	5.80	2.90	2.90
Taiwan			
1901-50	1.2	0.4	0.8
1952-66	3.3	−0.8	4.1
Mexico			
1921-40	−0.2	1.3	−1.5
1940-50	3.0	0.7	2.3
1950-68	1.8	0.0	1.8
United States			
1880-1900	1.1	1.2	−0.1
1900-20	.6	.5	.1
1920-40	2.2	1.5	.7
1940-60	5.8	4.2	1.6

[a] These figures are considerably lower than figures for this period reported by Hayami and Ruttan and somewhat lower than recent estimates for the period 1920 to 1935 by Saburo Yamada and Yujiro Hayami, "Growth Rates of Japanese Agriculture, 1880-1965" (Paper [and revisions thereof] prepared for the Conference on Agricultural Growth in Japan, Korea, Taiwan, and the Philippines at the East-West Center, Honolulu, Hawaii, February 1973), pp. 16, 17, 21.

SOURCE: Data from Montague Yudelman, Gavan Butler, and Ranadev Banerji, *Technological Change in Agriculture and Employment in Developing Countries,* OECD Development Centre (Paris, 1972) except figures for the U.S. from Yujiro Hayami and Vernon W. Ruttan, *Agricultural Development: An International Perspective* (Baltimore and London, 1971), p. 114. Their calculations refer to changes in output and area per male worker in agriculture rather than total farm labor force.

for Japan, the United States, Taiwan, and Mexico, four of the six countries that are examined in Chapters 5 and 6. As noted shortly, the aggregate figures for Mexico conceal the actual pattern of change and must be considered in the light of additional information. It will be observed that the growth of output per worker in both Japan and the United States was especially high in the most recent periods (1952-67 for Japan and 1940-60 for the United States). It was in this period that Japan's farm labor force finally began to decline at a rapid rate; and in the United States there was a marked acceleration in the rate of decline from just under 1 per cent per annum in the 1920-40 period to nearly 4 per cent between 1940 and 1960. The main contrast between Japan and Taiwan is in the relation between the rates of growth of farm output and output per worker. In Taiwan the rate of growth in output per worker has (until very recently) been roughly one percentage point less than the rate of growth of output because the farm work force was increasing at an annual rate of about 0.7 per cent between 1913 and 1937 and 1.1 per cent during the years 1946-68.[15] In Japan, apart from the 1952-67 period when the rate of increase in labor productivity was much more rapid than the growth of output because of the rapid decline in the farm labor force, the rates of growth of output and output per worker were essentially the same. (The reasons why Japan's farm labor force remained virtually unchanged between 1880 and 1940 are examined in Chapter 5.)

The sectorwide changes in output per worker, acreage per worker, and yield per acre in Mexico given in Table 4.1 obscure the principal contrast between Mexico's pattern of agricultural development and the growth paths in Japan and Taiwan. According to these average figures, increases in yield per acre have accounted for virtually all of the increase in labor productivity in Mexico's farm sector. But those average rates of change are a composite of the very different patterns of growth in Mexico's "modern" and "traditional" subsectors.[16] From the evidence reviewed in Chapter 6, it is apparent that in the modern subsector there has been considerable increase in acreage per worker as well as in yield per acre. Inasmuch as the sectorwide rate of change in acreage per worker between 1950 and 1968 was zero, it can be inferred that the cultivated area per worker declined somewhat in the traditional subsector, and the increase in yield in that subsector was probably considerably less than the average increase of 1.8 per cent per annum. The increase in Mexico's total and farm labor force in recent years has been more rapid than in Taiwan; between 1940 and 1960 the work force in the entire agricultural sector increased at an average rate of 2.4 per cent (compared to 1.5 per cent in Taiwan). It seems likely that the increase in output in the traditional subsector was only slightly more rapid than the rate of growth of the labor force in that subsector which would imply, of course, that rapid increase in output per worker in the modern subsector accounted for virtually all of the sectorwide increase in labor productivity.

The experience of Mexico and Taiwan illustrates the fact that in late-developing countries the farm labor force will tend to increase at a rate determined more or less exogenously by the rates of increase of the total labor force and of nonfarm employment. The demographic and structural characteristics of these countries thus constrain the possibilities for increasing output per worker in the agricultural sector. That is, to achieve rates of increase in output per worker (Y/L) comparable to those realized in developed countries, the rate of advance in agricultural output would have to be substantially larger to offset the growth in their farm work force. In fact, the rate of growth in aggregate farm output in underdeveloped economies will be higher than in developed economies—owing to more rapid growth in the consuming population and higher income elasticities of demand for food—if the latter are to avoid reliance on imports or sharp increases in prices. However, apart from small countries that are able to expand export production rapidly or a temporary phase of import substitution, the combination of unavoidable growth in farm labor force and a rate of growth of effective demand for agricultural products that is unlikely to exceed, say 4 per cent, means that the feasible rate of growth in output per worker is limited.

In many of the developing countries, especially in Asia, scarcity of agricultural land of satisfactory quality makes it difficult if not impossible to expand the cultivated area rapidly enough to keep pace with the growth of the farm labor force. But even in those parts of Latin America and Africa where there is still substantial unused land, a sectorwide increase in the acreage cultivated per worker would limit the scope for yield-increasing innovations. It would even foreclose that possibility if the rate of increase in acreage per worker was equal to the "feasible" rate of increase in output per worker as determined by the growth of effective demand and the rate of change in the farm work force. The "feasible" rate cannot be specified precisely because the propositions concerning a "maximum" rate of increase in output and an exogenously determined rate of growth of the farm labor force are only approximate. In a particular case, it may be possible to expand output a good deal more rapidly than the increase in domestic demand because of export expansion or import substitution. It may also be possible for marketed output to increase somewhat more rapidly than the rightward shift in domestic commercial demand. Because of the inelasticity of demand for farm products, this will mean a deterioration in agriculture's terms of trade; but especially in a situation where input-output relations are being improved by technical change, continued expansion of output may still be profitable in spite of a substantial decline in farm prices.

The proposition that a late-developing country cannot simultaneously achieve sizable increases in the acreage cultivated per worker and in yield per acre may at first seem surprising. It is actually a logical consequence of the fact that the "feasible" rate of increase in labor productivity in agriculture will be relatively low unless the nonfarm sector represents a large fraction of the total population.

These constraints that derive from the structural-demographic features of a late-developing country have highly significant implications for the choice of means for fostering agricultural progress. It now becomes clear why it is essential to consider the effects of alternative strategies on the sectorwide expansion path; to assess the benefits and costs of an individual project or to compare two innovations, without considering other options available, is apt to lead to erroneous conclusions. The purchasing power constraint also underscores the importance of distinguishing between external (purchased) inputs and the internal inputs that depend on farm-supplied resources of labor or land. Attempts to compare the "efficiency" of tractors and bullocks in isolation, rather than as elements of an agricultural strategy, are a good example. In that type of partial analysis, comparisons of the estimated costs and returns of the two sources of power almost invariably ignore the fact that bullocks and the resources required for their maintenence are *internal* costs whereas tractors are an *external* input. Similarly, it is usually assumed that the increased output of farm products made possible because of the acreage released from fodder production can be sold without difficulty at the market prices currently prevailing, an assumption that is valid for an individual farmer but not when one is considering mechanization as a component of a sectorwide strategy for agriculture. Because of the purchasing power constraint that applies to the agricultural sector, it would be more relevant to compare the returns to investments in tractors and related implements that are effective in enlarging the acreage cultivated per worker with investments that are efficient in increasing per-acre yields.

More generally, in designing an efficient agricultural strategy it is essential to strive for the best combination of programs and policies that are attainable given the problems of imperfect knowledge and the economic and political constraints that operate at a particular point in time. As noted at the beginning of this chapter, the relevant options embrace (a) programs of institution building to strengthen agricultural research, farmer training, and so on, (b) investment programs to expand and improve the agricultural infrastructure, (c) programs to improve product marketing and the distribution of inputs, and (d) policies related to prices, taxation, and land tenure. The relevant pricing policies apply, of course, to the prices of domestically manufactured or imported products purchased by farmers as well as those affecting prices of agricultural products. And it should also be emphasized that tax measures are frequently significant because of their influence on rural income distribution and on the size distribution of farm operational units as well as for their role in mobilizing resources for development purposes.

In the final analysis, each country must devise its own combination of programs and policies. Diagnosis of the factors currently limiting the expansion of output and an attempt to identify the most promising opportunities for technical progress can help to focus attention on the measures that are likely to make the largest contribution to attaining the objectives of an agricultural strategy.

Choice of Innovations: Divisibility and Complementarity

A central element of a unimodal strategy is the development and diffusion of highly divisible innovations that promote output expansion within an agrarian structure made up of operational units relatively equal in size and necessarily small because of the large number of holdings relative to the cultivated area. The divisibility factor, by rendering new technology applicable to these small units, permits the progressive modernization of an increasing proportion of a country's farmers. There will, of course, be differences in the speed and efficiency with which farmers seize new opportunities depending on their initial resources, ability, and desire. Moreover, technical progress will inevitably have an uneven impact on different regions and types of farming. Such differences, however, are much less significant than those that result from the polarization of agriculture into modern and traditional sectors employing drastically different technologies.

Progressive modernization based on widespread adoption of a sequence of innovations compatible with the constraints imposed by the structural-demographic characteristics stressed above makes it possible to exploit the large potential that exists for augmenting the productivity of the agricultural sector's internal resources of labor and land. The experience of four of the six countries considered in Chapters 5 and 6 demonstrates the considerable magnitude of this potential contribution to the expansion of farm output. And recent experience with the seed-fertilizer revolution provides further evidence of the significance of this source of increases in production.

If purchased inputs are primarily divisible inputs such as seed and fertilizer, the new technologies can be widely adopted in spite of the purchasing power constraint. Spread of such inputs coupled with changes in farming practices and growth of farm cash income will generate demands for improved equipment to increase the precision as well as reduce the time required for various farming operations; but with progressive modernization this demand will be directed toward simple and inexpensive implements. And if output expansion results from widespread increases in productivity among the small farm units which necessarily predominate when the farm labor force is large relative to the total cultivated area, the capital requirements for investment in labor-saving farm equipment will be limited. The relative profitability—private and social—of outlays for fertilizer and other current inputs as compared to capital equipment will be influenced by the type of agricultural strategy pursued. For example, electric- or diesel-powered pumpsets in India and Pakistan have represented an innovation that has been essentially complementary to the internal resources of labor and land; and in spite of the lumpiness of the investment, the practice of selling tubewell water to nearby farmers makes the input provided quite divisible. The institution of contract plowing can make the *services* of tractors divisible, and under certain circumstances, especially in semi-arid regions, mechanical cultivation can be complementary to yield-increasing inputs.[17] And when the decision to hire tractor services is made by the farmer or tenant operating a unit of average size, that is, small, there is a good chance that the input will also be a complement to the labor of family members in contrast to the labor-displacing consequences when tractor mechanization is introduced in a large operational unit.

Our emphasis on framing a strategy aimed at promoting more productive utilization of the abundant supply of labor in the agricultural sector is not to be equated with the notion of a "labor surplus" in the sense that there are individuals with zero marginal product. It is common to speak of a "labor surplus" in traditional agriculture when the population of working age appears to be larger than the number of "full-time workers" that would be required to maintain the level of production even with existing technologies. But those labor force concepts appropriate to a modern industrial economy are not really applicable. Particularly for the unpaid family labor that accounts for most of the rural work force, there is no institutionally determined workday and no clear dichotomy between "work" and "leisure."[18]

For any given "stock" of farm labor—in a household or in the sector—the actual "flow" of labor inputs into agricultural production is determined by a "subjective equilibrium" in the allocation of labor time. And the activities other than farming embrace pursuits such as handweaving and other types of cottage industry as well as leisure and a variety of "noneconomic" activities—litigation, ceremonies, hunting, and so on—many of which are readily *compressible* if altered circumstances make it attractive to increase the allocation of labor time to farming. In addition, agriculture is usually characterized by large seasonal variation in the demand for labor and farm work. Consequently, there is often considerable scope for increasing the number of hours worked per day, the number of workdays per year, and even the pace of work.[19] The increase in time devoted to farming activities may also result from a reduction in the allocation of labor to cottage industries as the products of those industries are replaced by purchased goods. In brief, there is "slack" that can be drawn into production if there is an increase in the marginal product attributable to additional inputs of labor or an increase in the marginal valuation that workers place on increments to income.

The prevalence of this labor slack in agriculture is a consequence of the economic structure and rapid growth of labor force in developing countries which make it inevitable that the farm work force will continue to grow in absolute size for many years. In fact, "labor slack" is merely a shorthand expression to describe a situation where the labor of a large part of the rural population of working age has a low opportunity cost. And because of rapid population growth the opportunity cost of labor is held down, or pushed even lower, unless a country's development strategy is generating new opportunities for productive employment at a pace more rapid than the rate of expansion of the labor force. The phenomenon is, of course, not confined to agriculture. Certain labor-intensive service trades characterized by

THE DESIGN OF AN AGRICULTURAL STRATEGY 151

easy entry also absorb part of the labor force that is unable to find jobs in firms that provide regular wage employment. John P. Lewis is describing a phenomenon that has its counterpart in most developing countries when he speaks of "the urban immigrant who, instead of doing absolutely nothing, joins Bombay's army of underemployed bootblacks or Delhi's throngs of self-appointed (and tippable) parking directors, who becomes an extra, redundant salesman in the yard goods stall of a cousin, who according to custom is going to have to provide him with bed and board anyway."[20] But with the exception of some of the semi-industrialized countries in Latin America, agriculture is the dominant "self-employment" sector and absorbs the majority of the annual additions to the labor force.

Because of the existence of labor slack, the impact on farm output of yield-increasing innovations goes beyond their effects on output per unit of labor input. Under a unimodal strategy, technical change and associated investments in infrastructure are likely to induce fuller use of farm labor and land as well as enlarged use of such inputs as fertilizer, because of the complementarity between the internal and external inputs. Taiwan's experience, reviewed in Chapter 6, gives an indication of the quantitative importance of more productive seed-fertilizer combinations and investments in infrastructure which increased the returns to additional labor inputs. Investments in irrigation and drainage not only raised yields directly, they also facilitated multiple cropping, thereby raising the year-round utilization of both labor and land. Those who have argued that "labor surplus" (in the sense of a zero marginal product) is an important feature of a traditional agriculture have often implied that the agricultural sector can be neglected in a development strategy. It should be clear from the foregoing that we are definitely not suggesting that agriculture can be neglected, but rather that a strategy of progressive modernization will have especially important advantages under those conditions.

If a strategy of progressive modernization has significant advantages in achieving both the economic and social goals of development, how are we to account for the act that so many developing countries appear to be pursuing bimodal strategies? A major objective of this book is to throw light on that question. But there are several pertinent points that it is convenient to introduce here.

In the absence of institutional arrangements to generate and diffuse innovations capable of raising yields on small farm units, a concentration of resources in a subsector of large and capital-intensive farms may appear to be the only feasible alternative. Tractors and their associated equipment constitute an innovation that is readily transferred. Their introduction is a powerful means of enlarging the area under cultivation, and it may also facilitate expansion of the planted area by increased multiple cropping. The large international corporations manufacturing tractors have considerable competence and strong incentive to promote sales and to organize distribution and service facilities in developing countries, and the local climate of opinion often favors special encouragement for the introduction of tractors because they are seen as a symbol of modernity.

Although the agricultural sector is necessarily subject to a severe purchasing power constraint until considerable structural transformation has taken place, a subsector of large farm units that accounts for most of the increase in commercial production is able to escape that constraint. (This means, of course, that the remaining farm units will continue to be subject to a purchasing power constraint that is now more binding.) It is also easy for such farms to realize the economies of scale associated with the use of tractors. In addition, reliance on rapid expansion of output by a "modern" subsector of large and "progressive" farm enterprises bypasses the problems and costs associated with involving a large fraction of the farm population in the modernization process.

This type of bias toward "reinforcing success" is often linked with the assumption that there is necessarily a sizable trade-off between growth and equity goals. William Nicholls, for example, asserts that Brazil "must unfortunately face a hard choice between equity and productivity," and he argues that "the present large holdings" must be relied upon to satisfy the growth of commercial demand.[21] Moreover, there is frequently a failure to recognize the extent to which bimodal and unimodal strategies are mutually exclusive alternatives.

THE DESIGN OF AN AGRICULTURAL STRATEGY 153

The advocacy of a bimodal strategy by Wyn Owen is of special interest because he is one of the few to recognize explicitly that reliance on a subsector of large and capital-intensive farms necessarily implies that most rural people will have to find their livelihood in what he terms a "surplus population-supporting sector."[22] The degree of structural transformation, as it affects the size of the commercial market for farm products and the availability of resources, is the major factor that determines the feasibility of pursuing simultaneously strategies that promote rapid expansion by a large-scale, commercial subsector and programs aimed at progressive modernization of a small-farm sector. Although a unimodal strategy has important economic and social advantages under the conditions that characterize a late-developing country, logical arguments and historical evidence will obviously not be the only factors determining a country's pattern of agricultural development. It is also necessary to take account of political factors to which we now turn.

POLITICAL CONSTRAINTS AND THE DECISION-MAKING PROCESS

Extremely difficult problems arise in trying to explain the decisions that determine whether political leaders and other policy makers in a country will opt for a unimodal or bimodal strategy. It is, of course, a gross simplification to suggest that a government "opts" for an agricultural strategy. Graham Allison applies the term "rational actor model" to describe the type of analysis which assumes that a government makes a choice with respect to a strategic problem in a manner analogous to decision making by an individual. Valuable insights can be obtained by assuming that a government has certain goals and determines its course of action by examining the options available and then weighing the costs and benefits associated with the alternatives. But to obtain a more complete understanding of the factors that determine an outcome, such as the pattern of agricultural development, it is necessary to supplement the "rational actor model" by other types of analysis. The two complementary models elaborated by Allison emphasize, first, the need to focus on specific organizations and organizational routines within specific organizations, and, second, the need to consider the action channels within a government and the role of key individuals as determined by their ability to influence government action.[23]

The so-called "induced development model" presented by Vernon Ruttan and Yujiro Hayami sheds some light on the decision-making process that determines the nature of a country's agricultural growth path. Their approach focuses on the role of many actors who are influenced strongly by their perception of relative factor prices.[24] Thus they hypothesize that relative factor prices will induce not only farmers and firms supplying inputs but also agricultural administrators and scientists to emphasize institutional and technical innovations that will economize on a country's scarce factors of production. In particular, they note that the contrasting patterns of technical change and output expansion in Japan and the United States represented appropriate responses to very different factor availabilities and prices. Their analysis is especially valuable in calling attention to the fact that prices which accurately reflect social opportunity costs are perhaps even more important in influencing the orientation of research and therefore the nature of technical change which conditions a country's agricultural growth path than in relation to short-run allocative efficiency. The mechanism is a dynamic process of factor substitution in response to trends in relative prices.

Lance Davis and Douglass North have elaborated a similar theory of institutional innovation.[25] They explain changes in institutional arrangements as a response to exogenous changes in knowledge, technology, prices, or other factors that create the possibility of profits that cannot be captured without new or altered institutional arrangements. The Davis-North theory is more ambitious in attempting to explain whether the new institutional arrangement will be an innovation by a private firm, by a group of individuals cooperating voluntarily, or by government acting through an existing or new agency or by providing legislative sanction for group action by private firms (e.g., the fruit and vegetable marketing orders that often have been used to regulate supplies of those commodities in the U.S.). In our opinion, the Davis-North approach is closer to reality than the Hayami-Ruttan "induced development model" in recognizing that the "primary action group" that perceives the possibility of capturing profits through a new institutional arrangement may be motivated by a group interest that does not coincide with society's interest in greater total income or other national goals.[26]

Davis and North make no reference to the Marxian view of the historical process which explains economic and social change in terms of the "contradictions" that arise between a society's "productive forces" and their interactions with its "relations of production, and with the whole relations of society." Albert Hirschman has suggested a reformulation of the Marxian concept that has some similarity to the Davis-North theory of institutional change. He suggests that it does not do undue violence to Marx's thought to equate his "productive forces" with economic factors and his "relations of production" with political factors. On that basis, he suggests the following formulation of the process of change:

At any one historical stage, the economy functions within a given political and institutional framework; on the basis of and owing to this framework, economic forces left to themselves can achieve some forward movement, but beyond a certain point further development becomes more difficult and eventually is held back by the unchanging political framework which, from a spur to progress turns into a "fetter"; at that point, political-institutional change is not only necessary to permit further advances, but is also highly likely to occur, because economic development will have generated some powerful social group with a vital stake in the needed changes.[27]

A noteworthy difference between Hirschman's version and Marx's formulation is related to the scale on which the alternation of economic and political forces brings about change. Marx was preoccupied with revolutions "that sweep away all of the institutions of whatever ancien régime needs to be done away with, and that then set up sociopolitical conditions ideal for the vigorous and unhampered unfolding of the 'productive forces' during a prolonged period until such time as the new batch of contradictions emerges." Hirschman argues that historical reality generally does not conform to the Marxian view of an alternation of sweeping changes affecting all dimensions of a society. Instead, the sociopolitical change induced by contradictions is likely to be "partial, grudging, and with a lot of unfinished business left behind, so that the need for further change makes itself felt once again in fairly short order."[28] The Marxian scheme thus reinterpreted has considerable relevance to the more limited but multifarious changes in institutions that are analyzed by Davis and North. And the propelling "contradiction" may simply be a result of technological change that opens up new economic opportunities provided that the necessary institutional rearrangements are made. It is also to be noted that a governmental bureaucracy with a vested interest in administering a system of direct controls can also become a "fetter" to economic advance. Moreover, it is a fetter that is politically difficult to remove because the control machinery is supported strongly by the large-scale enterprises that benefit from administrative rationing whereas the much more numerous industrial entrepreneurs and farmers that suffer the effects of counterproductive policies tend to be diffuse and poorly organized.[29]

Whenever redistributive aspects of institutional change are important, political power will inevitably be a determining influence. For this reason land reform represents the agricultural policy issue that lies most squarely in the political sphere, but the political aspect figures prominently in most decisions affecting agricultural development.

It was suggested earlier that it is a gross oversimplification to speak of a situation in which policy makers "opt for a unimodal or bimodal strategy." In a remarkably perceptive essay, Colin Leys notes that "the process of 'choice' rarely consists of an explicit 'moment' at which some appropriate person or committee reviews the alternatives, weighs their pros and cons and consciously selects one of them. It is, generally, a continual process of options foregone, through the passage of time, and through the taking of other decisions which have the often unforeseen consequence of closing off possibilities in spheres not considered at all in the context of the decision."[30]

Of equal importance is the need to recognize that decisions and policies are shaped by all sorts of conflicting interests. If there is any overriding concern it is preoccupation with staying in power, not the comparatively abstract goal of development. Leys goes so far as to suggest that the social structure normally associated with poverty tends "to produce a particular type of politics, which is the type least likely to set a high premium on so generalized an objective as national economic development. . . ."[31] Be that as it may, there is no doubt that political leaders in developing countries face a host of pressing problems and demands that are monumental in relation to what they are able to command in the way of "resources"—of money, votes, prestige, patronage, political allies, military force, and so forth.[32] Often the most fundamental problem confronting the government of a developing country is to achieve a modicum of national integration in a country divided by linguistic, cultural, racial, and religious differences. Government resources in the narrow sense of tax revenues are, of course, distressingly small; taxation that takes 15 to 20 per cent of national income often yields revenue that is the equivalent of only $10 or $15 per person.

To the outsider the problem of poverty might appear to be a supreme challenge and a spur to sacrifice and selfless action. But there is a large element of truth in the observation by Leys that the political and administrative elites in most developing countries "are rarely eager for measures that would entail redistribution of wealth or any threat to their own status or prospects." After all this tends to be true of elites in all countries, the principal difference in less-developed countries being the more limited force of "institutions which can hold these tendencies in check and make the elite give the public value for its privileges. . . ."[33]

Several conclusions might be drawn from this somber review of political constraints. In a situation where these obstacles to development seem especially severe, one might conclude that a revolution is a prerequisite to meaningful development. There are, of course, many instances in which military leaders have justified their seizure of power in terms of the need to replace selfish and corrupt leaders. There is, of course, no assurance that the new elite will be more determined or effective in furthering economic progress than the leaders that are replaced. Certainly few regimes have managed to emulate the success of a Mao Tse-tung and the other rulers of China in maintaining disciplined devotion to an attack on poverty. And to those who hold a value system that assigns substantial weight to individual liberties, the human costs of the Communist approach in both China and the Soviet Union have been high. The evidence, briefly summarized in Chapter 6, also indicates that the economic performance of agriculture in the Soviet Union has not been impressive. Communist China's experience is too brief and too poorly documented to infer much beyond the fact that egalitarian goals are being strictly pursued.

The general conclusion that Leys draws as a political scientist is that it is essential to assess realistically "what changes—social and political, as well as economic—are within the politicians' 'means,' and what are not; and what patterns or sequences of change, among those that are practical, will carry the process of economic development farthest and fastest at the least cost in the politicians' resources."[34] In fact, the common tendency is for economists to concentrate on drawing up a development plan on the blithe assumption that political "obstacles" to implementation can be readily overcome if political leaders will simply muster the "will to develop."

What bearing does this digression have on the problem of designing efficient agricultural strategies? Several general observations merit brief attention, and the interrelations between politics, land reform, and the pattern of agricultural development receive more extended treatment below.

On the most general level, we believe that it points to two seemingly contradictory conclusions. On the one hand, it points up the need for economists, administrators, and policy makers to take a broad view of the objectives of agricultural development and of the choice of strategy. Leys is certainly correct in emphasizing that the process of "choice" is a continual activity and that it is difficult to avoid decisions that have "the often unforeseen consequence of closing off possibilities" in spheres that are ignored in the context of the decision. But this is precisely why it is so important to emphasize that measures which foster a bimodal strategy foreclose the option of achieving the progressive modernization of agriculture on a broad front.

On the other hand, a realistic view of the political constraints on

THE DESIGN OF AN AGRICULTURAL STRATEGY

decision making emphasizes that it is often necessary to make progress in a piecemeal fashion. Inasmuch as most decisions are made in ad hoc fashion, usually punctuated at intervals by Five-Year Plans, it is especially important for advisors and decision makers to have the clearest possible conception of the pattern of agricultural development that will result from the mix of policies and programs that are adopted. Only then can a sequence of individual actions relating to research, extension programs, investments in infrastructure, and other elements of an agricultural strategy achieve a significant cumulative impact.

The extent to which political forces will impede the design and implementation of a pattern of agricultural development that furthers both economic and social objectives clearly depends on circumstances of time and place. Political constraints are likely to be less binding, however, if decisions are related to the goal of expanding farm output by means that are economically efficient and which also promote broad participation in improved income opportunities and a narrowing of inequalities in income. Although resistance is to be expected from large farm operators and others with a personal interest in a dualistic pattern, mounting concern with problems of income distribution and unemployment should strengthen support for a unimodal strategy. That outcome appears most probable if there is recognition on the part of the groups that shape opinion and policies that the basic requirement for progress in achieving both the employment and income distribution goals is a pattern of development that brings about a rate of growth in demand for labor, including the internal "demand" for the labor of members of farm households, that will exceed the rate of growth of the supply of labor seeking employment.[35] That is, the reduction of underemployment and unemployment and narrowing of the extreme income disparities that prevail because of miserably low returns to labor will depend primarily upon a sufficiently rapid expansion of opportunities for productive employment within and outside agriculture.

On the other hand, political constraints are likely to be considerably more serious if the response to concerns about employment and income distribution is concentrated on measures such as massive public works programs that treat efficiency and employment creation as separate objectives rather than viewing them as an integral part of the development strategy. Likewise, attempts to ameliorate the condition of low-income farm households by subsidized distribution of credit or by legislating "equitable" rates for land rental payments, which ignore the forces of supply and demand that determine what tenants are prepared to pay for the use of this scarce resource, are almost certain to be counterproductive.

In agrarian societies where land is scarce relative to the population that depends on it for a livelihood, the distribution of the ownership of land is obviously a very significant determinant of income distribution; and we will be arguing, subject to the proviso that it is politically feasible, that redistributive land reform is a desirable element of a unimodal strategy. However, the size distribution of operational units is not necessarily determined by the distribution of land ownership, and it is the former that is of decisive importance in determining a country's pattern of agricultural development.

The relative scarcity of labor vis à vis the nonlabor factors of production is the prime determinant of income distribution, but this relative scarcity is shaped by factors which are in varying degree policy variables. It is the nature of the technologies adopted and the success that is realized in transforming the economic structure of an agrarian society that are most critical and most likely to be capable of being influenced by the choice of policy instruments.[36] Although we question the wisdom of legislative action aimed at compelling landlords to reduce their rents, we do not question the desirability of reducing the rental share of income and raising the return to labor. However, that should be accomplished by operating on the underlying forces of supply and demand for land and labor in such a way as to raise the share of income accruing to labor in addition to enlarging total income. And a unimodal strategy will do precisely that.

Clearly, the rate of growth of demand for labor and the availability of alternative income opportunities, which determines the rental share which landowners will demand and that tenants are prepared

THE DESIGN OF AN AGRICULTURAL STRATEGY

to pay, will be influenced strongly by the nature of the agricultural technologies adopted and by the rate of structural transformation. Furthermore, the spread of yield-increasing, land-saving innovations tends to reduce the relative scarcity of land so that sectorwide rent is not as large as it would be in the absence of such innovations. That general tendency is obscured, however, by the fact that the initial increase in productivity will mainly increase the economic rent of land; and in vanguard areas (such as India's Punjab) which are able to exploit the new technologies successfully, there will be a tendency for landowners to retain a very large part of the initial increases in income (unless land taxes are raised so that much of the increased economic rent accrues to government instead). It is only as the seed-fertilizer revolution and an accelerated pace of agricultural development leads directly and indirectly to increases in the demand for labor and to increases in aggregate output that the process results in increases in labor earnings that result in changes in the functional as well as the personal distribution of income.[37] Even then economic rents in favored areas are likely to remain above their previous level, but that will be at the expense of the rent accruing to land in less favored areas.

In the next section we consider in summary fashion some of the main factors that determine the pattern of agricultural development. These factors receive further attention in the course of examining various historical patterns of agricultural development in Chapters 5 and 6 and in the two concluding chapters which focus on the modernization of agriculture in the contemporary late-developing countries.

FACTORS DETERMINING THE PATTERN OF
AGRICULTURAL DEVELOPMENT

The pattern of agricultural development that emerges in a country will depend on interactions between its agrarian structure and institutions and the nature of the new technologies that become available and are adopted. Success in orienting agricultural research toward the development and diffusion of biochemical innovations, inexpensive items of farm equipment, and other divisible innovations are a necessary but not a sufficient condition for achieving a unimodal pattern of development. The pattern of adoption will also be shaped by the functioning of farm-support institutions—the extension service, cooperatives or farmers' associations, and public or private firms distributing inputs and credit. Those supporting institutions can operate so as to either intensify or counter forces that lead toward a bimodal pattern of development.

A country's agrarian structure will influence the pattern of development in a number of ways. The existing distribution of land and other forms of wealth are a key factor that will be considered in some detail. With a strongly hierarchical organization of rural society, it is likely to be more difficult to create institutions that serve the needs of small as well as large farmers because of the tendency for politically powerful leaders at the local level to manipulate cooperatives and other organizations for their own purposes.[38] The seriousness of that type of obstacle to widespread rural progress will be especially pronounced when there are policy-induced price distortions. In a situation of excess demand and discretionary allocation of credit, import licenses, and inputs, those with greater wealth, power, and status will have preferential access to scarce resources and will be induced to substitute capital for labor beyond the point that is socially profitable.

Land Tenure Arrangements and the Size Distribution of Operational Units

The assertion is frequently made that land reform is a necessary condition for achieving agricultural development that insures wide participation of the rural population and satisfactory progress toward the social goals of employment and income distribution.[39] There is now a general consensus that "almost never does land reform decrease production, occasionally it has a neutral effect, most often it has a positive impact."[40] This conclusion applies to land reform which transfers property from large to small landowners. There is a common tendency to regard "tenancy reform" which imposes a legal ceiling on land rental payments as an almost perfect substitute for redistributive land reform. But the two types of land reform have very different consequences.

Although there are indications that in some countries conditions are becoming more favorable for implementation of redistributive land reform measures, it seems likely that such countries will continue to be the exception. Because of the great variation in the political structures and forces that prevail in various countries, however, it is impossible to generalize about the prospects for land reform. In many countries politically powerful groups are arrayed against it. This includes a number of countries in which there is a strong commitment to land reform at the level of public pronouncements and even legislation but a wide gap between the rhetoric and actual implementation. Moreover, there is a common tendency to regard redistributive land reform as too difficult, because of the strength of political opposition, and to shift the emphasis to "tenure reform" aimed at officially decreed ceilings on land rental payments accompanied by legislative enactments to insure security of tenure by preventing landowners from evicting their tenants without "due cause."

It is difficult enough to secure effective implementation of a program of land redistribution even though it involves a single transaction; and once title to a piece of land has been transferred the new owner has a keen interest in holding on to that valuable asset. But enforcement of a legal ceiling on land rent and of a prohibition against evicting tenants requires continuing surveillance at the local level where the power of large landowners is great and tenants are typically unorganized and often dependent upon a landlord for their livelihood. Particularly in an area where some landowners are already acquiring tractors and evicting their tenants in order to undertake direct cultivation, the greatest fear of a tenant is that he may be denied access to a piece of land that will provide work and a meager livelihood even though he is obliged to pay an "exorbitant" rent. Although outside observers may draw the conclusion that "rack renting" prevails because landlords are an exceptionally greedy lot, the average tenant recognizes all too well that rents are at a high level because of the paucity of alternative income opportunities. The result is that tenants or those seeking to become tenants are often as ready as landlords to ignore a rental ceiling. That is bad enough. The real problem, however, is that the possibility of future enforcement of rental ceilings and security of tenure provisions may reinforce other polarizing factors that encourage landlords to convert large ownership units presently cultivated by a number of tenants into large operational units.

The resulting change in the size distribution of operational units becomes a potent force inducing an excessively capital-intensive pattern of investment. The ease with which mechanical cultivation can be introduced on large holdings is a significant factor. But the main consideration is that the creation of large operational units increases the attractiveness of investing in labor-displacing mechanical equipment because of the difficulties of supervising a large farm labor force. In the first place, the costs of hired labor will normally exceed the opportunity cost of labor supplied by a tenant and members of his family. Moreover, the labor costs as *perceived* by a landowner undertaking direct cultivation are likely to be considerably higher than would be indicated by the going wage rate. A landowner will often have doubts about the reliability of hired labor, and he is therefore concerned about the costs that he will incur if labor is not available at a critical period in the farming calendar. More generally, the high degree of variability in agriculture poses special problems of management and decision making which cannot be centralized without duplication of effort because of the large number of "on-the-spot supervisory decisions" that must be made.[41] This arises because of the biological nature of the production process in agriculture which means that the operations to be performed are separated in time and space. Although this characteristic is usually cited as a factor that limits the economies of scale in agriculture, it also suggests that "shirking" and poor performance are likely when agricultural workers do not have a direct interest in the outcome of the farm enterprise. Indeed, a wealth of historical evidence attests to the fact that tenancy arrangements are the most efficient form of "hiring" the

THE DESIGN OF AN AGRICULTURAL STRATEGY

labor of farm households that possess little or no land to be applied to the fields of large landowners.

The reorganization of agricultural production in Japan in the late Tokugawa period is an interesting historical example of transition from fairly large operational units using sizable labor gangs made up of retainers and hired workers to small-scale family units, many of them tenant or part-tenant households. Particularly with the development of more productive but labor-using techniques, small units employing family labor were more efficient. Large landowners, being reluctant to sell their holdings, responded to the situation by renting their land to tenants who were prepared to apply the more intensive techniques that had been evolved. A writer of the late eighteenth century asserted that "all large holders have adopted tenant cultivation" and explained:

The reason for this is that the tenant by extraordinary diligence will cultivate twice as much land as hired labor, and he will provide his own fertilizer by the bitter work of gathering it. Thus he can make a bare living from a very small plot, even though he has no additional land of his own and no income from work outside his home.[42]

Whereas the imposition of rental ceilings has the effect of encouraging the creation of large operational units, a reform that redistributes land in excess of an acreage ceiling to small cultivators clearly has the opposite effect (although it may simply transfer title to tenants already cultivating the land). Thus the favorable effect in reducing income inequalities, through redistribution of this highly important asset, is associated with favorable economic effects because the more uniform size distribution of operational units encourages labor-intensive, yield-increasing technologies consistent with the high ratio of farm workers to cultivated area that characterizes the rural sector in a late-developing country. The social advantages of a more even distribution of land ownership are related in part to the fact that the economic rent that accrues to the owners of this scarce, nonreproducible resource is more widely distributed. Technological advances and other developments that increase the yield of land all tend to increase the rent accruing to landowners. For landlords, this implies a tendency to raise the share of output that will be demanded as rent from tenants, assuming that alternative earning opportunities available to tenants have not improved their weak bargaining position. And in a situation in which the farm labor force is increasing rapidly and the growth of demand for labor is slow, because of bias toward reliance on capital-intensive technologies in agriculture as well as industry, the bargaining power of tenants and the earnings of unskilled labor generally can be expected to remain at a very low level. But with the favorable effects of a unimodal strategy on the absorption of labor both in agriculture and in nonagriculture, the ability of landlords to extract high rents will be diminished because of this improvement in alternative earning opportunities.

In a situation of rapid technical change, owner cultivation has two economic advantages distinct from those relating to the size distribution of operational units.[43] In the first place, owner cultivation avoids the difficulties that can be expected to arise when landlords, responding to higher yields, raise the percentage share of output that they demand as rent. In fact, if landowners anticipate much resistance on the part of tenants to an upward adjustment of rent that leaves the residual income of tenants essentially unchanged, this may be a significant factor inducing them to evict their tenants and shift to direct cultivation. Second, owner cultivation avoids the division of responsibility that may make it difficult for landowners and tenants to arrive at joint decisions with respect to investments in land improvement even though they offer a high payoff because of the improved production possibilities. The uncertainty associated with rapid introduction of new innovations is also likely to accentuate the problems that arise because of the need for joint decision-making under tenant cultivation.

Given the significant economic and social advantages of redistributive land reform the key question that calls for a careful assessment is the question of political feasibility in a particular country. Princeton Lyman and J. T. French suggest that whether a government possesses "the will and the capacity to overcome political opposition" to land reform will depend upon the strength of outside pressures, the attitude of local elites not dependent upon support from anti-reform interests, and the extent of organized pressure from the rural masses who would benefit from land reform.[44] Given the numerical importance of the groups who would benefit it might appear that the necessary political support could be mobilized with ease. But this is unlikely because of the inherent difficulties of organizing large "latent groups," even though they have a strong common interest. The individual peasant has little incentive to give active support to an organization created to secure the enactment and implementation of land reform legislation. If the efforts of such a group bear fruit, the individual tenant will share in the benefits whether he has been an active participant or not. And his individual contribution to the success of the endeavor is likely to seem small indeed relative to costs that he can perceive all too clearly.[45] The possibility of tenants exerting significant pressure on a major political party is also compromised by the existing social structure at the local level. Speaking of the political system in the Philippines as an example, Leys argues that

the basis of party support is strictly an extension of the social relations governing life at the village level: people do not group themselves with others according to some specialized interest which they all share as a group—as farmworkers, for instance, or sharecroppers—but put their vote at the service of a local patron in return for material rewards—jobs, loans, intervention with the police, etc.[46]

His assessment may be overly pessimistic and the dominance of groups with wealth and status in the Philippines may be extreme.

It may also be true, as Doreen Warriner has argued, that land redistribution is especially difficult in a country like India where there is a "squirearchy" of relatively small landowners with 20 to 50 acres who are likely to be politically more important than large absentee landlords because they are so much more numerous.[47] On the other hand, the abrupt changes that have resulted from the seed-fertilizer revolution in areas such as the Punjab may bring about marked shifts in social relations and increased class consciousness of small farmers, tenants, and laborers, and alter the local power structure through new political alignments or rural agitation and violence. Francine Frankel, for example, argues that there is evidence that this has been occurring in both the Indian and Pakistani Punjabs.[48] Her analysis ignores the general problem of organizing "latent groups" and the fact that the differences that divide small farmers, tenants, and landless laborers may be more potent than their common interests. But the emerging consciousness of such groups may be a significant political force, particularly if it results in legislation for redistributive land reform that is really implemented and a move away from price policies and administrative rationing that make it difficult for small farmers to have access to inputs.

Viewing distributive land reform as an element in the design and implementation of a unimodal strategy emphasizes its probable contribution to both economic and social goals. At the same time it emphasizes that it is not an indispensable requirement since it is the size distribution of operational units rather than the pattern of land ownership that is critical.

Even the much-maligned institution of share tenancy has important advantages as compared to the organization of production in large operational units. In fact, the argument that is frequently encountered that share tenancy contracts are economically inefficient rests on a fallacious analysis and is grossly overstated. The argument is that such an arrangement dampens the incentive for tenant farmers to expand the use of labor, fertilizer, and other nonland inputs because the tenant bears the full cost of the input but receives only a part of the resulting increments to output. This analysis, which views a share tenancy contract as equivalent to an ad valorem excise tax, is incomplete. It ignores the fact that such an interpretation implies that the tenant's residual income will include a "rent" making it higher than his alternative earnings so that it is not an equilibrium solution. Steven Cheung undoubtedly goes too far in claiming to have demonstrated that resource allocation will be identical under share tenancy, a fixed rent arrangement, and owner-cultivation.[49] But the empirical evidence that he presents and other pieces of evidence

THE DESIGN OF AN AGRICULTURAL STRATEGY

emphasize the validity of his proposition that tenancy arrangements will include stipulations, such as the cropping pattern and land area rented to an individual tenant, that go beyond the rental percentage. Moreover, the costs of inputs such as fertilizer are likely to be shared between landlord and tenant.[50] This not only provides a relatively simple means of offsetting the alleged inefficiency of resource allocation under share tenancy but may actually have an advantage since the landlord has an incentive to overcome obstacles to expanded fertilizer use stemming from a tenant's lack of knowledge, shortage of capital, or risk aversion. Those advantages are unlikely to apply, however, in the case of absentee landlords.

The size distribution of operational holdings that emerges will also be influenced by the forces that determine the profits that landowners can earn by direct cultivation as compared to investing their financial and managerial resources in nonfarm enterprises. This has noteworthy implications for the pattern of industrial expansion. (See Chapter 7.) It also has implications with respect to policies which make agriculture artificially attractive by supporting farm prices above equilibrium levels. Furthermore, it underscores the importance of taxing the economic rent accruing to land for the twofold purpose of mitigating inequalities in rural income distribution and augmenting government resources available for development purposes.

Sequences of Change and Their Cumulative Effect on Rural Progress

It was noted earlier that satisfactory progress in achieving development goals requires a realistic assessment of the "patterns or sequences of change" which are feasible and which "will carry the process of development farthest and fastest. . . ."[51] In similar fashion Hirschman has emphasized the need to "think in terms of sequences in the course of which a forward step in one direction will induce others. . . ." Thus it may be counterproductive to condemn a policy that does not lead immediately to the most advanced land reform legislation or to an ideal reform of the agricultural tax system. In like manner, an emphasis on "uniquely correct policies and absolute priorities" should give way to a recognition of the need to emphasize "efficient sequences" and decisions about those patterns of change that are "most likely to achieve eventually certain objectives which are not within the direct reach of policymaking."[52]

It is easy to reach excessively pessimistic conclusions about the prospects for rural progress if one takes a narrow view of the development process and yields to the temptation to regard particular reforms as absolute prerequisites. The very circumstances that often seem to make land reform stand out as an indispensable condition for progress are likely to mean that the prospects for successful implementation of meaningful reforms will be poor. Therefore, if it is assumed that a politically powerful group of landowners will continue to maximize wealth, power, and status within a "closed loop" in which economic options are confined to farming, the prospects for significant improvement in rural well-being will appear to be very grim indeed.[53]

In the context of a modernizing society, however, it is likely to be very misleading to take a static view of rural institutions and the power structure at the local level. If rural elites with the resources to exploit new opportunities outside agriculture perceive and act upon such opportunities, because of rapid and decentralized growth of nonfarm production, their behavior and attitudes can be expected to change. Some fraction of the landlord group will no longer concentrate on maximizing wealth and power within farming and will no longer be motivated to stubbornly resist changes aimed at improving the income opportunities of small and medium farmers. Moreover, if reasonable success is achieved in promoting widespread technical progress so that more rapid growth of farm output puts pressure on agricultural prices, the more alert and aggressive members of the rural elites will turn to new and more rewarding areas of entrepreneurial activity.

A very different diagnosis may apply, however, to areas in which the concentration of land is particularly extreme. Thus Dale Adams has suggested that the prospects for redistributive land reform are probably very good in northeast Brazil because the landowning group is so small that its political power is considerably less than its economic power. This is a region "where 120 families own almost all of the high-quality land" and improved technology of itself "will do relatively little to ease the poverty and employment problems which exist among the millions of landless."[54] Where the owner of a large hacienda has a dominant economic position throughout a sizable area, the adverse effects on income distribution are likely to be especially severe. This is a consequence of the existing distribution of property and of the monopoly power that a large landlord is able to exert, both in renting land and hiring workers, and those conditions are difficult to modify except by redistributive land reform.[55]

There is a rich variety of ways in which changes in one sphere can set in motion sequences of change in behavior, attitudes, and institutions, but these aspects are likely to be ignored in elaborating formal models or even in drawing up development projects unless a serious effort is made to derive understanding from previous experience. In the course of studying a set of development projects in Latin America, Asia, and Africa, Hirschman was impressed by the significance of the social, institutional, and attitudinal changes which often emerged as unanticipated side effects from the implementation of a project. This prompted him to stress "the importance for development of what a country *does* and of what it *becomes* as a result of what it *does,* and thereby contests the primacy of what it *is,* that is, of its geography- and history-determined endowment with natural resources, values, institutions, social and political structure, etc."[56] Here he is expressing a more general view that has been increasingly emphasized by social scientists: "that behavioral change may lead more effectively to attitude change than vice versa"—and that the new modes of behavior can be expected to induce changes in social structure and institutions as well.[57]

The present proposition goes beyond the point made earlier that one objective to be considered in assessing an agricultural strategy concerns its effectiveness in fostering changes in attitudes and behavior that will have a favorable impact on social modernization. Under a unimodal strategy in which the mass of the country's rural households become involved in processes of technical and economic change, the resulting changes in behavior and attitudes are likely to have a cumulative effect in facilitating further progress in many directions.[58] The recent spread of the high-yielding varieties in a number of developing countries has confirmed earlier experience in Japan and Taiwan. The success of a few farmers who gain confidence in the possibility of expanding production by adopting new seed-fertilizer combinations tends to build that confidence in other farmers. Moreover, success gained in generating and diffusing such innovations tends to strengthen morale; it creates a sense of pride and dedication among research workers and extension staff. As farmers adopt a sequence of innovations their sense of fatalism is weakened. They become more alert to new opportunities for greater productivity. Enlarged demand for fertilizers and other new inputs increases the profitability of establishing or extending distribution facilities; because of a higher level of sales and increased competition farmers have more reliable access to inputs and at lower prices.

The changes that can be expected will vary enormously depending on the antecedent social structure and on current developments, including the spread of all-weather roads, bus service, electricity, and radios and newspapers "which link the village to the region and nation by creating whole new sets of economic and cultural transactions."[59] Concurrent spread of education can also be expected to lead to increased capacity of farmers to organize and strengthen the ability of the rural population to influence the institutions serving their needs. Those changes together with broad improvement in income-earning alternatives can also be expected to enhance the bargaining power of tenants as part of a more pervasive improvement in labor incomes.

This view of the development process which emphasizes sequences of change and the influence of a large number of technical and sociopolitical as well as economic factors confronts a very serious difficulty. The number of interacting variables is so large that it is difficult to reach a consensus concerning the factors that are of strategic importance. Indeed logical analysis alone is not sufficient to demonstrate the feasibility of a strategy aimed at progressive modernization of millions of small-scale, traditional farmers. The responsiveness of small-scale peasant farmers and the potential gains in factor productivity with widespread adoption of divisible and complementary innovations are, in the final analysis, empirical questions. It is therefore essential to go beyond the type of general arguments advanced in this and earlier chapters and examine relevant historical evidence.

The comparative method in history has been aptly described as "an exercise in imagination controlled and guided by available evidence."[60] The understanding to be derived from previous experience can be of great value in stretching the imagination and in deepening our understanding of the complex forces that determine the rate and pattern of agricultural development. Of the six countries considered in the next two chapters, the experience of Japan and Taiwan is of special interest in demonstrating the feasibility of achieving widespread productivity increases among small farmers, in illustrating the quantitative importance of the potential gains in factor productivity, and in clarifying the advantages of a unimodal strategy in accomplishing the formidable task of transforming an agrarian economy.

NOTES

1. In a cogent critique of the target-setting approach to agricultural planning, V. M. Dandekar argues that government planners in India, preoccupied with setting targets, have tended to concentrate on goals they could not influence and have neglected those areas where government action could be effective. V. M. Dandekar, "Planning in Indian Agriculture," *Indian Journal of Agricultural Economics* Vol. 22, No. 1 (January-March 1967). Finn Reisegg makes the same point in arguing that "planning for action," that is, an attempt to outline a detailed program to be followed and targets to be fulfilled, is an inappropriate approach to fostering the development of agriculture. The problem is instead one of "planning for decision-making," that is, analyses aimed at deciding the right approach for solving problems when several alternatives exist. Finn Reisegg, "Extent of Gaps Between Plans and Realization," in *Economic Models and Quantitative Methods for Decisions and Planning in Agriculture,* edited by Earl O. Heady (Ames, Iowa, 1971), pp. 462-63.

2. In a very useful book on project analysis, J. Price Gittinger of the World Bank's Economic Development Institute emphasizes that "project preparation

is not the only aspect of agricultural development or planning." J. Price Gittinger, *Economic Analysis of Agricultural Projects* (Baltimore and London, 1972), p. 1. To date, however, the World Bank seems to have given relatively little attention to the problems involved in designing and implementing agricultural strategies. It has taken a step in that direction by initiating "agricultural sector studies" intended to provide a framework for project evaluation. In addition, it has recently undertaken an "African Rural Development Study" to examine experience in that region to provide guidance for future Bank programs aimed at having a broader impact on rural development than was typical of past projects. A short paper by Uma Lele provides a very useful summary of the study and the principal lessons derived from it. ("Designing Rural Development Programmes: Lessons from Past Experience in Africa." (Paper prepared for the Second International Seminar on Change in Agriculture, Reading, England, September 9-19, 1974). A more comprehensive monograph is forthcoming.

3. Erik Thorbecke, "Sector Analysis and Models of Agriculture in Developing Countries," *Food Research Institute Studies* Vol. 12, No. 1 (1973), pp. 87, 88.

4. Albert Waterston, "Resolving the Three-Horned Planning Dilemma," *Finance and Development* Vol. 9, No. 2 (June 1972), p. 39.

5. See Kenneth J. Arrow, *The Limits of Organization* (New York, 1974), especially chapter 4; A. K. Sen, "Employment Policy and Technological Choice," mimeographed (Geneva: International Labour Office, World Employment Programme, 1973), p. 141; Kenneth E. Boulding (Richard T. Ely Lecture), "The Economics of Knowledge and the Knowledge of Economics," *American Economic Review* Vol. 56, No. 1 (May 1966), pp. 4-5, 10-11; and Richard R. Nelson, T. Paul Schultz, and Robert L. Slighton, *Structural Change in a Developing Economy: Colombia's Problems and Prospects* (Princeton, New Jersey, 1971), pp. 305-7.

6. The quoted passage is from a very pertinent essay of Olaf Helmer and Nicholas Rescher, "On the Epistemology of the Inexact Sciences," *Management Science* Vol. 6, No. 1 (October 1959).

7. A common defect of a project-oriented approach is the tendency to rely on an autonomous project authority that is staffed at a level which cannot be widely replicated. The CADU project in the Chilalo Sub-Province of Ethiopia is an interesting example of a comprehensive development unit that has been used to pioneer the introduction of innovations and administrative procedures that were later spread more widely as "minimum package" projects; but typically the emphasis on autonomous authorities is at the expense of neglect and even weakening of the regular field programs.

8. Alan Berg's recent book, *The Nutrition Factor* published by the Brookings Institution (Washington, D.C., 1973), provides an interesting treatment of the problems involved in devising programs that will have a significant impact in improving the nutritional status of population groups subject to malnutrition. He stresses especially the importance of reversing the trend in developing countries toward increased reliance on bottle rather than breast feeding. Berg also emphasizes the potential contribution of techniques for fortifying foods

THE DESIGN OF AN AGRICULTURAL STRATEGY 175

that are widely consumed with vitamins, minerals, or essential amino acids (which can now be manufactured at low cost). Many of the "commerciogenic" nutritious foods that have been promoted in recent years are, however, costly in comparison with the foods consumed by low-income households and have serious disadvantages. See Barry M. Popkin and Michael C. Latham, "The Limitations and Dangers of Commerciogenic Nutritious Foods," *American Journal of Clinical Nutrition* Vol. 26, No. 9 (September 1973), pp. 1019-20.

9. The East Pakistan program is described by Sunil Guha as having "reached proportions which must be deemed as massive . . ." in his comparative study of rural works programs in India and Pakistan. Sunil Guha, *Rural Manpower and Capital Formation in India* (New Delhi, 1969), p. 58. Walter P. Falcon's estimate of the employment impact of that program is reported in "Agricultural Employment in Less Developed Countries: General Situation, Research Approaches, and Policy Palliatives," mimeographed (Washington, D.C.: International Bank for Reconstruction and Development Economic Staff Working Paper No. 113, April 1973). For an interesting discussion of the problems and potential of a rural works program in the Indonesian context, see Richard Patten, Belinda Dapice, and Walter Falcon, "An Experiment in Rural Employment Creation: Indonesia's Kabupaten Development Program," mimeographed (Jakarta: BAPPENAS/Harvard Research Program, June 30, 1973).

10. John Stuart Mill, *Principles of Political Economy,* 5th London ed., Bk. 2 (New York, 1870), concluding paragraph of Chap. 7.

11. Eva Mueller, "Agricultural Change and Fertility Change: The Case of Taiwan," mimeographed (Ann Arbor: University of Michigan, 1971), pp. 37-38. In a more recent paper, Professor Mueller examines additional evidence on linkages between agricultural and demographic change. Eva Mueller, "The Impact of Agricultural Change on Demographic Development in the Third World," in *Demographic Growth and Development in the Third World,* book manuscript, International Union for the Scientific Study of Population, Belgium (1973). She notes that much of the evidence is contradictory but continues to stress the role of rising aspirations.

12. The contrast with Brazil and Mexico, where the pattern of agricultural development has been bimodal, is striking. In Taiwan there was a decline in the birthrate from 41 to 36 per thousand between 1947 and 1963 and a further decline to 26 per thousand by 1970. In South Korea, the decline was from 45 to 30 per thousand between 1950 and 1970. In contrast, the reduction in Brazil over the same 20-year period was only from 41 to 38 per thousand and the decline in Mexico was from 44 to 41 per thousand. See James E. Kocher, *Rural Development, Income Distribution, and Fertility Decline,* Occasional Paper of the Population Council (New York, 1973), pp. 64-65. Clearly many factors contribute to those contrasts. Some would stress the absence of family planning programs in Mexico and Brazil and the role of the Catholic Church and other cultural influences; but the French peasantry that impressed Mill by its "prudence" was predominantly Catholic yet it practiced family planning on a significant scale at a time when birth control technology was very primitive.

13. Richard A. Musgrave, "Cost-Benefit Analysis and the Theory of Public

Finance," *Journal of Economic Literature* Vol. 7, No. 3 (September 1969), p. 804.

14. Earl O. Heady, "Welfare Implications of Agricultural Research," in *Resource Allocation in Agricultural Research*, edited by Walter L. Fishel (Minneapolis, Minnesota, 1971), pp. 128-29.

15. T. H. Lee and Y. E. Chen, "Growth Rates and Taiwan's Agriculture, 1911-1970" (Paper prepared for the Conference on Agricultural Growth in Japan, Korea, Taiwan, and the Philippines at the East-West Center, Honolulu, Hawaii, February 1973).

16. Instead of simply partitioning the increases in output per worker into acreage per worker and yield per acre, in this case it would be more instructive to examine changes over time in a modern subsector and a traditional subsector, each weighted by its influence on the sectorwide productivity of agricultural labor.

17. The influence of intercountry variability on the design of an efficient agricultural strategy is taken up in more detail in Chapter 9.

18. For an interesting review of a good deal of relevant evidence and general discussion of the applicability of the work-leisure dichotomy as used in industrial societies and of the concept of underemployment, see Edgar Raynaud, "The Time Concept in the Evaluation of Rural Underemployment and Leisure Time Activities," *Social Science Information* Vol. 8, No. 3 (June 1969). See also the summary account by William O. Jones of a Conference on Competing Demands for Time and Labor in Traditional African Societies sponsored by the Social Science Research Council, "Labor and Leisure in Traditional African Societies," *Items* Vol. 22, No. 1 (March 1968).

19. See Chihiro Nakajima, "Subsistence and Commerical Family Farms: Some Theoretical Models of Subjective Equilibrium," in *Subsistence Agriculture and Economic Development*, edited by Clifton R. Wharton, Jr. (Chicago, 1969); John W. Mellor, "Toward a Theory of Agricultural Development," in *Agricultural Development and Economic Growth*, edited by Herman M. Southworth and Bruce F. Johnston (Ithaca, New York, 1967); A. K. Sen, "Peasants and Dualism With or Without Surplus Labor," *Journal of Political Economy* Vol. 74, No. 5 (October 1966); Paul Zarembka, *Toward a Theory of Economic Development* (San Francisco, 1972), Chap. 1; Don Winkelmann, *The Traditional Farmer: Maximization and Mechanization*, OECD Development Center Studies, Employment Series No. 7 (Paris, 1972), Chap. 3; William J. Barber, "Some Questions About Labour Force Analysis in Agrarian Economies with Particular Reference to Kenya," *East African Economic Review*, n.s., 2, No. 1 (June 1966).

20. John P. Lewis, *Quiet Crisis in India* (Garden City, New York, 1964), p. 53n.

21. William H. Nicholls, "The Brazilian Food Supply: Problems and Prospects," *Economic Development and Cultural Change* Vol. 19, No. 3 (April 1971), pp. 387-88.

22. Wyn F. Owen, *Two Rural Sectors: Their Characteristics and Role in the Development Process*, Indiana University International Development Research

Center, Occasional Paper No. 1 (Bloomington, 1971). The argument by Owen advocating a bimodal strategy is examined in more detail in Bruce F. Johnston (with the assistance of John M. Page, Jr. and Peter Warr), "Criteria for the Design of Agricultural Development Strategies," *Food Research Institute Studies* Vol. 11, No. 1 (1972).

23. Graham T. Allison labels these two styles of analysis an "organizational process model" and a "governmental politics model." Graham T. Allison, *Essence of Decision: The Cuban Missile Crisis* (Boston, 1971). We return to these alternative ways of viewing governmental decision making in Chapter 9.

24. Vernon W. Ruttan and Yujiro Hayami, "Strategies for Agricultural Development," *Food Research Institute Studies* Vol. 11, No. 2 (1972).

25. Lance E. Davis and Douglass C. North, *Institutional Change and American Economic Growth* (New York, 1971).

26. An analysis of the returns to research on cotton in São Paulo in Brazil provides an interesting illustration: Harry W. Ayer and G. Edward Schuh, "Social Rates of Return and Other Aspects of Agricultural Research: The Case of Cotton Research in São Paulo, Brazil," *American Journal of Agricultural Economics* Vol. 54, No. 4 pt. 1 (November 1972), pp. 56-67. Their answer to the question, why did São Paulo invest so heavily in cotton research and so sparingly in other products such as food crops, hinges on the fact that at the time the heavy investments were made "the state legislature was in the hands of rural landowners and farmers." And those groups perceived that since cotton was an export crop, increased production due to technical change would have only a limited impact on the price of cotton so that "the benefits of technical change would be realized as a producer surplus, as contrasted to a consumer surplus with domestic food crops."

27. Albert O. Hirschman, *A Bias for Hope* (New Haven and London, 1971), pp. 16-17.

28. Ibid. p. 18.

29. We are indebted to Raj Krishna for this point. On the general question of government commitment to administrative controls that are often counterproductive, see Jagdish N. Bhagwati and Padma Desai, *India: Planning for Industrialization* (London, 1970), Chap. 9.

30. Colin Leys, "Political Perspectives," in *Development in a Divided World*, edited by Dudley Seers and Leonard Joy (Middlesex, England, 1971), p. 137.

31. Ibid. p. 111.

32. A recent book by Warren F. Ilchman and Norman T. Uphoff places major emphasis on analyzing the "resources" available to political leaders as a factor influencing the decision-making process in developing countries. The Ilchman-Uphoff approach and recent books by W. Howard Wriggins and Nathan Leites and Charles Wolf, Jr. are examined in a very useful and provocative review article by Raymond F. Hopkins, "Securing Authority: The View from the Top," *World Politics* Vol. 24, No. 2 (January 1972).

33. Leys, "Political Perspectives," p. 125.

34. Ibid. p. 133.

35. For an interesting discussion of some conditions under which the efforts

of populist regimes to increase the share of income accruing to labor may in fact exacerbate the problem of income distribution, see Nelson, Schultz, and Slighton, *Colombia's Problems and Prospects,* pp. 310-12.

36. Our view is similar to E. Preiser's in emphasizing that "the distribution of income does by and large correspond to marginal productivity" while at the same time rejecting the claim that the theory of marginal productivity reveals a "natural" distribution of income. E. Preiser, "Property, Power and the Distribution of Income," in *Power in Economics,* edited by K. W. Rothschild (Middlesex, 1971), pp. 124, 135. Preiser emphasizes that the distribution of property influences the functional as well as the personal distribution of income, noting for example that widespread ownership of land increases the elasticity of the supply of farm labor (by increasing the "economic power" of workers to offer or withhold their labor).

37. An interesting analysis by Albert Fishlow of the highly skewed pattern of income distribution in Brazil places major emphasis on inequalities in access to formal education. Albert Fishlow, "Brazilian Size Distribution of Income," *American Economic Review* Vol. 62, No. 2 (May 1972). However, the evidence which he presents also makes it clear that rural poverty is a prime cause of the inequality in income distribution. We do suggest that a unimodal strategy is likely to strengthen forces that lead to more equal access to education, but we believe that in the earlier phases of development other features of a unimodal strategy are more crucial in reducing rural poverty.

38. The terms unimodal and bimodal have occasionally been used to characterize different rural societies. We reject that use of the terms because we feel that it incorrectly implies that the existing rural social structure inevitably determines the pattern of agricultural development which will emerge.

39. This brief treatment does not do justice to the great diversity in land tenure situations. Doreen Warriner's book provides much valuable detail on the range of problems and experience. Doreen Warriner, *Land Reform in Principle and Practice* (London, 1969). An essay by Philip Raup is especially valuable in examining the various ways in which land tenure arrangements can influence agricultural output, capital formation, and technical change. Philip Raup, "Land Reform and Agricultural Development," in *Agricultural Development and Economic Growth,* edited by Southworth and Johnston.

40. The quoted statement is by Dale Adams, "The Economics of Land Reform: Comment," *Food Research Institute Studies* Vol. 12, No. 3 (1973), p. 134. In commenting on a recent paper by Doreen Warriner, Adams provides a concise review of the available evidence and finds considerable support for this general conclusion.

41. The quoted phrase is from a classic article by John Brewster, "The Machine Process in Agriculture and Industry," *Journal of Farm Economics* Vol. 32, No. 1 (February 1950). See also Nurul Islam, "Employment and Output—as Objectives of Development Policy," *Fifteenth International Conference of Agricultural Economists, São Paulo, Brazil, August 1973* (Oxford, 1973), especially p. 77.

THE DESIGN OF AN AGRICULTURAL STRATEGY 179

42. Quoted by Thomas C. Smith, *The Agrarian Origins of Modern Japan* (Stanford, California, 1959), p. 128.
43. The discussion in the text applies to situations where individual ownership of land is already established. In much of tropical Africa, however, households are assigned cultivation rights but individual ownership is not recognized. Under those circumstances, a weakening of the traditional social structure may lead to a dual-size structure of farm units because powerful individuals are able to obtain large allocations or establish individual ownership of large units. Uncritical support for "owner cultivation" can, in those circumstances, lead to a bimodal pattern which is difficult to reverse.
44. Princeton N. Lyman and Jerome T. French, "Political Results of Land Reform" (Paper prepared for the Agency for International Development, Spring Review of Land Reform, Washington, D.C., June 2-4, 1970), p. 40.
45. This weakness of "latent groups" is a central thesis in Mancur Olson's book, *The Logic of Collective Action* (Cambridge, Massachusetts, 1964).
46. Leys, "Political Perspectives," p. 119.
47. Warriner, *Land Reform*, p. 139.
48. Francine R. Frankel, "The Politics of the Green Revolution: Shifting Patterns of Peasant Participation in India and Pakistan," in *Food, Population, and Employment: The Impact of the Green Revolution*, edited by Thomas T. Poleman and Donald K. Freebairn (New York, 1973).
49. Steven N. S. Cheung, "Private Property Rights and Sharecropping," *Journal of Political Economy* Vol. 76, No. 6 (November/December 1968); idem, *The Theory of Share Tenancy* (Chicago, 1969). A recent paper by Newbery gives a more general demonstration of the reasons for expecting share tenancy contracts to compare favorably with fixed rent contracts in allocative efficiency. He seems to effectively refute the arguments advanced by Bardhan and Srinivasan against Cheung's analysis. See David Newbery, "The Choice of Rental Contract in Peasant Agriculture," in *Agriculture in Development Theory*, edited by Lloyd Reynolds, forthcoming; and P. K. Bardhan and T. N. Srinivasan, "Cropsharing Tenancy in Agriculture: A Theoretical and Empirical Analysis," *American Economic Review* Vol. 61, No. 1 (March 1971). In a 1950 paper by D. Gale Johnson, which anticipated Cheung's argument, it is noted that under share tenancy there are three techniques "available to the landlord for enforcing the desired intensity of cultivation. The first is to enter into a lease contract that specifies in detail what the tenant is required to do. A second is to share in the payment of expenses to the same extent as in the sharing of the output. The third is to grant only a short-term lease, which makes possible a periodic review of the performance of the tenant." Both Cheung and Newbery note that, because of the significance of the third of those techniques, short-term leases are likely to lead to a closer approximation to efficiency than long-term leases. D. Gale Johnson, "Resource Allocation under Share Contracts," *Journal of Political Economy* Vol. 58, No. 2 (April, 1950), p. 118.
50. According to a survey of share tenancy in two districts of Bangladesh, the

cost of fertilizer was either shared equally by tenants and landowners or paid entirely by the landowner on over half of the farms studied. And in all but six cases among the 54 farms in the sample purchasing irrigation water, those costs were either shared equally by landowners and tenants or paid entirely by the landowner. In his highly interesting report on this survey, M. Raquibuz Zaman presents the standard argument for expecting sharecroppers to use inputs less intensively than owner-cultivators. He recognizes, however, that this implies that sharecroppers will thereby gain an "economic rent" and that in practice family labor is likely to be used "up to the limit imposed by the production possibility curve" because of the lack of alternative job opportunities. Furthermore, he notes that "The results of the survey do not provide any conclusive proof of significant yield differences in the owner-operated and sharecropped land." M. Raquibuz Zaman, "Sharecropping and Economic Efficiency in Bangladesh," *Bangladesh Economic Review* Vol. 1, No. 2 (April 1973), p. 152. See also C. H. Hanumanth Rao, "Uncertainty, Entrepreneurship, and Sharecropping in India," *Journal of Political Economy* Vol. 79, No. 3 (May/June 1971), p. 593n.

51. Leys, "Political Perspectives," p. 137.

52. Hirschman, *Bias for Hope,* pp. 19-20.

53. For example, the pessimistic conclusions suggested by Carl Gotsch are clearly influenced by his familiarity with the hierarchical rural structure in (West) Pakistan ("The Distributive Impact of Agricultural Growth: Low Income Farmers and the 'System' [A Case Study of Sahiwal District, West Pakistan]" [Paper prepared for a Seminar on Small Farmer Development Strategies sponsored by the Agricultural Development Council and the Ohio State University, Columbus, September 13-15, 1971]).

54. Adams, "Economics of Land Reform," p. 136.

55. This is one of two extensions of Preiser's analysis of the determinants of income distribution which may be highly significant in the context of a developing country. Preiser recognizes the influence of monopoly power, especially the fact that the "market form" is able to influence distribution locally "and for a short time even over the whole market." He argues, however, that it is of little importance for the long-term distribution of the social product because "a comprehensive monopoly is inconceivable in the case of any of the three large classes of income receivers." See Preiser, "Property, Power and the Distribution of Income," p. 124. Within a situation in which owners of large haciendas are able to act as monopolists, peasants in the area are likely to find it difficult to rent land to enlarge their smallholdings, and they therefore remain under strong pressure to work for the landlord for extremely low wages. Thus the distribution of property and monopoly power jointly exert a persistent influence on income distribution. A less dramatic but more widespread situation arises when there is artificial cheapening of capital, and often of inputs such as fertilizer, so that it is necessary to resort to administrative rationing to cope with an excess demand situation. Under those circumstances, the status and the economic and political power of large farmers and other

THE DESIGN OF AN AGRICULTURAL STRATEGY

privileged groups can have a long-term influence on income distribution.

56. Albert O. Hirschman, *Development Projects Observed* (Washington, D.C., 1967), p. 5.

57. The quoted phrase is from Elihu Katz's comment on John Brewster's essay on "Traditional Social Structures as Barriers to Change" ("Comment," in *Agricultural Development and Economic Growth*, edited by Southworth and Johnston). Hirschman's formulation of this view that "attitudinal change can be a consequence of behavioral change rather than its precondition" has been related particularly to the theory of "cognitive dissonance" originated in 1957 by Leon Festinger (*Bias for Hope,* pp. 323-26).

58. Arthur Mosher describes the cumulative effects discussed in this paragraph as "self-generating resources" because they are "augmented rather than consumed by use" (*Technical Cooperation in Latin-American Agriculture* [Chicago, 1957], p. 268).

59. The quotation is from George Dalton, *Economic Anthropology and Development* (New York, 1971), pp. 276-77.

60. William N. Parker, "Sources of Agricultural Productivity in the Nineteenth Century," *Journal of Farm Economics* Vol. 49, No. 5 (December 1967), p. 1466.

5 | Historical Patterns: England, The United States, and Japan

Throughout the long history of agriculture, the international diffusion of crops and technologies has been important. In contemporary developing countries, this process takes on special significance because of the cumulative advances in science and technology that have produced an enormous backlog of transferable innovations. For the countries considered in the present chapter, however, indigenously evolved innovations and institutions played the dominant role.

The evolutionary aspect of agricultural change was especially pronounced in Britain's experience which is examined in the first section. Although we focus on the extended period from 1750 to 1875, a number of the innovations that spread during that period had emerged earlier. The balance of the chapter reviews the patterns of agricultural change in the United States and Japan. In spite of striking contrasts, most notably in the relative abundance of land in the United States, there are also significant similarities. In particular, the rates of growth of farm output and productivity over the 80-year period from 1880 to 1960 were broadly similar, and in both countries industrial progress made increasingly important contributions to productivity growth in agriculture.

In a brief overview of the similarities and contrasts between agricultural change in the United States and Japan, which constitutes the second section of the chapter, it is emphasized that the process of structural transformation began much earlier in the United States. It is for that reason that the third section, which summarizes the

HISTORICAL PATTERNS: ENGLAND, THE UNITED STATES, JAPAN 183

highlights of agricultural change in the United States, covers the long span from 1820 to 1960. The section on Japan that follows concentrates on the 1880-1960 period and gives considerable attention to agriculture's role in facilitating industrial growth. A concluding section focuses on the changes in total factor productivity in the two countries and the lessons to be derived from their experience.

EVOLUTIONARY CHANGE IN ENGLAND, 1750-1875

There is a lack of quantitative evidence concerning changes in farm productivity and aggregate output in Great Britain during the 125 years ending in 1875, the period in which agricultural change appears to have had the most significant influence on the country's industrial development. There is, however, a wealth of descriptive material that provides a tolerably accurate picture of the changing character of British agriculture.[1] In his influential treatise on *English Farming Past and Present,* Lord Ernle singles out the period 1780 to 1813 as one of "exceptional activity in agricultural progress." The high prices which prevailed during that period, in part as a result of the Napoleonic wars, stimulated food production: "Landlords and farmers were spurred to fresh exertions and a great outlay of capital and labour by the large returns on their expenditure."[2] This was by far the most active period of enclosure; just over a million acres of common pasture and waste were enclosed by Acts of Parliament between 1793 and 1815, nearly twice the total enclosed during the preceding 65 years.[3] Enclosures were frequently followed by the introduction of better crop rotations, improvement of livestock herds, and other innovations associated with more competent farm management. This was also the period in which the writings of the prolific Arthur Young and his associates, the activities of the semiofficial Board of Agriculture (founded in 1793), and local farm clubs made notable contributions toward spreading knowledge of improved practices and a wider application of the "high farming" developed by earlier innovators.

Until fairly recently the English agricultural revolution has been described mainly in terms of the towering contributions of a handful of innovators. Thus Lord Ernle emphasizes the role of Jethro Tull and the techniques advocated in his book, *Horse-Hoeing Husbandry*, published in 1731, which in Ernle's view provided "the principles on which was based an agricultural revolution in tillage." Stress is also placed on the development of the famous Norfolk four-course rotation, often attributed to Lord Townshend, dubbed "Turnip Townshend" because of the importance he attached to turnips as a fodder root in the rotation employed on his estate in Norfolk. Subsequent research has emphasized that these and other "traditional heroes of the agricultural revolution" were essentially popularizers, whose greatest contribution was to stimulate and diffuse an interest in improvement and in scientific enquiry.[4] Moreover, there is now much greater emphasis on the general shift away from "the ancient division of the cultivated area between permanent arable and permanent grass which tended to undermine the fertility of both."[5] The Norfolk rotation was only one of a number of forms of "convertible agriculture" based on the alternation of arable crops and grass on the same land. In addition, the grass was sown with clover or other leguminous crops which increased soil fertility directly as well as making it possible to maintain larger herds of cattle and sheep. Turnips or other fodder roots provided winter feed which also contributed to increased production; and the work of pioneers in livestock breeding, such as Robert Bakewell, increased the size and quality of the animals reared. A highly significant by-product of these advances was the better quality and increased availability of manure which contributed to the maintenance of soil fertility and to notable increases in grain yield, especially on the lighter soils in the south and east of England which became the most progressive agricultural regions.

These innovations were the forerunners of numerous developments in the nineteenth century. During the first half of the century there were marked improvements in techniques of drainage, aided by the manufacture of clay pipe (initiated in 1845) and by Government Drainage Loans. Improved drainage was often a prerequisite for the increased use of fertilizers which became significant from about 1840. Enlarged use of commercial fertilizers was stimulated by a process, patented by Sir J. B. Lawes in 1843, for treating pulverized bones with sulfuric acid; the technique soon had a much larger impact when it was applied to phosphate rock. Domestic supplies of fertilizers rich in nitrogen were also augmented by imports of guano beginning in 1835 and rising to 200 thousand tons by 1847. The development of the seed drill in the eighteenth century was followed in the nineteenth century by numerous advances in farm machinery. An all-iron plow and all-iron harrow came into manufacture in 1830, and from about 1850 stationary steam engines came into use for threshing grain, pumping, and other farm operations.

Those who have chronicled agricultural change in England stress the spread of technical knowledge and the application of efficient farming methods during the two decades following the repeal of the Corn Laws in 1846. Although considerable progress had been made by a handful of enlightened farmers, the general level of farming was still extremely backward in 1846.[6] The large gap between occasional examples of "high farming" and the generally low level of practice at this time seems to have involved more than the inevitable lag between the methods of progressive and backward farmers in a community. There had been notable advances in knowledge of crop rotations, fertilizers and fertilizer use, and other practices, but these advances derived almost entirely from the slow empirical process of trial and error. More important, however, results were often misinterpreted because the scientific principles underlying practice were not well understood. By experience and intuitive judgment the best farmers were following practices that could not be improved upon for many years, but in the absence of scientific understanding to resolve differences of opinion it was easy for conservative farmers to persist in the use of outmoded practices.

Progress in various fields of basic science was a necessary condition for the establishment of sound principles to guide the choice of rotations, fertilizer use, and other aspects of farm management. Better understanding of plant nutrition was clearly of fundamental importance, and Sir A. D. Hall, an eminent British agriculturalist, dates modern agricultural science from 1840. This was the year that the German chemist, Liebig, published his famous report setting forth the principles that were to provide the basis for this field of agricultural science. With the work of Liebig and his successors, the analysis and use of plant nutrients was given a scientific basis that facilitated the wider and more effective application of commercial fertilizers. It was not until 1886, however, that the special value of leguminous crops in rotations was clarified by the discovery that legumes have a distinctive capacity to "fix" nitrogen.

In 1843, just three years after the publication of Liebig's treatise on the principles of plant nutrition, Lawes and Gilbert initiated a program of research at the now famous Rothamsted Experimental Station. This was an epochal event because it marked the first time that systematic agricultural experiments were launched along lines which have become the mainstay of agricultural experiment stations throughout the world. However, this institutional innovation was to achieve its most significant results in other countries. In England this was the heyday of laissez-faire, and the work at Rothamsted was financed personally by Lawes throughout the nineteenth century.[7] This was related also to the English tradition which emphasized the role of country gentlemen, such as Jethro Tull, Lord Townshend, and Thomas Coke, in pioneering agricultural improvements. It was also related to the conviction, challenged by John Stuart Mill but generally holding sway in England, that large estates, owned by the landed gentry and operated by farmers (a term that was originally synonymous with tenant), were essential for realizing agricultural progress.

This belief in the inherent superiority of England's organization of agricultural production in large units seems to be a persistent view. Thus E. L. Jones declares that "The growth of an estate system where the owners often possessed large extra-agricultural resources which they were willing to invest in land was crucial in raising English agriculture from the rut of capital-starvation in which the continental peasantry remained struck."[8] It seems probable that this type of disparaging comparison between England's "larger and better-equipped holdings" and the "continental peasantry" has been influenced unduly by an emphasis on "modernity" and technical efficiency. A comparison in terms of economic efficiency, taking account of the rates of increase in total factor productivity, would undoubtedly yield conclusions much more favorable to the small-scale farming of the continent.[9] That British agriculture of the nineteenth century was able to use relatively large amounts of capital even in the first half of the nineteenth century is not surprising in light of the substantial structural transformation that had taken place by midcentury. In 1851 only 22 per cent of the British labor force was in agriculture; in most of the continental countries some 50 per cent or more of the labor force was still engaged in agriculture as late as 1880. Some justification for this argument could be found in the conditions prevailing in English agriculture at this time. The gentry were able to force enclosure which was a potent device for breaking with the rigidities of the old three-course rotation, the open-field system, and village commons. Moreover, the concept, much less the practice, of publicly financed experiment stations and extension services to foster productivity advance among small and medium farmers had not yet emerged. Although the first publicly supported agricultural experiment station was established in Germany (at Möckern in Saxony in 1852), it was in Japan and the United States that this institutional "invention" was to record its first major achievements.[10]

Jones emphasizes three aspects of agriculture's "Contributions to Economic Development" in England during the eighteenth and nineteenth centuries: the supply of food and raw materials, the release of factors of production, and the income effects of agricultural change in the development of a market for industrial goods.[11] It is apparent that considerable increases in farm productivity and output were necessary conditions for England's economic growth which was accompanied by what used to be regarded as "explosive growth" of population. From 1700 to 1800 the population of England and Wales grew from about 5.8 to 9.2 million. Between the first and last decades of the century England switched from being a small net exporter of grain to a net importer, but only about one-sixth of the extra grain needed to satisfy the requirements resulting from the 57 per cent increase in population came from imports.[12] Between 1801 and 1831 population increased by approximately 50 per cent and domestic food production must have increased by as much or more since food imports were relatively unimportant during those years. During the period 1831-71 there was a further increase in population of close to 60 per cent. Although there was substantial expansion of food imports during those years, it is possible that the increase in total domestic production of farm products was as large or larger than the increase in population since there is clear evidence of an improvement in diet in this period, notably in the shift from the cheaper cereals and potatoes toward livestock products.

Contemporary historians no longer stress the role of the enclosure movement in making available an abundant supply of cheap labor for the growing manufacturing industries. The newer systems of farming, and the land reclamation, hedging, building of farm roads, and other improvements that accompanied enclosure all demanded considerable labor, and it is also pointed out that the work force engaged in agriculture, forestry, and fishing increased—from 1.7 to 2.1 million between the first census in 1801 and the census of 1851.[13] But this increase was much less, both proportionally and absolutely, than the increase in the total working population. Agriculture's share in the total labor force declined from 36 per cent in 1801, already a remarkably low figure by international comparisons, to a mere 22 per cent in 1851.[14] Thus in spite of the increase in absolute numbers in agriculture, there was substantial migration to urban areas.

It is difficult to generalize about the extent to which people were "pushed" out of agriculture as a result of losing their land or grazing rights on the commons and as a response to low agricultural wages; by 1851 some 70 per cent of the male workers in agriculture were hired laborers.[15] During much of the nineteenth century there was certainly a strong "pull" exerted on agricultural labor, drawing it into railway construction, manufacturing, and other nonfarm occupations.

Jones emphasizes that because the agricultural innovations of the eighteenth century favored the light soil regions, "Regional differences in agricultural prosperity intensified as the south and east became increasingly superior at producing grain and fatstock." He goes on to suggest that "Northern and some Midland districts became more industrial precisely because the readier uptake of the 'new' crops on light land in the south had made them relatively poorer agriculturally." He also reports that the quickening of the growth of manufacturing in the northern districts occurred before the discovery of coal which stimulated heavier industries based on the steam engine or coke-smelted iron. The earlier expansion of manufacturing in these districts "was important as a supplement to inadequate farm incomes, or in cases like Midland hosiery a remedy for the loss of agricultural work among those dispossessed by the enclosure of parishes which were laid down to pasture."[16] In his contemporary account of the wage differentials in the mid-nineteenth century, James Caird emphasizes "the proximity of manufacturing and mining enterprises" and notes that the line of demarcation "is distinctly drawn at the point where coal ceases to be found." Whatever the reasons, it is an arresting statistic that in the northern district wages had increased by 66 per cent since 1770 whereas in the south the rise was only 14 per cent.[17] In a dynamic view of the growth process, it should be emphasized that " 'North' and 'South' thus evolved as complementary markets which it became worthwhile linking by better communications." And improvements in transportation—the extension of turnpikes, "the canal mania of the 1790s," and the railway boom that began in the 1840s—provided a stimulus to increased production in both agriculture and industry.[18]

Transportation improvements outside the boundaries of England were to play a decisive role in ushering in the changes of the 1870s that marked the end of the period of "high farming." For several decades it had appeared that increased productivity in English agriculture would provide a substitute for the protection that came to an end with the repeal of the Corn Laws in 1846. But the end of the American Civil War, the impact of the railroads in reducing the cost of moving grain from the American Midwest to eastern ports, and the steamships that drastically reduced the cost of ocean transport exposed British agriculture to competition that brought to an end to the "golden age" of English farming.[19] Not surprisingly, we will find that in contrast the 1870s were a period of exuberant expansion of American agriculture.

Although agriculture did not play as strategic a role in the industrial development of England as it did in the United States and Japan, increased farm productivity was clearly a necessary condition for the first triumph of the Industrial Revolution. In his chronicle of industrial development in Western Europe, David Landes notes "the fundamental contrast between self-generated change" as represented by Britain and the "emulative response" of the Continent.[20]

AGRICULTURAL DEVELOPMENT IN THE UNITED STATES AND JAPAN: AN OVERVIEW

By contrast with the evolutionary changes that transformed British agriculture, it might appear that the development of agriculture in the United States and Japan were examples of "emulative response." We shall see, however, that in both the United States and Japan "self-generated change" was of pre-eminent importance.

Knowledge of European and especially English experience was widely disseminated in nineteenth century America by the agricultural press, at meetings of agricultural societies, and in the firsthand knowledge brought by immigrants. As farmers in the East, especially in New England, encountered problems of depleted soil fertility and declining yields, they resorted to some of the techniques reviewed above. An 1837 issue of *The Cultivator* (published in Albany, New York) described a new system, based on English practice, consisting of "draining, manuring, alternating crops, the culture of roots and artificial grasses, the substitution of fallow crops for naked fallows, the application of lime, marl, and other earthy matters to improve the mechanical condition and the fertility of the soil, and the blending of tillage and grass husbandry—of cattle and grain."[21] But in general the European prescriptions did not meet the needs of America's agricultural economy. Drainage was too expensive to find much application. The cultivation of roots was rejected almost everywhere because maize, the "corn" of the New World, "was a far more certain and profitable crop, requiring less labor for larger returns, while the fact that it was a hoed crop, like roots, served the purpose of clearing the land of weeds."[22] Most fundamental of all, however, America's farmers were intent on opening up an empty continent and, by comparison with Europe, land was abundant and cheap, labor scarce and dear. This difference in factor prices led to a widespread tendency to give low priority to the maintenance of soil fertility by manuring, an attitude described succinctly in the 1852 *Transactions* of Michigan's State Agricultural Society: "But little attention is paid to saving or applying manure; we are aware of its utility, we haul it to our fields if we find time; the low price of lands and high price of labor will not warrant the operation in all cases." According to Clarence Danhof, this remained true until after 1870; and we will find in fact that fertilizers did not become a significant input in American agriculture until the 1930s.[23]

The innovations that led to increased agricultural productivity in Japan in the half-century following the Meiji restoration of 1868, drew upon scientific advances in Europe, especially the improved knowledge of plant nutrition that stemmed from Liebig's pioneer work. But the technology that emerged was a highly successful mixture of indigenous and borrowed elements. In comparison with the course of events in today's late-developing countries, it too was fundamentally a case of "self-generated change."

In spite of the striking differences between the United States and Japan in factor endowment, their rates of growth in agricultural output were remarkably similar over the 80-year period from 1880 to 1960. Even the differences in the rates of increase in labor productivity were fairly small; the annual rate of increase in output per male worker in the United States at 2.4 per cent was just over 25 per cent more rapid than the 1.9 per cent rate of increase in Japan.

Table 5.1. Index numbers of output, area, yield, and of area and output per worker in the United States and Japan

	1880	1960	Annual (compound) rate of increase
Output (net of seeds and feed)			
United States	100	340	1.5
Japan	100	358	1.9
Arable land area			
United States	100	238	1.1
Japan	100	128	0.3
Output per hectare of arable land			
United States	100	143	0.4
Japan	100	280	1.3
Number of male workers			
United States	100	50	−0.9
Japan	100	79	−0.3
Arable land area per male worker			
United States	100	476	2.0
Japan	100	162	0.6
Output per male worker			
United States	100	680	2.4
Japan	100	453	1.9

SOURCE: Data from Yujiro Hayami and Vernon W. Ruttan, *Agricultural Development: An International Perspective* (Baltimore and London, 1971), p. 114 except that the rate of increase in arable land per worker in Japan, printed there as .9 has been corrected to .6. The output figures for Japan that Hayami and Ruttan use are based on a careful revision of the official crop statistics published in Mataji Umemura et al., *Agriculture and Forestry*, Vol. 9, *Estimates of Long-Term Economic Statistics of Japan Since 1868*, edited by Kazushi Ohkawa, Miyohei Shinohara, and Mataji Umemura (Tokyo, 1966).

But the nature of the growth paths in the two countries differed drastically. It is apparent from the comparative figures in Table 5.1 that in the United States the expansion of cultivated area accounted for most of the growth of output, whereas in Japan the increase in yield per acre was the dominant factor. It is because of the more rapid rate of growth of crop yields that the increase in output per worker in

Table 5.2. Man-land ratios and the relative price of land in the United States and Japan

	1880	1960
Arable land per male farm worker (hectares/worker)		
United States	10	46
Japan	.61	.97
Agricultural land area per farm worker		
United States	25	109
Japan	.70	1.13
Relative prices of land and labor (days of work required to purchase one hectare of arable land)		
United States	181	108
Japan	1,559	3,216

SOURCE: Data from Yujiro Hayami and Vernon W. Ruttan, *Agricultural Development: An International Perspective* (Baltimore and London, 1971), p. 113 who show the comparisons in considerably greater detail.

Japan was not a great deal less than in the United States even though the arable area per male farm worker in Japan increased by just over 60 per cent compared with close to a fivefold increase in acreage per worker in the United States.

The contrast between the man/land ratios in the two countries and in the relative prices of land and labor are summarized in Table 5.2. It is especially striking that in 1960 the arable land area per male farm worker in the United States was 47 times as large as in Japan compared with a 17-fold differential in 1880. Although the more rapid expansion of crop area in the United States was a major factor, the much greater reduction in the number of farm workers was almost as important in accounting for this increase in the man/land differential. By 1960 there were only half as many male workers in United States agriculture as in 1880 whereas in Japan the decline was just over 20 per cent.

It is apparent from Figure 5.1 that the share of the total labor force in United States agriculture declined substantially between

194 AGRICULTURE AND STRUCTURAL TRANSFORMATION

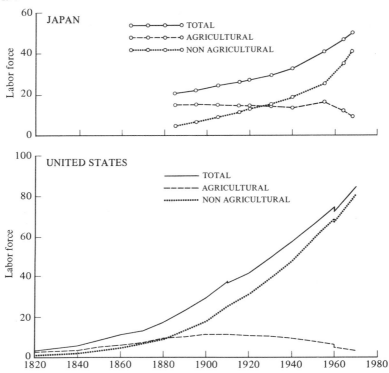

Figure 5.1 Total agricultural and nonagricultural labor force in the United States from 1820, and in Japan from 1885 (million people).
SOURCE: Data from Appendix Tables I and II.

1820 and 1880 even though the "structural transformation turning point," when the absolute size of the farm work force began to decline, was not reached until 1910. Agriculture's share of the labor force in Japan in 1880 was over 75 per cent, about as high as in the United States in 1820. Considering its heavy weight in the total labor force, it is somewhat surprising to note that Japan's farm work force registered a slight decline whereas the farm labor force in the United States increased considerably between 1880 and 1900.[24] The principal factor responsible for this outcome was the substantially more rapid growth of the total labor force in the United States, which

HISTORICAL PATTERNS: ENGLAND, THE UNITED STATES, JAPAN 195

was growing at rates comparable to those that prevail in the contemporary developing countries whereas Japan's population and labor force were increasing at the relatively moderate rates that characterized the demographic transition in the United Kingdom and other European countries. The growth of nonfarm employment in the United States during the late nineteenth century, and especially during the 1880s, was close to the most rapid rate ever recorded in the United States or in any country. Expansion of nonfarm employment in Japan in the late nineteenth and early twentieth centuries was also very rapid. And since rapid growth of nonfarm employment was associated with moderate growth of the total labor force, Japan's "coefficient of differential growth," which is simply the difference between the two rates, was exceptionally high.[25] The following tabulation, extracted from Appendix Tables I and II, compares the growth rates of the nonfarm and total labor force and the coefficients of differential growth for the two countries (annual compound rates in percent):

	United States				Japan		
Period	Nonfarm (1)	Total (2)	Coefficient of differential growth (1)-(2)	Period	Nonfarm (3)	Total (4)	Coefficient of differential growth (3)-(4)
1880-90	4.66	2.98	1.68	1885-95	3.53	.90	2.63
1890-1900	2.67	2.23	.44	1895-1905	2.83	.86	1.97

For reasons that are examined later, there was a slackening of the rate of growth of nonfarm employment in Japan in the 1920s and 1930s which had the effect of delaying any significant decline in the size of the farm work force. Following a temporary reversal of the transformation process immediately after World War II, Japan's farm labor force began to decline at a rapid rate in the mid-1950s. The growth of nonfarm employment between 1955 and 1968 was even more rapid than during the late nineteenth century and more than twice as high as the rates of increase during the 1920s and 1930s.

In the concluding section of this chapter we examine in some detail the changes in total factor productivity in the two countries. The growth of factor productivity over the 80-year period from 1880 to 1960 was substantial in both countries, although somewhat higher in Japan. There were, however, marked differences in the timing of the periods of rapid and relatively stagnant growth in productivity. Before comparing the growth paths of the two countries in more detail, it is essential to review the salient features of agricultural change in each country.

HIGHLIGHTS OF AGRICULTURAL CHANGE IN THE UNITED STATES

Throughout most of the nineteenth and into the twentieth century a major aim of agricultural policy in the United States was the opening up of virgin land to make possible the creation of new family farms. In the decades prior to the Homestead Act of 1862, which gave settlers the right to 160 acres of federal land by clearing it and establishing a farm, abundant federal land was available at $1.25 per acre or even less. Under the Homestead Act and other provisions for disposing of the public domain, approximately a billion acres passed into private ownership, an area about three times as large as the total acreage now under crops.[26] The nation's labor force more than doubled between 1850 and 1880, and nearly half of the increase represented additions to the work force in agriculture. During those three decades, the share of agriculture in the labor force declined only from 55 per cent in 1850 to 51 per cent in 1880 whereas it had dropped abruptly from 79 to 55 per cent during the three decades before 1850.

During the next three decades the total labor force nearly doubled once again, but only about 15 per cent of the increase was absorbed in agriculture. Thus by 1910 the share of agriculture in the labor force had declined to 31 per cent. Although 1910 was the "structural transformation turning point" when the farm labor force began to decline in absolute size, 1880 was also a significant turning point for United States agriculture in marking the end of a prolonged period in which the farm labor force increased almost as rapidly as the total. In commenting on that turning point, Stanley Lebergott notes that the superintendent of the census had observed that it was in the 1880s that there ceased to be "continuity in the line of settlement," an event that the historian Frederick Jackson Turner was to describe more dramatically as "the end of the frontier."[27] Of more fundamental importance, however, was the fact that by the late nineteenth century American industry had come of age, giving rise to greatly increased demand for labor in manufacturing, construction, and in supporting service industries. At the same time, the rapid spread of two-bottom, five-horse plows, stationary threshers, and other mechanical innovations made it much easier for agriculture to release labor.

Investment was required to translate the availability of virgin land into an economic asset. But much of this was accomplished by the work of the settlers and the draft animals that they brought to their homesteads. Thus new land was cleared and brought into cultivation year by year with the aid of simple tools.

Creating a transport network was a crucial element in the opening up of the new lands and linking farms throughout the country to the growing urban markets at home and to the export markets in Europe. Steamboats provided economical transportation on navigable rivers and gave added impetus to the rapid expansion of canals. Extension of railroad transport was the decisive factor in linking the rapidly expanding farming areas to the growing urban markets of the East and to markets overseas. In the northern states there were only 73 miles of railroad in 1830, but this increased to 3328 miles within a decade and reached 34,776 miles by 1870. The importance of the expanding transport network in lowering transportation costs and in raising the farm gate prices of farm products was of immense importance. A contemporary observer writing in the *American Agriculturalist* of 1868 declared that "if the farmers had taxed themselves to build all the railroads in this country, and given them away to any companies who would stock and run them, the . . . increased values of their lands would have well repaid all the outlay."[28]

Foreign investment was of considerable importance in financing the expansion of the transport network. There was also an important inflow of capital from abroad embodied in the immigrants whose cost of rearing had been borne by their European homeland and who brought their energy, knowledge of farm work, and other skills to the task of building the new economy. This tide of immigration reached flood proportions in the late nineteenth and early twentieth centuries—over six million immigrants during the decade of the 1880s and a record inflow of eight million during the first decade of the twentieth century.

The growth of the total labor force in the United States, augmented as it was by immigration as well as by natural increase, averaged about 3 per cent per year between 1820 and 1890 and close to 2.5 per cent during the next two decades before its rate of growth fell off sharply (Appendix Table I). Concern about problems of unemployment, however, seems to have been confined to the cyclical crises that periodically interrupted the process of economic growth, although resentment on the part of industrial workers against the influx of cheap immigrant labor was often acute. The absence of serious concern about problems of "labor force absorption" was, of course, a result of the large reserves of untapped resources waiting to be exploited and reliance on technologies that did not have the great capacity to displace labor which characterizes modern technologies. The fact that millions of new entrants to the labor force had the option of making their own farms out of virgin land was an especially important possibility during the period of rapid westward expansion in the latter half of the nineteenth century. Effective demand for farm products rather than availability of land was the factor limiting the expansion of income opportunities in farming, and the expansion of agricultural exports assumed great importance.

Commercialization of American Agriculture

In the later decades of the nineteenth century there appears to have been mounting concern to improve access to foreign markets to sustain a demand for the increasing output of agricultural products that emerged as the productive capacity of American agriculture was increased by westward expansion and rising productivity. In the South cotton exports dominated the cash economy, but in general the growth of domestic demand in urban markets was the major factor that sustained the profitability of expanded production and led to the increases in farm cash income that transformed American agriculture from a semisubsistence to a commercial orientation. Danhof estimates that the proportion of agricultural output sold in urban markets increased from about 20 per cent in 1820 to 40 per cent in 1870. It is even more difficult to estimate the increase in commercial sales, including purchases of farm products by members of the rural nonfarm population as well as urban residents, but Danhof suggests that the increase on that broader definition may have been from 25 per cent or slightly more in 1820 to 50 or possibly 55 per cent of total farm output sold in 1870.[29]

Agricultural exports were the chief source of foreign exchange earnings throughout the nineteenth century; they accounted for 83 per cent of total merchandise exports in 1820 and 81 per cent half a century later. Their importance as a source of farm cash income as well as foreign exchange seems to have reached a peak during the last three decades of the century. The total value of exports doubled during the decade of the 1870s, an increase that was almost entirely due to rapid expansion of agricultural exports. Figures relating to the value of agricultural exports naturally overstate the contribution of production for export to value added in agriculture, but it is nonetheless significant to note that the value of agricultural exports in 1880, close to $700 million, was more than a quarter as large as total value added in agriculture ($2.6 billion in 1879 in current prices according to Robert Gallman's estimate).[30]

It is apparent that the rate of growth of agricultural output realized in the late nineteenth century was made possible in important degree by the expansion of agricultural exports. American farmers and the political leaders who represented them were keenly aware of this fact. As early as 1846 a Senator made the extravagant claim:

Illinois wants a market for her agricultural productions; she wants the market of the world. Ten counties of that state could supply all the home market. We want a foreign market for our produce which is now rotting in our granaries.[31]

Thus agriculture was able to play an important role as a "leading industry" during that period because of the extent to which grain and other commodities produced at low cost in the United States were able to find export markets in Europe where costs were higher in spite of substantially lower wage rates.[32]

The highly commercial character of United States agriculture is now of such long standing that it is easy to overlook the fact that the country's agriculture still had a "semi-subsistence" character until well into the nineteenth century. Between 1820 and 1870 there was a highly significant transition from an agricultural economy largely oriented to the subsistence needs of farm households to production for market. The expansion of domestic and foreign markets and the growth of farm cash income during that period led to noteworthy changes in the attitudes and behavior of American farmers.

Until well into the nineteenth century "money expenditures were held to a minimum, partly because opportunities to sell produce for cash were usually limited and thus money was difficult to come by. . . ."[33] Many contemporary observers remarked on the more commercial orientation that was spreading, leading to changes that were sometimes deplored but by midcentury more often hailed as essential to progress. Thus Danhof quotes an acute observer in the 1850s writing with reference to conditions a generation earlier: "The great effort then was for every farmer to produce anything he required within the circle of his own family; and he was esteemed the best farmer, to use a phrase of the day, 'who did everything within himself.'" During that earlier period when farmers were obliged to rely so heavily on farm-supplied resources, "necessity was converted into a virtue," as Danhof aptly comments, and "the disapproval that had long attached to the purchase of anything that could be produced persisted for some time, operating to restrict the amount of specialization that was acquired."[34]

The extended cash market enabled farmers to specialize by doing one thing and doing it well. In addition to becoming a specialist producer instead of a jack-of-all-trades, a growing number of farmers became adept at appraising alternatives in terms of costs and profits. Many also became much more innovative and experimental in their approach.

Mechanical Innovations and Acreage Expansion

Growth of market outlets and increased readiness to innovate would not have accounted for much, however, if the nation's farmers had not acquired the means to expand the area under cultivation. It was not until the 1930s that increases in yield per acre began to make a significant contribution to the growth of output and productivity. Prior to that there was a long period in which crop yields declined, partly as a result of some decline in soil fertility, but mainly because of the expansion of crop areas into drier regions.

The large increases in acreage cultivated per farm worker in the United States have been associated with a host of mechanical innovations which drastically reduced farm labor requirements long before the tractor appeared on the scene. The following estimates by Danhof indicate that a sizable reduction in the man-hours of labor required for wheat production had already taken place by 1850, and the reduction in labor requirements per acre between 1850 and 1880 was remarkable:

Man-hour requirements in wheat production
(*Per acre*)

Date	Preparation and seeding	Harvesting	Threshing	Total
Prior to 1830	26	20	29	75
1850	25	10	8	43
1880	10	2	1	13

These figures overstate the impact of mechanical innovations on labor requirements in American agriculture because cereal crops such as wheat were most affected by the introduction of labor-saving equipment. Furthermore, these estimates "are highly generalized in character and indicate minimum hours required with the use of the best available equipment."[35] There is no doubt, however, that the actual changes were very great. According to the detailed analysis by William Parker and Judith Klein, there was a fourfold increase in output per man-hour in grain production in the United States between 1840-60 and 1900-10; and those calculations indicate that virtually all of this increase is to be attributed to mechanization in combination with regional shifts in the location of grain production.[36] The rapid expansion of grain production in the Midwest, where farms more easily attained the "threshold acreage" required to make it profitable to harvest grain with a reaper-binder, was a powerful factor contributing to the rapid increase in labor productivity.[37]

In brief, the strategic factors that led to rapid increases in output and labor productivity in American agriculture were the interacting influence of the opening up of new lands and the availability of a wide range of increasingly sophisticated and efficient implements. Although the development of the internal combustion engine in the twentieth century greatly increased the energy that could be applied to farming, most of the basic principles embodied in farm equipment were evolved before mechanical power became available. Danhof notes that "in the 40 years following 1820 the technology of agriculture was revolutionized by the successful or more effective application of horsepower to every critical task in growing crops." This progress resulted from the ingenuity and persistence of numerous blacksmiths, mechanics, and tinkerers and from "the zeal of the widely scattered farmers who purchased the machines as they were offered and operated them under difficult conditions of poor design, awkward and crude construction, inadequate maintenance and repair facilities, and their own lack of familiarity with mechanical devices."[38]

The feedback between farmers and those who were designing and manufacturing farm equipment was of great importance in directing inventive activity toward meeting the most critical needs of farmers and in eliminating the defects of early models. Even at the present

HISTORICAL PATTERNS: ENGLAND, THE UNITED STATES, JAPAN 203

time much of the significant R&D work is performed by small, local machine shops, working closely with farmers. The large machinery manufacturers devote substantial resources to R&D, but the small firms working with more direct feedback from farmers tend to have an advantage in evolving new designs. Thus many of the products which are mass produced by large corporations such as John Deere or International Harvester are based on designs and models produced by a small machine shop which then sells the rights to the product to one of the large corporations interested in initiating large-scale production.

As a result of the combined effects of strong commercial demand for farm products, abundant land, and rapid decline in the relative and (from 1910) absolute size of the farm population, there was a growing need to economize on the time required for performing farm operations. This need was intensified when timeliness was critical, but it derived more fundamentally from the economic pressure to reduce labor inputs per unit of output.

In large measure the mechanical innovations that have progressively changed the character of American agriculture were evolved in response to emerging problems and opportunities and changing cost-price relationships. In particular, the steady progress in improving farm machinery represented a response to a situation characterized by the increasing scarcity and rising cost of labor.

The pattern of development in the United States was probably less unimodal than in Japan, where the rice-based agricultural economy is relatively homogeneous and the size of operational units clustered around the median size of about 2.5 acres. Even in the American Midwest where egalitarianism has been a conspicuous feature of the rural economy, there have been large variations in the size, progressiveness, and profitability of farm units. Nevertheless in most agricultural regions in the United States the concurrent changes in the country's economic structure and in the capacity of farm equipment led primarily to an increase in the average size of farm units without any marked change away from the dominant position of the "family farm." Until recently large corporate farms were confined mainly to California and Florida. In the period since World War II, however, there has been a marked increase in the importance of corporate farming. It appears, however, that with the exception of certain enterprises such as poultry production for which scale economies have become significant, this trend has been induced primarily by governmental policies that have increased the attractiveness of corporate investments in farming as a "tax shelter" or for similar reasons.[39]

The American South, where the plantation system and the institution of slavery left a strong imprint, represents the principal exception to the progressive modernization of United States agriculture characterized by an essentially unimodal expansion path. World War II marked the end of a long period of stagnation. Because of a combination of forces, including rapid transfer of technologies from other regions, the pace of technical and economic change in the South during the past quarter-century has been more rapid than in the rest of the country. In 1945 only 14 per cent of the farms in the South had adopted tractors, compared with 56 per cent in the North, but the gap had narrowed considerably in 1964 when the percentages were 66 and 80 per cent, respectively.[40] Introduction of tractors in the Mississippi Delta has been followed by mechanical cotton pickers and chemical herbicides with the result that the rural labor force has been reduced drastically.

An analysis of the "demise of the sharecropper" in the Mississippi Delta by Richard Day provides valuable insights concerning the likely impact of farm mechanization in the less-developed economies.[41] Of particular interest is the way in which the adoption of new technologies had very different effects on the demand for labor during the period 1940-49 as compared to 1949-57. In the earlier period the off-farm demand for labor increased sharply, and in the immediate postwar era the increase in cotton acreage raised the derived demand for labor about as fast as labor-saving techniques reduced it. In the initial stage of mechanization, tractors replaced mules in land preparation, but mules were still used for interrow cultivation, and picking of cotton and corn was by hand. In the next stage there was complete mechanization of preharvest operations except some handweeding of cotton and maize, and except for handpicking of cotton, harvest operations were completely mechanized. In the third stage, mechanical cotton pickers were adopted, and the cropping pattern became less labor-intensive, for example, in the substitution of soybeans for cotton and maize.

Those different stages of mechanization differed not only in their effects on the total demand for labor but also in the seasonal pattern of labor demand. The chief effect of initial stages of technical change was to push sharecroppers off the farm but not out of the region. The seasonal peak labor demands were actually increased, but the sharecropping system was no longer attractive to landowners. The outcome was "a push of sharecroppers off the farm itself (where they had to be maintained year around) to the village (where they provided a conveniently located labor pool that could be inexpensively transported to surrounding plantations and farms)."[42] When the final stage of mechanization was reached, with extensive use of cotton pickers and chemical weed control, the forces pushing labor out of agriculture and the region became very powerful, this is indicated on an annual basis by Day's estimates of labor input requirements for cotton. Between 1940 and 1949 the labor input per unit of output declined from 33.5 to 19.4 hours per hundredweight; but by 1957 only 2.4 hours of labor were required per hundredweight of cotton. The changes associated with the final stage of mechanization were especially significant in eliminating the seasonal peak in labor requirements which had been accentuated, mainly because heavier use of fertilizer had increased cotton yields and the per-acre labor requirements for picking.

The decline in the Delta's farm population between 1940 and 1950 was moderate. Between 1950 and 1960 there was a 54 per cent reduction, and it appears that the really sharp reduction in farm labor inputs began in 1964.[43] On many farms in the Delta advanced technologies had not been adopted by 1960 even though they had become highly profitable to farm operators. It appears that the Freedom Summer of 1964, and other changes set in motion by the Civil Rights

Movement, had the effect of accelerating the adoption of labor-displacing innovations. These changes presumably raised the cost of hiring farm labor as *perceived* by the farm operator above the actual cost as determined by the prevailing wage rate and also weakened the force of noneconomic considerations that had previously slowed the rate of adoption.[44]

Considering the size and absorptive capacity of the nonfarm sector in the United States, one might have expected the workers displaced by farm mechanization in the South to have been easily absorbed in alternative, higher-productivity employment. Nevertheless, most observers believe that the rapid exodus of farm laborers and their families from the South has been an important factor contributing to recent problems of unemployment and unrest in urban areas. The problems of absorbing these uprooted families were accentuated, however, because most of them were black and were at a disadvantage because of poor education and racial discrimination.

The exceptionally rapid pace of agricultural change in the Delta during this recent period was possible because of the technological backlog available. Many of the biological-chemical innovations such as the use of weedicides had been worked out elsewhere. Even though some of the mechanical innovations had to be adapted to the special problems of the Delta, the techniques that had been evolved from purposive R&D activity by private firms and by public institutions had greatly reduced the time required for the research and development process.

It is of interest to contrast that instance of accelerated regional development in the post-1940 period with the much slower, more empirical process that changed the character of United States agriculture during the nineteenth and early twentieth centuries. On the basis of his extensive research on technological change in American agriculture, William Parker has observed that:

On close examination, most improvement before 1910 turns out to be either a market-induced diffusion of practices long in existence or a market selection out of countless rather blind experiments engaged in by the producers themselves. The technology for achieving technical change remained what it had been over most of the world's history—an evolutionary process proceeding with great loss and waste, and subject to accelerations in rate and slight changes in direction without change in essential character, under changes in the natural or economic environment. An increase in the rate of improvement in the nineteenth century was not due to any sharp improvement in the art of acquiring new knowledge.[45]

And in the final section of this chapter we will find that in the four decades between 1880 and 1920 the substantial increase in farm output in the United States was associated with an almost equally large increase in total farm inputs.

AGRICULTURAL DEVELOPMENT AND ECONOMIC GROWTH IN JAPAN

It has already been noted that yield-increasing innovations were far more important in Japan than in the United States. And they became important much earlier. There was a brief time during the early years of the Meiji period (1868-1912) when efforts were made to introduce farm equipment which had been developed in the United States and in England. Because this equipment had been designed to meet the needs of agricultural economies characterized by drastically different man/land ratios and much larger fields than prevailed in Japan that attempt was a failure. Only in Hokkaido, with its relatively sparse population, did the imported equipment find a place.

Research and Technical Innovations

In their pragmatic and farsighted approach to problems of agricultural development, Japan's leaders recognized the inappropriateness of mechanical innovations developed in countries with factor endowments that differed so greatly from conditions in Japan. Attention was then shifted to generating an early precursor of the "seed-fertilizer revolution." Max Fesca, who worked in Japan from 1882 to 1895, and other German advisors brought knowledge of Liebig's pioneering work on plant nutrition. This was only one of many areas in which agricultural science in Japan benefited from the accumulating body of scientific knowledge in Europe and the United States, but it was of special significance. Although the international transfer of technology played a greater role in Japan than in the United States, it should be kept in mind that the new technologies that evolved were tailored to Japanese conditions and the outcome was a distinctive synthesis aptly described as the "Meiji Technology."

Much of the early success in raising yields and factor productivity in Japan was based on increasingly wide diffusion of relatively high-yielding, fertilizer-responsive varieties and simple improvements in cultivation techniques that had been evolved by progressive and experimentally minded farmers during the course of many decades preceding Japan's period of modern economic growth. Severe restrictions on internal movement and communication between prefectures during the Tokugawa period had limited the spread of these improved varieties and techniques. When the Tokugawa rule was brought to an end by the Meiji Restoration, those feudal restrictions were removed and purposeful government action was initiated to facilitate the diffusion process. Under those circumstances it proved possible to increase crop yields substantially as a result of the spread of known techniques and varieties throughout the country. Rapidly expanded use of commercial fertilizers began as early as 1880.[46] From roughly the same date there appears to have been an increase in land improvement activity—mainly small-scale projects aimed at improving water control by realigning paddy fields and irrigation channels and providing drainage for individual fields. Inasmuch as this type of investment is underreported in the official statistics used in estimating changes in inputs, a part of the "unexplained" increases in farm output during the Meiji period is accounted for by these significant but unrecorded investments in the agricultural infrastructure.

It is not altogether clear how early in the Meiji period organized agricultural research began to have a substantial influence on farm productivity and output in Japan. Parker's observation that the "increase in the rate of improvement in the nineteenth century was not due to any sharp improvement in the art of acquiring new knowledge" may have been as applicable to Japan as to the United States. The evidence seems to suggest that from about 1880 an increased emphasis on research and the development of problem-solving capabilities began to have a considerable influence on the level of productivity in Japanese agriculture. The work on fertilizer requirements and practices, initiated with the "technical assistance" of a few German scientists, was probably the first significant development.

An interesting example of an early innovation was the technique of placing rice in salt water to separate sound from immature seed, which was devised in 1882 by Tokitaka Yokoi, the Director of the Fukuoka Agricultural Experiment Station. Not only was this a simple device but it was essentially a refinement of a practice that Yokoi had observed among a few innovative farmers. The example illustrates the way in which intimate knowledge of the best of traditional methods was the starting point for research in this early period and also the emphasis on improvements in the cultivation of rice, the country's dominant crop. Efforts were made to determine the most efficient techniques for raising seedlings in nursery beds, for plowing and preparing paddy fields for transplanting, for weeding, and for applying irrigation water. Determining optimum rates and techniques of fertilizer application and changes in plant population required to take advantage of higher levels of soil fertility also received major attention.

Simple mechanical innovations were important both in easing labor bottlenecks and in permitting certain operations to be performed more efficiently. The introduction in 1892 of a rotary cultivator-weeder pushed by hand, in combination with the planting of seedlings in rows lengthwise and crosswise, reduced the time required for effective weed control. The introduction a few years later of the rotary foot-pedal thresher reduced the seasonal labor peak at harvesting time, and the introduction of an improved, short-soled plow facilitated deeper plowing that was important in realizing the yield potential of the new varieties and high levels of fertilizer application.[47]

Research staff at the prefectural experiment stations were responsible for directing the extension activities of the agricultural associations which helped to insure that the research was relevant and widely applied. The research techniques available were, of course, quite primitive compared, for example, with the capabilities of modern plant breeders working in a team with geneticists, entomologists, pathologists, soil scientists, and other specialists. Yet impressive results were achieved because the strategy of concentrating efforts on fostering an efficient "fertilizer-consuming rice culture" was appropriate to the nation's factor endowment.

The contributions of research and technical innovations to the spectacular increases in output and productivity in Japan's silk industry merit special attention. The 17-fold increase in output of raw silk between the 1880s and the 1930s was more than twice the increase in cocoon production which in turn was nearly twice as large as the expansion in area planted to mulberry trees. Between 1880 and 1910 the increase in cocoon production was only a little larger than the increase in mulberry area, although even during that period the growth in silk output was appreciably larger than the increase in cocoon production. Basic discoveries made in 1909 at the Tokyo Imperial University led to the development of hybrids between Chinese and Japanese races of silkworms which were more vigorous, less susceptible to disease, and spun larger cocoons. The yield of raw silk per metric ton of cocoons rose from about 75 kilograms to nearly 140 kilograms between 1908-12 and 1938-42.

At the same time, better cultural practices and higher rates of fertilization led to heavier production of mulberry leaves, and their feeding value was augmented by better methods of handling the leaves. Progress was also realized in the techniques of hatching the silkworm eggs and in rearing the silkworms. The development of techniques for hatching the eggs artificially was especially significant because this made possible an autumn crop of cocoons which became almost as important as the spring crop. This innovation appears to have been a major factor responsible for the 60 per cent increase in cocoon production between 1911-20 and 1931-40 that was associated with an increase in mulberry acreage of less than 25 per cent. The even more striking increase of nearly 150 per cent in the output of raw silk during the same period owed much to increased specialization and efficiency in producing silkworm eggs, organizational innovations such as the introduction of forward purchasing contracts between large silk breeders and individual farmers or associations of sericulturists, and other measures that led to increased efficiency of well over a million farm households engaged in rearing silkworms and in producing cocoons of standardized quality.

These increases in productivity in Japan's sericulture industry were particularly significant because of the strategic importance of silk and silk products in earning foreign exchange to finance the imports of machinery and raw materials that were essential to the country's development. Between 1868 and 1930 the share of silk and silk fabrics in total merchandise exports averaged 42 per cent; and the share was nearly 46 per cent during the final five-year period.[48] In fact, these figures somewhat understate the importance of sericulture as an earner of foreign exchange. Silk and silk products, together with tea which was a relatively minor export item except in the early years of Meiji, were produced almost entirely with indigenous resources whereas cotton textiles and other major exports required sizable imports of raw materials so that their net contribution to foreign exchange availability was less than their share in export proceeds.

Not surprisingly, the rapid expansion in the volume of exports of silk and silk products was associated with a considerable decline in the barter terms of trade. The movement in the single-factoral terms of trade was, however, much more favorable because of the rapid increase in productivity. The impressive rate of technical advance in the sericulture industry sustained the profitability of silk production until competition with nylon and the emergence of more profitable alternatives in Japanese agriculture finally led to the decline of the industry. Although reliance on silk exports was subject to the usual disadvantages of primary exports, it is extremely doubtful whether Japan's indigenous resources could have been employed in an alternative way to generate a comparable expansion of foreign exchange proceeds during the 60-year period ending in 1930.

Agriculture's Role in Development

The development of Japanese agriculture—most notably between the Meiji Restoration of 1868 and World War I—was a potent force in propelling the overall development of the economy. There seems to be general agreement that three features of the "Japanese model" are especially significant. First, agricultural output was increased within the framework of the existing small-scale farming system. Second, the bulk of the nation's farmers were involved in increases in agricultural productivity. Thus the growth of output was characterized by substantial increases in factor productivity because widespread adoption of technical innovations and new inputs enhanced the efficiency of the on-farm resources of labor and land.

Third, agricultural and industrial development went forward together in a process of "concurrent" growth, and the various interactions between agriculture and nonagriculture had profound implications for growth in both sectors. Expansion in the nonagricultural sectors has, of course, been considerably more rapid than expansion in agriculture so that the overwhelmingly agricultural structure of the economy has been transformed.

The fact that agricultural output was increased with very small demands on the critically scarce resources of capital and foreign exchange was clearly of strategic importance in making possible a substantial increase in savings and investment available for industrial expansion. Most students of economic development in Japan have stressed agriculture's role in financing investments in infrastructure and in the new manufacturing, commercial, and transport enterprises which became dominant elements in the Japanese economy. Thomas C. Smith has observed that:

If funds cannot be had from foreign sources, they must be taken from the domestic economy—which in most cases means agriculture: thus the ability to modernize comes to depend largely on the productivity of agri-

HISTORICAL PATTERNS: ENGLAND, THE UNITED STATES, JAPAN 213

culture and the willingness of the peasantry to part with current income for distant and half-understood goals.[49]

Some may question the "willingness" of Japan's peasantry to part with their current income. Particularly in the earlier decades of the country's modern economic growth, taxation of the agricultural sector represented the principal mechanism by which resources were transferred from agriculture to the more rapidly growing sectors of the economy. Agriculture's share of government tax revenue was approximately 85 per cent during the years 1888-92 and still accounted for some 40 per cent in 1918-22.[50]

It is apparent that agriculture's contribution was significant even if we confine our attention to government flows. Investment by the government represented about 30 per cent of gross domestic fixed capital formation during the extended period from 1887 to 1936; and that figure excludes military investment. The government's investment outlays were mainly devoted to extending and improving the rail network, establishing "model" factories, subsidizing the creation of a merchant marine; and the reverse flow of government funds to agriculture was extremely limited.

It is not possible to trace the intersectoral flows of capital through private channels in Japan, but it seems clear that there was a net outflow. Studies of rural financial institutions and investment patterns during the Meiji period indicate that savings by agricultural landowners were substantial and that they played a major role in establishing and operating financial institutions and in launching many of the small-scale factories that were a conspicuous feature of rural Japan. Evidence of a net outflow of private funds from agriculture is also provided by studies which show that the deposits of farmers in cooperative banks and other financial institutions were in aggregate much larger than the sums borrowed by farmers.[51]

Retarded Growth, 1920-40

This summary account has stressed the favorable features of the development strategy pursued in Japan. It is instructive, however, to consider the period between 1920 and 1940 when agricultural progress and economic transformation were seriously retarded. During the 1920s, especially, the rate of increase in agricultural output was slow in comparison with earlier decades, and there was a sharp reduction in the rate of increase in total factor productivity in the 1930s as well as in the 1920s.[52]

This picture of relative stagnation also applies to the rate of change of labor productivity in agriculture. By 1920 considerable structural transformation had taken place, and the nonagricultural labor force was nearly as large as the farm labor force. Because the nonfarm sectors weighed much more heavily by 1920—48 per cent of the total compared to only about 25 per cent in the 1880s—the agricultural work force would have begun to decline in absolute size during the 1920s if the growth of nonfarm employment had continued at the rapid rates that prevailed during the earlier decades. In fact, as was noted earlier, the effect of the increased weight of nonfarm employment in the labor force was offset by marked retardation in the growth of employment opportunities outside agriculture. The decline in the increase in nonfarm employment was from a rate of 2.9 per cent in the decades prior to 1920 to a rate of 1.8 per cent during the 1920-40 period; and much of the increase in the off-farm labor force was in "self-employment" in low-productivity service activities. (See Appendix Table II.)

To understand the reasons for the slow growth of agricultural labor productivity after 1920 it is necessary to consider two sets of factors—those that were responsible for the slow growth of farm output and those that limited the contraction in the farm labor force. The most obvious factor limiting the growth of demand for farm output in Japan was the expansion of food imports from Taiwan and Korea which satisfied most of the increase in demand after 1920. High prices, which provoked the so-called "rice riots" at the end of the First World War, gave rise to concern about the country's "food problem" and led to the adoption of government policies aimed at holding down the price of rice. Vigorous and effective measures were launched in Taiwan and Korea to expand rice production and exports to Japan with the result that the "food problem" quickly gave way to an "agricultural problem"—concern with the low prices and depressed economic conditions affecting Japanese agriculture. The price of rice declined at an average annual rate of 2 per cent between 1920 and 1935 and domestic production grew at a rate of only .4 per cent, so farm cash receipts from this major crop obviously declined.[53]

The growth of domestic demand for agricultural products was remarkably slow for a country with the low levels of per capita income that still prevailed during the 1920s and 1930s; the elasticity of demand for food with respect to income was actually considerably higher in the 1950s even though per capita income had risen substantially—about .5 to .6 compared with .3 or .4 between 1922 and 1940 and also between 1878 and 1922.[54] This sluggish increase in effective demand for agricultural products was probably mainly due to a traditional diet—with rice as the "staple food" and other items as "side dishes"—that to some extent restricted marginal changes in the pattern of food consumption and therefore delayed a shift in the direction of a more costly "Western" diet characterized by increased consumption of expensive items such as meat and dairy products.

Although the prevailing ideas and motivations were very different, there seem to have been certain similarities between Japan's economic policies and their effects during the 1920s and the beginning of the 1930s and the contemporary situation in many developing countries. Specifically, Japan's exchange rate was consistently overvalued during the 1920-32 period. At the end of the First World War Japan found itself with large foreign exchange balances and gold reserves—and an inflated cost, price, and debt structure. A major policy objective of the nation's financial authorities was to return to the Gold Standard with the yen at prewar parity with the dollar and the pound sterling. To achieve that objective, finally realized in January 1930, the yen was pegged at a rate higher than its equilibrium price and deflationary policies were applied during most of the decade of the 1920s. To overcome the adverse effects of the overvaluation on the competitive position of Japanese exports, both industry and government adopted policies aimed at the "rationalization" of industry, including emphasis on concentrating production in larger and more capital-intensive enterprises.

It has been argued that in spite of the abundance of cheap labor, the industrial sector was forced to adopt relatively capital-intensive techniques because of rigidities in the technical coefficients in industry and the need "to cope with severe international competition."[55] It seems likely, however, that the emphasis on capital-intensive technologies, and the accentuated dualism in Japanese industry which became marked in that period, was carried to excess because of the persistence of an overvalued exchange rate and the pursuit of deflationary policies.

It appears that the expansion of nonfarm employment was slowed as the result of changes in both the level and the character of investment. Henry Rosovsky's estimates indicate that gross investment declined from 20 per cent to 14.5 per cent of net national product between 1920 and 1930; and the decline in private investment was even more pronounced because the share of government in total investment showed a marked increase.[56] This was mainly a result of the large outlays for reconstruction following the 1923 earthquake, expenditures which did not create continuing job opportunities.

A considerable increase in the concentration of capital formation in large-scale, capital-intensive firms was at least equally important in reducing the rate of expansion of new job opportunities. To emphasize the range of variation that characterizes Japanese industry, Kazushi Ohkawa has suggested that a distinction be made between a "modern" sector comprising large-scale, capital-intensive firms paying relatively high wages and a "semi-modern" industrial sector made up of small- and medium-scale firms, using substantially less capital per worker, and paying wages only a little above earnings in the agricultural sector.[57] It appears that expansion during the 1920s and 1930s was concentrated excessively in the capital-intensive modern sector.

An alternative and probably more satisfactory way of describing

HISTORICAL PATTERNS: ENGLAND, THE UNITED STATES, JAPAN 217

this change in the pattern of capital formation is to say that investment and expansion in the semimodern sector was unduly depressed because the deflationary policies during the 1920-31 period mainly affected the growth of firms in that sector. In Japan the banking system has played a dominant role as a source of finance for industry. Hence, because of the close links between the banks controlled by the Zaibatsu—the large financial-industrial conglomerates such at Mitsui and Mitsubishi—and firms in the "modern" sector of industry, it can probably be assumed that those enterprises fared well in the rationing of available credit whereas firms in the "semimodern" sector bore the brunt of the tight money policies. W. W. Lockwood reports that because of the bank failures and mergers of the 1920s, the smaller firms became increasingly dependent on the big financial institutions which were closely affiliated with the large industrial concerns. He further suggests that this gave the large firms a financial advantage that was often decisive, and the centralized control over the supply of loanable funds by big business and government meant that the smaller firms were confronted with a dearth of credit and very high interest rates.[58]

Thus the impact of the slowing down of the overall rate of investment and growth was felt mostly by those branches of industry that were labor intensive and which might otherwise have offered a major outlet for surplus farm labor and mitigated the financial hardship, unrest, and social tension that prevailed in rural Japan during the 1920s and 1930s. Studies of the emergence of extremist groups in the 1920s and 1930s suggest that there was probably an important relationship between this damming up of population in the countryside and the successful seizure of power by the militarist clique that carried Japan into the disastrous adventures that began with the invasion of Manchuria in 1931 and ended with the nation's defeat in World War II.[59] Needless to say, a great many other factors were also important. Even confining our attention to economic factors, reference should be made to the unimpressive expansion of world trade during the 1920s and the adverse effects of economic policies of the major European powers and the United States. The barriers erected against

Japan's economic expansion were certainly important influences contributing to the seizure of power by leaders advocating military expansion and creation of a Japanese-dominated Co-Prosperity Sphere in Asia.

Although various external influences were certainly important, there seems to be considerable justification for stressing the role of national economic policies. The remarkably rapid rates of growth of output and of industrial employment that Japan achieved in the 1950s and 1960s seem to support the view that the process of structural transformation and the rates of growth of industrial output and employment were retarded to an unnecessary and undesirable extent in the 1920s and the early 1930s. And the adverse effects on Japan's economic growth during the interwar period resulting from an overvalued currency, deflationary policies, and credit rationing, all of which restricted primarily the expansion of the smaller and more labor-intensive firms, would seem to have some relevance to contemporary less-developed countries.

Agriculture and the Postwar Turning Point

The rapid pace of change in Japan's economic structure in the postwar period has led both directly and indirectly to noteworthy changes in the country's agriculture and its agricultural policies. That the mid-1950s marked a significant "turning point" in Japan's economic history is beyond dispute. This was not only a "structural transformation turning point" in the simple sense that it marked the beginning of rapid decline in the absolute size of the farm labor force; it was also marked by an upward shift in the marginal productivity of labor and of real wages in agriculture and by a sharp decline in the elasticity of supply of labor to the nonfarm sectors.[60]

Two government measures have had a strong impact on agriculture in the postwar period so that the observed changes in Japan's agricultural economy are not a simple consequence of accelerated economic growth and structural transformation. The postwar Land Reform, carried out in response to a directive of the Allied Occupation Headquarters but with considerable support from Japanese who believed that such a reform was overdue, has had highly significant economic and political consequences. The most apparent results, which stemmed from the fact that former tenants no longer had to make large rental payments, were a positive effect on farmer incentives and increased purchasing power among the mass of the rural population. The second measure of agricultural policy that has represented a new departure in the postwar period has been the maintenance of the price of rice at a level well above world prices as a device to support farm incomes.

The most notable change affecting agricultural production directly has been the rapid spread of power tillers of good design adapted to the small farms and even smaller plots that characterize Japanese agriculture. Between 1955 and 1959 the number of power tillers in use increased from 89,000 to 514,000. Their number reached a million in 1961 and 2.5 million in 1965.[61] More recently there has also been a rapid spread in the use of small mechanical reapers and considerable adoption of simple machines that reduce labor requirements in transplanting rice.

Rapid decline in the farm labor force has been associated with a tremendous expansion of part-time farming. This phenomenon had expanded considerably in the late 1930s as the beginning of the war economy increased the availability of nonfarm employment for members of farm households. But as a result of the enormous postwar increase in off-farm job opportunities within commuting distance, this practice has spread and become a highly significant feature of the rural economy. In fact, as early as 1964 the off-farm income accruing to members of farm households exceeded their income from agriculture. Because of the spread of power tillers and other types of labor-saving equipment, together with continuing progress in developing and applying yield-increasing innovations, a declining number of farm households was able to achieve rapid growth of agricultural production even though nearly half of the "labor time" of farm households was devoted to off-farm occupations.[62]

The new and complex issues of agricultural policy that Japan is now facing are the problems of a developed economy and need not be considered in detail here. It should be noted, however, that the recent policies which led to a sharp rise in the price of rice represented a reversal of a policy that had been followed throughout Japan's era of modern economic growth, that is, preventing any significant increase in the price of this major wage good. Yujiro Hayami emphasizes that the policy shift in the 1960s reflected the fundamental economic changes in the postwar economy—the virtual trebling of per capita income in a decade and transformation of the country's industrial structure with a marked rise in capital intensity.[63] As a result wages and the cost of living have become much less critical factors affecting the competitive power of Japanese industry. Rice, which still accounted for more than 10 per cent of total consumer expenditure in households of urban workers in 1959, dropped to 4.3 per cent of the total in 1969 in spite of the fact that the agricultural price index increased during the 1960s by about 80 per cent against a 2 per cent increase in manufacturing prices.[64]

The rapid increase in the price of rice, together with the rapid increase of off-farm income of members of farm households, achieved the objective of maintaining parity between farm and urban incomes —but at a heavy cost. By the end of the decade, costly surplus stocks of some eight million tons of rice had been accumulated. And the high price of rice, roughly three times the world price, encouraged inefficient resource allocation in agriculture and discouraged the reduction in the number of farm households and the reorganization of agricultural production. Similarly, as has been emphasized by Kazushi Ohkawa and Shigeto Kawano, the effect of the Land Reform in establishing a rigid structure of small-scale units has now become a negative factor impeding required adjustments.[65] Japan at long last is confronted with the need and opportunity to move toward a pattern of agricultural production based on larger units in order to make efficient use of more powerful tractors and associated equipment and thereby realize the economies of scale which become important with the use of capital-intensive technologies. The fact that Japan *now* has this opportunity is due in no small measure, however, to the fact that the country's development was served so well by increasingly productive small-scale farm units that are only now becoming inappropriate for a modern, industrial economy.

INCREASES IN PRODUCTIVITY IN THE UNITED STATES AND JAPAN: SIMILARITIES AND CONTRASTS

Considering the similarity in the growth of farm output and productivity in the United States and Japan over the entire period from 1880 to 1960, the contrast between the performance of the countries during the first half and the second half of the period is truly remarkable. The following tabulation repeats the 1880 and 1960 figures for output expansion in the two countries, and it also shows the index numbers for output in the 1920s along with the figures that summarize the rates of increase in inputs and in total factor productivity.[66]

Output, inputs, and productivity in the United States and Japan, 1880, 1920, and 1960

	United States			Japan		
	1880	1920	1960	1880	1920	1960
Output (net of seed and feed)	100	180	340	100	232	358
Total inputs	100	172	190	100	119	156
Total productivity (output per unit of total inputs)	100	105	179	100	195	229

It is apparent that the rate of growth of output in Japan was considerably more rapid during the four decades between 1880 and 1920 whereas the increase in use of inputs during that period was much more rapid in the United States. But during the next four decades the picture is reversed.

The contrasting patterns of growth of output and in the use of inputs naturally has a magnified effect on the changes in total factor productivity in the two countries. Thus we see that in Japan factor productivity virtually doubled between 1880 and 1920 whereas, according to the Hayami-Ruttan calculations, factor productivity in

United States agriculture increased by only 5 per cent during the 40-year period. Conversely, during the next four decades a 70 per cent increase in factor productivity explains a major part of the expansion of output in the United States whereas in Japan the increases in use of inputs was not much less than the growth of output and the increase in factor productivity was only 17 per cent.

It is likely that the actual increase in factor productivity in the United States between 1880 and 1920 was somewhat more than the 5 per cent indicated by the calculations presented above.[67] It seems clear, however, that the large increase in agricultural production in the United States between 1880 and 1920 was associated with similarly large increases in the labor force, land area, and capital inputs utilized in the production process.

It is not easy to identify with confidence the reasons for this marked contrast between the United States and Japan in the extent to which increased production between 1880 and 1920 resulted from increases in factor productivity. But the sharp contrast between the two countries in the relative importance of yield increases and expansion of crop area appears to be a significant factor. In the United States the arable land area increased 2.5 times between 1880 and 1920 whereas output per hectare of arable land declined; but in Japan the acreage increase was only 26 per cent whereas yields rose by 84 per cent. This contrast in yield trends was obviously influenced by the predominance of rainfed agriculture in the United States and by shifts in crop acreage to areas of lower rainfall; but subsequent experience has demonstrated that those were not the only relevant factors.

The presumption that the great importance of increases in factor productivity in Japan during those decades was related to the differing emphasis on yield-increasing innovations is strengthened by the experience of both countries between 1940 and 1960. Agricultural production in Japan fell drastically during World War II, the sharply reduced availability of chemical fertilizers being a major causal factor. By the late 1940s, however, fertilizer consumption in Japanese agriculture began to rise above the high levels reached in the prewar period, and the effects of higher levels of soil fertility were reinforced by new advances in varietal selection and in farming techniques associated with the availability of much more effective chemicals for pest control and also new inputs of industrial origin, notably power tillers and vinyl sheeting for nursery beds.

In the United States, World War II acted as a stimulus to increases in agricultural output and especially increases in productivity. The fact that farm output increased at an annual average rate of 1.9 per cent between 1940 and 1960, when the rate of increase in total inputs was a mere .2 per cent, must be attributed to a complex of interacting factors that led to increases in output and reductions in some resource inputs. General buoyancy in economic conditions enabled the large nonfarm sector to absorb the workers who were moving out of agriculture at an unprecedented rate—an average decline in the farm labor force of 2.9 per cent per year over the two decades. There was even a slight decrease in the arable land area, probably to be attributed mainly to acreage limitations associated with farm price support programs.

Another striking change, already evident in the 1920-40 period, was that American agriculture's long history of steady or declining crop yields had given way to a period characterized by substantial increases in per-acre yields. Whereas output per acre had registered a decline of just over 1 per cent per year during the first two decades of the century, there was an average yield increase of 1.4 per cent between 1920 and 1940 and a still higher rate of 2.1 per cent between 1940 and 1960. In view of the dominant position of maize production in American agriculture, there can be no doubt that the introduction of hybrid maize and the rapid expansion in fertilizer use that began in the mid-1930s were major factors responsible for this upsurge in crop yields.

Thus biological and chemical inputs began to exert a major influence on crop yields in the United States at a much later date than in Japan. In Japan the acute shortage of land suitable for agriculture and the density of the farm population meant that relative factor prices, and the very limited scope that existed for acreage expansion, induced farmers and policy-makers to emphasize yield-increasing innovations from an early period. In contrast, the pressure to raise crop yields in the United States was much less. Public policy and the concerns of farmers were directed mainly at expanding the cultivated area and particularly the acreage per farm worker. Furthermore, plant breeding strategies in the United States during the earlier period were for the most part not very effective. The major emphasis was on protective research, for example in developing rust-resistant varieties of wheat to maintain yields when existing varieties lost their resistance or when new strains of rust appeared; and relatively little attention was given to varietal crosses or hybridization aimed at the development of fertilizer-responsive varieties. The success of "horizontal expansion" based on advances in mechanical technology coupled with the attitudes of farmers and the relatively slow development of scientific research of high caliber at the land-grant institutions contributed to this comparative neglect of yield-increasing innovations in the United States until the 1930s.

The contrasts between Japan and the United States in the relative importance of biological and chemical innovations as compared to mechanical innovations is mirrored in the contrasting patterns of change in the use of farm inputs. (See Figure 5.2.) As early as 1920 tractors in the United States began to significantly augment the draft power provided by horses, and by 1930 the tractor horsepower on farms had slightly exceeded the number of horses and other work animals. But in Japan tractor power was negligible until 1955; there was a slight increase in the number of draft animals which continued until 1955, but the number of horses and bullocks per male worker never exceeded .5. Consequently, the availability of power per worker in the United States was much greater even before the enormous expansion of petroleum-based energy with the spread of tractors.

The earlier expansion in the use of fertilizers in Japan is equally apparent (Figure 5.2). Between 1940 and 1950 fertilizer consumption per hectare of cropped land in the United States rose from 11 to 25 kilograms of plant nutrients. But even the 49 kilograms per

HISTORICAL PATTERNS: ENGLAND, THE UNITED STATES, JAPAN 225

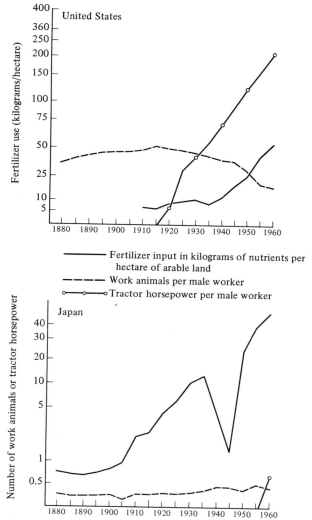

Figure 5.2 Fertilizer use per hectare and work animals and tractor horsepower per male worker, the United States and Japan, 1880-1960.

SOURCE: Data from Yujiro Hayami and Vernon W. Ruttan, *Agricultural Development: An International Perspective* (Baltimore and London, 1971), pp. 338-41.

hectare consumed in 1960 was only a little above the 45 kilograms per hectare used in Japan in 1915 and was less than one-fifth of the 272 kilograms of nutrients per hectare of arable land consumed in 1960.

Parallel Advances in Manufacturing Productivity

It is high time to emphasize that the expansion of farm output and productivity in these countries depended to a large and increasing extent on parallel advances in productivity in their manufacturing sectors which lowered the cost and raised the efficiency of farm inputs of industrial origin. The significance of the parallel advances in productivity in agriculture and in industries producing farm inputs can be summarized concisely by examining changes in what, following Folke Dovring, can be termed "aggregate labor productivity." A common expectation is that a large reduction in "direct" labor inputs, applied at the farm level, will be associated with a substantial increase in "indirect" labor inputs used in the manufacture of inputs purchased by farmers. There are formidable statistical problems in calculating those "indirect" labor inputs, but the evidence available for the United States and Japan suggests that the increase has been extremely small relative to the decline in "direct" labor inputs.

Estimates for the United States in terms of man-hours by W. F. Gossling, summarized in Table 5.3, indicate a decline between 1920 and 1930 in the "indirect" labor used in agricultural production and, in spite of a considerable increase between 1940 and 1960, the quantity of indirect labor embodied in agricultural inputs in 1960 was a little less than in 1920. However, figures published by Dovring using a somewhat different method indicate a modest increase in the indirect labor used for agricultural production from 1.5 million man years or somewhat more in 1920 to 2.0 million man years in 1960.[68] This increase of half a million man years or less was accompanied by a decline in the direct (on-farm) labor force from 10.8 to 6.0 million. (These are Lebergott's estimates reported in Appendix Table I;

HISTORICAL PATTERNS: ENGLAND, THE UNITED STATES, JAPAN 227

the decline was even greater according to Dovring's estimates in terms of labor inputs rather than labor force.)

Estimates for Japan also show a decline in indirect labor use between 1920 and 1930 and then a rise, with the level of 1960 slightly higher than prevailed in 1920.[69] Since commercial fertilizer was the principal external input in Japan, the sizable reduction in "indirect labor" between 1920 and 1930 was influenced mainly by significant advances in manufacturing technologies for chemical fertilizers which came to dominate fertilizer purchases during the 1920s. (See Table 5.3.) Inasmuch as the increase in farm output in the United States was associated with a sharper reduction in the farm labor force, it is not surprising that we find a much greater increase in "aggregate labor productivity"—260 per cent in the United States compared to an increase of not quite 60 per cent in the case of Japanese agriculture. In the 1955-60 period, when Japan's farm labor had begun to decline rapidly, the annual rate of growth of aggregate labor productivity was 4.9 per cent compared with a 6.2 per cent rate for the same period in the U.S. But over the four decades between 1920 and 1960 the U.S. rate was more than twice as high—3.3 per cent compared to an average of 1.5 per cent in Japan.

Factors Influencing the Agricultural Growth Paths in the United States and Japan

In both Japan and the United States governmental policies and programs, the decisions of individual farmers, and the activities of firms manufacturing farm inputs appear to have been well adapted to the underlying resource endowment and relative factor prices. The experience of the two countries thus provides considerable support for the Hayami-Ruttan "induced development model" which hypothesizes that changes in relative prices induce not only farmers and firms supplying inputs but also agricultural administrators and research scientists "to search for technical alternatives which save increasingly scarce factors of production."[70] They conclude their examination of the role of science and technology in Japan with the

Table 5.3 "Direct" and "indirect" labor inputs for agricultural production and aggregate labor productivity: United States and Japan, 1920-60

Year	United States				Japan			
	Direct labor	Indirect labor	Total labor	Aggregate labor[a] productivity ($1920=100$)	Direct labor	Indirect labor	Total labor	Aggregate labor[a] productivity ($1920=100$)
	(million man-hours)				(1,000 persons)			
1920	23,995	4,503	28,498	100.0	13,939	1,488	15,427	100.0
	(84.2)	(15.8)	(100.0)		(90.4)	(9.6)	(100.0)	
1930	22,921	3,124	26,045	112.9	13,944	937	14,881	114.3
	(88.0)	(12.0)	(100.0)		(93.7)	(6.3)	(100.0)	
1940	20,472	2,904	23,376	145.2	13,549	953	14,501	121.1
	(87.6)	(12.4)	(100.0)		(93.4)	(6.6)	(100.0)	
1950	15,137	4,391	19,528	209.7	15,250[b]	1,504[b]	16,754[b]	87.8[b]
	(77.5)	(22.5)	(100.0)		(90.0)	(9.0)	(100.0)	
1955	12,808	4,343	17,151	267.7	15,410	1,661	17,071	124.6
	(74.7)	(25.3)	(100.0)		(90.3)	(9.7)	(100.0)	
1960	9,825	4,203	14,028	361.3	13,390	1,516	14,905	158.4
	(70.0)	(30.0)	(100.0)		(89.8)	(10.2)	(100.0)	

a Calculated by dividing agricultural gross output by the total of "direct" and "indirect" labor hours. The productivity index is given by Gossling with 1957-59 as the base years.
b For 1951.

SOURCE: United States data for direct labor hours from United States Department of Agriculture, *Changes in Farm Production and Efficiency*, Economic Research Service, Statistical Bulletin No. 233 (Washington, D.C., 1964), Table 15, p. 33; indirect labor hours from W. F. Gossling, "A New Economic Model of Structural Change in U.S. Agriculture and Supporting Industries" (Ph.D. dissertation, University of Illinois, 1965), Appendix E, Table 2, p. 251. The estimates for Japan were calculated by Mr. Yoshimi Kuroda using estimates of direct labor (gainfully employed workers in agriculture) from Mataji Umemura et al., *Agriculture and Forestry*, Vol. 9, *Estimates of Long-Term Economic Statistics of Japan Since 1868*, edited by Kazushi Ohkawa, Miyohei Shinohara, and Mataji Umemura (Tokyo, 1966) on the assumption that indirect labor inputs used in the manufacture of agriculture's current inputs were in the same proportion of the nonfarm labor force as the percentage share of current farm inputs in nonfarm national product. A similar assumption of proportionality was used in calculating the labor inputs associated with the capital inputs used in agriculture.

assertion that the country was able to evolve the highly productive Meiji Technology because of "the dialectic interaction among farmers, scientists, and agricultural supply firms in response to relative factor prices which reflected Japan's resource endowments. . . ."[71]

Clearly, the strong emphasis on yield-increasing innovations in Japan was related to the scarcity and costliness of land. Whereas the price of land relative to the agricultural wage rate in the United States in 1960 was only a little over half the ratio in 1880, in Japan there was a twofold increase in the price of land relative to the price of labor over the 80-year period. And as a result of continuing advance in fertilizer manufacturing technologies, there was a far greater change in the land/fertilizer price ratio. During the half-century ending in 1930, there was a twelvefold increase in the price of arable land, but the price of fertilizers increased by only about 25 per cent.[72]

It is important to emphasize that prices were not seriously distorted in Japan so that price changes reflected underlying changes in the demand and supply of products and factors. It is also important that there was effective interaction among farmers, public research institutions, and agricultural supply firms. An interesting episode in Japan's economic development, reported by Hayami and Ruttan, suggests, however, that much more was involved than simply a response to changing prices:

> In the 1880's, under the depression due to the monetary reform by the Finance Minister Masayoshi Matsukata, there was strong agitation for the reduction of the newly established land tax, an essential revenue source for Japanese industrial development. At that time the *Nogakukai* (Agricultural Science Association) issued the *Konoronsaku* (A Treatise on the Strategy of Agricultural Development) in which they rejected the argument for a land tax reduction and advocated "more positive measures to develop agriculture such as agricultural schools, experiment stations, itinerate lectures, and agricultural societies" to reduce the burden of farmers. The establishment of the National Agricultural Experiment Station represented the response to this plea. In retrospect the policies advocated by the Agricultural Science Association were remarkably successful.[73]

HISTORICAL PATTERNS: ENGLAND, THE UNITED STATES, JAPAN 231

The decisions that were taken at that time required impressive foresight to initiate the "positive measures" needed to realize the potential that existed for relatively inexpensive gains in agricultural productivity. But why were the leaders in Meiji Japan able to make and effectively implement policy decisions which appear to have been so appropriate to the goal of economic development? And why was the response and performance on the part of the mass of the people so energetic?

There is a rich literature that throws light upon those questions.[74] It is sufficient for present purposes to note that Japan's policy makers were keenly aware of the need to implement a realistic set of policies in order "to secure first the independence and then the fullest possible economic and military development for their country."[75] Japan's first "development plan," a massive document entitled *Kōgyō Iken* or *Advice for the Encouragement of Industry* that was completed in 1884, recognized the importance of improving the functioning of the country's market economy. The Meiji leaders were aware that economic advance on a broad front was dependent on the decisions and energy of a large number of entrepreneurs, including some five million farm operators, and their response to product and factor prices. The development strategy set forth in *Kōgyō Iken* was based on careful study of the strengths and weaknesses of the economy and a recognition of the need to begin wherever possible with small-scale units employing techniques that did not represent a sharp departure from familiar modes of production and organization. There was also awareness of the advantages of fostering advances in productivity based on research and wide diffusion of new technical knowledge and new equipment or inputs. In their interesting analysis of this remarkable document, Ichirou Inukai and Orlon R. Tussing emphasize that "The planners understood that Japan had to become an industrial and military power by her own resources and that virtually her only resources were her indigenous industries and abundant labor. If development was to occur, it had to reflect the planning of the governing elite, but it was the people themselves who had to do the practical innovating and work."[76] In brief, and the evidence is by no means confined to this document, there was a probing analysis of the implications of different patterns of development and a conscious decision to implement what we have dubbed a unimodal agricultural strategy.

Experience in the United States may come closer to representing a "pure" case of the "induced development model." The activities of the inventors and manufacturers that produced a succession of mechanical innovations in the nineteenth century were obviously influenced by price signals which reflected the growing scarcity of farm labor, the availability of cheap land waiting to be brought into cultivation, and the growing commercial demand for farm products. And there was a large and steady decline in the price of farm machinery relative to the price of labor (interrupted only during the Depression of the 1930s when farm wage rates fell more sharply than the price of machinery).

It is also plausible to argue, as Hayami and Ruttan have done, that the somewhat belated emphasis in the United States on yield-increasing innovations beginning in the 1930s was influenced significantly by perceived changes in relative prices. The price of land began to rise at the turn of the century, and following World War I there was a marked upturn in the price of land and also in farm product prices. Over the same period, there were sizable increases in federal and state allocations in support of agricultural research. Although the Morrill Act which granted the states federal land to subsidize the establishment of colleges of "agricultural and mechanical arts" was enacted in 1862, funding for research was niggardly—less than $2.0 million in 1900 and still less than $15 million in 1920.[77] Clearly the major emphasis was on the "mechanical arts," an area dominated by the private sector; vigorous activity and substantial investments by individual inventors and firms were motivated by the profits to be realized from the development of improved items of farm equipment. For the biological arts, however, private R&D was of slight importance, largely because the gains from such research generally cannot be appropriated by the innovating firm. It was the state experiment stations, together with studies at the Carnegie Institution, that made the breakthroughs that provided the scientific basis for the breeding programs for hybrid maize in the 1920s which in the 1930s led to widespread commercial production of hybrid seed adapted to various localities. But the adoption of hybrid varieties by farmers and the doubling of the average yield of maize cannot be explained solely by the advances in plant breeding and seed production techniques. Since hitting a peak in 1920, fertilizer prices have declined almost continuously while the prices of farm products have risen moderately and the prices of farm land and farm wages have increased sharply[78]:

Product and input prices in United States agriculture

Year	All crops (Index: 1910-14 = 100)	Daily wage rate ($/day)	Value of arable land ($/ha.)	Fertilizer price ($/m. ton of nutrients)
1920	188	3.30	352	309
1930	105	2.15	247	202
1940	101	1.60	180	153
1950	249	4.50	389	202
1960	225	6.60	711	168

Clearly, relative prices had an important influence in Japan and in the United States in shaping their agricultural expansion paths. But it seems equally clear that for the contemporary late-developing countries, there is a wealth of supplementary evidence that needs to be consciously evaluated to supplement price signals as guidelines for the design of development strategies. In formulating the agricultural strategy that was implemented in Taiwan, Japanese officials in the newly acquired colony were undoubtedly guided by earlier success at home in accelerating technical advance in agriculture by a "seed-fertilizer revolution" supported by investments in water control. And surely the Rockefeller Foundation scientists that laid the groundwork for spectacular increases in wheat yields in Mexico during the 1950s and 1960s were influenced strongly by the demonstrated capacity of agricultural scientists to alter dramatically the production functions available to farmers.

NOTES

1. Official estimates of agricultural production were not instituted until 1884, although unofficial estimates by Lawes and Gilbert for wheat date from 1852. See J. A. Venn, "An Inquiry into British Methods of Crop Estimating," *Economic Journal* Vol. 36 (September 1926).
2. Lord Rowland E. P. Ernle, *English Farming Past and Present* (London, 1922), p. 210.
3. E. L. Jones, "Editor's Introduction," in *Agriculture and Economic Growth in England 1650-1815,* edited by E. L. Jones (London, 1967), p. 13.
4. The quoted phrase is from C. Peter Timmer, "The Turnip, the New Husbandry, and the English Agricultural Revolution," *Quarterly Journal of Economics* Vol. 83, No. 3 (August 1969), who provides an excellent summary of the "traditional" and "modern" views of England's agricultural revolution. See also Jones, "Editor's Introduction" and J. D. Chambers and G. E. Mingay, *The Agricultural Revolution 1750-1880* (London, 1966).
5. Ibid. p. 4.
6. See the contemporary account of James Caird, *English Agriculture in 1850-51* (London, 1852), p. 370; and also Ernle, *English Farming,* pp. 354-70; and W. H. R. Curtler, *A Short History of English Agriculture* (Oxford, 1909), pp. 271-88.
7. Yujiro Hayami and Vernon W. Ruttan, *Agricultural Development: An International Perspective* (Baltimore and London, 1971), p. 137.
8. Jones, "Editor's Introduction," p. 14.
9. Denmark is no doubt exceptional in the success achieved in fostering increased efficiency among small- and medium-scale farm units, but an examination of the impressive gains in farm output and productivity in Denmark between 1880 and 1920 certainly casts doubt on the view that large estates have any inherent efficiency advantage. See Bruce F. Johnston, "Agricultural Development and Economic Transformation: A Comparative Study of the Japanese Experience," *Food Research Institute Studies* Vol. 3, No. 3 (November 1962), pp. 259-65. In fact, Doreen Warriner states that "Denmark, by every standard of farming efficiency, has long headed the list of European countries." Doreen Warriner, *Land Reform in Principle and Practice* (London, 1969), p. 392.
10. Hayami and Ruttan, *An International Perspective,* p. 137.
11. Jones, "Editor's Introduction."
12. Timmer, "The Turnip, the New Husbandry," p. 382.
13. Jones, "Editor's Introduction," pp. 21-22; J. D. Chambers, "Enclosure and Labour Supply in the Industrial Revolution," in *Agriculture and Economic Growth,* edited by Jones, pp. 112-13.
14. Stanley Lebergott, "Labor Force and Employment, 1880-1960, in *Output, Employment, and Productivity in the United States after 1880,* National Bureau of Economic Research, Studies in Income and Wealth, Vol. 30 (New York, 1966), p. 119.

HISTORICAL PATTERNS: ENGLAND, THE UNITED STATES, JAPAN   235

15. Ernle, *English Farming,* p. 459.
16. Jones, "Editor's Introduction," p. 37.
17. Caird, *English Agriculture,* p. 511.
18. Jones, "Editor's Introduction," pp. 32, 37.
19. According to Chambers and Mingay, who provide an excellent account of these changes, the cost of shipping grain from Chicago to Liverpool was reduced by nearly 75 per cent between the 1870s and the end of the century (*Agricultural Revolution,* p. 180).
20. David S. Landes, *The Unbound Prometheus* (London, 1969), p. 39.
21. Quoted by Clarence H. Danhof, *Change in Agriculture: The Northern United States, 1820-1870* (Cambridge, Mass., 1969), p. 255.
22. Ibid. pp. 255-56.
23. Ibid. p. 260.
24. According to Mataji Umemura's recently revised estimates of the number of gainfully employed workers in agriculture and forestry, there was a small increase from 15.55 million workers in 1880 to a peak of 15.97 million in 1907. See Saburo Yamada and Yujiro Hayami, "Growth Rates of Japanese Agriculture, 1880-1965" (Paper [and revisions thereof] prepared for the Conference on Agricultural Growth in Japan, Korea, Taiwan and the Philippines at the East-West Center, Honolulu, Hawaii, February 1973), pp. 34-35.
25. It will be recalled from Chapter 2 that the "coefficient of differential growth" indicates the rate at which the percentage share of the nonagricultural labor force will increase.
26. Harold G. Halcrow, "Public Policy for Food and Agriculture," book manuscript (1971), Chap. 3.
27. Lebergott, "Labor Force and Employment," p. 127.
28. As quoted in Danhof, *Change in Agriculture,* p. 5.
29. Ibid. p. 2.
30. U.S. Department of Commerce, Bureau of the Census, *Historical Statistics of the United States, Colonial Times to 1957* (Washington, D.C., 1960).
31. Senator Sidney Breeze as quoted in W. A. Williams, *The Roots of the Modern American Empire* (New York, 1969), p. 2.
32. Brinley Thomas reports that the cost of wheat production in Rhenish Prussia was twice as high as in the United States in 1887 in spite of the fact that wages on wheat farms in the northwestern United States were four times as high ("General Comment," in *Output, Employment and Productivity,* National Bureau of Economic Research).
33. Danhof, *Change in Agriculture,* p. 16.
34. Ibid. pp. 16-17.
35. Clarence H. Danhof, "Agricultural Technology to 1880," in *The Growth of the American Economy,* edited by Harold F. Williamson (New York, 1944), p. 137.
36. William N. Parker and Judith L. V. Klein, "Productivity Growth in Grain Production in the United States, 1840-60 and 1900-10," in *Output, Employment, and Productivity,* National Bureau of Economic Research.

37. Paul David, "The Mechanization of Reaping in the Ante-Bellum Midwest," in *Industrialization in Two Systems: Essays in Honor of Alexander Gerschenkron*, edited by Henry Rosovsky (New York, 1966).
38. Danhof, *Change in Agriculture*, pp. 181, 229.
39. Recent papers by Philip M. Raup provide a good deal of documentation of the extent to which the trend toward corporate farming has been a response to changes made in the Internal Revenue Code in the 1950s which opened up very significant tax advantages to corporate investment in agriculture. He also argues cogently that if government policies continue to encourage this trend the result will be "private gains and public losses" because of the adverse effects on the level and orientation of research and investment, and he further predicts a tendency for labor and management to collude in price and market dominance if the tax incentives encouraging the trend toward corporate farming are not modified. Philip M. Raup, "Corporate Farming in the United States," *Journal of Economic History* Vol. 33, No. 1 (March 1973) and "Public Concerns and Policy Issues on Corporate Agriculture," University of Minnesota, Department of Agricultural and Applied Economics Staff Paper P73-15 (St. Paul, May 1973). A paper by Kenneth R. Krause and Leonard R. Kyle emphasizes that in addition to the tax-avoidance opportunities the trend toward large corporate farms has been encouraged by the possibility of such firms securing higher product prices and lower input prices. They report that as late as 1929 large-scale farms in the United States accounted for only 5 per cent of total production; but in 1964 they accounted for 44 per cent of the total. Kenneth R. Krause and Leonard R. Kyle, "Economic Factors Underlying the Incidence of Large Farming Units: The Current Situation and Probable Trends," *American Journal of Agricultural Economics* Vol. 52, No. 5 (December 1970), p. 749.
40. Nicholas P. Sargen, "Technical Change in Farm Power: 'Tractorization' in the U.S. and Its Relevance for Developing Countries" (draft Ph.D. dissertation, Stanford University, 1971).
41. Richard H. Day, "The Economics of Technological Change and the Demise of the Sharecropper," *American Economic Review* Vol. 57, No. 3 (June 1967).
42. Ibid. p. 442.
43. Ibid. It is argued later (Chapter 8) that the Delta's experience has considerable relevance to assessing the probable effects of mechanization on the demand for farm labor in India, Pakistan, and other developing countries; and estimates of the changes in farm labor use during the years 1960 to 1967 are introduced at that point.
44. Carl H. Gotsch, "Technical Change and the Distribution of Income in Rural Areas," *American Journal of Agricultural Economics* Vol. 54, No. 2 (May 1972), p. 340.
45. William N. Parker, "Sources of Agricultural Productivity in the Nineteenth Century," *Journal of Farm Economics* Vol. 49, No. 5 (December 1967), p. 1464.

46. Initially organic fertilizers—fish meal and soybean cake—were the major commercial fertilizers and farm-supplied manure and compost were of great importance. Only in the 1920s did chemical fertilizers become available in large quantities and at prices that became increasingly advantageous in comparison with the cost of commercial organic and farm-supplied fertilizers. The supplies of the latter were much less elastic, and collecting and applying manure and compost represented a demand for farm labor that could be applied more profitably in other enterprises.

47. The volume *Agricultural Development in Modern Japan*, prepared under the auspices of the Japan FAO Association, is particularly valuable as an English-language account of technical change in Japanese agriculture (ed. Takekazu Ogura [Tokyo, 1963]). This section draws heavily on that volume and Johnston, "Agricultural Development."

48. Kenzō Hemmi, "Primary Product Exports and Economic Development: The Case of Silk," in *Agriculture and Economic Growth: Japan's Experience*, edited by Kazushi Ohkawa, Bruce F. Johnston, and Hiromitsu Kaneda (Tokyo, 1969), p. 310.

49. Thomas C. Smith, *Agrarian Origins of Modern Japan* (Stanford, California, 1959), p. 211.

50. For additional detail and references, see Johnston, "Agricultural Development," pp. 239-40; idem, "Agriculture and Economic Development: The Relevance of the Japanese Experience," *Food Research Institute Studies* Vol. 6, No. 3 (1966), p. 283.

51. Yuzuru Katō, "Mechanisms for the Outflow of Funds from Agriculture into Industry in Japan," *Rural Economics Problems* Vol. 3, No. 2 (December 1966), pp. 8-11.

52. Recent calculations based on revised estimates of output and of inputs give the following breakdown into time periods. See Yamada and Hayami, "Growth Rates," p. 16 revised.

	Annual compound rates of growth		
Period[a]	Total output	Total inputs	Total factor productivity
1880-1900	1.6	0.4	1.2
1900-1920	2.0	0.5	1.5
1920-1935	0.9	0.5	0.4
1955-1965	3.6	0.7	2.9

[a] Growth rates between five-year averages centered on the years shown.

53. Hayami and Ruttan have made some interesting hypothetical calculations which suggest that without the rapid increase in rice imports from Taiwan and Korea, the rate of growth of rice production in Japan between 1920 and 1935 would have been at least twice as rapid. Under one set of assumptions they calculate that the decline in the price of rice over that period would have

averaged only .2 per cent instead of 2 per cent and that the rate of increase in domestic production would have been about .8 instead of .4 per cent. Under an alternative assumption that, in the absence of the increased reliance on rice imports, the rate of improvement in rice varieties would have continued at the same pace as during the 1890-1920 period, they calculate that Japan's rice production would have increased at a rate of 1 per cent but the moderating effect on the rate of decline in rice prices would not have been so pronounced (*An International Perspective*, pp. 221-26).

54. Hiromitsu Kaneda, "Long-Term Changes in Food Consumption Patterns in Japan," in *Japan's Experience*, edited by Ohkawa, Johnston, and Kaneda, pp. 426-27.

55. Kazushi Ohkawa, "The Pattern of Japanese Long-Term Economic Growth," mimeographed (1960), p. 23.

56. Henry Rosovsky, "Japanese Capital Formation: The Role of the Public Sector," *Journal of Economic History* Vol. 19, No. 3 (September 1959), pp. 354, 367.

57. Kazushi Ohkawa, "Agriculture and Turning-Points in Economic Growth," *Developing Economies* Vol. 3, No. 4 (December 1965).

58. William W. Lockwood, *The Economic Development of Japan* (Princeton, New Jersey, 1954), p. 293.

59. See for example, R. A. Scalapino, *Democracy and the Party Movement in Prewar Japan: The Failure of the First Attempt* (Berkeley, 1953), pp. 370, 389-92. A somewhat more extended treatment of this period of retarded growth and additional citations to some of the relevant literature are given in Johnston, "Agricultural Development." See also Hayami and Ruttan, *An International Perspective*, pp. 218-28.

60. Ryōshin Minami, "Turning Point in the Japanese Economy," *Quarterly Journal of Economics* Vol. 82, No. 3 (August 1968); reprinted as "The Supply of Farm Labor and the 'Turning Point' in the Japanese Economy," in *Japan's Experience*, edited by Ohkawa, Johnston, and Kaneda.

61. Keizō Tsuchiya, "Economics of Mechanization in Small-Scale Agriculture," in *Japan's Experience*, edited by Ohkawa, Johnston, and Kaneda, p. 156.

62. For an interesting analysis of this phenomenon, see Takeo Misawa, "An Analysis of Part-Time Farming in the Postwar Period," in *Japan's Experience*, edited by Ohkawa, Johnston, and Kaneda.

63. Yujiro Hayami, "Rice Policy in Japan's Economic Development," *American Journal of Agricultural Economics* Vol. 54, No. 1 (February 1972).

64. Ibid. pp. 21, 27.

65. Kazushi Ohkawa, "Phases of Agricultural Development and Economic Growth," in *Japan's Experience*, edited by Ohkawa, Johnston, and Kaneda, p. 34 and Shigeto Kawano, "Effects of the Land Reform on Consumption and Investment of Farmers," in *Japan's Experience*, edited by Ohkawa, Johnston, and Kaneda.

66. Hayami and Ruttan, *An International Perspective*, p. 114.

67. The statistics relating to labor inputs in American agriculture that were

available to Hayami and Ruttan probably overstate the increase in the labor component. See Lebergott, "Labor Force and Employment," pp. 157-61. But rough computations suggest that the overestimation in that component was only about 10 per cent and the overstatement of the increase in total inputs would naturally be considerably less.

68. Folke Dovring, *Productivity of Labor in Agricultural Production,* University of Illinois College of Agriculture, Agricultural Experiment Station Bulletin No. 726 (Urbana, 1967), pp. 20, 22.

69. We are indebted to Mr. Yoshimi Kuroda, graduate student in the Food Research Institute, Stanford University, for these estimates.

70. Hayami and Ruttan, *An International Perspective,* p. 57.

71. Ibid. p. 160.

72. This is roughly the midpoint of two indexes for the price of fertilizer nutrients. Ibid. p. 342.

73. Ibid. p. 164.

74. For a review of some of the pertinent literature, see Johnston, "Agriculture and Economic Development," pp. 254-65.

75. G. B. Sansom, *The Western World and Japan* (New York, 1950), p. 441.

76. Ichirou Inukai and Arlon R. Tussing, "Kōgyō Iken: Japan's Ten Year Plan, 1884," *Economic Development and Cultural Change* Vol. 16, No. 1 (October 1967), p. 65.

77. Hayami and Ruttan, *An International Perspective,* p. 144.

78. Ibid. pp. 339-40.

6 | Agriculture's Role in Three Latecomers: Taiwan, Mexico, and the Soviet Union

The concept of "lateness" is relative. Japan's agricultural development and industrial expansion were "late" as compared to the United States, still more so as compared to the United Kingdom. However, it is the experience of Taiwan and Mexico, involving rates of population growth in excess of 2 per cent and a high degree of initial technological backwardness, that is perhaps most directly pertinent to the situation faced by contemporary late-developing countries. In both countries purposive transfer of technology shaped their patterns of agricultural development—and gave rise to the very different patterns of growth that will be examined shortly. In addition, they were among the first countries to experience the rapid reductions in mortality that have resulted in the type of explosive growth of population that now impedes the transformation process. The rate of natural increase in Taiwan reached an annual rate of 2.2 per cent between 1925 and 1930 and exceeded 3 per cent during the first two decades following World War II. In Mexico, the rate of population growth began to accelerate in the 1930s after a period of slow growth caused by the Civil War and the economic disorganization that followed the Revolution. From an average of 2.0 per cent in the 1930s, the rate rose to 2.8 per cent in the 1940s and 3.1 per cent in the 1950s.

Economic development in the Soviet Union has been characterized by many unique features, but it seems useful to classify it as a late-developing country. Although many students of Russia's economic history have emphasized the quickening pace of economic development in the decades preceding the First World War, the agricultural strategy that was launched with the collectivization drive that began in 1928 represented the response of a late-developing country. The evidence suggests that the choice of strategy for agriculture was influenced as much by political as by economic considerations; but it also seems clear that the approach adopted would not have been feasible had it not been possible to rely on the rapid introduction of the "American system" in the very specific and limited sense of heavy reliance on tractor cultivation.

An examination of Taiwan's pattern of agricultural modernization in the first section of the chapter is followed by a short review of Mexico's approach. Both countries represent "success stories" because of their rapid growth of agricultural production; and science-based technological progress was a major source of the gains in farm productivity and output. In spite of those similarities, there is a sharp contrast between the progressive modernization of agriculture in Taiwan and Mexico's essentially bimodal pattern of development. For both countries, the task of transforming the structure of predominantly agrarian societies has been formidable because of extremely rapid growth of population and labor force. A net flow of capital from agriculture appears to have contributed to the growth of nonfarm output and employment in the two countries, although the percentage of farm output that represented a net outflow was substantially larger in Taiwan.

The treatment of Soviet agriculture in the final section of the chapter focuses on the decades following the decision to collectivize the agricultural sector, a decision that was implemented with great speed in the early 1930s. The approach that was followed can be viewed as a "success" in terms of the Soviet goal of rapid industrialization with emphasis on heavy industry, but the economic and human costs were high. The "extractive" approach that was followed accomplished the objective of assuring that food shortages would not interfere with industrial expansion. But in spite of the severity of the "squeeze" on agriculture, it seems probable that the net outflow of capital from agriculture was, in relative terms, considerably less than the outflow in Taiwan. In contrast with both Taiwan and Mexico, increases in factor productivity contributed very little to the expansion of farm output in the Soviet Union because of an environment that was not conducive to rapid technological progress.

Rates of population growth in the Soviet Union have been moderate compared to those in Taiwan and Mexico—an average of 1.2 per cent between 1927 and 1939, a 1.7 per cent rate during the 1950s, and a 1.2 per cent rate in the 1960s.[1] However, those relatively low rates are to a considerable extent a consequence of high mortality associated with the famine that struck the countryside in the 1930s and the high level of war-related deaths during World War II. A decline in population during the 1940s reduced birthrates in the following decades. Those abnormal circumstances also affected the rates of growth of the country's labor force. Consequently, no attempt is made to examine changes in the sectoral distribution of the labor force that accompanied structural transformation in Russia, whereas those changes in Taiwan and Mexico receive considerable attention.

AGRICULTURAL DEVELOPMENT IN TAIWAN:
THE JAPANESE PATTERN REPEATED

Development of agriculture in Taiwan, even more than in Japan, has demonstrated the potential that exists for increasing agricultural output by widespread introduction of yield-increasing innovations. The rates of increase in output and factor productivity were both higher than in Japan. Crop production grew at an average annual rate of 3.5 per cent in both the prewar (1911-15 to 1936-40) and postwar periods (1951-55 to 1961-64); and factor productivity increased at an average rate of about 2.5 per cent between 1920 and 1939 and at about the same rate in the post-1952 period.[2]

Labor Force Growth and Structural Change

A distinctive feature of Taiwan's experience was the rapid growth of population and labor force. As early as the 1930s Taiwan's total labor force was increasing at an annual rate of 2.3 per cent with the result that the farm labor force increased by more than 15 per cent between 1930 and 1940 in spite of accelerated growth of nonfarm employment that was sufficient to reduce agriculture's share in the labor force from 68 per cent at the beginning of the decade to 62 per cent in 1940. The farm labor force increased at an even higher rate in the postwar period and by 1966 was 70 per cent larger than in 1930 even though its share in the total labor force had declined to 53 per cent (Appendix Table III).

It is also of considerable interest that the successful development of agriculture was "induced" by the implementation of an agricultural strategy that was a modified version of Japan's unimodal approach. And because the expansion path of Taiwan's agricultural sector made it possible to increase output at relatively low cost the agricultural sector was able to make significant positive contributions to transforming Taiwan's overwhelmingly agrarian economy. During the past decade nonfarm employment opportunities have expanded rapidly, a structural transformation turning point has been reached, and the long-term trend toward reduction in the amount of cultivated land per farm worker has been reversed. Taiwan's agricultural sector has entered a phase of fairly rapid improvement in income levels resulting from the growth of sales of farm products and enlarged off-farm income earned by members of farm households. Farm cash receipts more than doubled between 1950-55 and 1966-69. The farm labor force increased by about 15 per cent during that period, but that was much less than the 30 per cent increase in the total labor force. In the past few years the farm labor force has begun to decline in absolute size, and a substantial rise in real wages paid agricultural workers provides collateral evidence that the "labor slack" in agriculture has been reduced markedly.[3]

Taiwan's remarkably rapid economic growth since the early 1950s has benefited from the relatively large volume of economic aid received from the United States—a total of nearly $1.5 billion during the period from 1951 to 1965 when the aid program was terminated.[4] Moreover, there appears to have been an unusually effective working relationship between the AID Mission to Taiwan and the national authorities responsible for economic planning and development programs. Most important, the resources obtained under the aid program were effectively utilized, and the government's economic policies became increasingly effective in promoting rapid growth. Although the supplementary resources received as aid were clearly a favorable factor, the evidence is strong that the pattern of agricultural development and Taiwan's economic policies were of more fundamental importance in facilitating the rapid growth and structural transformation that has been achieved. The principal features of the country's agricultural strategy are examined in the following sections. In the next chapter we consider the economic policies related to industrialization, intersectoral resource flows, and the strengthening of financial intermediation.

The redistribution of agricultural land certainly improved the income position of former tenants, but this only reinforced the influence of the country's unimodal agricultural strategy in fostering rapid economic growth which, unlike the situation in most of the contemporary developing countries, has been associated with increased equality in income distribution.[5]

The Agricultural Growth Path

The pattern of productivity growth in Taiwan's agriculture can be usefully summarized in terms of the changes in the land/man ratio (A/L) and changes in output per unit of cultivated land (Y/A) that have taken place. The productivity of labor in agriculture (Y/L) is defined (as was noted in Chapter 4) by the product of those two ratios, that is,

$$\frac{Y}{L} = \frac{A}{L} \cdot \frac{Y}{A}$$

where Y is net output of agriculture, A is the input of cultivated land, and L is input of labor in man units. The historical growth path of agricultural productivity in Taiwan is summarized in Figure 6.1 which shows the changes in land productivity (Y/A) on the vertical

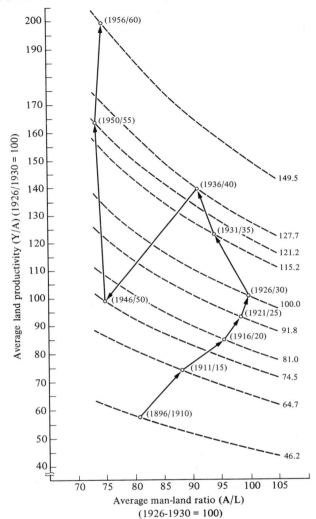

Figure 6.1 Historical growth path of farm labor productivity in Taiwan, 1896-1960.

SOURCE: Reproduced from Cristina M. Crisostomo et al., "The New Rice Technology and Labor Absorption in Philippine Agriculture" (Paper prepared for the Conference on Manpower Problems in East and Southeast Asia, Singapore, May 22-28, 1971). It is adapted from T. H. Lee, *Intersectoral Capital Flows in the Economic Development of Taiwan, 1895-1960* (Ithaca, New York, 1971).

axis; changes in labor productivity (Y/L) are shown by isoquants drawn through the points that represent the combinations of A/L and Y/A that prevailed during successive periods of development in Taiwan.[6] The three variables are expressed as index numbers, with the five-year average 1926-30 taken as 100.

It will be observed that the doubling of labor productivity from an index of 46 in 1896-1910 to 100 in the 1926-30 quinquennium was associated with a substantial increase in land productivity and a considerable improvement in the land/man ratio. During the early decades of Japanese rule in Taiwan, considerable scope existed for expanding the cultivated area, and the growth in the farm labor force and number of farm households was fairly moderate. Since that time, however, there has been very little scope for expanding the cultivated area, and by 1946/50 the farm labor force had increased substantially because of accelerated growth in the total labor force.[7] Thus the doubling of farm labor productivity between 1946-50 and 1956-60 resulted entirely from a doubling of the yield per unit of cultivated land. The increase in farm labor force was associated with an approximate doubling of the number of farm households between 1930 and 1960 and the average farm size declined from approximately five acres (1.97 hectares) to about 2.5 acres (1.05 hectares). Moreover, only about 6 per cent of the farm units, other than sugar plantations, were larger than eight acres and most operational units were close to the average size. A central feature of agricultural development in Taiwan is the extent to which a sequence of yield-increasing innovations led to substantial increases in productivity affecting virtually all farm households. In fact, net farm income per acre is consistently higher in the smaller size units.[8]

Although the development and widespread introduction of improved varieties and expanded use of fertilizer were the critical factors in the increase of farm productivity in Taiwan as in Japan, there are some important differences to be noted. At the time that Taiwan was ceded to Japan in 1895, irrigation facilities were of primitive design and limited extent. A major objective of Japan's development policy in Taiwan was the extension of irrigation, drainage, and flood control systems. Large-scale irrigation projects were carried out directly by the colonial government, but grants, loans, and technical assistance to irrigation associations for the construction of small-scale systems were even more important. The percentage of irrigated land to the total cultivated area increased from about 32 per cent in 1906 to 64 per cent in 1943.[9] Further extension of irrigation facilities, improvements in their design and management, and land improvement have been important features of agricultural advance since World War II. These improvements in water control for agriculture were a necessary condition for the widespread introduction of new varieties and the rise in cropping intensity to be noted shortly.

The increases in area, yield, and production of rice and of sugarcane, the second most important crop, are summarized in the following tabulation (index numbers with 1901-10 = 100)[10]:

Period	Rice			Sugar		
	Area	Yield	Production	Area	Yield	Production
1901-10	100	100	100	100[a]	100[a]	100[a]
1911-20	112	104	117	323	95	306
1921-30	128	120	154	371	164	608
1931-40	152	145	220	387	298	1155
1941-50	150	125	187	361	197	710
1951-60	180	168	302	306	303	927
1961-70	180	222	401	310	326	1015

[a] 1902-10 = 100.

The much more rapid expansion of sugar production during the prewar decades can be attributed in part to the priority that was given to developing Taiwan as a major sugar producer within the yen bloc. Various subsidies and other inducements were provided to stimulate the expansion of cane production and the establishment of modern sugar mills by Japanese corporations. By 1929 Taiwan's exports reached 750,000 tons and provided nearly all of Japan's sugar supplies. Although processing became a large-scale industry, the production of cane was mainly by small-scale Taiwanese farmers. The threefold increase in cane yields between the first and fourth decades of the century benefited greatly from the spectacular achievements in cane breeding in Java and Barbados in the late nineteenth century. Particularly noteworthy were the POJ varieties developed in Java after 1910; by 1930 virtually all of the cane acreage in Taiwan was planted to POJ varieties.

The very large expansion of rice production during the 1950s and 1960s was absorbed by the domestic market which expanded rapidly as a result of the influx of population from the Mainland and a high rate of natural increase. The increase in crop area resulted mainly from increased double-cropping, although there appears to have been some shift of acreage from sugar to rice. It is noted later, that new crops have enabled Taiwan to substantially expand its foreign exchange receipts from agricultural products in spite of the drastic curtailment in the traditional exports of sugar and rice.

Distinctive Features of Taiwan's Agricultural Development

In many respects the policies of the Japanese administration in Taiwan were typical of those pursued by the European powers in their colonies. During the first few years subsidies from Japan accounted for a substantial fraction of expenditures for general administration and development in Taiwan, but local sources of revenue were quickly developed and were soon sufficient to cover the current and investment expenditures of the administration in Taiwan. Until the 1930s there was heavy emphasis on developing Taiwan as an exporter of sugar and rice to Japan and as a market for manufactured exports.

There were, however, certain distinctive features of the economic and agricultural policies pursued by the Japanese in Taiwan which contributed to the success of the strategy of progressive modernization whereby the productivity of Taiwan's small-scale, labor-intensive farm units was steadily increased. One student of the development policy of Japan's colonial government in Taiwan has observed that "it was the combination of its practical knowledge of local institutions, its attention to details, and its painstaking supervision of research and extension work, that made the government so influential in guiding Taiwan's agricultural development."[11]

The first major step in laying the foundation for agricultural progress in Taiwan was a land survey initiated in 1898 to identify ownership and to provide a basis for computing land values for tax purposes. Much of the land was operated under an archaic three-level tenancy system; property rights were unclear and land transactions and tax collections were difficult. In 1905, after completing the land survey, the Japanese administration introduced a land reform that simplified the situation by terminating the rights in land of some 40,000 top level landlords (*ta-tsu hu*), compensating them with government bonds. The so-called "tenant landlords" became the legal owners of the land and assumed direct responsibility for the land tax. The distribution of land ownership remained highly skewed in favor of the larger landowners, with some 90 per cent of farm households owning only about 40 per cent of the cultivated land.[12] With a fixed land tax that was scrupulously and honestly collected, the landowners had an incentive to make their land more productive, and they were required by the government to share in the costs of land improvements carried out by tenants.

Another indigenous institution that was used by the Japanese to promote agricultural development as well as to maintain law and order, was the system known as *pao-chia* (or *hō-kō* in Japanese). Virtually all Taiwanese were assigned to a group of perhaps a dozen households (a *chia*) which in turn were grouped into village units (*pao*), and the heads of those units were responsible for fulfilling various obligations, including the mobilization of labor for road building and irrigation projects and the dissemination of information concerning improved farming methods. Particularly in the early period of Japanese rule there was considerable antagonism on the part of the Taiwanese population to the alien administration, and government officials including the police at the local level often intervened directly to implement government measures, including agricultural programs. The use of the structure of *pao* and *chia* enabled the Japanese "to apply sanctions against wrongdoing more selectively and less frequently. Penalties fell on those persons in positions to exercise a deterrent influence on others."[13]

Reference has already been made to the irrigation associations that performed an important role in organizing and partly financing the construction of local irrigation systems and in managing and maintaining those facilities. A network of agricultural associations (*nōkai*) also performed important functions in promoting technical advances in Taiwanese agriculture, particularly in providing a mechanism that enabled the government to carry out an effective extension program at relatively low cost. Large numbers of extension workers and technicians were employed by those organizations, and government subsidies covered only a part of their salaries. Until their reorganization following the land reform carried out in the early 1950s, the agricultural associations were dominated by landlords. But inasmuch as both landlords and tenants had an interest in making the numerous, small-scale farm units more productive, the conflict of interest did not prevent the associations from serving a useful purpose.

Agricultural Research and Investments in Infrastructure

Clearly, the most fundamental factor underlying the success of agricultural modernization in Taiwan was the substantial and effective support that was given to research. A Central Agricultural Research Bureau was established in 1903 and agricultural experiment stations were created in each of the major regions.[14] Research and other agricultural programs employed large numbers of specialists from Japan, and many of these were men of high calibre who pursued their work in Taiwan as a challenging lifetime career. It was thus a major "technical assistance" program with a good deal of continuity in personnel, unlike virtually all other aid programs except the effort in Mexico. Although the Japanese moved fairly slowly in expanding educational opportunities for the Taiwanese population, by the 1930s appreciable numbers were being trained in agricultural vocational schools and universities in Japan and Taiwan in preparation for work in agricultural research and extension programs. With the retrocession of Taiwan to the Republic of China following World War

II many scientists and other agricultural administrators from the Mainland moved into senior positions previously occupied by Japanese. But many Taiwanese, who had acquired training and experience during the period of Japanese rule, appear to have contributed to the continuity in research.

Determined efforts were made to raise rice yields, a crop which accounted for half of the total value of agricultural output, but special problems had to be overcome. Efforts at varietal improvement based on selection of the native *indica* varieties led to some increase in yields, but the first significant progress followed the development of *japonica* varieties and techniques of growing them that were adapted to Taiwan's conditions. Approximately a decade was required to select adapted *japonica* varieties and to develop agronomic practices that made it possible to grow them successfully under the low latitude, tropical conditions of Taiwan. These varieties (referred to as *ponlai* in Chinese and *hōrai* in Japanese) were still being grown only on an experimental basis in 1922, but 10 years later approximately one-third of the total rice area was planted to *ponlai* varieties.

In important respects the contributions of research have been even more impressive in the postwar than in the prewar period. In 1957 a major breakthrough was made in developing stiff-strawed, fertilizer-responsive *indica* varieties with yield characteristics similar to the *japonica*-type *ponlai* varieties. One of these varieties, Taichung Native No. 1, was introduced on a considerable scale in other countries in Asia and in tropical Africa. Under more humid conditions, notably in India, Taichung Native No. 1 has often encountered serious disease problems; but a dwarf *indica* variety from Taiwan was one of the parents of IR-8, the first of the improved varieties released by the International Rice Research Institute.

Although the introduction of high-yielding varieties of rice and sugarcane have been singled out, the major point to be emphasized is that the research programs in Taiwan have generated an impressive stream of innovations that have been profitable and adapted not only to the physical environment but to the needs of small-scale farmers. For example, the development of systems of "relay-interplanting"—

the succession planting of crops such as sweet potatoes, melons, and vegetables along with rice—have received considerable emphasis in the years since World War II as a means of increasing cropping intensity and thereby raising farm incomes in spite of the substantial reduction in the size of farm units. Numerous simple but useful mechanical innovations have also made a notable contribution to increased farm productivity in Taiwan. The R&D activity on farm equipment was, however, very closely related to the growth of Taiwan's metalworking industries and it is therefore more appropriately examined in Chapter 8.

The other major government effort to foster agricultural development in Taiwan was its direct and indirect support for creating the infrastructure on which expanded farm output depended. Outlays by the colonial administration for fixed capital formation averaged about one-fourth of total government expenditures (which increased rapidly as tax receipts expanded). Of these expenditures one-half or more was allocated to the construction and improvement of a rail network, harbors, and roads, and by the 1920s most points of the islands had access to inexpensive transportation facilities.[15] Of even greater significance for agriculture were the substantial outlays for irrigation and flood control. Total investment in irrigation facilities rose sharply during the 1920s and accounted for nearly 15 per cent of total capital investment in Taiwan during that decade. The level of investment in irrigation facilities was more than twice as high during the 1956-60 quinquennium but represented only about 7.5 per cent of total investment because by that time the nonfarm sectors were so much more important.[16]

Farmers' Response and Changes in Output and Inputs

A number of the most important changes in farm output and in various inputs are summarized in Table 6.1. It is striking that farm output increased 3.4 times between 1911-15 and 1956-60, whereas the cultivated land area increased by only about 27 per cent. As noted earlier, the cropped area almost doubled as a result of an increase in the index of cropping intensity from 116 in 1911-15 to 180

Table 6.1. Changes in farm output and various inputs in Taiwan, 1911-15 to 1956-60
(*Index numbers except as otherwise indicated*)

Period	Total farm output	Cultivated land area	Cropped area	Farm labor force	Labor inputs in working days
1911-15	100	100	100	100	100
1956-60	337	127	196	149	198

Period	Working days Per cultivated hectare	Per cropped hectare	Per worker	Fertilizer consumption (*1000 metric tons*)	Total current inputs[a]
1911-15	195	167	117	50.8	100
1956-60	305	170	155	663.5	512

[a] In contrast with Japan, livestock feed has long been an important component of current inputs in Taiwan. It accounted for 57 per cent of current inputs in 1911-15 and 41 per cent in 1956-60 when fertilizer represented 45 per cent of the total.
SOURCE: Data from T. H. Lee, *Intersectoral Capital Flows in the Economic Development of Taiwan, 1895-1960* (Ithaca, New York, 1971).

in 1956-60. And as a result of the introduction of higher-yielding varieties and a 13-fold increase in fertilizer consumption, the yield per cropped acre also rose substantially.

One of the most significant features of Taiwan's agricultural development, reflected in the lower panel of Table 6.1, is the effect of the unimodal strategy in bringing about fuller utilization of the farm labor force. Between 1911-15 and 1956-60, the number of farm workers increased by about 50 per cent but the labor input measured in working days virtually doubled. It is apparent that this was closely correlated with the increase in the cropped area as the average number of working days per cropped hectare was essentially unchanged.

Underlying all of these changes was the behavior of the Taiwanese farmers who acquired the knowledge, skill, and managerial ability to exploit the income-earning opportunities that became available with changes in their technical and economic environment. In attempting to account for the widespread and vigorous participations of Taiwan's farmers in technical and economic advance, it seems plausible to suggest that in the early years coercion and economic pressure were of considerable importance. For tenants and part-tenants, the obligation to pay a high rent meant pressure to raise yields. At the same time landlords had an incentive to undertake land improvements and to encourage the adoption of innovations and use of yield-increasing inputs by their tenants that would increase the amount of rice delivered as share rent. Owner-cultivators as well as tenants felt pressure to raise their cash income to pay for fertilizer and other essential inputs, to pay water fees and taxes, and to pay for the consumer goods and services that became increasingly important components of the standard of living in rural areas. The most general and pervasive force at work, however, seems to have been the desire of farm households to enlarge their net income in spite of the difficult conditions imposed by the lack of land and, for many, heavy rental payments.

In the 1920s and 1930s the Japanese officials placed considerable reliance on the "encouragement method" for promoting the adoption of new varieties, the main subsidies being for fertilizer and free distribution of seed. Farmers in Taiwan have become highly receptive to innovations. It has become common for virtually all farmers in an area to adopt a new variety within two or three years. It was reported, for example, that Taichung Native No. 1 had been adopted by 90 per cent of the farmers in Ta-Chia District near Taichung within two years of its introduction.[17] And the rapid expansion of exports of canned mushrooms and canned asparagus in the 1960s is striking evidence of the rapidity with which large numbers of farmers have been prepared to seize new income-earning opportunities and acquire the relevant technical knowledge. Accumulated experience with technical change and the spread of education were presumably important factors contributing to this receptivity to change. Although the Japanese colonial administration moved slowly in expanding opportunities for higher education, primary school enrollment increased rapidly after World War I. The percentage of children of school age (6-14) enrolled in school reached 33 per cent in 1930/31 and 71 per cent in 1943/44.[18] In the post-World War II period the percentage enrolled in primary schools reached 95 per cent in 1960 and the increase in percentage of graduates enrolled in the next higher level of schools has been striking.[19]

Postwar Land Reform

A noteworthy development of the postwar period was the redistributive land reform carried out in the early 1950s. A "Farm Rent Reduction Program" in 1951 was followed in 1953 by the so-called "Land to the Tiller Program." Under this program landlords were forced to sell their land in excess of a very small acreage ceiling (three hectares in the case of medium-grade paddy), for which they were compensated in bonds (denominated in rice and sweet potatoes as a hedge against inflation). Most observers agree that this postwar land reform contributed to the impressive increases in productivity of the post-1952 period inasmuch as the newly created owner-cultivators had even stronger incentives to increase the yield of their land.[20]

Although the episode provides strong evidence for the proposition that redistributive land reform can reinforce an efficient unimodal strategy, it should be recognized that unique circumstances had considerable influence on the decision to carry through such an effective land reform program. The administration of General Chiang Kaishek had just gone through what John Brewster has aptly termed a "catastrophic learning experience" in their defeat by the Chinese Communists and expulsion from the Mainland; and one of the lessons learned by painful experience was the importance of maintaining the support of the farm population.[21] The fact that virtually all of the administrators who took that decision and implemented it so forcefully were Chinese from the Mainland, whereas the landlords obliged to sell their land were Taiwanese, minimized the problems of conflict of interest. Those problems are bound to be serious in a country like India where so many of the officials and members of Parliament and local legislative bodies own land that would be affected by redistributive land reform. It also seems likely that the decision was facilitated by the availability of substantial bilateral aid from the United States and the fact that some of the influential United States officials in Taiwan were impressed by the success of the postwar land reform in Japan in which the role of General MacArthur's Allied Headquarters was a decisive factor.

Intersectoral Capital Flows and Agriculture's Contributions to Development

Rapid expansion of farm output in Taiwan facilitated overall economic growth in many ways. The country's experience appears to be unusual, however, in the extent to which increases in agricultural output contributed to financing investments outside agriculture. Furthermore, because of the availability of long-term economic statistics and T. H. Lee's empirical study, it is possible to examine Taiwan's intersectoral capital flows over an extended period. We return to that aspect of Taiwan's experience in Chapter 7.[22]

The net resource outflow from agriculture represented slightly over 30 per cent of the total value of agricultural production in 1911-15 and was still equal to 21 per cent of the value of output in 1931-35, by which time the real value of the sector's output had increased more than two and one-half times. Moreover, during this period virtually all of the net real capital outflow represented a net outflow of funds, specifically, an outflow of funds in payment of land rent and interest, taxes, and transfers through financial institutions in excess of the inflow of funds.[23]

Such a large net transfer of resources from agriculture was possible only because the increases in agricultural production were achieved with remarkably small increases in the use of purchased inputs. The increase in sales of farm products in the 1920s and 1930s was unusually rapid in Taiwan because of the rapid expansion of exports of sugar and rice to Japan. Even so, outlays for purchased inputs represented only about 18 per cent of the value of total agricultural production as late as 1936-40. This was 35 per cent of total farm purchases, and virtually all of it represented outlays for the purchase of fertilizer and other variable inputs; the expenditures for fixed capital amounted to only about 10 per cent of the total outlays for external inputs.

Given the level of farm cash sales, sectoral outlays for inputs might have been higher if expenditures on consumer goods had been less or if there had been a smaller net outflow of funds. Considering the persistence of low rural consumption levels in prewar Taiwan, the 65 per cent share of farm purchases allocated to consumer goods certainly does not seem high. Although the increase in rural consumption levels in the prewar decades was held down by the heavy rental and tax payments that farmers were obliged to make, it is apparent that this burden did not frustrate the development of agriculture. It seems likely that it would have done so in the absence of the technical progress and key investments in infrastructure that made possible large increases in factor productivity.

A rice-fertilizer barter scheme administered by the Provincial Food Bureau was responsible for a major part of the invisible capital outflow from agriculture that was a significant feature of the postwar period. From the standpoint of economic efficiency, this rice-fertilizer barter program clearly represented a very undesirable device for "taxing" agriculture since the unfavorable rate at which farmers were obliged to deliver rice in exchange for fertilizer maximized the disincentive effect on the use of a highly productive input. The fact that fertilizer use and crop yields increased in spite of that "negative subsidy" emphasizes the powerful influence of favorable environmental conditions and the availability of fertilizer-responsive varieties developed by Taiwan's agricultural research stations.

THE DEVELOPMENT OF MEXICAN AGRICULTURE, 1940-65[24]

There is a striking contrast between the unimodal pattern of agricultural development in Taiwan and the predominantly bimodal pattern pursued in Mexico. But, in spite of significant contrasts, similarities in the role of research and infrastructure investments in the two countries are probably of more fundamental importance.

Another significant similarity should be mentioned. Mexico like Taiwan seems to have pursued economic policies that have avoided most of the adverse effects on growth associated with "financial repression." Particularly in contrast with other Latin American countries, considerable success has been achieved in controlling inflationary pressures. As a result, real rates of interest have probably not been much below an equilibrium rate in spite of the ceilings that have been imposed on deposit rates and on interest rates on loans. This has meant that lending through organized capital markets has not been a mere conduit for channeling subsidies to borrowers, as in many Latin American countries where the officially regulated interest rates have so often represented negative rates in real terms. The favorable effects of a reasonably stable price level have also been reenforced by the free convertibility of the Mexican peso and policies that have avoided overvaluation, at least since 1954. As a result saving has not been discouraged by an expectation of devaluation giving rise to either a large risk discount or a strong preference for placing savings in financial institutions abroad. The net effect of these favorable factors has been a considerable increase in the real stock of money, including time and savings deposits, and a growth of financial intermediation that has facilitated the expansion of output in both agriculture and industry.[25]

Expansion of farm output in Mexico since 1940 has been rapid— an annual rate of 4.7 per cent for the 1940-53 period and 3.7 per cent during the years 1954-65.[26] Especially in the 1940-53 period, this increase in output was associated with rapid expansion of land, working capital, fixed capital, hired labor, and other inputs; but the 3 per cent rate of increase in total inputs was considerably less than the growth of output implying a rate of increase in total factor productivity of 1.7 per cent. During the 1954-65 period all except the variable inputs increased at a considerably slower rate, and it is estimated that the annual increase in factor productivity was 1.9 per cent, thus accounting for slightly over one-half of the 3.7 per cent annual increase in output.[27]

Research and Investments in Infrastructure

In Mexico as in Taiwan research-based increases in crop yields, associated with rapid expansion in fertilizer consumption, have accounted for much of the growth in farm output. Not surprisingly, this is most striking in the case of wheat. The greatest success of the Office of Special Studies, created within the Ministry of Agriculture in 1943 as a cooperative venture of the Rockefeller Foundation and the Mexican government, was the development of high-yielding varieties of wheat. The early work on rust-resistant strains was an important step, but the major breakthrough came with the development of short-stemmed, stiff-strawed, fertilizer-responsive varieties. The development of those varieties, which are now having such a major impact on wheat production in India, Pakistan, and many other parts of the world, was facilitated by the introduction of genes from high-yielding, semidwarf varieties from the Pacific Northwest in the United States (which in turn had incorporated the attractive attributes of plant material introduced from Japan shortly after World War II). The decisive factor in that and other research achievements in Mexico was the competence and continuity of the staff of agricultural scientists recruited initially in the United States and progressively augmented by Mexican agricultural scientists selected and trained as an integral part of the program. The success of that program led to the dissolution of the Office of Special Studies and the creation of a National Institute of Agricultural Research (I.N.I.A.) that is now responsible for Mexico's agricultural research programs. The Rockefeller Foundation staff and some of the Mexican agricultural scientists provided the nucleus for the International Maize and Wheat Improvement Center (CIMMYT) that was established in 1966.

The development of the high-yielding varieties of wheat was by no means the only achievement of the research program carried out cooperatively by the Ministry of Agriculture and the Rockefeller Foundation. A number of maize hybrids were developed to meet the ecological requirements of different areas, and by 1960 over 300,000 hectares were planted to hybrids with an average yield approximately 75 per cent above the yield for open-pollinated varieties. However, that represented only about 6 per cent of the acreage planted to ordinary maize, and part of the yield differential must be attributed to the fact that 32 per cent of the hybrid maize was under irrigation compared to only 8 per cent of the area planted to ordinary maize. Perhaps even more important has been the knowledge accumulated about the numerous races of maize that is now facilitating efforts to raise the yield of open-pollinated varieties by recently improved techniques of selection which are discussed later. Notable success also was realized in developing disease-resistant varieties of white potatoes, although those achievements are having a greater impact in the Andean countries of South America where potatoes are a more important crop than in Mexico. For cotton also great strides were made in varietal improvement which, in combination with some related changes, led to a 150 per cent increase in cotton yields from the mid-1930s to the early 1960s. As a result of the sharp increase in yield and the substantial acreage expansion, cotton became Mexico's most important export. The mechanism by which new cotton technologies were transferred was, however, quite different from the program for food crops and will be considered later.

The rapid expansion of wheat and cotton production was facilitated enormously by the expansion of irrigation. Production of both crops is concentrated in the arid regions of northern Mexico and the expansion of output has therefore been dependent on large public investments in irrigation. As of 1960/61, the North Pacific Region accounted for over 65 per cent of the land served by government irrigation projects, and the North Region accounted for most of the remainder.[28] Rapid expansion of irrigation in those two regions permitted a large increase in crop area and facilitated the speedy adoption of new varieties and enlarged use of purchased inputs, notably mechanical equipment and chemical fertilizer. Between 1940 and 1960 the number of tractors in use on farms in Mexico rose from less than

5000 to nearly 55,000, largely concentrated in the two northern regions.[29] Consumption of nitrogen fertilizer in Mexico averaged only 10,000 nutrient tons during the years 1948/49-1952/53 but reached 345,000 tons in 1968. The regional concentration of the increase in fertilizer consumption, however, was undoubtedly less pronounced than in the case of machinery.

The Bimodal Character of Mexico's Agricultural Development

The pattern of agricultural development in Mexico can be characterized as bimodal because large-scale, highly commercial farm units in northern Mexico have accounted for the bulk of the increase in farm output and an even larger fraction of the growth of commercialized production. Donald Freebairn suggests on the basis of his interpretation of data from the 1960 Census of Agriculture that less than 15 per cent of all farm units accounted for about 75 per cent of all sales of agricultural products.[30] This is based on his calculation that 68,000 of the larger private holdings accounted for half of total crop sales and 321,000 farm households in *ejidos,* where operational units averaged 10 hectares or more of crop land, accounted for another 25 per cent of sales.[31] Taking a somewhat different approach, Delbert Myren has suggested that some 20 per cent of the country's farm households constitute a modern, commercial sector, perhaps 35 per cent are traditional, predominantly subsistence households, and roughly 45 per cent are in an intermediate transitional sector.[32] All that can be said with confidence is that the two northern regions accounted for a disproportionate share of the increase in output between 1940 and 1960, and that large-scale, relatively capital-intensive farm units were of predominant importance in those regions and of limited importance elsewhere.

The contrast between the two northern regions and the Central Region was especially marked; crop output in the Central Region increased at an annual rate of a little over 3 per cent between 1940 and 1960 compared to rates of about 8 per cent and 11 per cent in the North and Pacific North regions.[33] The increase in output in the South Pacific Region, however, rivaled the rate of increase in the Pacific North, both regions registering more than a fivefold increase in output between 1929 and 1959. This comparison has considerable interest because the 5.8 per cent annual increase in output in the Pacific North during the 30-year period is almost entirely attributable to the 5.6 per cent rate of increase in total inputs whereas the 2.9 per cent rate of increase in inputs in the South Pacific Region "explains" just over half of the 5.7 per cent rate of increase in output.[34]

The large increase in factor productivity in the South Pacific is no doubt to be attributed to a considerable extent to substantial investments in land clearing and planting of coffee and other tree crops that were underestimated in the capital input figures. Even though that probably accounts for much of the "unexplained output," it is significant that this region was able to make important contributions to output and foreign exchange earnings by fuller and more productive utilization of supplies of land and labor in the region and with relatively small claims on the types of capital that are especially scarce in a developing country.

For the three decades between 1929 and 1959, the unaccounted for portion of the growth rate was 1.3 per cent for the entire country compared to the 2.8 per cent rate in the South Pacific Region and only .2 per cent in the Pacific North.[35] The investments in irrigation facilities in the latter region, which were concentrated in the 1930s and 1940s, had a fairly long gestation period. Hence, it is not surprising that the rate of increase in output in the final decade was considerably higher and the growth of output "unexplained" by growth of inputs was about 6.0 per cent in the North Pacific in the 1949-59 decade compared with 2.3 per cent in the South Pacific and a countrywide rate of 1.9 per cent. The increase in factor productivity in the Pacific North may have been even higher in the 1960s because of the notable increase in wheat yields and the growing concentration of wheat in that region.

Land Reform and the Economics of Farm Size

Acute discontent over the unequal distribution of land was a major force underlying the Mexican Revolution, and seizure of land by armed peasants was an important feature of the period from 1911 until the early 1920s. The goal of agrarian reform was given official standing in the Constitution of 1917; and by 1940 approximately half of the cultivated land had been distributed to peasants grouped in *ejidos*.[36] Given the strong commitment to land reform, it is surprising that the pattern of agricultural development has had an essentially bimodal character. One result has been a tendency to emphasize the positive *indirect* effects of land reform in fostering development. Some scholars have also argued that establishing *ejidos* fulfilled an important social goal whereas the emergence of large private farm enterprises was essential to the achievement of economic goals because of the belief that efficient expansion of agricultural output required the creation of large units. After examining those propositions, we turn to some other factors that may well have been more important in accounting for the bimodal strategy that was implemented.

The view that the most important positive effects of Mexico's land reform were indirect appears to command fairly general agreement. Edmundo Flores, for example, has argued that land reform contributed indirectly to overall economic growth by giving the country "a government with a new concern for the people and the nation" and because of its effects in increasing mobility, destroying the feudal-type of caste system, instilling the idea of progress and personal ambition, and helping to create a climate favorable to road building, irrigation programs, and industrialization.[36a] It has been noted by Clark Reynolds that the political climate created by the agrarian reform program made it easier for the government to undertake major programs of irrigation development and highway construction, programs which accounted for a quarter of public investment between 1925 and 1935 and rose to 44 per cent of the total between 1935 and 1945. Although the benefits accrued mainly to large operators in the modern sector, *ejidos* in the favored regions also benefited. He also advances the more general argument that Mexico's "dual strategy" for agriculture was advantageous because the policy of redistributing land in small parcels to millions of *ejidatarios* "satisfied income security and distribution criteria essential to maintain political stability, while the policy of public investment satisfied productivity criteria designed to spur the rate of growth of agricultural production.[37]

There seems to be a widespread view among students of Mexican agriculture that from the standpoint of economic efficiency the performance of the *ejido* units has been unsatisfactory. In his review article on economic policy and the views of Mexican economists, Leopoldo Solís states that "Most opinions concur that the *ejido* is in crisis or stagnant and is not an institution that can provide a satisfactory solution to the agrarian problem."[38] Various factors are cited such as the inflexibility and uncertainty associated with the tenure system, the lack of credit to the *ejido* members (since they cannot mortgage their land), and the small size of the individual plots. The last factor in particular is often stressed. Several of the economists whose views are summarized by Solís argue that "the small plots constitute the main problem of the agricultural sector today" and that because of their small size they "hinder the formation of capital as well as an increase in productivity, and maintain the technological level of the rural sector as stagnant."[39] And Reynolds seems to be expressing a prevalent view when he speaks of the loss of potential output because "some of the most productive large holdings were fragmented into inefficiently small units, and the inalienability of *ejidal* tenure perpetuated whatever allocative inefficiency resulted."[40]

Concern over underemployment and the highly unequal distribution of income that characterize Mexican agriculture has, however, led to a reconsideration of the alleged inefficiency of small farms under the conditions that prevail in Mexico. There is increasing recognition that industrial expansion leading to "the absorption of a surplus rural population by secondary and tertiary activities" can only be a long-run solution.[41] The extremely rapid growth of the total labor force makes it virtually impossible to forestall some further increase in the working force in agriculture even though Mexico's nonagricultural sectors now employ something over half of the labor force.[42]

Only Flores de la Peña, of the economists whose views are reported by Solís, seems to question the usual criticism of the inefficiency of small units; and because of the rural population problem he argues for emphasis on "small farms with an intensive use of labor as the predominant mode of agricultural production."[43] Although the *ejidos* face special problems because of their inability to obtain mortgage credit, it seems likely that the apparent superiority of the large-scale units is mainly in technical rather than economic efficiency. According to a comparative analysis by Folke Dovring, Mexico's small-scale units are more efficient than the large, capital-intensive farms in terms of output per unit of external inputs. A somewhat similar conclusion is reached in a recent study of agrarian structure and agricultural development directed by Sergio Reyes Osorio and Rodolfo Stavenhagen.[44] An analysis of yield levels by state for each of the major crops based on 1960 census data indicates that large private farms had a significant yield advantage only for wheat. And for most crops the increase in yield between 1950 and 1960 was more rapid for the *ejidos* than for the large farms in spite of their greater use of purchased inputs.[45] Finally, it appears that farmers in *ejidos* have often been prevented from cultivating the most profitable crop combinations because of restrictive policies applied by the National Ejidal Credit Bank, the only source of institutional finance available to them.[46]

Certain features of the physical environment along with the proximity to the United States seem to go far to explain why Mexico has followed an essentially bimodal pattern of agricultural development in spite of the national commitment to agrarian reform. The existence of large amounts of sparsely populated, unutilized land in the Pacific North and North regions that could be made highly productive with irrigation offered an attractive means of rapidly expanding agricultural production. Moreover, the scope that existed for rapid expansion of cotton production for export and of wheat production for import substitution insured that for some years at least demand constraints would not impair the profitability of the sizable investments in farm machinery that accompanied the very large investments in irrigation facilities. The attractiveness of those investments was increased by the availability of capital at relatively low rates of interest from the United States and from the World Bank and by the availability of easily transferred agricultural technologies in the American Southwest.

The ready availability of "technical assistance" and capital from the United States had a particularly important effect on the expansion of cotton. Large cotton merchandising firms in the United States, in particular Anderson-Clayton and Company, played an active role in stimulating the growth of production and exports in northern Mexico in the 1940s and 1950s. Technologies in use in America's Southwest were taken up by producers south of the border, and the technical expertise and capital provided by the field offices of the American firms fostered the process whereby Mexico more than doubled its cotton production from an annual average of 450,000 bales in 1945-49 to over a million in 1950-54 and an average of just over two million during the years 1955-59. This was accompanied by a 150 per cent increase in cotton yields (from 1934-38 to 1961-65); in both percentage and absolute terms the yield increase was appreciably larger than in the United States.[47] United States price support policies and acreage restrictions stimulated that development by the "umbrella" effect on world prices (especially before 1956 when the United States began its export subsidy payments) and in giving an incentive for cotton merchandising firms in the United States to expand their activities in Mexico and other Latin American countries.[48]

These forces also influenced the technologies used to achieve rapid expansion of wheat production. The potential for increased output of wheat opened up by investments in irrigation in the arid northern regions could be realized most rapidly by large, mechanized units. To a considerable extent cotton and wheat are grown on the same farms so that tractors and other equipment introduced initially for cotton were also used for wheat. Although wheat in Mexico is basically a domestic food crop, demand conditions were favorable for the more than threefold expansion of output that occurred between 1948-52 and the 1960s. Mexico had depended on imports for approximately half of its wheat supplies so that there was considerable scope for import substitution, and total demand was increasing rapidly because of population growth. Partly because of the importance that was attached to achieving self-sufficiency in wheat, the large-scale wheat growers were able to demand and receive highly favorable treatment in the allocation of credit at relatively low interest rates. Maintenance of attractive prices for wheat (including a transport subsidy on wheat shipped from the Pacific North Region to Mexico City), development of hydroelectric power, and credit and subsidies made available for construction of deep wells for supplementary irrigation also contributed to the rapid growth of wheat production.

Crop Improvement Programs for Wheat and Maize

The relatively slow growth of output that has characterized the Central Region and many other areas where agriculture is dominated by small-scale farm units is also to be attributed in part to some significant contrasts between the crop improvement programs for wheat and maize. Maize is the dominant crop in the traditional and transitional subsectors that continue to provide employment and livelihood for the bulk of the rural population. Although the increase in maize

Table 6.2. Highest and lowest annual average yields of maize and wheat in Mexico for selected periods
(*Kilograms per hectare*)

	Corn		Wheat	
	Lowest	Highest	Lowest	Highest
1950-54	721	854	863	1098
1955-59	803	880	1063	1592
1960-64	946	1133	1471	2056
1965-67	1090	1204	2400	2800

SOURCE: Reproduced from Delbert T. Myren, "The Rockefeller Foundation Program in Corn and Wheat in Mexico," in *Subsistence Agriculture and Economic Development,* edited by Clifton R. Wharton, Jr. (Chicago, 1969), p. 439.

production has been limited compared to the spectacular expansion of wheat output, Mexico's experience in increasing maize production during the past two decades has been fairly impressive compared to the stagnant situation that prevailed during the preceding half-century and which continues to characterize many less-developed countries. It is no mean achievement that production of the country's major staple food increased to keep pace with the growth of population which virtually doubled from 26 million in 1950 to 49 million in 1969; and the increase in yields has been about as important as acreage expansion in accounting for the growth of maize output. It is clear from the comparison of maize and wheat yields in Table 6.2 that the results of the efforts to introduce high-yielding varieties of maize have been unimpressive in comparison with the spectacular increases in wheat yields. It is clear from Figure 6.2 which shows the annual changes in wheat yield that there has been a strong upward trend since the early 1950s. The first distribution of improved seed in 1948 did not lead to a perceptible effect on average yield for several years. And the distribution of the first semidwarf variety in 1962 did not visibly affect the upsurge that followed Mexico's last serious epidemic of stem rust in 1959. The threefold increase in wheat yield is, of course, a notable achievement. But it is also significant, especially in assessing the impact of the more recently initiated seed-fertilizer revolutions, that this was the result of continuing advances in plant breeding and agronomic practice that extended over an 18-year period.

The contrasts between the wheat and maize programs have been influenced by the increasing concentration of wheat production in the irrigated areas of northwest Mexico, technical differences between the maize and wheat plants, and differences between the type of farm units growing the two crops. By 1964 the Pacific North accounted for 55 per cent of the wheat area and 72 per cent of production compared with 30 per cent of the acreage and 38 per cent of the harvest in 1950.[49] It is estimated that maize is grown on at least two-thirds of all farms in Mexico or by about two million farm households whereas wheat is grown by fewer than 50,000 farmers. And the average

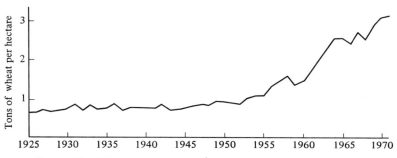

Figure 6.2 Historical movement of wheat yields, Mexico 1925-71.

SOURCE: Data reproduced from Dana G. Dalrymple and William I. Jones, "Evaluating the 'Green Revolution'" (Paper prepared for the joint Meeting of the American Association for the Advancement of Science and the Consejo Nacional de Ciencia y Technologia, Mexico City, June 20, 1973), p. 12.

wheat acreage per farm is between 15 and 20 hectares whereas the average for corn is only about three hectares.

With production concentrated geographically and carried on mainly by large, commercially oriented farmers, the scientists working on wheat were able to carry knowledge of the new varieties and associated agronomic practices directly to the farmers—who were increasingly "looking over their shoulders" at experiment stations and field trials. In contrast, a former director of the maize program reports that there was a concentration on "the problem of developing the many varieties of hybrids needed for the great number of ecological situations in Mexico and we carried this program to the point of producing foundation seed for the National Corn Commission" whereas "the wheat program . . . was concerned not only with the development of rust resistant, high yielding varieties but with seed production, the use of higher amounts of fertilizer, and adoption by farmers."[50] Because of the need for annual replacement of seed, the limited range of adaptability of maize hybrids, and the problems of selling seed to a huge number of small producers in diverse ecological zones, the problems of seed distribution were considerably more difficult for maize. The self-pollination of wheat means that a farmer can buy a small quantity and mulitiply it himself and use it for many years whereas there is a drastic reduction in yield if a farmer replants his own hybrid maize seed. (This applies to the usual pure-line hybrids but not the "varietal hybrids" that are discussed in the next section.)

Agriculture's Role in Mexican Development

The rapid expansion of agricultural output that has been achieved in Mexico has made a number of vital contributions to the country's overall economic development. In addition to meeting the growing demand for food, and eliminating dependence on sizable imports of wheat, the expanded production of farm products has been a major factor in enlarging foreign exchange receipts. Mexico's merchandise exports increased at an average rate of 8.5 per cent between 1940 and 1963 and rapid growth of agricultural exports accounted for most of this increase.[51] In 1940 agricultural and forestry products represented a mere 20 per cent of Mexico's commodity exports, which were then dominated by mineral products; by 1950 their share had increased to 52 per cent and to a still higher percentage in 1960.[52] Cotton and coffee have been the major export commodities, but in recent years sugar and meat have also been important. Still more recently sales to the United States and Canada of tomatoes, fresh and frozen strawberries, and other fruits and vegetables have expanded rapidly, so rapidly in fact that Mexico has instituted voluntary restraints to forestall more drastic restrictions by the United States. Mexico's share of the United States fresh tomato winter market increased sharply from 40 per cent in 1968-69 to 70 per cent in 1969-70, so a desire to avoid flooding the market and a sharp decline in prices was an additional motive for acting to limit exports.[53]

The evidence available indicates that there has been a net flow of resources from agriculture to the rest of the economy, but the transfer appears to have been relatively small compared to the net capital outflow from agriculture in Taiwan. In terms of government expenditures and receipts, the evidence indicates that there was a net flow of funds into agriculture. Mainly because of the large government-financed investments in irrigation, public expenditures in agriculture have generally exceeded tax revenues collected from agriculture. For the years 1942-61, the net flow of public revenues into agriculture was some three billion 1960 pesos, the amount by which taxes collected from agriculture during this period fell short of the 19.1 billion pesos spent in the agricultural sector. The net flow of public resources into agriculture was especially large in the 1940s, and the substantial acceleration in the growth of agricultural output generated sufficient savings in the agricultural sector in excess of investments in agriculture so that there has been a substantial net outflow of funds through financial institutions.

The net outflow of funds through the banking system alone appears to have been a little less than the net inflow of public funds. But it seems likely, according to Reynolds, that if allowance is made for financial flows through nonbank intermediaries as well as through the banking system the net private outflow was greater than the net inflow of public funds.[54] Reyes Osorio and his associates have argued that allowance should also be made for a sizable invisible outflow of resources from agriculture associated with unfavorable shifts in agriculture's terms of trade. In fact, it has been calculated that the transfer associated with a shift in relative prices against agriculture was somewhat greater than the net inflow of funds on public account.[55] It can be argued that a shift of relative prices resulting from differential rates of change in productivity and demand should not be regarded as a resource transfer. But in any event, the fact that nonfarm consumers experienced a decline in the relative price of food products was clearly favorable for industrial expansion in contrast to the situation that would have prevailed if scarcity of food had led to a rise in the relative price of this basic wage good. It is worth noting that the decline in food prices has been especially marked. Both the farm wheat and the consumer prices of wheat flour fell by about a half, in real terms, between the early 1950s and the early 1970s.[56]

Although land redistribution and the creation of *ejidos* did a great deal in providing security and at least a minimum level of income for a large fraction of the country's rural population, there is now a good deal of concern with increasing inequality of income distribution. Nonfarm employment has been growing rapidly in Mexico, reflecting the growth of manufacturing and expansion of the service industries stimulated by tourism as well as greater interdependence and rising per capita incomes. The labor force employed in manufacturing doubled between 1940 and 1950 and increased another 50 per cent between 1950 and 1960. By that time manufacturing employment had reached nearly 1.6 million out of a total nonfarm labor force of close to 5.2 million which represented some 46 per cent of the total labor force. But the farm work force increased by approximately 60 per cent between 1940 and 1960, even though its share in the total declined from 65 to 54 per cent, because the total labor force was increasing at well over 3 per cent per year. (See Appendix Table IV.) It is therefore not too surprising that problems of labor force absorption and underemployment in agriculture are viewed with considerable concern in spite of the impressive performance of Mexico's nonagricultural sectors.

As a result of the increased concern with problems of income distribution and rural underemployment, a good deal of attention has been given to programs to accelerate increases in output and productivity among small-scale farmers. An interesting example is the so-called Puebla Project, a major pilot project aimed at achieving "a breakthrough in ways of efficiently channeling knowledge, credit, and modern production inputs to a vast number of farmers."[57] The Puebla Project is focused on achieving a large increase in the level of yield of maize, by far the most important crop for farmers in the project area.

The decision to undertake the Puebla Project resulted in part from increased awareness of the difficult problems of multiplying and distributing hybrids. This recognition coincided with the development of more efficient techniques for recurrent mass selection of open-pollinated varieties. The yield potential of the "synthetic varieties" developed with this improvement strategy is only a little less than that of hybrids. And because of their diverse parentage these high-yielding varieties can be crossed to produce "varietal hybrids" which experience a much smaller yield reduction than pure-line hybrids when farmers replant their own seed. Although this modified breeding strategy has produced impressive results in some areas, Kenya being an especially interesting example, varietal improvement has so far been of slight importance in the Puebla Project. Up to the present time, the efforts to improve upon the surprisingly high yields obtainable with local varieties have not been successful. In large measure this is because the local varieties are very responsive to high levels of soil fertility, and impressive results have been achieved in increasing yields simply through heavier application of fertilizer, closer spacing, and other changes in agronomic practices.[58]

A benefit/cost analysis of the Puebla Project by Delbert Myren and Jairo Cano published in 1970 reported remarkable progress; and on the basis of a highly optimistic assessment of future prospects, they estimated an incredibly high benefit/cost ratio of 7.8.[59] A later study by Cano and Don Winkelmann was based on very conservative assumptions in order to provide "lower bound" estimates of benefits.[60] They assume, for example, that the yield increase for those participating in the project would not rise beyond the increase of 895 kilograms per hectare that was obtained in 1970 and that the area on which increased yields would be obtained would also remain at the 1970 level (12,661 hectares) throughout the 1971-76 period. In fact, preliminary reports for 1971 which they cite indicate a 16 per cent expansion in area. Although that increase was not negligible, it was much less than the expansion assumed in the 1970 study by Cano and Myren which projected expansion to 20,000 hectares in 1971 and further increases in subsequent years to 64,000 in 1975. It should also be noted that the 1972 calculations by Cano and Winkelmann include an estimate of the additional labor inputs involved in adopting the improved technology—mainly the extra time required for applying more fertilizer (including a split application for nitrogen), increasing the plant population from about 20 to 50,000 plants per hectare, better weed control, and harvesting and handling a heavier crop). They assumed that this labor would be provided by family members and that the opportunity cost of this family labor would be substantially less than the wage rate for agricultural workers and accordingly calculated the cost of the additional labor at one-half the agricultural wage rate prevailing in Puebla State. Cano and Myren did not include this item in their estimate of associated costs. They argued that fuller and more productive utilization of the large farm labor force in the region represented an improved income-earning opportunity and should not be treated as a cost from the viewpoint of regional development, a viewpoint that is not unreasonable in view of the prevailing "labor slack" in Mexican agriculture. The lowest of 12 benefit/cost ratios computed by Cano and Winkelmann was only 1.13, but the ultra-conservative assumptions on which that figure was based included a price of maize of only $49.50 per ton, an "export price" that took account of transport cost to Europe, whereas the guaranteed price for maize in Mexico is $75 per ton. Even their "high" estimate of a benefit/cost ratio —2.88—appears to be a rather conservative figure.

It remains to be seen how rapidly the yield-increasing innovations for maize will spread in the Puebla Project area and how widely the approach can be extended to other areas in Mexico. Difficulties are likely to be encountered in areas of unreliable rainfall because of the reluctance of small farmers to risk substantial cash outlays for inputs that would yield little or no return in a year of below average rainfall; and the administrative problems of extending a crop insurance program to such cultivators are considerable.[61] It is always a formidable problem to reach large numbers of small-scale, traditional farmers and Mexico's progress in strengthening farm extension programs has not been nearly as impressive as the achievements in creating a capacity for agricultural research.

It also seems likely that the success already achieved in expanding farm output under a bimodal strategy will compromise the prospects for a successful shift to a more unimodal approach. At least, the constraints imposed by the rate of growth of effective demand make it doubtful whether the Mexican government will be prepared to commit substantial resources to an expanded effort to promote increased output by smallholders. Because of the rapid expansion of farm output, the government's preoccupation with agriculture appears to have shifted from concern with a "food problem" to concern about an "agricultural problem"—using the terms in the same sense as in the earlier discussion of Japan's experience during the 1920s. Some worsening of agriculture's intersectoral terms of trade has already occurred. From 1957 to 1967 the index of agricultural production increased at the rapid rate of 5.0 per cent, but the 3.8 per cent annual rate of increase in sectoral GDP was appreciably less. This divergence arose partly because inputs per unit of output purchased from outside the agricultural sector increased; but it also reflected the fact that the 2.9 per cent annual increase in crop prices over that period was considerably less than the 4.4 per cent rate of increase in the general price level. As noted earlier, the real price of wheat fell by about one-half between the early 1950s and the early 1970s. And in addition a two-price system was instituted in the late 1960s whereby a lower price was paid to producers in the North Pacific states to dampen the rate of expansion of wheat production in order to avoid the need to stockpile or export at a loss.[62]

A recent study of Mexican agriculture suggests that those trends are likely to be accentuated in the 1970s. Possibilities of import substitution are virtually exhausted, and rapid expansion of agricultural exports will compensate only in part for the domestic demand constraint. Mexico's exports of wheat and maize depend upon a government subsidy and therefore pose a budget problem. And as previously noted, the rapid expansion of exports of fruits and vegetables to the United States has already encountered problems.[63]

It could be argued with considerable cogency that Mexico's bimodal strategy was well suited to the particular set of circumstances that the country faced. The irrigation potential in sparsely populated arid regions in the North, the availability of capital from the United States and the World Bank at relatively low interest rates, the demand conditions which made it socially as well as privately profitable to expand output at a rapid pace were all forces that encouraged the reliance on bimodal strategy. And they were especially potent forces because a number of the most powerful political leaders of the post-Revolutionary period were from the North and had a special interest in fostering the development of the two northern regions.

AGRICULTURAL DEVELOPMENT IN THE SOVIET UNION:
ABUNDANT USE OF CAPITAL AND LABOR

The Soviet Union has been selected as an example of agricultural development in a centrally planned economy because of its intrinsic importance and because there is now a substantial amount of scholarly documentation of Soviet experience covering a period of four decades. It was noted earlier that Soviet agricultural policies were successful in insuring that food shortages did not impair the realization of the goal of rapid industrialization with a strong emphasis on establishing heavy industry. It was also noted that the human and economic costs were high, and there is much evidence, from Russian as well as Western sources, that agriculture has been a chronic problem area in the Soviet economy. Its performance has been much less impressive than the Soviet achievements in rapidly raising the level of industrial output and technology.

The limited evidence currently available seems to suggest that Communist China has managed to avoid or minimize many of the problems that have hampered Soviet efforts to develop the agricultural sector. This seems especially true of the period since the modifications of Chinese agricultural policy following the setbacks of the late 1950s and early 1960s associated with the "Great Leap" and the initial policies applied to the rural communes that were created at that time. But because the period is very brief and poorly documented, we believe that it is more useful to focus on the Soviet experience. It should be recognized, however, that a number of the deficiencies of "command farming" as it has been developed in the Soviet Union might not be so pertinent to the Chinese situation where agricultural strategy appears to have been more pragmatic and with somewhat less emphasis on centralized control. It is also significant that Mao Tse-tung and most of the other leaders have had long and intimate association with the Chinese peasantry, especially during the Yenan period. In contrast, Lenin, Stalin, and most of the other Soviet leaders had very weak links with the Russian farm population.

The Collectivization of Soviet Agriculture

It is well-known that since the collectivization drive that began in 1929, Soviet agriculture has had a bimodal and dual-size structure of a very special character—though it is one that has been repeated in varying degree in the countries of Eastern Europe that have followed the Soviet model. From the early 1930s up until the 1960s the collective farms (*kolkhozy*) dominated agricultural production in the Soviet Union. It was apparently late in 1929 that Stalin made the decision to force drastically the pace of collectivization. Collective organizations, mainly of a looser type than the *kolkhoz*, accounted for only 1.7 per cent of peasant households and 2.3 per cent of the crop area in 1928. By 1938, 93.5 per cent of the households and 99.3 per cent of the planted area had been collectivized.[64]

In implementing that decision, the fiction was maintained that it represented a "spontaneous" movement of peasant households to join the collectives. However, during a short period when coercion was relaxed following the publication of an article by Stalin in March 1930 condemning the excesses committed by local officials in their zeal to force the pace, the proportion of the peasant population collectivized fell from a reported 55 per cent in March to only 24 per cent in June. But the rapid pace was quickly resumed; 53 per cent of the peasants' households and 68 per cent of the crop area were collectivized in 1931 and the corresponding figures reached 83 and 94 per cent by 1935.[65] Initially, there were a great many instances in which livestock as well as land was collectivized. As a result of shortages of feed, mismanagement, and a widespread tendency of peasants to slaughter their livestock for their own use rather than surrender it to the authorities, there was a sharp decline in all types of livestock. By 1932, the cattle population was down by 50 per cent; the decline in the number of sheep and pigs was even greater.[66] In Stalin's *Pravda* article of March 1930, it was stated that "small vegetable gardens, small orchards, the dwelling houses, a part of the dairy cattle, small livestock, poultry, etc., are *not socialized*," although in fact officials at many levels issued directives collectivizing all types of livestock.[67] Apart from some exceptions in 1930 and 1931, small private plots of about one-quarter hectare have been permitted, and these have accounted for a considerable proportion of total output, especially of livestock products.

In the early period of collectivization, state farms (*sovkhozy*), which were operated as state enterprises with hired labor, were relatively unimportant. But in recent years state farms have accounted for a large part of the increase in cultivated area that has resulted from the opening up of the virgin lands, and some collectives have been converted into state farms. The relative importance of the various types of farm units is summarized in the following tabulation; the figures refer to all Soviet territory as of the given date:[68]

Sown area
(*millions of hectares*)

	1928	1937	1956	1959	1962
Collective farms	1.4	116.0	152.1	130.2	114.4
State farms	1.7	12.2	35.3	58.8	94.8
Private holdings of collective peasants and state employees	1.1	6.24	7.25	7.2	6.6
Private land, individual peasants	108.7	0.86	0.03	0.01	...

Employees of state farms, railway workers, and even teachers and local officials in rural areas often cultivate a small plot and possess some livestock. These holdings increased somewhat between 1959 and 1962, whereas the land allotted to peasant households on collective farms declined from 5.3 to 4.2 million hectares. Although the private holdings represent only a minute fraction of the total cultivated area, they have accounted for a sizable fraction of output of vegetables and also of livestock products as summarized in the following tabulation:[69]

Per cent of total output

	1940	1950	1957	1962
Meat, total private	72[a]	67	53	44.2
of which:				
Collective-farm peasants	(46)	(50)	(39)	...
Milk, total private	77[a]	75	54	44.9
of which:				
Collective-farm peasants	(44)	(51)	(37)	...
Eggs, total private	94[a]	89	86	26.4
of which:				
Collective-farm peasants	(58)	(61)	(57)	...

[a] Includes an unusually large number of individual peasants in newly annexed areas. These are not significant in other years.

It is reported that as late as 1965 private plots accounted for 32 per cent of gross agricultural output even though they accounted for only 3.2 per cent of the sown area. Private plot holders are, however, frequently able to use free hay, straw, and pasture of the collective farm, so their share of total inputs is greater than their share of sown area.[70]

There has been continuing tension between official policy aimed at maximizing the output of the collective farms—especially the collection of grain at low prices for resale to the urban population—and the continued existence of the private plots. Two principal factors seem to explain the decision reached in 1931 to reopen markets in towns and cities at which *kolkhoz* members were permitted to sell products from their private plots and the reluctant parallel decision to accept this coexistence of private and collective production. In the first place, the failure of the collectives in their attempts to manage livestock enterprises, for which individual incentive, initiative, and interest are paramount, could not be ignored. Second, it must have quickly become obvious that the incomes received by members of collective households as compensation for their work on the collective farm was usually so low that it was essential to allow the individual households to augment their incomes by intensive cultivation of a small plot and by keeping a cow, a sow, and perhaps a few chickens.

Because of the drastic reduction of the availability of work animals, sheer necessity as well as an ideological commitment to large-scale, mechanized farming dictated a rapid expansion in the use of tractors on the collective farms. Thus the number of tractors in use rose from just over 25,000 in 1928 to nearly half a million in 1938, with similarly sharp increases in the number of tractor-drawn plows, combines, threshers, and other items of farm equipment. Until 1958, the equipment used for cultivation on the collective farms was operated by the Machine Tractor Stations which also played a major role in the compulsory procurement of grain. The prices paid for quota deliveries were set at an extremely low level. The compulsory procurement price for wheat in 1936, inclusive of handling cost, was only 15 rubles per ton. Since this wheat was sold to the state milling enterprises at 107 rubles per ton, the "turnover tax" that accrued to the government amounted to 92 rubles or almost nine-tenths of the wholesale price inclusive of tax.[71] This compulsory collection of grain appears to have been the principal means by which the agricultural population was forced to bear a large part of the real cost of financing the rapid industrialization that was initiated in 1928 with the adoption of the first Five-Year Plan.

The collective farms pay their members on the basis of "workday units" (*trudoden*) which are accumulated according to the quantity and quality of work performed.[72] Detailed norms are recommended to provide a basis for determining these differentials. The daily norm for an unskilled occupation such as night watchman might be fixed at half of a "workday unit" whereas skilled workers might earn two and a half times the norm. There is also a complicated system of bonuses awarded to brigades or teams. The actual value of a workday unit depends on the amount available for distribution at the end of the year, divided by the total number of workday units earned by all members of the collective, including the chairman and other *kolkhoz* officials who receive an allocation of workday units in addition to a fixed salary. But the income that all other members receive from the collective farm is determined as a residual. We will see that a major problem associated with the Soviet system is the enormous variation in the residual income accruing to members of collectives in different regions. Regional variations in the amount of supplementary income from private plots is also great because of differences in the quality of land and in access to markets.

The collectivization of Soviet agriculture with the coexistence of mechanized production by the collective farms and the use of primitive techniques on the private holdings of *kolkhoz* members resulted in a pattern that Theodore W. Schultz has described as "an absurd, bimodal structure of farm sizes, that is, exceedingly large state and collective farms and tiny plot farms, a bimodal structure based on big tractors and many hoes."[73] Under this dual-size structure there is obviously intensive use of labor on the private plots. Although farming carried out by the collectives is highly mechanized, the level of labor inputs is surprisingly high even for enterprises such as production of wheat and other small grains that are particularly well adapted to mechanical cultivation. As of 1960 labor use in grain production on collective farms was 10 times as high as the labor input per unit of output in the United States whereas the mechanical energy available per hectare was almost half that available in the United States.[74] Exceptionally large investments in agriculture in the late 1950s and during the 1960s led to a substantial reduction in labor requirements. The reduction in labor requirements between 1960 and 1968 for grain and certain other products was more rapid than the corresponding reduction in labor requirements in the United States during that period, although the reverse tended to be true when the 1960 differential was less than seven or eight times. D. Gale Johnson estimates that the overall reduction in labor requirements per unit of output in Russia was about 30 per cent, a significant reduction to be achieved in an eight-year period although "the investment costs of achieving such a reduction appear to be very high in comparison to the costs of an equal reduction in the United States."[75] Noteworthy changes resulting from the heavy investments during the decade ending in 1968 were an increase in the number of tractors from 924,000 to 1.82 million and in the supply of chemical fertilizers from 2.5 to 8.3 million tons.[76]

Although collectivization and the rapid introduction of tractors made it easy to release labor from agriculture to meet rapidly expanding needs for labor for industry and construction as industrial development was accelerated during the 1930s, the reduction in the absolute and relative size of the agricultural labor force in the postwar period has been sluggish compared to the countries of Western Europe. Thus the 1959 census indicated a farm work force of 38.4 million or close to 40 per cent of the total labor force.[77] Inasmuch as income payments to the members of a collective are determined as a residual, there is in fact very little incentive for *kolkhoz* managers to economize on the use of labor.

The pricing of labor is only one of a number of ways in which prices are determined in such fashion that they fail to provide appropriate signals and adequate incentives to encourage efficient allocation of resources. In the course of describing the variation in product prices for (a) sales against a compulsory quota, (b) over-quota sales, (c) commission sales to consumer cooperatives, and (d) free-market sales, Alec Nove notes that the government's policies result in "a bewildering multiplicity of prices." Government purchase prices "change little or not at all in response to shortage or abundance" and relative prices have little economic meaning.[78]

A problem of equity as well as efficiency in resource allocation arises because there is no satisfactory substitute for differential rent. Until 1958, the government extracted a form of differential rent from the collective farms located on more valuable land (because of soil quality or site value) by appropriate variations in the scale of payments demanded for the services of the Machine Tractor Stations and in the quotas for compulsory deliveries at low prices.[79] But with the abolition of the Machine Tractor Stations and that part of the multiple price system, the government lost the principal means available for correcting for differences in natural advantage between areas. The zonal differentiation of prices is a gesture in that direction, but the differentials are inadequate to offset the very large differences in cost. In documenting this problem, Nove presents figures reported by the Soviet economist S. Nedelin which indicate that costs of grain production in Kirov in northern Russia were three and a half times higher than on collective farms in Krasnodar with more fertile land, and this in spite of the fact that members of collectives in Kirov were paid only four or five rubles (in cash and in kind) per man-day work unit (*trudoden*) compared to 11 or 12 units per *trudoden* in Krasnodar. The lack of a mechanism that reflects the differential value of land also makes it difficult to achieve an efficient pattern of regional specialization. Because of the adverse effects of the present system on efficiency and equity, the problem of land rent is being vigorously debated by Soviet economists.[80]

Many of the difficulties that have made Soviet agriculture a problem area are now acknowledged by Soviet economists, although there does not appear to be an emerging consensus concerning the remedial measures that would be acceptable and effective. And there is, of course, still a tendency to extol the virtues of the Soviet approach. K. P. Obolenski, a Soviet economist participating in a 1965 conference in Rome on economic problems of agriculture in industrial societies, was understandably at pains to emphasize the advantages of the organization of agricultural production in the Soviet Union. The principal claim that he advanced was the advantage of being able to *plan* the level and composition of farm output in the Soviet system. In fact, the evidence seems clear that in agriculture there has been only a very loose relationship between plans and performance. Obolenski asserted that the problems that limited the effectiveness of agricultural planning in the past had been overcome, but his arguments were not very persuasive and do not seem to have been borne out by subsequent experience.[81] This is, of course, not surprising because of the inherent difficulty in reconciling decentralized decision making, which is so important in agriculture, with centrally determined plans that fix specific output targets. And of course the problem of variability of output because of weather conditions is an intractable one; and the effects of adverse weather are perhaps especially acute in the absence of strong local initiative to act promptly and vigorously to minimize the effects of weather conditions.

The Decision to Collectivize and Agriculture's Role in Development

Given the evidence that the performance of agriculture has been so unimpressive, a fundamental question arises: why did the Soviet leadership opt for the policy of compulsory collectivization? It is clear that the question cannot be answered definitively; the motivations were complex and the decision was made privately by Stalin and a few close associates.[82] The immediate precipitating forces were related to a crisis in grain supplies for the urban areas. Jerzy Karcz and M. Lewin have argued that that crisis was largely a consequence of mismanagement, ill-advised policies based on an incorrect analysis of peasant behavior, neglect of measures that could have fostered increased production.[83] The decision to collectivize must also have been influenced to some extent by a major tenet of Marxian ideology which emphasizes the superiority of large-scale farms.[84]

Writers as opposed in their general outlook as Maurice Dobb and Naum Jasny seem to agree, however, that the collectivization drive was motivated primarily by a desire to insure food supplies for the urban population by controlling the disposition of farm production.[85] The actions which forced the pace of collectivization were also influenced by the political objective of establishing governmental control over the rural population so that an independent peasant class would not constitute a threat to the regime.[86] Hence, many party leaders were determined to eliminate individual peasants—and more especially the *kulaks* because they were regarded as the chief potential threat to the regime. And a less-drastic approach would have been difficult to implement because the leaders of the Soviet regime had such weak ties with the rural population.

Many scholars have argued that the collectivization policy must be assessed as an integral part of the "Stalinist strategy" of accelerated industrialization with its primary emphasis on heavy industries to produce "the means of production" that were considered the key to rapid growth.[87] In Abram Bergson's terse phrase, "steel was a final good to Stalin, and bread an intermediate one."[88]

The overriding objective of agricultural strategy, from this point of view, was the extraction of a surplus of good and raw materials to satisfy the requirements of industry and an expanding urban population and to earn foreign exchange to finance essential imports. A corollary of this strategy of surplus extraction was that agriculture should make a maximum contribution to domestic saving and therefore the reverse flow of inputs and consumer goods to agriculture should be held to an absolute minimum.

Two facts which are beyond dispute lend credence to this interpretation. The Soviet Union has been successful in transforming a relatively underdeveloped economy into a modern industrial power. And the exceedingly low prices paid for grain delivered against compulsory quotas and in payment of the services provided by the Machine Tractor Stations represented a significant flow of capital to the nonagricultural sectors made possible by a form of forced saving imposed on the rural population.

The fact that rapid industrialization was linked historically with measures that lowered the standard of living of the rural population does not prove, however, that agriculture made a large net contribution to the capital requirements of other sectors. To consider only the "surplus" that was extracted from agriculture is clearly not sufficient to settle the issue. James R. Millar has emphasized that the evidence required to estimate the magnitude of the net flow is not available. He suggests, however, that the net capital contribution obtained from agriculture was probably very modest because the reverse flow of resources into agriculture, including the budget grants that financed the Machine Tractor Stations and interest-free capital grants to state farms, may have been nearly as large as the expansion of agriculture's sales to nonagriculture.[89]

Although the magnitude of the net flow of resources out of agriculture is in doubt, the fact remains that the forced procurement policies did insure that urban food shortages did not interfere with the goal of rapid industrialization with prority to heavy industry. Even in years of reduced production, industrial workers were buffered from the effects of a short fall in farm output because, as noted earlier, under the Soviet system farm households had become the residual claimants for the grain supplies available. That is, food supplies for the nonfarm population were assured because compulsory deliveries of grain had become a "First Commandment," in the terminology that gained currency during the collectivization drive in the 1930s.

It might be claimed that in the context of the Stalinist strategy neglect of agriculture was rational since the record demonstrates that the overall policies were successful in transforming a predominantly agrarian society into a modern industrial state. That view is, however, subject to several qualifications. First, it should be noted that considerable industrial development had taken place in Russia prior to World War I, a sizable rail network had been built, and the country had small but well-qualified technical, scientific, and statistical cadres so that it is wrong to picture Russia on the eve of the revolution as a country at a very early stage of economic growth.

Much more important, however, are the considerations that suggest that the economic as well as the human costs of the development process were in some sense unnecessarily high. The most obvious factors to be noted in that regard are the direct effects of compulsory collectivization—a sharp drop in farm output, an unknown but substantial loss of human life in the famine of 1933, and an enormous waste of capital in the form of the draft animals that perished during the early years of the collectivization drive. Handicraft production and small-scale industries were also a casualty of that period, and their destruction accentuated the fall in living standards. The rejection of criteria based on conventional concepts of economic rationality and the heavy reliance on "command farming" and a "campaign approach" led to substantial waste and inefficiency.

Of greater significance than the costs in terms of static efficiency, however, are the adverse effects of the Soviet strategy on the process of technical change that can give rise to substantial increases in factor productivity. The estimates available seem to indicate clearly that, apart from the late 1950s when economic incentives were abruptly improved, increases in factor productivity in Soviet agriculture have made virtually no contribution to the expansion of agricultural output. Johnson's estimates of changes in agricultural output and inputs between 1928 and 1938 point to a decline in factor productivity of between 3 and 13 per cent depending on the assumptions used in the measurement of inputs; and estimates of changes between 1928 and 1939 by Karcz indicate a similar decline.[90]

It is hardly surprising that the environment of "command farming" has proved hostile to the introduction of a range of new inputs such as improved seed-fertilizer combinations and associated changes in techniques. The refusal for many years to introduce hybrid maize, because of the ideological objections of Lysenko, is an extreme example but other types of problems have probably had a greater negative influence. In particular, the structure of incentives and the limitations on decentralized decision making must have impeded the adoption of a sequence of innovations well adapted to local circumstances, including the use of complementary factors such as tractors of varying size and a variety of implements which were often simply not available because firms manufacturing farm inputs lacked the awareness, incentive, and capacity to respond to the diverse needs of farm units.

The failure to exploit the potential for advances in factor productivity based on technical change is especially striking because of the strong emphasis on research and the training of scientists. Even in the late nineteenth and early twentieth centuries, Russian scientists had made notable contributions in several fields of agricultural research. And under the Soviet regime there has been strong and increasing emphasis on research institutes and expanded training of research workers in institutions of higher education. A Soviet scholar has recently reported that "the U.S.S.R. is now in first place as regards number of scientific workers. Every fourth scientist in the world holds a Soviet passport." And in 1972, *Izvestia* reported that the number of employees in the country's scientific research organizations had grown six times faster than the total number of workers.[91] It is clear that a large proportion of Soviet scientists are working on top priority projects such as development of the hydrogen bomb and space exploration; but the principal explanation for the limited contribution of agricultural research in fostering advances in farm productivity and output seems to be related to characteristics of the Soviet farm economy. The decision-making framework for agricultural management at both the macro and micro level has the effect of discouraging innovation and specialization.[92]

The Relevance of the Soviet Experience

Two aspects of agriculture's role in the development of the Soviet economy appear to have particular relevance to the contemporary developing countries. The Soviet experience emphasizes once again the critical importance of parallel development of agriculture and industry and the fact that it is likely to be essential for agriculture to make a net contribution to the large capital requirements for industrial expansion, infrastructure, and the development of educational and other institutions required for modern economic growth. At the same time it illustrates the disadvantages of an agricultural strategy that does not foster the types of technological change that permit substantial increases in factor productivity.

The second aspect, the failure to exploit the potential for increases in factor productivity, is especially significant. Most of the contemporary developing countries are subject to more binding resource constraints because the potential for expanding production through extending the area under cultivation is so much more limited than in the Soviet agricultural economy. There was an additional type of "slack" that characterized the Soviet food economy which is also much more limited in the contemporary late-developing countries (and was also more limited in Japan and Taiwan during the early decades of their modern economic growth). The reliance on the low-cost sources of calories and nutrients in the developing countries is such that there is much less possibility of offsetting reductions in total food supplies by increased reliance on grain and potatoes, starchy staples that are the cheapest sources of energy and a number of essential nutrients. In addition, the task confronting the contemporary countries in transforming their economic structure is made much more difficult because their farm work force as well as total labor force are increasing so rapidly.

Given the stringent resource base in Japan and Taiwan, it is most unlikely that the agricultural sector would have been able to make such large contributions to the financing of industrial expansion if it had not been for the success achieved in fostering technical progress and increases in factor productivity. It is also clear that the increases in agricultural productivity, and more particularly the increases in farm labor productivity, in Japan and Taiwan would not have been possible without the concurrent growth of manufacturing and other nonfarm sectors.

Some years ago Clifford Geertz stressed that aspect in contrasting the experience of Japan following the Meiji restoration and Java's experience in the late nineteenth and early twentieth centuries. In both countries considerable technical advance was achieved; but whereas in Japan the traditional labor-intensive, small-scale farming system "came to be complementarily related to an expanding manufacturing system in indigenous hands . . . Javanese peasant agriculture came to be complementarily related to an expanding agro-industrial structure under foreign management." Geertz's final conclusion is that "the real tragedy of colonial history in Java after 1830 is not that the peasantry suffered. It suffered much worse elsewhere, and, if one surveys the miseries of the submerged classes of the nineteenth century generally, it may even seem to have gotten off relatively light. The tragedy is that it suffered for nothing."[93]

Considerable progress has been made in raising crop yields in Java through the development of irrigation, varietal improvement, and considerable use of fertilizer. But because of population growth in an economy where close to 70 per cent of the economically active still find their livelihood in agriculture, there has been appalling fragmentation of crop land. In the Jogjakarta Region of Central Java where population density is especially high, the average density per square kilometer rose from 492 in 1930 to 784 in 1970. Areas with fertile, well-irrigated lowland soils have a disproportionate concentration of population. The 164 families in one village have access to 29.5 hectares, equivalent to an incredible density of 2350 persons per square kilometer.[94] The average holding for families *with land* was less than one-quarter of a hectare; and 28 families had no land at all. Those families and others with minuscule plots struggle to survive by working as laborers or by tapping coconut trees and producing sugar at returns which at best provide bare subsistence. There is strong evidence of considerable hunger and malnutrition, and the relatively low rate of population growth (an average of about 1 per cent in central Java between 1930 and 1961) seems clearly to be a consequence of the grim "positive checks" postulated by Malthus.[95] Java is rivaled only by Bangladesh as an example of the dangers of "partial modernization"—that is, a situation in which advances in agriculture, infrastructure, and public health are unaccompanied by structural change. In consequence, the task of transforming Java's predominantly agrarian structure has become even more formidable because of the severe population pressure and poverty in the countryside and the intensification of production that has already taken place.

It can be said of the Soviet Union, as of Japan, Taiwan, and Mexico, that although "the peasantry suffered" they did not suffer for nothing, which underscores the necessity of linking the development of agriculture with a process of economic transformation. But it is our contention that the unimodal strategy as exemplified by Japan and Taiwan is more efficient in attaining that objective, while simultaneously contributing to the goals of improving the well-being of the rural population and fostering attitudinal and behavior change on which the demographic transition and other aspects of social modernization depend.

NOTES

1. The rate for the earlier period is an adjusted estimate by Frank Lorimer, *The Population of the Soviet Union: History and Prospects,* League of Na-

tions, Economic, Financial, and Transit Department (Geneva, 1946), p. 112; the estimates for the later periods are from the United Nations, *Demographic Yearbook, 1971* (New York, 1972).

2. Raymond P. Christensen, *Taiwan's Agricultural Development: Its Relevance for Developing Countries Today,* U.S. Department of Agriculture, Economic Research Service, Foreign Agricultural Economic Report No. 39 (Washington, D.C., 1968), pp. 16, 21. For the period 1952-68, T. H. Lee reports a 6 per cent rate of increase in gross output and a 5.4 per cent annual increase in net output. His estimates of the rate of increase to be attributed to technological change based on a Solow-type model, are similar to Christensen's estimates which are based on the difference between the rates of change of output and total inputs ("Intersectoral Capital Flows in the Economic Development of Taiwan, 1895-1960" [Ph.D. dissertation, Cornell University, Ithaca, New York, 1968], pp. 73-80 and *Intersectoral Capital Flows in the Economic Development of Taiwan, 1895-1960* [Ithaca, New York, 1971], p. 49).

3. Employment estimates based on Household Registration data show a slight increase in agriculture through 1969, but those figures are affected by a lag in registering changes in occupation. According to estimates based on a Quarterly Labor Force Survey that was instituted in 1963, agriculture's share in the labor force fell below 50 per cent in 1966 and the absolute size of the farm work force declined at an annual rate of 1 per cent during the 1967-70 period. *Quarterly Report on the Labor Force Survey in Taiwan,* January 1971, Labor Force Survey Research Institute, Taiwan Provincial Government, Taichung, and sponsored by the Council for International Economic Cooperation and Development; cited in T. H. Lee, "Strategies for Transferring Agricultural Surplus Under Different Agricultural Situations in Taiwan," in *Agriculture and Economic Development: Structural Readjustment in Asian Perspective,* Vol. 2, Japan Economic Research Center, Center Paper No. 17 (Tokyo, 1972), p. 411.

4. Mo-Huan Hsing, *The Philippines and Taiwan—Industrialization and Trade Policies,* OECD Development Centre, Paris (London, 1971), p. 192.

5. David J. Turnham, "Income Distribution: Measurement and Problems" (Paper prepared for the Society for International Development Twelfth World Conference, Ottawa, May 16-19, 1971).

6. The labor input figures refer to the farm labor force and the land input refers to the cultivated area rather than the planted or cropped area. As noted shortly, the increases in output per farm worker were associated with increases in the number of days worked per year, and the increase in output per cultivated acre reflected increased multiple cropping as well as yield increases for individual crops (e.g., in the "first crop" and "second crop" of rice).

7. The decline in land productivity between 1936/40 and 1946/50 was a result of the disruptions of World War II and its aftermath. Consumption of chemical fertilizers which had reached a prewar peak of 518,000 tons in 1938, had only recovered to 290,000 tons by 1950; and the deterioration in irrigation and drainage facilities had not yet been made good. See S. C. Hsieh and T. H. Lee, *An Analytical Review of Agricultural Development in Taiwan: An Input-*

Output and Productivity Approach, Joint Commission on Rural Reconstruction, Economic Digest Series No. 12 (Taipei, 1958), p. 38.

8. Joint Commission on Rural Reconstruction, *Taiwan Agricultural Statistics 1901-1965,* Economic Digest Series No. 18 (Taipei, 1966), p. 219.

9. Samuel P. S. Ho, "The Development Policy of the Japanese Colonial Government in Taiwan, 1895-1945," in *Government and Economic Development,* edited by Gustav Ranis (New Haven, Connecticut, 1971), p. 319.

10. Data for 1901-51 from Joint Commission on Rural Reconstruction, *Taiwan Agricultural Statistics,* pp. 23, 47; for 1952-70 from Republic of China, Council for International Economic Cooperation and Development, *Taiwan Statistical Data Book 1972* (Taipei, 1972), pp. 49-52.

11. Ho, "Japanese Colonial Government in Taiwan," p. 318.

12. Ramon H. Myers and Adrienne Ching, "Agricultural Development in Taiwan under Japanese Colonial Rule," *Journal of Asian Studies* Vol. 23, No. 4 (August 1964), p. 559.

13. G. W. Barclay, *Colonial Development and Population in Taiwan* (Princeton, 1954), p. 51.

14. Myers and Ching, "Agricultural Development in Taiwan," p. 563.

15. Ho, "Japanese Colonial Government in Taiwan," p. 314.

16. Lee, "Intersectoral Capital Flows," p. 110.

17. The foregoing draws particularly on an interview in January 1971 with the head of the Extension Section of the Ta-Chia Farmers Association. His account was based on 23 years of experience with that Association and observations during the mid-1930s when he was in his teens.

18. Ho, "Japanese Colonial Government in Taiwan," p. 309.

19. Republic of China, Council for International Economic Cooperation and Development, *Taiwan Statistical Data Book 1971* (Taipei, 1971), p. 170.

20. Chao-chen Chen, "Land Reform and Agricultural Development in Taiwan," in *Conference on Economic Development of Taiwan* (Taipei, 1967); T. H. Shen, *Agricultural Development on Taiwan Since World War II* (Ithaca, New York, 1964), pp. 40-46.

21. John M. Brewster, "Traditional Social Structures as Barriers to Change," in *Agricultural Development and Economic Growth,* edited by Herman M. Southworth and Bruce F. Johnston (Ithaca, New York, 1967).

22. See Lee, "Intersectoral Capital Flows"; idem, *Intersectoral Capital Flows;* idem, "Strategies for Transferring Agricultural Surplus."

23. Ibid. pp. 415-16.

24. We are indebted to Victor Horcasitas and Bernard Pillet, graduate students in the Food Research Institute, Stanford University, for assistance in the preparation of this section.

25. We are grateful to Clark W. Reynolds for calling our attention to these financial effects on real growth in Mexico. (For additional detail, see Dwight S. Brothers and Leopoldo Solís, *Mexican Financial Development* [Austin, Texas, 1966] and Robert L. Bennett, *The Financial Sector and Economic Development: The Mexican Case* [Baltimore, 1965].) Reynolds points out, however, that intersectoral capital flows between agriculture and the rest of the

economy seem to have been inhibited to some extent in Mexico by the lack of flexibility in credit policies which fail to allow for regional differentials in the cost of financial intermediation. Since interest rate ceilings on deposits and loans are based on conditions in the major urban areas, rural saving and investment have been discouraged. These policies have also encouraged some outflow of savings to United States financial institutions; farm operators are often not aware of the alternative of investing in Mexican bonds (marketed primarily in urban areas) which would have given a better return even with an allowance for a somewhat larger risk premium.

26. Reed Hertford, "Mexico: Its Sources of Increased Agricultural Output," in *Economic Progress of Agriculture in Developing Nations,* U.S. Department of Agriculture, Economic Research Service, Foreign Agricultural Economic Report No. 59 (Washington, D.C., 1970), p. 99. Leopoldo Solís's "Mexican Economic Policy in the Post-War Period: The Views of Mexican Economists," *American Economic Review* Vol. 61, No. 3 Part 2 (June 1971), pp. 4-5 gives even higher rates of increase.

27. Hertford, "Mexico: Increased Agricultural Output," p. 99.

28. William O. Freithaler, *Mexico's Foreign Trade and Economic Development* (New York, 1968), p. 151.

29. C. John Fliginger et al., *Supplying U.S. Markets with Fresh Winter Produce: Capabilities of U.S. and Mexican Production Areas,* U.S. Department of Agriculture, Economic Research Service, Agricultural Economic Report No. 154 (Washington, D.C., 1969), p. 46.

30. Donald K. Freebairn, "The Dichotomy of Prosperity and Poverty in Mexican Agriculture," *Land Economics* Vol. 45, No. 1 (February 1969), p. 35.

31. Land expropriated from haciendas and redistributed under Mexico's agrarian reform laws has been assigned to members of nearby communities, and the property rights are vested in the community—the *ejido*—as a group. The *ejidatario* (head of an *ejidal* household) is given the use of the land for his lifetime, and he can pass it on to an heir. *Ejidatarios* are not permitted to sell, mortgage, or lease their land, although it is reported that renting of *ejidal* land is not uncommon. Each *ejidal* parcel was supposed to consist of four hectares, but many are smaller. In a few cases *ejidal* land is farmed collectively, but in general the parcels are farmed as separate operational units. Private landowners were permitted to keep 100 hectares of irrigated land and larger amounts of rainfed or pasture land; but in practice many private holdings exceed the acreage ceilings.

32. Delbert T. Myren, "Integrating the Rural Market into the National Economy of Mexico," mimeographed (Madison: University of Wisconsin, Land Tenure Center, LTC No. 46, June 1968).

33. W. Whitney Hicks, "Agricultural Development in Northern Mexico, 1940-1960," *Land Economics* Vol. 43, No. 4 (November 1967), p. 396.

34. In the South Pacific Region the rate of increase in capital inputs was actually less than the rate of growth in output so that the capital/output ratio fell from .3 to .2 whereas in the North Pacific the increase in capital inputs was more than twice as rapid as the growth of output so that the capital/output

ratio rose over the three decades from .9 to 2.5. See Clark W. Reynolds, *The Mexican Economy* (New Haven, Connecticut, 1970), pp. 94-127.

35. Ibid. p. 124.

36. See footnote 34 for additional detail on the *ejidos* and Reynolds's *Mexican Economy*, Chap. 4 for a brief analysis of the agrarian reform.

36a. Edmundo Flores, *Land Reform and the Alliance for Progress*, Princeton University, Center of International Studies Memorandum No. 27 (Princeton, New Jersey, May 1963), p. 7.

37. Reynolds, *Mexican Economy*, pp. 154-55.

38. Solís, "Views of Mexican Economists," p. 11.

39. Ibid. pp. 12-13.

40. Reynolds, *Mexican Economy*, p. 152.

41. Solís, "Views of Mexican Economists," p. 14.

42. The 1970 Census, which unlike previous censuses was carried out in January when employment in agriculture is at a seasonal low, overstates the decline in the farm labor force, although its share may well have declined from 54 per cent in 1960 to about 46 per cent. See Donald B. Keesing, "Mexico's Development: Modernization and the Labor Force Since 1803," book manuscript (1971).

43. Solís, "Views of Mexican Economists," p. 14.

44. Folke Dovring, "Economic Results of Land Reforms," Agency for International Development, Spring Review of Land Reform (Washington, D.C., June 2-4, 1970), p. 16; Sergio Reyes Osorio et al., *Estructura Agraria y Desarrollo Agrícola en México*, 3 vols., Centro de Investigaciones Agrarias (Mexico, D. F., 1970), all references are to Vol. 1.

45. The analysis of yield levels takes into consideration irrigation levels and the relative acreage of a crop in *ejidal* and private holdings in the various states. It should also be noted that the more rapid increase in yields for the *ejidos* represented a "catching up" process as the *ejido* yields in 1950 were clearly lower. Bernard Pillet, "Land Tenure and Agricultural Productivity in Mexico," mimeographed (Stanford, California: Food Research Institute, Stanford University, March 1973).

46. This type of policy-induced inefficiency in resource allocation is suggested by Hugh Stringer's study of agriculture in the state of Morelos. He found that there was misallocation of resources in *ejidos* because farmers are forced to devote much of their acreage to sugar and rice, two of the least profitable crops, as a consequence of legal requirements and a policy of restricting credit to the growing of these crops ("Land, Farmer and Sugar Cane in Morelos, Mexico," *Land Economics* Vol. 48, No. 3 [August 1972]).

47. Freithaler, "Mexico's Foreign Trade," pp. 72, 75.

48. Ibid. pp. 74, 78.

49. Delbert T. Myren, "The Rockefeller Foundation Program in Corn and Wheat in Mexico," in *Subsistence Agriculture and Economic Development*, edited by Clifton R. Wharton, Jr. (Chicago, 1969), p. 442.

50. Sterling Wortman as quoted in Myren, "Corn and Wheat in Mexico," p. 441.

AGRICULTURE'S ROLE IN: TAIWAN, MEXICO, SOVIET UNION   295

51. Freithaler, "Mexico's Foreign Trade," pp. 62-65.
52. The figures in terms of "agricultural products" based on the official Mexican classification, which are somewhat lower than the figures in the text which are based on a United Nations classification, show a peak of 51 per cent in 1955 and a decline to 43 per cent in 1965. See Timothy King, *Mexico: Industrialization and Trade Policies since 1940*, OECD Development Centre, Paris (London, 1970), p. 20.
53. William L. Rodman, "Mexico's Restraints on Shipments of 1970-71 Winter Fruits and Vegetables to the United States Have Mixed Results," *Foreign Agriculture* Vol. 9, No. 22 (May 31, 1971), p. 2.
54. Reynolds, *Mexican Economy*, pp. 177-79.
55. Reyes Osorio et al., *Estructura Agraria*, p. 261.
56. Dana G. Dalrymple and William I. Jones, "Evaluating the 'Green Revolution' " (Paper prepared for the joint Meeting of the American Association for the Advancement of Science and the Consejo Nacional de Ciencia y Technologia, Mexico City, June 20, 1973), p. 17.
57. Myren, "Integrating the Rural Market," p. 10.
58. Leobardo Jiménez Sánchez, "Strategies for Increasing Agricultural Production on Small Holdings: The Puebla Project" (Paper prepared for the Food Research Institute Conference on Strategies for Agricultural Development in the 1970s, Stanford University, Stanford, California, December 13-16, 1971). According to a recent report on the Puebla Project, two native varieties that have been very important in the project area were selected over a period of years by a local dairy farmer in a small area that had been well fertilized. It is therefore not so surprising that they were highly responsive to fertilizers. Carroll P. Streeter, *Reaching the Developing World's Small Farmers*, The Rockefeller Foundation (New York, 1973?), pp. 9-10. It is also significant that the original hearth of the maize plant is only a few hundred miles away from Puebla, and farmers in the region have been growing and selecting maize varieties in that environment for several thousand years.
59. Jairo Cano and Delbert T. Myren, "Benefit-Cost Analysis of the Puebla Project," in *Strategies for Increasing Agricultural Production on Small Holdings*, edited by Delbert T. Myren (Puebla, Mexico, 1970).
60. Jairo Cano and Don Winkelmann, "Plan Puebla: análisis de beneficios y costos," *El Trimestre Economico* Vol. 39, No. 4 (October-December 1972).
61. Myren, "Integrating the Rural Market," p. 5. Some farmers and groups of farmers in the project area are beginning to install tubewells for supplementary irrigation and thus lessen the risk of inadequate or poorly timed rainfall. It is reported that this is feasible in three of the project's five zones. Streeter, *Reaching the Developing World's Small Farmers*, p. 11.
62. Dalrymple and Jones, "Evaluating the 'Green Revolution,' " p. 17.
63. The study referred to in the text was carried out by John Duloy and Roger Norton of the World Bank in cooperation with the Mexican government. It projects an increase in agricultural exports at an annual rate of 6.8 per cent between 1968 and 1974, with exports accounting for nearly a third of sector income in the later year. Nevertheless, the projected rate of increase

in sector income is only 3.2 per cent, substantially less than the projected 4.7 per cent rate of increase in production ("CHAC, A Programming Model of Mexican Agriculture," in "Multi-Level Planning: Case Studies in Mexico," edited by Louis M. Goreux and Alan S. Manne, book manuscript, World Bank and Stanford University [1972], Chap. 4.3, pp. 387-91).
64. Lorimer, *Population of the Soviet Union*, p. 104.
65. Alec Nove, "The Decision to Collectivize," in *Agrarian Politics and Problems in Communist and Non-Communist Countries*, edited by W. A. Douglas Jackson (Seattle and London, 1971), pp. 88-91.
66. Jerzy F. Karcz, "Comparative Study of Transformation of Agriculture in Centrally Planned Economies: The Soviet Union, Eastern Europe and Mainland China," in *The Role of Agriculture in Economic Development*, edited by Erik Thorbecke, National Bureau of Economic Research (New York, 1969), p. 241.
67. Alec Nove, *The Soviet Economy*, 3rd printing (New York, 1967), pp. 88-91.
68. Ibid. p. 29.
69. Ibid. p. 59.
70. Philip M. Raup, "Some Consequences of Data Deficiencies in Soviet Agriculture," in *Soviet Economic Statistics*, edited by Vladimir G. Treml and John P. Hardt (Durham, North Carolina, 1972).
71. Nove, *Soviet Economy*, p. 105.
72. Since 1966 collective farms have been shifting gradually to a monthly wage. Raup, "Consequences of Data Deficiencies," p. 274.
73. Theodore W. Schultz, *Transforming Traditional Agriculture* (New Haven, Connecticut, 1964), p. 123.
74. The energy available per 100 hectares in the Soviet Union in 1971 averaged 153 h.p. on the *kolkhozes* and 147 h.p. on the *sovkhozes* compared to a United States average of 418 h.p. per 100 hectares in 1967. *Voprosy ekonomiki* No. 12 (1969), p. 70.
75. D. Gale Johnson, "Soviet Agriculture Revisited," *American Journal of Agricultural Economics* Vol. 53, No. 2 (May 1971), pp. 259-60.
76. Ibid. p. 258.
77. Folke Dovring, "Soviet Farm Mechanization in Perspective," *Slavic Review* Vol. 25, No. 2 (June 1966), pp. 288, 292. In spite of the large work force engaged in agriculture, Karl-Eugen Wädekin argues that labor shortages have been hampering efforts to expand farm output in the Soviet Union. He notes that a rapid outflow of farm labor between 1959 and 1964 was halted in the latter year, and between 1964 and 1966 the farm labor force actually increased slightly (from 25.2 to 25.4 million) with favorable effects on production. Wädekin also suggests that labor shortages will become a more serious factor because of the aging of the labor force and the unduly slow increase in "mechanizers" and other specialists which limits the effectiveness of capital investments intended to substitute for labor ("Manpower in Soviet Agriculture—Some Post-Khrushchev Developments and Problems," *Soviet Studies* Vol. 20, No. 3 [January 1969]).

78. To illustrate this conclusion, Nove cites an example that must be rather extreme. For reasons of flexibility, delivery regulations often permit product substitutions, for example, the substitution of butter for milk. Since the pricing mechanism fails to signal consumer demand, Nove reports, "deliveries of milk are generally made in the more readily transportable and less perishable form of butter, and liquid milk is notoriously short at many times of the year in most Soviet cities. Thus in 1958 no less than 65 per cent of all 'milk' delivered to the state in the USSR was in fact butter, over 80 per cent in some republics." See Nove, *Soviet Economy*, pp. 144, 194.

79. J. Wilczynski cites as an example the fact that collective farms in the fertile Krasnodar Region were charged 150 kilograms of grain for plowing one hectare whereas those in Byelorussia paid the Machine Tractor Station only 35 kilograms per hectare ("Towards Rationality in Land Economics Under Central Planning," *The Economic Journal* Vol. 79, No. 315 [September 1969], p. 542n).

80. It is reported that a drastic change in land legislation was enacted in December 1968 which provided for the evaluation of land. Although implementation has apparently lagged, this measure to put a price on land will presumably have a significant impact on farm management and crop production plans. Raup, "Consequences of Data Deficiencies," p. 272.

81. K. P. Obolenski, "Agricultural Planning in U.S.S.R.," in *Economic Problems of Agriculture in Industrial Societies*, edited by U. Papi and C. Nunn (New York, 1969).

82. See Nove, "Decision to Collectivize" and M. Lewin, *Russian Peasants and Soviet Power: A Study of Collectivization* (Evanston, 1968).

83. Karcz, "Transformation of Agriculture in Centrally Planned Economies"; and Lewin, *Russian Peasants*.

84. Karl Wittfogel gives a concise account of the views of Marx, Kautsky, and Lenin concerning the superiority of large-scale agriculture ("Communist and Non-Communist Agrarian Systems, with Special Reference to the U.S.S.R. and Communist China: A Comparative Approach," in *Agrarian Policies and Problems*, edited by Jackson, pp. 10-18).

85. Maurice Dobb, *Soviet Economic Development since 1917* (New York, 1948); Naum Jasny, *The Socialized Agriculture of the USSR: Plans and Performance* (Stanford, California, 1949).

86. See Lewin, *Russian Peasants*, especially pp. 192, 252, 258, and 288; and Nove, "Decision to Collectivize," p. 78.

87. The Soviet economist Gatovski makes this point in general terms in a 1960 article which rejects marginalism and reliance on market signals of scarcity as guides to resource allocation because that would mean "a reduction in growth tempos of our economy, a change in the pattern necessary for such growth, and in particular the superior growth of production of means of production." Quoted by Nove, *Soviet Economy*, p. 293.

88. As quoted by Anthony Tang in an article which is especially interesting in arguing that Soviet agricultural policies were an appropriate element of a Stalinist strategy of development ("Agriculture in the Industrialization of

Communist China and the Soviet Union," *Journal of Farm Economics* Vol. 49, No. 5 [December 1967], p. 1118).

89. James R. Millar, "Soviet Rapid Development and the Agricultural Surplus Hypothesis," *Soviet Studies* Vol. 22, No. 1 (July 1970).

90. Johnson, "Soviet Agriculture Revisited"; Jerzy F. Karcz, Soviet Agriculture: A Balance Sheet," *Studies on the Soviet Union,* n.s., Vol. 6, No. 4 (1967), pp. 113, 127; idem, "Transformation of Agriculture in Centrally Planned Economies," pp. 242-43. A study of the Ukraine by A. G. Frank also finds virtually no increase in factor productivity in the agricultural sector whereas the contribution of increases in productivity to the growth of industrial output in the Ukraine were similar to those reported for the United States ("General Productivity in Soviet Agriculture and Industry," *Journal of Political Economy* Vol. 66, No. 6 [December 1958]).

91. The quotation is from *Neva* No. 1 (1973), p. 173 and the *Izvestia* report was in the issue of December 5, 1972.

92. Raup offers a concise analysis of why "the resulting matrix in which planning and management decisions are made is heavily biased toward caution and conservatism" ("Consequences of Data Deficiencies").

93. Clifford Geertz, *Agricultural Involution: The Process of Ecological Change in Indonesia* (Berkeley, 1963), pp. 135, 141, 143.

94. This is Miri, a village in one of the most heavily populated subdistricts (Srihardjo) of the Jogjakarta Region.

95. Masri Singarimbun, "Some Consequences of Population Growth in Java," mimeographed (Jogjakarta: 1973?).

7 | Agriculture-Industry Interactions

This chapter and the next view the process of structural transformation and choice of agricultural strategies from the perspective of the manufacturing sector. Because the study of variable linkages between the agricultural economy and industry in the early stage of economic development is a comparatively unexplored field, our analysis will have to go forward without the benefit of a rich historical literature to draw upon. In this chapter and the next we will focus our analysis on the contemporary experience of three Asian countries —Taiwan, India, and West Pakistan. The subject of this chapter will be various macroeconomic elements of the agriculture-industry relationship, including the pattern of demand for producer and consumer goods, factor proportions, resource transfers, and the role of exports. Chapter 8 will examine from a microeconomic viewpoint the two principal farm input supply industries, chemical fertilizers and farm equipment, with a focus on comparative advantage and technology adaptation.

AN OVERVIEW OF INTERSECTORAL RELATIONSHIPS

When we turn to the development of industry and its interactions with the agricultural sector, we find that many of the analytical perspectives used earlier hold here as well. Given the savings limitation of a low-income economy, sustained expansion of manufacturing output requires an output mix and choice of production techniques that utilize relatively more labor than capital. Indeed, in analyzing the rate of growth of manufacturing output we can apply the same type of identity we used in agriculture, substituting capital per worker (K/L) for cultivated acreage per worker: $Y/L \equiv K/L \cdot Y/K$. This says that output per worker in manufacturing is determined by average productivity per unit of physical capital (analogous with yield per acre), times the number of capital units per worker. The term Y/K is controlled by all those factors which bear on productivity other than the quantum of material capital, namely technology, labor skills, and organization. Rewriting the identity in terms of aggregate output emphasizes the fact that output depends on the total number of workers employed (L) as well as the capital/labor and output/capital ratios, that is $Y \equiv K/L \cdot Y/K \cdot L$. And subject to keeping costs down to market-clearing prices, the lower K/L the larger L, i.e., the number of workers able to obtain employment in the manufacturing sector. Paralleling the earlier conclusion that agricultural policies should be aimed at raising yields with maximum labor input per cultivated acre, the implication for industry is to set policy instruments so as to raise capital productivity (Y/K) and to minimize capital intensity (K/L). All else being equal, this will tend to maximize both output and employment.

The parallels between the development of agriculture and industry are not limited to this basic identity. The purchasing power constraint in the farm sector has its counterpart in the foreign exchange constraint in manufacturing. With a few exceptions, capital-intensive processes are more demanding in terms of equipment complexity, the degree of processing of intermediate inputs, and high-level technical skills. This means that as with tractor-mechanized farming, capital-intensive modes of manufacturing production tend to have a high import content relative to more labor-intensive modes of production. Accordingly, the expansion of industrial output is constrained by the availability of foreign exchange as well as by the availability of investment funds.

Another similarity is the presence of a dual structure of producers. We have noted in earlier chapters this duality or bimodalism among farm producers in various Asian and Latin American countries. The dualism in the industrial sector is more universal, based in part on the lack of an intermediate technology heritage treated in our "On Being Late" discussion. The industrial economy may be roughly characterized as being comprised of a semitraditional subsector and a modern subsector. The former is made up of a large number of small firms, utilizing low-wage and/or family labor and producing simple, unstandardized goods. In the other subsector there is a smaller number of much larger firms utilizing capital-intensive modern technologies and relatively high-wage labor. In the first instance market structure is characterized by atomistic competition and in the second by tariff-buttressed monopoly or concentrated oligopoly. The result is a sharp inequality between the two subsectors in wage and profit income (and thereby saving capability). Although the nature and causes of this industrial dualism differ somewhat from that in the agricultural sector,[1] in industry as in agriculture the detrimental aspects of dualism are often exacerbated by government policies which provide a "modern" subsector privileged access to scarce inputs.

The critical difference between agriculture and industry is that manufactures are not subject to the severe demand limitation that applies to farm produce. First, given the composition of imports, the possibilities for import substitution are much greater for manufactured goods. Second, the potential export demand for labor-based manufactures is more buoyant than normally is the case for unprocessed food and fiber. Third, and most fundamental, is the differential income elasticity of demand: in contrast to the demand pattern for food, as per capita output in the economy rises a growing share of household expenditures are devoted to manufactured and processed commodities.[2] It is this absence of a significant demand limitation, in conjunction with the trend toward specialization, which makes industry the fastest growing sector in an expanding economy and the major recipient of resource transfers from slower growing sectors, especially agriculture.

Despite the potentially favorable demand prospects for industrial output there are many eventualities which can slow or halt the enlargement of this sector. Many of these eventualities arise in the domain of agriculture-industry interactions. Lagging farm output raises food prices and thereby industry's wage bill. Faltering primary exports tighten the foreign exchange constraint. Excessive absorption of investment funds by agriculture holds down capital formation in the potentially faster growing sector. A pattern of rural demand which favors sophisticated, capital-intensive goods stimulates industries that lack a basis in comparative advantage. (The contrary of these developments correspondingly promotes industrial expansion.) In this chapter and the next we shall examine evidence not only on these intersectoral connections but also on the effects of various allocational policies that bear on efficient specialization and interaction within the manufacturing sector itself.

THE DEMAND FOR MANUFACTURED GOODS

The first of agriculture's interactions with industry that we shall examine is the demand it generates for manufactured goods. From the perspective of industrial development, farm demand for industrial commodities has two aspects, its aggregate level and its composition. The aggregate level of demand is determined by cash sales less net savings. Sales of farm products are made to the domestic market (its size being constrained by the nonfarm labor force ratio) and to export markets. There being neither empirical nor a priori grounds for assuming that intersectoral capital transfers or primary exports vary in any systematic fashion with a particular pattern of agricultural development, we may take the aggregate level of rural demand for manufactures to be potentially the same under either a unimodal or a bimodal strategy. This leaves the composition of demand, both for producer and consumer goods, as the factor that can be significantly influenced by economic policy.

In Chapter 2 we presented data on farm cash disbursement patterns in the United States, Taiwan, and Ethiopia. It will be recalled that in Ethiopia expenditures on manufactured consumption goods were many times higher than for manufactured producer goods; in the case of Taiwan, specialization having gone much further, the margin of consumer over producer goods was a good deal narrower. In the United States, where structural transformation is extremely advanced, purchases of externally produced inputs have risen to a point where they are some 40 per cent larger than consumption outlays. Within this broad trend, for any given stage of structural transformation there will be a certain degree of variation in the balance between consumption and production expenditures. Specifically, the more labor-intensive are agricultural production methods, the larger the share of consumer goods and the lesser the share of capital goods. This follows both from the substitution of labor inputs for capital inputs and from the high propensity to consume from labor income. Moreover, within each of the two categories the composition of goods will vary.

Let us first consider producer goods. These include (a) capital equipment such as cultivation implements, pumpsets, and transport and (b) intermediate inputs such as fertilizers, fuel, and cement and other construction materials. A pattern of agricultural development that favors maximum utilization of available labor supplies stimulates the demand for those producer goods which complement labor. This means enlarged markets for muscle-powered farm and transportation equipment and conversely constricted markets for their labor-saving counterparts. In terms of specific inputs, draft animals and their feed, bullock-drawn steel plows, knapsack sprayers, foot-pedal threshers, hand-cranked winnowers, and the like substitute for tractors, gasoline and diesel fuel, tractor-drawn equipment, and combine harvesters. Similarly, in the construction of housing, farm buildings, and irrigation channels, simpler and less-processed materials are combined with greater quantities of labor (including subsequent maintenance labor) to produce the desired functional structure.

There are two producer goods for which market size is not affected by the choice of agricultural strategy. Fertilizer and water are yield-increasing inputs complementary to both a labor-using and a capital-using pattern of development. In the production of both these inputs, the far-greater capacity of the capital-intensive techniques—inorganic fertilizer factories and motorized pumps—provide an overwhelming advantage vis-à-vis the animal manure and muscle-or-wind power alternatives.

The industrial significance of the two contrasting sets of capital goods is that their production characteristics are not identical. Indeed, in their manufacture there are systematic differences in technical skills, investment, foreign exchange content, employment, and technology-diffusing effects. We shall be examining several representative packages of farm equipment for just this set of characteristics in Chapter 8.

The second and larger class of goods is consumer items. As noted above, total consumption expenditures are larger under the unimodal pattern because of the more sparing use of capital inputs and the higher propensity to consume out of labor income. Part of this larger expenditure will be directed to purchased food (as distinct from increased consumption of self-produced food) and services. The favorable employment and welfare consequences of the high-income elasticity of demand for food were noted in earlier chapters. In the case of manufactured goods, the critical difference between the unimodal and the bimodal pattern lies in the composition of the products which are purchased.[3]

While the contrasting composition of demand for producer goods derives from differences in the production function under the two patterns of agricultural development, in the case of consumer goods the cause is the difference in the size distribution of income among rural households. Where income is more or less evenly distributed over broad segments of the population, the result is large markets for comparatively simple goods. Production technology for these commodities consists, in most cases, of highly standardized operations requiring little technical and managerial sophistication; typically domestic intermediate products constitute a larger input than in the case of more complex products. By contrast, with a skewed distribution of income that would be associated with the intensive development of a small subsector of large farmers, the resultant demand situation is one of small markets for expensive goods which for reasons of intermediate inputs, scale, and technology are not suited for efficient local manufacture.

Examples of the type of purchases that low- and medium-income rural households are likely to make as their incomes rise—and here we draw on our personal observations in various African and Asian countries—are such items as cosmetics, combs, brushes, plastic and leather sandals, cotton textiles, light fixtures, wooden furniture, and bricks and paint for home improvement. In the Indian and Pakistan Punjab in the households of the large-scale mechanized farmer one typically observes such consumer durables as an airconditioner, a car, and a television set; on a small farm the comparable items are an electric fan, a bicycle, and a transistor radio.

Of available empirical studies, an analysis of Indian rural expenditure data by John Mellor and Uma Lele comes closest to providing the degree of disaggregation in products and in income stratification that is required to test our proposition about varying demand patterns. Their principal findings are summarized in Table 7.1 below. Collating consumption expenditures with the National Sample Survey of land holdings, the authors report that the bottom two decile classes of expenditure correspond to landless laborers, the sixth, seventh, and eighth deciles correspond to holdings of 5-10 acres, and the upper half of the tenth decile corresponds with farms of 30 acres and over. For our purposes the latter two categories are roughly indicative of the predominant demand pattern under a unimodal and a bimodal regime, respectively.[4]

With respect to agricultural commodities, the greatest difference is the very much lower demand for food grains in the highest expenditure class. This documents the greater scope that exists for exploiting the potential of the seed-fertilizer revolution (which to date has had its major impact on wheat and rice) when rural income is more equitably distributed. A labor-using agricultural strategy would, of course, also channel more income to consumers in the lowest expenditure deciles where the marginal propensity to consume

Table 7.1. Division of incremental expenditure among expenditure categories, by rural expenditure class, India 1964-65

	Bottom 2 deciles (mainly landless ag. and nonag. laborers)	6th, 7th, and 8th deciles (5-10 acres)	Upper ½ of 10th decile (30+ acres)
Mean per capita monthly expenditure	8.93	24.13	85.84
Allocation of an additional rupee of expenditure			
A. Agricultural commodities	0.78	0.51	0.34
Food grains	0.55	0.15	0.02
Milk and milk products	0.08	0.13	0.09
Meat, eggs and fish	0.02	0.03	0.03
Other foods[a]	0.02	0.09	0.17
Tobacco	0.02	0.02	...
Vanaspati	...	0.02	0.01
Other oils	0.05	0.03	0.01
Sweetners	0.04	0.04	0.01
B. Nonagricultural commodities	0.22	0.49	0.66
Cotton textiles	0.09	0.07	0.04
Woolen textiles	...	0.01	0.02
Other textiles	...	0.01	0.02
Footwear	...	0.01	...
Durables and semidurables	0.01	0.02	0.05
Conveyance[b]	0.01	0.02	0.10
Consumer services[c]	0.02	0.03	0.06
Education[d]	0.01	0.03	0.11
Fuel and light	0.08	0.06	0.03
House rent[e]	...	0.02	0.08
Miscellaneous[f]	...	0.17	0.15

See adjacent page for notes

AGRICULTURE-INDUSTRY INTERACTIONS

food grains is even higher. Of industrially processed foods there is greater marginal consumption of milk products, tobacco, vanaspati, edible oils, and sweeteners by the intermediate income group. Beyond the very important case of textiles, the nonagricultural commodity classifications are so wide as to preclude valid inferences about differential demand for specific products.

PRODUCTION CHARACTERISTICS

Having demonstrated the differential demand pattern, Mellor and Lele proceed to examine the capital-labor ratios for the processing or manufacture of the products they have isolated. They find, with two exceptions, that all the above mentioned commodities, plus footwear, exhibit capital-labor ratios substantially below the average for manufacturing as a whole. Even in the case of cigarettes and milk products, the two exceptions, the authors suggest that much of rural consumption is in a less-processed form, supplied by small-scale producers utilizing less capital-intensive techniques than those associated with the higher income, large-scale urban markets. This is an instance of the product variation phenomenon discussed in Chapter

---

[a] Includes spices, salt, vegetables, fruits and nuts, beverages, refreshments, jam, jelly, pickles.
[b] Includes expenses on transportation by bus, taxi, train, airplane, steamer, boat, motor car, motorcycle, scooter, rickshaw, bullock cart, horse car, including conveyance charges incurred by children for going to school.
[c] Includes medical care, litigation and domestic work, barbers, washermen, dry cleaners, carpenters, blacksmiths, priests, plumbers, gardeners, gold and silversmiths, and drivers.
[d] Includes expenses on books, journals, newspapers, periodicals, stationery, school fees, private tutor's fees.
[e] Includes expenditure incurred on rented house. No imputation of rent for residential houses owned by the sample households was made.
[f] Includes biscuits and confectionery, intoxicants, pan, medicines, toiletry, sports and amusements, sundry goods (details unspecified in the study), ceremonials and gifts. This item is estimated *as a residual*.
SOURCE: Data from John W. Mellor and Uma J. Lele, "Growth Linkages of the New Foodgrain Technologies," USAID-Employment and Income Distribution Project, Cornell University, Department of Agricultural Economics, Occasional Paper No. 50 (Ithaca, New York, May 1972).

3. The single most important consumption item, textiles, provides a particularly useful illustration of the favorable demand effects of a broad-based agricultural strategy. Cotton cloth on which the expenditures of the 6-8 decile group are concentrated is substantially more labor intensive than are other textiles which are purchased in considerable quantity by the top 5 percentile group. Their figures are as follows:[5]

	Total capital per worker (*rupees*)	Fixed investment per worker (*rupees*)	Per cent of all manufactured output (*per cent*)
Cotton textile	4,843	2382	23.7
Wool textile	9,259	2729	0.7
Art silk	11,427	5279	1.3

Somewhat more information on production characteristics of goods related to agricultural sector demand is available for (West) Pakistan and Taiwan. A returns-to-capital approach, which uses payments for factor services rather than the stock of capital, differentiates three production inputs—physical capital, labor skills, and raw labor. In this framework, value-added per worker is a measure of overall material capital and skill intensity. If the wage component of value-added per worker in a particular industry is absolutely large, considerable labor skills are being employed. If the nonwage component is large, substantial capital inputs are being utilized. If neither the average wage or the nonwage value-added is sizable—that is total value-added per worker is low—the inputs are primarily the services of unskilled labor. In an underdeveloped economy it is this latter type of industry, economizing on scarce physical material and human capital inputs, that is economcially the most efficient. Viewed from an import substitution perspective, the lower the intensity of skilled labor and physical capital, the more competitive the local product will be, *ceteris paribus,* with the imported counterpart.

Nurul Islam has applied these measures to census of manufactur-

Table 7.2. Value-added per employee in (West) Pakistan manufacturing 1964-65

	Total		Wage		Nonwage	
Industry	Rs.	Rank[a]	Rs.	Rank[a]	Rs.	Rank[a]
Petroleum refining	84,236	1	3873	3	80,363	1
Fertilizer	19,244	6	2168	15	17,067	5
Alcoholic beverages	17,200	4	2200	7	15,000	3
Paint	13,492	11	2047	17	11,445	10
Other electrical products	13,017	13	2032	18	10,985	12
Industrial chemicals	12,226	15	3030	5	9,196	17
Vehicle manufacturing	11,666	16	2142	16	9,524	16
Pumps and compressors	5229	41	1538	40	3691	38
Cotton textiles	4504	49	1210	67	3294	48
Electric fans	4051	54	1301	56	2750	52
Bakery products	4011	55	1079	69	2932	50
Cycles	3971	58	1353	52	2618	55
Metal products	3807	60	1589	32	2218	62
Heating and lighting	3761	62	1384	49	2377	61
Wooden furniture	3728	63	1606	29	2122	64
Textile machinery	3580	65	1504	43	2076	66
Agricultural machinery	2522	77	1044	70	1478	76
Utensils	2465	78	975	75	1490	75
Rice milling	1550	82	538	81	1012	79
Clay products (bricks)	1535	83	994	74	541	82

[a] Rank in a total of 84 industries.
SOURCE: Data from Nurul Islam, "Factor Intensities in Manufacturing Industries in Pakistan," *Pakistan Development Review* Vol. 10, No. 2 (Summer 1970), table 3.

ing data for Pakistan. Some of his results, ranking industries by their total value added per worker, are presented in Table 7.2. Petroleum refining emerges as Pakistan's least-efficient industry. With a value-added per employee of 84,236 rupees, of which 80,363 rupees were payments for capital and 3873 rupees were wages, it ranks first in overall capital intensity, third in average wage or skill intensity, and first in physical capital intensity. At the bottom end of the scale, ranking 83rd, is clay products (bricks), Pakistan's most efficient industry; value-added per worker is 1535 rupees of which 994 rupees are paid for labor services and 541 rupees represent profit, interest, and rent.[6]

The Pakistan data in Table 7.2 show that of the 84 industries petroleum refining and fertilizer use the first and sixth largest amounts of scarce human and physical capital per employee. In neither case does the employment-sacrificing investment result in a product which is as cheap as the import alternative. Consumer goods for which the demand is likely to be greater under a bimodal agricultural strategy—motor vehicles, airconditioners, electrical appliances—also appear to have unfavorable factor intensities. On the other hand, the strategy which makes maximum use of abundant resources in the production of farm products appears to stimulate demand for products with similarly favorable factor proportions—bicycles,

Table 7.3. Factor intensity in Taiwan manufacturing, 1966
(*Thousands NT$ except as otherwise indicated*)

Industry	Value added per employee			Capital per employee	Value added per million NT$ assets	Persons engaged
	Total	Wage	Nonwage			
Petroleum refining	228.4	25.6	202.8	566	403	9,40
Fertilizer	122.0	22.0	100.0	630	197	9,93
Agricultural machinery	50.0	12.5	37.5	82	386	2,67
All manufacturing	38.2	12.5	25.7	131	257	589,70
Motor vehicles	37.3	13.8	23.5	124	227	12,29
Cotton textiles	23.4	10.6	12.8	183	126	49,60
Wood furniture	16.6	11.7	4.9	30	545	3,5
Agricultural implements	15.0	9.0	4.0	28	543	6

SOURCE: Data from The Republic of China, Commission of I.C.C.T., *General Report the Third Industrial & Commercial Census of Taiwan*, Vol. 3, *Manufacturing* (Taipei, J 1968).

wooden furniture, metal utensils, and agricultural machinery (no tractors were produced at this time).

The second, third, and fourth columns of Table 7.3 present comparable data for Taiwan. The same extreme capital intensity of petroleum refining and fertilizers appears. Agricultural machinery, since here it is largely power tillers, ranks somewhat higher than average in capital intensity; agricultural implements, however, are low. Wooden furniture, as before, is also low. The only anomaly in its relative labor intensity is motor vehicles; this seems to be the result of a wider classification which includes motorcycles and repair activities. The fifth column of Table 7.3 presents the more traditional measure of physical capital intensity, total assets per worker. (This same ratio for (West) Pakistan is shown in Table 7.4.) By this measure Taiwan's fertilizer industry surpasses petroleum refining in capital intensity.

Some Consequences of Price Distortions

We have frequently pointed out for Pakistan and India that (a) policies relating to foreign exchange, rationing of scarce intermediate products and rate setting for utilities have resulted in underpriced inputs for privileged users; (b) governmentally controlled interest rates in the organized lending market have brought about the same results for capital; and (c) institutionally supported urban wage levels in the modern sector have overvalued labor services relative to their supply price. Azizur Khan has carried out various calculations for Pakistan which strongly suggest that the expected consequences of such policies have in fact been realized. Khan's results shown in Table 7.4, in addition to confirming the general pattern depicted by the value-added approach, highlight the importance of raising the rate of plant utilization, both for providing more employment and for lowering unit costs.[7] A second point documented in the fourth column of the table is the far more economical use of investment resources in the small-scale sector as shown by their much lower capital/labor ratios. As noted in the Indian case and in Chapter 3, goods produced in small-scale establishments are frequently less standardized and

Table 7.4. Capital/labor ratios in (West) Pakistan manufacturing
(*Thousand rupees per man-year*)

Industry	1962-63 Large-scale Full capacity Utilization	1962-63 Large-scale Actual	Small-scale actual	1965-66 Large-scale actual
Fertilizer	178.1	178.1	...	217.2
Coal and petroleum products	58.0	58.0	...	...
Edible oil	26.4	26.4	...	25.2
Cement	19.9	21.9	...	85.2
Cigarettes	16.2	24.9	0.6	11.5
Sugar refining	15.4	19.7	...	29.9
Cotton textile	8.2	11.6	1.3	15.4
Other chemicals	7.8	19.6	...	18.1
Transport equipment	5.2	12.3	2.6	15.6
Rubber products	5.0	13.3	3.4	16.2
Other food, drink	4.3	8.7	...	18.4
Paper and printing	3.7	5.0	2.5	...
Basic metals	3.1	7.4	3.8	13.4
Leather products	2.1	5.6	1.8	4.1
Machinery	2.1	4.9	3.7	8.0
Metal products	1.6	4.7	1.6	8.2
Wood products	1.3	3.1	1.9	7.4

SOURCE: Data from Azizur Rahman Khan, "Capital-Intensity and the Efficiency of Factor Use—A Comparative Study of the Observed Capital-Labour Ratios of Pakistani Industries," *The Pakistan Development Review* Vol. 10, No. 2 (Summer 1970), pp. 254, 258, 260, 268.

utilize more domestic raw materials; their principal customers come from the lower income groups. A development strategy which favored a less-concentrated distribution of income would lead to an expansion of the small-scale sector, *a fortiori* if these producers are given equal access to the scarce, technology-carrying inputs.

Because there is greater or lesser possibility for varying the proportions of capital, labor, and other inputs in the production of most commodities, measures comparing factor intensities between countries can provide useful information as to how well a country is deploying its productive resources. Paralleling the selection of industries to be established in conformance with comparative advantage, the industrial sector as a whole will achieve a higher level of output the more intensively abundant factors are utilized (primarily labor and local raw materials for developing countries); and conversely, output will be maximized the more sparing and extensive the use made of scarce inputs. We have two sets of data which throw some light on this issue for Pakistan and Taiwan.

In addition to ranking Pakistan's industries, Khan compared capital/labor ratios found in his country with Japan and the United States. Since both of these countries are capital-rich and labor-scarce relative to Pakistan, the investigator predicted that fixed capital per worker industry-by-industry would be lower in Pakistan. He found, however, in two of the seven industries for which he had data, chemicals and leather goods, that capital intensity in Pakistan slightly exceeded the United States figure; in comparison with Japan, Pakistan had more assets per worker in seven out of eight industrial groupings. What this suggests is that Pakistan's foreign exchange and interest rate policies resulted not only in the establishment of inappropriate industries but also in higher capital/labor ratios in virtually all industries than would have prevailed under true scarcity factor pricing. Khan observes that foreign aid policies and the inflexibility of foreign investors from capital-rich countries may be additional contributing causes to this excessive capital intensity.

All the foregoing evidence on Pakistan's excessive capital intensity makes it clear that considerable national output has been lost by diverting too many investment resources into the large-scale sector industries that have been established. The same facts also imply that industrial output will be produced at a very high cost—that is, it will be priced far above competitive imports. Systematic studies by Stephen Lewis and Gary Hufbauer have disclosed that manufacturing, both for the home market and for exports, has received implicit subsidies ranging from 40 to 98 per cent of the value of net output.[8]

The real cost of these subsidies is most strikingly revealed in the fall in the share of large-scale manufacturing in GDP from 7.0 per cent when valued at internal prices to 0.4 per cent when valued at world prices.[9]

Taiwan, by contrast, has to an unusual degree kept its factor prices in alignment with its resource endowment. Interest rates have never fallen below 15 per cent, which has insured that capital can only be employed in its most productive uses as well as providing encouragement for saving. Trade union pressures to raise urban wages have been resisted. Protection deriving from all forms of foreign trade restrictions has been moderate. Thus in 1965 the downward adjustment in the share of manufacturing in GDP when valued at world prices was only from 18.7 to 16.0 per cent. And, of course, efficiently produced output has been based upon maximum use of Taiwan's abundant factor of production—labor. The final two columns of Table 7.5 compare labor's contribution to manufacturing

Table 7.5. Wages and salaries as a per cent of value-added in selected industries, Taiwan and West Pakistan

Industry	Taiwan			West Pakistan
	1952	1957-60	1965-68	1967-68
Food	81.0	43.5	58.4	19.1
Textiles	63.1	53.8	51.3	34.6
Wood and wood products	71.1	63.7	80.9	43.6
Paper and paper products	70.3	58.1	60.0	52.4
Chemicals and chemical products	55.4	49.6	42.6	19.0
Nonmetal mineral products	61.2	60.6	56.0	19.9
Metal and metal products	81.7	63.4	60.7	31.1
Electrical products	58.3	70.7	49.0	29.3

SOURCE: Data from Mo-Huan Hsing, *The Philippines and Taiwan—Industrialization and Trade Policies,* OECD Development Centre, Paris (London, 1971), p. 172; and Government of Punjab, Bureau of Statistics, *Census of Manufacturing of West Pakistan 1967-68* (Lahore, 1970). The value-added figures for Taiwan include indirect taxes whereas the net figures have been used for West Pakistan.

output in selected industry groups in the two countries. Although declining with continuing capital accumulation and rising rates of pay, wages and salaries still account for twice as large a share of output as in Pakistan in 1968.

As the data in Table 7.5 reveal, Taiwan has managed to achieve an extraordinary level of labor intensity in her industrial production. With expensive capital, noninflated urban wage rates, and a progressively more open economy from 1959 onward, large-scale firms began to turn to the manufacture of labor-intensive exports; the driving organizational abilities of management in these firms insured that every commercially feasible possibility for substituting labor for capital was exploited. In the small-scale sector, firms producing apparel, footwear, and a wide range of wood and metal products were able to supplement their labor supply with part-time agricultural workers, women, and teenagers. Under a regime of finely differentiated market wage rates it was possible to expand employment and output up to a point where the marginal product of labor was very low. On the demand side, expansion of these industries characterized by low capital/labor ratios was supported by purchases of the lower income, labor-providing rural and urban households.[10] Intensive use of the low-cost resource not only made possible an average rate of growth of industrial output of 13.5 per cent per year over the period 1952-66, it also created over 200,000 new jobs (an increase of 75 per cent), and this does not allow for entrained employment in the service sector.

INTERSECTORAL RESOURCE TRANSFERS

We now turn to another aspect of industry-agriculture interactions, the transfer of investible resources. As described in our analysis of farm cash disbursements in Chapter 2, agriculture's gross transfer of resources to other sectors is composed of that portion of taxes, voluntary savings, and payments of rent and interest made by farm households which go to recipients outside of the agricultural sector. To this must be added any invisible transfer that derives from a rise in the average price of nonagricultural products purchased by farm households relative to the average price of goods they sell. Against these outflows must be set the inflow of resources into agriculture from other sectors: government outlays for "public goods" such as research and extension that benefit farmers, input subsidies, investment in rural infrastructure, private investment by the nonfarm sector in agriculture, the provision of loan funds through financial intermediaries, and income payments received by members of farm households from the nonfarm sector. Reversing the previous case, a rise in the price of farm products relative to farm-purchased commodities represents an invisible inward flow of resources.[11]

As we have noted many times before, because agriculture is both the largest and the slowest growing sector of an underdeveloped economy, the optimal net flow of resources will, over the long run, be from agriculture to those sectors where the growth potential and returns on investment are higher. This does not mean there may not be periods when a net resource transfer into agriculture will have the highest payoff. One such period for many countries is likely to be at the onset of the seed-fertilizer revolution, when high-yielding seed varieties greatly raise the social profitability of investment in irrigation, storage, and transport facilities. Even when there is a net outflow of resources—say in the form of rent and voluntary savings—it may be optimal for government to invest more in agricultural infrastructure and research than it collects in taxes. Moreover, the composition of resource transfers, in whatever direction, has important effects both on incentives to increase output and on the distribution of farm income.

The transfer of invisible resources as a result of a change in the terms of trade can be very large. A decline in the relative prices of farm products may come about because growth in productivity exceeds that of demand or as a result of government pricing policies. We have earlier spent a good deal of time explaining how one such set of government policies which restrict manufactured imports and underprice foreign exchange for large-scale, import-replacing manufacturing firms turn the terms of trade against agriculture. While these policies improve the terms of trade for one set of industrial producers, they do not do so for all. Similarly, underpricing of foreign exchange hurts cultivators producing export crops more than those growing foodstuffs for the domestic market, and it actually subsidizes those farmers who can purchase untaxed imported farm equipment (notably tractors). Our conclusion is that changes in the intersectoral terms of trade describe the net outcome of a complex set of forces. The attention of policy makers should not focus on the terms of trade per se, but on all those productivity movements, pricing and tax policies which lay behind shifts in relative product prices.

Because a net flow of visible resources out of agriculture (e.g., taxes, savings, rent) must be associated with a surplus of farm sector sales over its purchases, the best method for estimating the magnitude of these transfers is to calculate overall commodity flows between agriculture and the rest of the economy. This approach has the additional advantage of illuminating the effects of the farm purchasing power constraint and the mix of inputs associated with a particular pattern of agricultural development. Of the three countries we have been concentrating on, aggregate statistics on farm receipts and expenditures are available only for Taiwan. T. H. Lee, in pioneering studies, has provided long-run estimates of farm output, farm sales, farm purchases, and resource transfers to the nonagricultural sectors.[12] These data covering the six-decade period beginning in 1911 are summarized in Table 7.6.

The top row of Table 7.6 records the movement of total agricultural output over the 60-year period. Even if we set aside the most recent decade when annual growth exceeded 5 per cent, during the previous half-century agricultural output advanced at an average rate of 3 per cent per year. Despite a swelling of the farm population from 2.1 million in 1911 to 5.2 million in 1960, output per man grew at an annual rate of 1.8 per cent. This performance was achieved with remarkably limited external purchases of capital goods as can be seen from the third-to-bottom row. As described in Chapter 6, the principal contributor to labor productivity growth since 1930

Table 7.6. Intersectoral resource flows in Taiwan, 1911-69
(Millions of Taiwan dollars at 1935-37 prices)

	1911-15	1921-25	1931-35	1936-40	1950-55	1961-65	1966-69
Agricultural output	162.9	238.0	361.4	422.5	513.3	801.6	1,044.9
Marketed share (*per cent*)	56.3	63.8	71.7	71.4	58.0	60.6	61.9
Resource transfer share (*per cent*)	30.5	26.1	24.8	21.1	22.0	13.4	13.8
Total farm cash sales	91.6	151.7	259.3	301.6	297.8	485.8	646.8
Percentage breakdown							
Sales to nonfarm households	32.6	26.5	23.2	22.6	46.4	40.6	42.5
Sales to foreign countries	16.9	23.2	34.4	32.3	5.5	7.4	8.2
Sales to processors	50.5	50.3	42.4	45.1	48.1	52.0	49.3
Total	100.0	100.0	100.0	100.0	100.0	100.0	100.0
Total farm purchases	42.1	92.6	169.8	212.5	185.0	378.5	502.4
Percentage breakdown							
Current inputs	18.3	27.4	32.3	31.6	32.2	32.6	35.6
Fixed capital	2.3	7.9	5.6	3.6	3.3	10.4	15.6
Consumer goods	79.4	64.7	62.1	64.7	64.5	57.0	48.8
Total	100.0	100.0	100.0	100.0	100.0	100.0	100.0

SOURCE: Data from T. H. Lee, *Intersectoral Capital Flows in the Economic Development of Taiwan, 1895-1960* (Ithaca, New York, 1971); idem, "Strategies for Transferring Agricultural Surplus Under Different Agricultural Situations in Taiwan" (Paper prepared for the Japan Economic Research Center Conference on Agriculture and Economic Development, Tokyo and Hakone, September 1971). The five-year periods omitted here for brevity are included in the original sources.

has been the rise in yields; this was made possible by an 11-fold increase in chemical fertilizers, the major item in the current inputs category.

In terms of the process of structural transformation, the most striking feature of Taiwanese agricultural development is revealed in the second row of Table 7.6. The share of market sales in total production measures the degree to which agriculture stimulates growth in the rest of the economy. This stimulation may take the form of generating demand for output from other sectors or of transferring financial resources for investment in nonagricultural enterprises. (In the Taiwanese case emphasis was on the latter.) Thus in the early 1920s, when only 30 per cent of the population was living outside of agriculture, exports of food contributed approximately 105 million Taiwanese dollars or twice as much to farm cash earnings as did domestic sales. Sales to foreign markets thus lifted the ceiling on output expansion that otherwise would have been imposed by the small proportion of the population in the nonfarm sectors. In 1921-25, for example, without exports total agricultural production would have been some 45 per cent lower than it actually was. At no time prior to the late 1950s did domestic sales account for as much as half of farm cash earnings. These exports are recorded both in the "Sales to foreign countries" and "Sales to processors." Sugarcane, citronella, soybean, tea, pineapple, jute, pigs, and tobacco were (and are) resold in their processed form to both foreign and domestic buyers; however, the overwhelming bulk of this category until the late 1950s was comprised of sugarcane destined for sales abroad. Agricultural exports, by releasing the constraint on farm cash earnings, have played a truly key role in Taiwan's structural transformation.

A second point concerning structural transformation worthy of brief note is the changing composition of farm demand. From the data on farm purchases one can discern, despite fluctuations in marketed share of farm output owing to export variation and the postwar dislocations, the predicted pattern of a falling share of outlays for consumer goods and a concomitant rise in production expenses as a result of a declining farm population ratio and the increased use of externally produced inputs. Allowing for wartime setbacks between 1940 and 1950, production expenditures have grown faster than output, reflecting the process of specialization and technical advance described in Chapter 2.

This brings us to our principal concern, the resource transfer shown in the third row of Table 7.6. Clearly a heavy squeeze was put on the Taiwanese farmer.[13] Although the absolute amount of the income transfer has increased with the level of agricultural development, the proportionate squeeze has varied inversely with the level of farm productivity. Beyond political factors, several permissive economic considerations should be noted: (a) export sales enlarged the marketed share from which financial transfers are drawn, (b) within the marketed share, a comparatively small fraction of sales income was devoted to production expenditures, and (c) a high overall rate of output growth permitted a rising rate of rural consumption (0.9 per cent per annum) despite the squeeze.

What were the constituent elements of this resource transfer? Up until 1940 some three-quarters of the funds transferred out of agriculture consisted of land rent and, to a much lesser degree, interest payments. Following land reform in 1953 these payments dropped to about one-quarter of the financial outflow while taxes and irrigation fees rose from one-fifth to over one-half during the 1950s. During the 1960s, with the income of farm households sharply up, voluntary savings became the major vehicle for intersectoral financial transfers, accounting for about two-thirds of the total. Invisible resource transfers through adverse movements in the terms of trade are included in Lee's calculations. From 1911 to 1950 there was a moderate invisible outflow from agriculture which, apart from one five-year period, ranged from one-twentieth to one-quarter of the total resource transfer. After 1950 there was a dramatic change; the terms of trade turned sharply against agriculture, so that the invisible transfer surpassed the visible component by as much as 50 per cent.

Taiwan's record of very large and uninterrupted resource transfers from agriculture to other sectors of the economy is indeed a remarkable one. Other developing countries, with different social and political conditions and less richly provisioned with skillful public administrators, may not be able to engineer capital transfers quite so large or so continuous.[14] Nevertheless, the significance of Taiwan's experience for choice of agricultural strategy is clear. It demonstrates conclusively that a labor-intensive pattern of agricultural development is not incompatible with high rates of growth in output and the generation of substantial financial resources for nonfarm investment.

THE ROLE OF EXPORTS

Taiwan's experience vividly illustrates the contribution agricultural exports can make to structural transformation in general and to the development of manufacturing in particular. By raising the money incomes of farmers, exports generate incremental demand for domestic manufactured goods and/or create additional potential for transferring investible resources from agriculture to the industrial sector. Second, the foreign currency earned by expanding exports eases the foreign exchange constraint on both new investment and on the rate of utilization of existing industrial capacity as discussed in the first section of this chapter.

The history of Taiwan's exports reveals her fortunate position vis-à-vis Japanese markets and her success in altering her economic structure as technically demanding foods and industrial products have in recent years become the major foreign exchange earners. Between 1911-15 and 1936-40 agricultural exports at constant prices increased fourfold. In 1938 Japan was the destination for 80 per cent of foreign sales; by 1960 this figure was 37 per cent. Until 1958 the traditional commodities of sugar and rice still accounted for two-thirds or more of all exports. Since then their importance has declined sharply, from 78 per cent of export proceeds in 1957 to 3 per cent in 1970. Total exports have risen from 165 million United States dollars in 1958 to 1.6 billion in 1970, with the tremendously rapid growth of textiles, electronic products, and metal and machinery raising the share of industrial products to 78 per cent of all exports. However, earnings from agricultural items have also risen absolutely owing to such new products as bananas, canned pineapple, canned mushrooms, and canned asparagus.[15]

There is one major qualification, however. The potential contribution of export earnings to structural transformation through a dual impact on the farm purchasing power constraint and the foreign exchange constraint is far more limited for large countries. This follows from the simple fact that an equal proportion of a large country's farm production devoted to a particular export commodity has a greater impact on total market supply and is therefore more likely to depress the price. Even a small country may face difficulty in expanding its export earnings if its major crop accounts for a large share of world exports, for example, Ghana's cocoa industry. As documented earlier in Table 2.5, there is a sharp dichotomy in per capita agricultural exports between countries with small populations (under 10 million) and those with large. Not only is the share of exports in national output lower in large countries, but in recent years their rate of growth has also been slower. Of a sample of 45 low-income countries that were grouped by Daniel Sisler according to their export performance during the 1960s, all 17 large countries fell into the three categories whose mean growth rates were significantly less than the average rate of export expansion of 6.4 per cent for all underdeveloped countries.[16] His results are summarized in Table 7.7.

It should be noted that the statistics in Table 7.7 include manufactures as well as primary exports. While the same increased probability of adversely influencing the terms of trade exist for a manufactured good, the growth in world demand for many of these products is higher than for agricultural commodities. Moreover, as a class manufactures are more openended and therefore face more favorable long-run demand prospects than does food and fiber, the more so because shifts from one manufactured product to another can be effected more readily than shifts from, say, tea to cocoa. In this connection, the marked acceleration of Taiwan's export growth since 1965 has coincided with the compositional shift to industrial prod-

Table 7.7. Classification of 45 developing countries according to export performance in the 1960s

Group	Countries	Annual percentage growth rate 1960-61–1968-69		Exports as a per cent of GNP 1968-69	Trade characteristics
		Exports	Per capita GNP		
I	Hong Kong, Israel, Korea, Taiwan	16.7	6.5	16.1	Exports are mainly labor-intensive manufactured products. Taiwan exports a significant value of processed agricultural products.
II	Iran, Kuwait, Libya, Saudi Arabia	15.3	8.1	37.6	Mainly dependent on petroleum exports.
III	Costa Rica, Guatemala, Honduras, Ivory Coast, Nicaragua, Panama, People's Republic of the Congo, Togo	10.6	2.8	16.9	Small countries that depend on agricultural exports. Central American countries are increasing exports of light manufactures.
IV	Bolivia, Chile, Jordan, Liberia, Peru, Zambia	9.9	4.1	24.9	Mainly dependent on mineral and metal exports.
V	Brazil, Colombia, Malaysia, Morocco, Pakistan, Tunisia, Sudan	4.0	2.4	9.3	Mainly dependent on traditional agricultural exports: coffee, rubber, jute, and cotton. Synthetics have curtailed demand for several commodities.
VI	Algeria, Argentina, Ecuador, India, Mexico, Nigeria, Philippines, U.A.R., Uruguay, Venezuela	3.8	1.4	5.4	Exports are varied, but agricultural products dominate. Rapidly expanding internal demand creates problems in producing an exportable surplus
VII	Burma, Ceylon, Ghana, Indonesia, Mauritius, Thailand	0.1	0.8	14.3	Exports are highly concentrated in a small number of commodities. Exports depend mainly on traditional agricultural products.
	Total	6.1	2.6	8.4	

SOURCE: Data reproduced from Daniel G. Sisler, "International Trade Policies and Agriculture," mimeographed (Ithaca, New York: Cornell University, Department of Agricultural Economics, 1971), p. 198; the underlying statistics were from AID, *Gross National Product 1969* and various issues of GATT, *International Trade*.

ucts. Indeed, the exports of all four countries in Group I are dominated by labor-intensive manufactured goods.

A second and more fundamental point to note is that larger countries, with slower growing exports, have stayed with their traditional crops. By contrast, Taiwan, the Ivory Coast, and Costa Rica have shifted toward new lines, such as fruits and vegetables, where demand prospects have been more favorable. Part of the reason that some smaller countries have shown flexibility in product switching is that they have kept their internal price structure more in line with world prices. Countries with sizable internal markets, on the other hand, are not so swiftly penalized when they ignore comparative costs. However, as we have seen time and again, the longer run effects of failing to bring factor and product prices into line with their true opportunity costs are no less potent in an India than in a Ghana. This point is forcefully made in Table 7.7 by the close correlation between rate of growth in exports and the rate of growth of GNP.

While agricultural exports from large countries can not have the same proportionate impact on farm output and intersectoral commodity flows, growing foreign exchange earnings are nevertheless an essential ingredient for their development. The fact that large countries are in most cases supplying a diminishing share of world exports in individual commodity markets suggests that their rates of export growth could be substantially raised without serious effects on the terms of trade.[17] As discussed above, the possibilities are more favorable in the long run for expanding light manufactures as opposed to food and fiber. The recent experience of Korea and Taiwan has demonstrated that such exports, beyond their contribution to pushing up per capita income, can markedly accelerate the growth of nonfarm employment.[18] And the degree to which these labor-intensive products are competitive in world markets hinges heavily upon agriculture's ability to supply cheap foodstuffs to the urban labor force.

NOTES

1. The process of biological growth provides a degree of uniformity to agricultural production functions that is absent in manufacturing. The differences in skill requirements, capital/labor ratios, and scale of output for optimum-

sized producers of (say) wheat, sheep, and oranges are far smaller than they are for (say) furniture, automobiles, and chemical fertilizer. Likewise with respect to change over time. The changes in needed skills, capital-intensity, and scale for the production of maize between 1875 and 1975 are far less marked than those associated with steel. The net result at any one point in time is that technology alone will tend to generate great variation in the size and factor-intensity of industrial establishments. These technological attributes create differential barriers to entry which condition market structure.

2. The income elasticity of the demand for food is measured at farm gate and therefore excludes the rising proportion of household food expenditures that goes to processing, packaging, and distribution. A part of the higher demand elasticity for manufactures is a consequence of the openendedness of this category, so that the scope for increasing per capita expenditures is much greater than in the case of food products.

3. It also seems safe to assume that total rural demand for *manufactured* consumer goods will also be higher under a unimodal regime. Only if there is a consumption bias toward services among lower income groups would this not hold—and the evidence reviewed in Chapter 2 and Table 7.1 below indicates just the opposite.

4. John W. Mellor and Uma J. Lele, "Growth Linkages of the New Foodgrain Technologies," USAID-Employment and Income Distribution Project, Cornell University, Department of Agricultural Economics, Occasional Paper No. 50 (Ithaca, New York, May 1972).

5. Ibid. p. 20.

6. These measures, which are based upon the supposition that value added consists only of the opportunity earnings of the labor and capital employed, are subject to error due to excise taxes and surplus factor earnings stemming from noncompetitive product and input markets. The presence of these imperfections distorts the absolute values of factor intensity while their uneven incidence distorts the ranking of industries. The principal sources of differential distortion are excise taxes (which are relatively easy to identify, e.g., cigarettes, cosmetics) and import restrictions, multiple foreign exchange rates for imported inputs, and monopoly (the effects of which are extremely difficult to disentangle). As an indication of the reliability of nonwage value-added as an ordinal measure of material capital intensity, Nurul Islam found a rank correlation coefficient between it and reported book value of capital stock per employee of .63 ("Factor Intensities in Manufacturing Industries in Pakistan," *Pakistan Development Review* 10, No. 2 [Summer 1970]).

7. Azizur R. Khan, "Capital-Intensity and the Efficiency of Factor Use: A Comparative Study of the Observed Capital-Labour Ratios of Pakistani Industries," *Pakistan Development Review* Vol. 10, No. 2 (Summer 1970).

8. Stephen R. Lewis, Jr., *Pakistan Industrialization and Trade Policies,* OECD Development Centre (London, 1970), pp. 80-84; and Gary C. Hufbauer, "West Pakistan Exports: Effective Taxation, Policy Promotion, and Sectoral Discrimination," mimeographed (Lahore: Harvard Development Advisory Group, Research Memorandum, 1969), pp. 50-52.

9. Ian Little, Tibor Scitovsky, and Maurice Scott, *Industry and Trade in Some Developing Countries* (Oxford, 1970), p. 73.
10. For a full statistical documentation of these points, see K. K. Fung, "Maximum Labor Participation and Economic Growth in a Labor Abundant Economy: A Case Study of Post-War Taiwan," *Academia Economic Papers* Vol. 1, No. 1 (March 1973).
11. For a full discussion of the complexities of intersectoral resource transfers, both visible and invisible, see Stephen R. Lewis, Jr., "Agricultural Taxation and Intersectoral Resource Transfers," *Food Research Institute Studies* Vol. 12, No. 2 (1973).
12. T. H. Lee, *Intersectoral Capital Flows in the Economic Development of Taiwan, 1895-1960* (Ithaca, New York, 1971); idem, "Strategies for Transferring Agricultural Surplus Under Different Agricultural Situations in Taiwan" (Paper prepared for the Japan Economic Research Center Conference on Agriculture and Economic Development, Tokyo and Hakone, September 1971).
13. Lee's resource transfer calculation somewhat overstates actual "savings" by agriculture. This is due to the very narrow definition of the agricultural sector, excluding as it does noncultivating landlords, farmers' associations, irrigation societies, traders, moneylenders, and all other persons in the rural economy engaged in nonfarming activity. As the net income of the latter, as well as some fraction of interest payments, are required to support basic consumption, these resource transfer computations overestimate the discretionary income that was mobilizable for capital formation.
14. Indeed, it could certainly be argued that in some sense the net outflow of capital from Taiwan's agriculture in the 1920s and 1930s was "excessive." Although the rapid commercialization of agriculture associated with large exports to Japan provided an important stimulus to the modernization of Taiwan's agriculture, it should also be noted that to a considerable extent the transfer of resources accrued to Japan. This meant that the effects of the net outflow in accelerating development of Taiwan's own nonfarm sectors was not as great as is implied by the magnitude of the resource transfer.
15. The dramatic changes are summarized in the following tabulation which shows the overall growth in exports and the percentage distribution by commodity groups:

	Index of all exports	*Percentage Distribution of Exports*		
		Industrial products	All farm products	Sugar and rice
1955	100	8	92	76
1960	129	34	66	45
1965	370	46	32	22
1970	1,167	78	22	3

16. Daniel G. Sisler, "International Trade Policies and Agriculture," mimeographed (Ithaca, New York: Cornell University, Department of Agricultural Economics, 1971).

17. For a full review of existing country-shares in the principal world commodity markets and the prospects for raising the export growth rate of individual countries, see Little, Scitovsky, and Scott, *Industry and Trade,* Chap. 7.

18. Between 1960 and 1966 Korea's manufactured exports grew at an annual rate of 40 per cent. Using an input-output matrix to estimate both the direct and induced employment effects of this expansion, Youngil Lim estimated that the employment elasticity of export manufacturing output was 1.03 for the industrial sector and 0.55 for all sectors ("Impacts of Export on Output and Labor Absorption in South Korea," *Economic Development and Cultural Change,* forthcoming).

8 Backward Linkages: Fertilizer and Farm Equipment

In this chapter we focus on the manufacture of two specific farm inputs, chemical fertilizer and farm equipment. These represent two of the three major categories of farm production expenditures, the omitted category being cement and other building materials used in the construction of irrigation works and farm buildings.[1]

As agricultural development gets underway chemical fertilizers become the largest backward linkage and by a considerable margin. The level of demand for fertilizer is not sensitive to the choice of a particular agricultural strategy; moreover, there is little scope for adjusting the factor proportions associated with its production. Thus the principal issue here is whether to import or to manufacture locally. In the case of farm equipment, however, the choice of agricultural strategy has a major influence on the volume of expenditures, the type of products that are produced, and the character of technological spillovers within the industrial sector.

FERTILIZERS

The purchase of chemical fertilizer represents the single largest potential input linkage from agriculture to the industrial sector. In 1971-72, farmers in developing countries purchased 16 million metric tons of chemical fertilizer (expressed in terms of contained nutrients $-N$, P_2O_5, $+ K_2O$). This represented more than a fourfold increase over the level of a decade earlier. In terms of volume of expenditure, fertilizer outlays were probably somewhat larger than the combined outlays for farm equipment and irrigation.[2] Slightly more than two-fifths of this fertilizer was imported from industrial countries.

The technology of fertilizer production was described at length in Chapter 3. The production process for both nitrogen and phosphate involves extremely large-scale, capital-intensive plants. As we saw in the preceding chapter (Tables 7.2-7.4), chemical fertilizers are among the most capital-intensive commodities made by man. They also require certain natural resource inputs. Where an underdeveloped country possesses both abundant financial resources and the requisite feedstock—such as is the case of Indonesia, Venezuela, Nigeria, and some Middle Eastern countries—the production of ammonia-based fertilizers can contribute significantly to economic development. Where neither capital nor raw materials are abundant, domestic production of these products exacts an inordinately high price in foregone manufacturing output and employment. And, of course, local manufacture under such conditions results in a higher fertilizer price to the farmer which in turn restricts farm output and raises food prices.

The concern of developing countries with fertilizer manufacturing has not been related to industrial efficiency, but rather with achieving self-sufficiency with respect to an indispensable ingredient for agricultural progress. Without growing supplies of nitrogen, phosphate, and potash to maintain steadily rising crop yields, the process of structural transformation will be halted and difficulties in providing minimum food supplies for the expanding population will soon follow. The recent experience in Asia examined in Chapter 9 has underscored the vital importance of reliable sources of fertilizer supplies.

Developments in the World Fertilizer Market[3]

Fertilizer consumption in the developing countries rose rapidly during the 1960s, at an average rate of 13.6 per cent as compared with 8.0 per cent for developed countries (Table 8.1). While pro-

Table 8.1. Trends in world fertilizer consumption
(*Millions of metric tons*)

Location	1962-63		1971-72		Estimated 1980-81	
	N	P+K	N	P+K	N	P+K
Developed countries						
North America	3.7	5.5	7.7	8.8	14.1	14.1
Western Europe	4.0	7.5	6.8	10.8	9.3	13.7
Eastern Europe	2.4	3.7	3.4	4.8	6.9	6.9
U.S.S.R.	...	...	5.2	4.8	8.5	6.8
Other	0.8	1.9	1.2	2.9	1.5	3.6
Total	10.9	18.6	24.3	32.1	40.3	45.2
Developing countries						
Asia and Middle East	1.2	0.4	3.7	2.1	11.0	6.4
Latin America	0.5	0.6	1.4	1.8	3.0	3.2
Africa	0.1	0.2	0.8	0.5	1.4	1.0
Socialist Asia	...	...	3.4	2.3	5.8	2.2
Total	...	...	9.3	6.7	21.2	12.8

SOURCE: Data from International Bank for Reconstruction and Development, *Fertilizer Requirements of Developing Countries*, World Bank Group (Washington, D.C., May 1974), Annex 1, Table 3 and Food and Agriculture Organization of the United Nations, *Review of Trends and Prospects for Fertilizer Supplies and Prices* (Rome, October 1973), Table 4.

duction of fertilizers in developing countries grew at a somewhat faster rate (16.7 per cent) than consumption, imports from industrial countries grew from 1.7 million tons of plant nutrient in 1962-63 to 4.1 million tons in 1971-72. Many factors contributed to this rapid expansion in fertilizer use—the introduction of the new high-yielding varieties, fertilizer subsidy programs, cost-reducing technological changes in fertilizer production and transportation, and the availability of fertilizer imports under bilateral aid agreements.

Like any industry characterized by a high degree of capital intensity and a long interval between the decision to invest and production start-up, the fertilizer industry is subject to wide swings in price and profitability. This has been particularly true over the past dec-

BACKWARD LINKAGES: FERTILIZER AND FARM EQUIPMENT

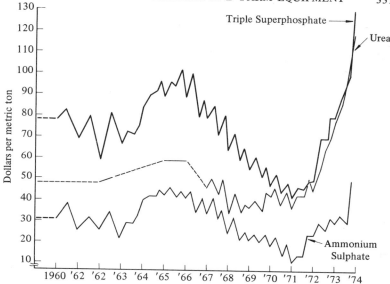

Urea: bagged, f.o.b. Northern Europe.
Ammonium sulphate: bulk, f.o.b. Northern Europe.
Triple superphosphate: bulk, f.o.b. U.S. Gulf Port.

Figure 8.1 Fertilizer export prices, 1960-1973.
SOURCE: British Sulphur Corporation.

ade and a half. As described in Chapter 3, the technical advances achieved in the early 1960s greatly reduced unit costs of ammonia and phosphoric acid. At the favorable market prices then ruling for nitrogen and phosphate fertilizers, investment in the new large-scale plants promised very high rates of return. Between 1963 and 1966 construction of some 75 plants was begun; most of them were located in the industrialized countries. With continuing growth in demand, fertilizer prices rose until 1966, the year the new capacity began to come on stream. From 1966 to 1971 output exceeded current demand, stocks accumulated, and prices fell continuously as more and more of the post-1963 factories came into production. As can be seen in Figure 8.1, by 1970 export prices of urea, now the most widely used of the nitrogen fertilizers, had fallen to half its 1965 level, and no longer covered the full cost of production. The fall in the prices of ammonium sulphate, triple superphosphate, and other fertilizer materials was only slightly less dramatic.

In 1972 the trend began to reverse. World demand continued to grow at 7 to 8 per cent. New capacity for the early 1970s depended upon investments being undertaken in 1967-70: with the exception of a few small projects in Asia and eastern Europe, none were. Indeed, depressed prices led to the closure of many older and less efficient plants in Japan, Europe, and the United States. The return to the sellers' market was accelerated by the drought in the U.S.S.R., Northern Europe, and Asia in 1971-72. The sharp rise in the price of foodgrains which followed the drought, plus deliberate measures to expand grain production, led to a sudden surge in demand for fertilizers. The emergence of China as the world's largest importer of nitrogen fertilizers was a contributing factor, her foreign purchases rising from 0.8 to 1.5 million nutrient tons between 1968 and 1972. The temporary disappearance of anchovy off the coast of Peru—a major source of fish meal for livestock—further added to demand pressures. By the end of 1973 f.o.b. export prices of phosphate and nitrogen fertilizers were soaring at levels 20 to 100 per cent above their previous peaks in 1965.

At the same time that demand began to outrun supply, the cost of producing and transporting fertilizer was rising at an unprecedented rate. Rising prices in the industrialized countries of naphtha and natural gas—the feedstock for ammonia—pushed up the cost of nitrogen fertilizers. Pollution control measures added to costs for both phosphate and nitrogen producers. As a result of the sharp increase in demand for shipping that resulted from the Russian and Chinese grain purchases, by late 1973 the cost of ocean freight for fertilizer imports had risen fourfold from its 1969 level.

At the present time it is difficult to forecast the future of fertilizer prices. On the brighter side, as capacity is brought into balance with demand over the next few years, downward pressure will be exerted on price and profit margins once again. Moreover, ocean freight rates and the contractor cost of plant construction can be expected to moderate as excess demand conditions ease in these sectors. Working in the other direction, the effects of worldwide inflation which began in 1972 have permanently raised the money cost of all inputs —construction, spare parts, power, feedstocks, and labor. Expenditures for environmental control with respect to emissions and water heating, now mandatory, also add to capital requirements. And, of course, there is the energy crisis. Although comprising a smaller portion of total cost than capital, the potential volatility of the cost of energy and hydrocarbon feedstocks suggests that these items will indeed play a major role in determining future fertilizer prices, especially nitrogen fertilizer prices. The issue here is the strength of the Organization of Petroleum Exporting Countries (OPEC) cartel in maintaining a monopolistic world price for petroleum. However these same oil-producing countries may, in a possible new role as major exporters of ammonia-based chemicals, exert countervailing downward pressures on nitrogen fertilizer prices.

Fertilizer Production in Three Asian Countries

We shall return to this most important question of the geographic location of future nitrogen capacity after reviewing the record of fertilizer manufacture in our three countries. Their experience is of considerable interest since they were among the first underdeveloped countries to undertake production; quantitatively they account for approximately half of all the fertilizer produced in Asia and the Middle East.[4]

Of the three countries Taiwan was the first to undertake the production of chemical fertilizers. While the bulk of the island's plant nutrient requirements were supplied by Japan over the entire colonial period, two small superphosphate plants and a cyanamide factory were built between 1920 and 1942. By the end of the period total output was in the neighborhood of 50,000 metric tons of calcium cyanamide (20 per cent N) and calcium superphosphate (18 per cent P_2O_5)—or about one-seventh of the country's fertilizer consumption. When the Nationalist Chinese government established the Taiwan Fertilizer Corporation (TFC) after the war, these three facilities were rehabilitated and expanded. Over the years additional units have been added: another calcium cyanamide factory in 1951 (40,000 metric tons), a small urea facility in 1958 (75,000 metric tons), and a nitrochalk factory in 1960 (60,000 metric tons). The Kaohsiung Ammonium Sulphate Corporation (KASC), another government concern, began production in 1950; with periodic expansions, its capacity has grown from 6000 to 180,000 metric tons of ammonium sulphate (21 per cent N).

The manufacturing processes utilized by TFC and KASC to produce nitrogen were the cyanamide process, water-electrolysis and the gasification of coal, and to a lesser extent, fuel oil. These are costly and outdated technologies. The cyanamide and electrolysis processes were replaced in the mid-1960s by partial oxidation units utilizing crude oil as the feedstock. Two small ammonia-producing units of KASC (60 and 90 tons per day) were operated on the basis of refinery off-gas. In 1960 a natural gas reserve at Chinsui was discovered, and in 1963 a joint venture between the Mobil Oil Company and Allied Chemical Corporation began production. This complex, with a 326 ton-a-day ammonia plant based on natural gas and the efficient steam reforming process, has an annual nitrogen capacity of 88,216 tons; in terms of fertilizer materials it produces 100,000 metric tons of urea (46 per cent N) and 45,000 tons of liquid ammonia (82 per cent N) for use in TFC's factories producing ammonium sulphate. With the discovery of another gas field, a second ammonia-urea complex was established at Hsinchu by TFC in 1969. With a single train and a 545 ton-a-day ammonia plant utilizing a centrifugal compressor, this factory was the first in Taiwan to incorporate all the advances of the post-1963 technology described in Chapter 3. In 1970 Taiwan achieved self-sufficiency in both nitrogenous and phosphate fertilizers.

In India and West Pakistan the production of nitrogenous fertilizers did not commence until 1947 and 1958, respectively. The pattern of the industry's development in these two countries has been similar to that of Taiwan. Early plants were small and for the most part based on outdated technology. The public sector has played the principal entrepreneurial role. Differing from Taiwan and India, plentiful natural gas has been discovered in West Pakistan which provides the potential for low-cost nitrogen production. By 1971 there were 13 nitrogen fertilizer factories in India and four in West Pakistan, producing 978,000 and 170,000 metric tons of plant nutrient nitrogen; the figure for Taiwan was 240,000 tons. Comparable tonnages of nutrient phosphate produced in the three countries were 308,000, 5,000, and 44,000, respectively. In both West Pakistan and India, consumption exceeds production by 40 to 60 per cent, the difference being made up by purchases from industrialized countries.

In assessing whether a country should undertake fertilizer production, decision-makers in developing countries and in international lending agencies tend primarily to be concerned with two questions: is there an adequate market and can the project be located near a feedstock source or port. A full consideration of comparative cost is not given, rather the emphasis is on a simple calculation of foreign exchange savings. Yet, given the nature of fertilizer manufacture, economic viability also depends critically upon high levels of capacity utilization and a low-cost capital input. The latter is composed of three elements: the installed cost of the physical plant annualized as a depreciation flow, an interest rate on the investment cost which reflects the productivity of these funds in their best alternative use, and a discount rate for technological obsolescence (i.e., the writedown in capital value that will occur when competitors introduce more efficient production processes).

What has been the practice in these matters? Because both the domestic government and foreign aid agencies typically ignore obsolescence considerations and, more importantly, make loan capital available to such projects at interest rates far below the opportunity cost of capital in the borrowing country, relative scarcity or abundance of resources comes into play only for private equity capital, labor, and feedstocks. With respect to investment in equipment and structures, feasibility studies for policy making purposes have relied on *ex ante* engineering estimates for a similar facility in an industrialized economy, plus a 40 per cent markup to cover such extra items as long distance transport, insurance, and supplementary investment in personnel housing, transportation facilities, and the like. With respect to the calculation of foreign exchange savings, it has been assumed that the plant will be operated at 80 to 90 per cent of capacity.

The nearly quarter-century of experience in the construction and operation of fertilizer plants in our three countries presents a substantial body of evidence against which to test the realism of these assumptions. We begin by reviewing actual investment costs and the extent to which they overran the original contract price.

In West Pakistan investigation of the possibility of fertilizer production began in 1949, one year after partition. In 1950 plans were drawn up by the West Pakistan Industrial Development Corporation (WPIDC) for a small ammonium sulphate plant (10,824 metric tons of nitrogen per annum) at Daudkhel, based on local coal and gypsum.[5] Although coal was no longer the preferred feedstock for ammonia, neither naphtha nor natural gas was available. A Belgian engineering firm contracted to construct the factory and finance was provided under United States foreign aid. Construction was begun in December 1952 and scheduled to be completed within 42 months. The cost of the factory, inclusive of housing and facilities for processing gypsum, was to be 61.0 million rupees. A further 2.5 million rupees was allocated for development of the colliery 26 miles away.

In the event the factory was not completed until February 1958, five years and four months after construction began and seven years after project authorization. The final investment cost had risen by some 49 per cent to 91.0 million rupees ($19 million)—of which approximately 60 per cent represented foreign exchange. The overrun was accounted for by original omissions (import duties, working capital, railway extension, staff training, insurance) and underestimations (number of European contractors, administration, price of equipment). Additional outlays were required to shore up sinking foundations and to modify the gasifiers owing to a lower quality coal than the tests had indicated—high ash content, unfavorable coking properties, and a large percentage of fines. It was the problems with the coal that accounted for most of the delay.

BACKWARD LINKAGES: FERTILIZER AND FARM EQUIPMENT

With the discovery of the Sui gas fields in the mid-1950s, WPIDC undertook to establish a urea and ammonium nitrate factory at Multan (73,260 tons of nitrogen).[6] In November 1957 a contract was signed with a French concern to erect the factory for operation in April 1961. Finance was obtained from the contractor and from the government of Pakistan, at 5.5 and 6 per cent, respectively. The approved estimates placed the cost of the project at 173 million rupees of which 113 million was foreign exchange.

In fact, the plant was not ready for operation until April 1963 (five and one-half years) and the cost had escalated to 229 million rupees; and the ammonia plant could not produce at the required output so that an additional 60 ton-a-day ammonia unit had to be installed at a cost of 27 million rupees. Thus the aggregate overrun was 48 per cent, giving a total investment of $53 million. The sources of increased costs were similar to those at Daudkhel: increases in equipment prices, duties, and wage costs. The contractor insisted on lavish expenditures on housing and training. The quality of gas was lower than promised with the result that decarbonization and desulphurization plants had to be introduced. During the 1961 trials, leakages in the production line and excessive consumption of catalysts necessitated further work which eventually took two years. Interest payments to the contractor during this period added 14 million rupees to the investment cost.

West Pakistan's two largest fertilizer factories are in the private sector. The Esso urea plant at Dharki was planned in 1964 shortly after the company discovered natural gas at Marri. Although larger and employing a more advanced technology than the Multan factory, the scale of output (81,180 tons of nitrogen per annum) was not sufficient to permit use of the centrifugal compressor in ammonia production. The estimated cost in 1964 was $25 million. Construction began in 1966 and was completed in November 1968. The final cost of the project was $20 million more than the initial estimate. Of the total $45.5 million, foreign exchange expenditures accounted for $24.6 million. The Dawood-Hercules urea factory—the country's largest (169,125 tons nitrogen) and most efficient plant—is also natural gas-based and it does employ a centrifugal ammonia compressor. The Dawood-Hercules gestation period—planned in 1968, construction begun in 1969, start-up in 1971—set a record for the Indian subcontinent. The final cost of the project was $79 million, an overrun of only $1 million above the 1968 estimate. This figure represented just double the cost of a similar facility in the United States.[7]

The history of plant construction in India is quite similar to that of West Pakistan. The country's first sizable plant, initially based upon wood gasification, was established by Fertilizers and Chemicals at Alwaye; it commenced production in 1947. This company (FACT) and the Fertilizer Corporation of India (FCI) are both owned by the government of India, and both have become major engineering contractors in erecting public sector fertilizer plants. FCI owns factories at Sindri, Nangal, Trombay, and Gorakhput, details of which are given in Table 8.2. The other two public sector plants are owned by Hindustan Steel (Rourkela) and the Neyveli Lignite Corporation.

With the exception of 30 small phosphate plants, having an installed capacity of 228,980 tons of P_2O_5, and eight ammonium sulphate units utilizing by-products from the steel industry, with a capacity of 28,130 tons of N, all fertilizer production derives from the 14 plants shown in Table 8.2.[8] In addition to the plants in operation in 1971, there were another nine projects under construction. Two of these projects are in the private sector, one in the cooperative sector, and six in the public sector.

All of the public sector plants have cost considerably more than their original estimates.[9] Gestation periods have been extremely long, averaging over five years. Approximately two years have been required after the investment decision to let contracts, acquire land, and arrange for licenses. As reported in the third column of Table 8.2, the time actually taken in erecting factories has been considerably longer than for the private sector. Stephen Merrett's chronicle of these projects reveals a familiar range of impediments: unfulfilled time schedules of civil works contractors and equipment manufacturers, delays in issuing foreign exchange licenses, unjustified

Table 8.2. Principal Indian fertilizer plants, 1970

Plant	Start-up	Feedstock	Years under construction	Investment (millions of rupees)	Workers employed	Ammonia plant (tons/day)	Nutrient capacity (thousand tons/year)	
							N	P_2O_5
Public sector								
Alwaye	1947	Naphtha	4	393	6428	355[a]	92	36
Sindri	1951	Coal	5	469	7139	463[a]	117	...
Nangal	1961	Electricity	3	312	3284	307	80	...
Rourkela	1963	Off-gas	...	...	1708	...	120	...
Trombay	1965	Naphtha	4	456	2107	350	90	45
Neyveli	1966	Lignite	6	388	1594	285	70	...
Gorakhpur	1969	Naphtha	5	349	2013	350	80	...
Namrup	1969	Natural gas	6	243	2074	200	45	...
Private sector								
Varanasi	1959	Coal	...	55	...	40	10	...
Ennore	1963	Naphtha	...	84	756	66	16	10
Baroda	1967	Naphtha	...	630	1624	950[a]	230	55
Visakhapatnam	1968	Naphtha	...	487	945	325	85	75
Kota	1969	Naphtha	2	464	1199	450	120	...
Kanpur	1969	Naphtha	3	610	992	830	207	...

[a] In two plants.

SOURCE: Data from Fertilizer Association of India, *Fertilizer Statistics, 1971-72* (New Delhi, 1973) and USAID, Office of Capital Development, *Status of Fertilizer Projects as of January 1970* (New Delhi, 1970).

technical risks, rectification of defective work, replacement of defective equipment, accidental explosions, additional facilities to handle unexpected feedstock impurities, and assorted technical difficulties.[10] For the two private sector plants for which there is information, speedier execution—paralleling the experience of Esso, Dawood-Hercules, and Taiwan's Mobil-Allied—seems to be explained, inter alia, by far more careful project planning, by greater reliance on imported capital goods and expert foreign contractors (hence, higher foreign exchange costs), and by less encumbered, more determined entrepreneurial follow-through.

In addition to the high cost of investment springing from the inefficiency of plant construction itself, an additional burden for public sector plants has been generous investment in housing and township facilities. "Evidently, all the projects have been lavish with the use of land. At Sindri there is one house constructed per acre of land, the argument being that land is cheap. Even at Trombay [adjacent to a large urban area], FCI has provided housing to 97 per cent of its workers. The cost of township formed 12.6 per cent of total project cost at Sindri and 12 per cent at Nangal."[11] Not only are public sector undertakings more prone to build townships when they are not absolutely necessary, but because of extensive overstaffing the townships are a good deal larger than they would otherwise be. And this in turn gives rise to higher noncapital costs as well: 11 per cent of the FACT and FCI labor force is employed in staffing schools, hospitals, and other municipal services.[12]

Much less information is available on the history of plant construction in Taiwan.[13] A good portion of the present capacity of TFC and KASC has been achieved by numerous small expansions of existing facilities; it seems that many of these were completed within 12 to 24 months. For at least three big projects—TFC's first coal-based urea plant and its Hualien nitrochalk factory, and KASC's first expansion—the gestation period was five years or more. By contrast the private investor-executed $23 million urea project at Miaoli holds the record for Asia's shortest gestation period. The agreement between Mobil Oil, Allied Chemical, and the Chinese Petroleum

BACKWARD LINKAGES: FERTILIZER AND FARM EQUIPMENT   341

Corporation was signed in August 1961. Planned and engineered by Allied and the Badger Company, respectively, construction was begun the following July with start-up 15 months later. This 26-month period was accomplished despite a United States longshoremen's strike and a typhoon.[14] Ingenious planning and faultless execution was rewarded with an extremely low-investment cost and subsequent trouble-free operation.

Table 8.3 attempts to bring together roughly comparable investment costs per ton of nitrogen capacity for fertilizer plants in our three countries and a composite figure for 17 United States firms producing urea. This computation involves adjusting reported investment costs for the overvaluation of domestic currencies and for changes in the price level between the time of the investment and 1970. The figures are probably an underestimate of true investment cost for the Asian plants. First, a large number of the projects received loans on which no interest charges were levied during the construction period. Second, our choice of shadow prices for domestic content (extremely low as an *average* for the periods they cover) and our assumption that local purchases were completely free of foreign exchange content also introduce a downward bias. The data for the United States were collected in a very careful investigation by a team of researchers at Michigan State University.[15] The 17-firm composite refers to a single train urea plant based on a natural gas ammonia facility utilizing the centrifugal compressor technology.

The results reported in the final column of the table reveal investment costs in Asia which range from 75 to over 600 per cent above that of the American composite. Much of the explanation for those investment costs above $1000 per ton is related to inefficient technological processes for ammonia production involving coal, lignite, or water electrolysis. Among the more recent Asian plants, private sector undertakings have clearly been less expensive. The extraordinary achievement of the 1963 Mobil-Allied investment is once again evident. The Esso-Dharki factory is closest in vintage to the United States composite; the investment cost differential is 172 per cent. In addition to the absence of special infrastructural require-

Table 8.3. Investment cost per ton of nitrogen capacity

Plant	Start-up	Nitrogen capacity[a] (thousand tons/year)	Investment cost[b] (millions of dollars)	Domestic content (per cent)	Investment cost at SER[c] (millions of dollars)	Inflation adjustment to 1970[d] (1970 prices)	Investment cost per metric ton[e] (dollars)
Pakistan							
Daudkhel	1958	11	19.1	40	15.3	1.612	2,227
Multan	1963	73	53.8	35	44.4	1.316	800
Esso-Dharki	1968	81	45.5	46	35.0	1.062	459
Dawood-Hercules	1971	169	79.0	42	62.5	1.000	370
Taiwan							
Mobil-Allied	1963	88	23.0	43	23.0	1.135	296
India							
(Public)							
Sindri	1951	117	98.5	40	78.8	2.156	1,452
Nangal	1961	80	65.5	54	47.9	1.829	1,095
Neyveli	1966	70	81.5	52	60.3	1.660	1,430
Namrup	1969	45	32.4	70	24.8	1.239	683
Gorkhpur	1969	80	46.5	59	37.4	1.078	504
(Private)							
Kanpur	1969	207	81.3	65	63.9	1.085	335
Kota	1969	120	61.9	50	51.6	1.085	467
American							
17-firm Composite	1967	262	40.1	100	...	1.104	169

[a] 330 days per annum.
[b] Converted to dollars at official exchange rates: Pakistan rupee, $1 = 4.76 Rs; Indian rupee, $1 = 4.76 Rs prior to 1967 and 7.5 Rs after. The investment cost of Mobil-Allied was reported in dollars.
[c] Investment cost when domestic content revalued at shadow exchange rates (SER): Pakistan rupee, $1 = 9.52 Rs; Indian rupee, $1 = 9.52 Rs prior to 1967 and 11.25 Rs after: No overvaluation in the case of the new Taiwan dollar.
[d] Wholesale price index based on the mid-year between construction start and on-stream.
[e] SER Investment cost $\times$ Inflation adjustment $\div$ Nitrogen capacity.

SOURCE: Data from Fertilizer Association of India, *Fertilizer Statistics, 1971-72* (New Delhi, 1973); USAID, Office of Capital Development, *Status of Fertilizer Projects as of January 1970* (New Delhi, 1970); United Nations, *Statistical Yearbook* (New York, 1961 and 1973); D. R. Henderson, G. R. Perkins, and D. M. Bell, *Simulating the Fertilizer Industry: Data* (East Lansing, 1972); and Republic of China, Council for International Economic Cooperation and Development, *Taiwan Statistical Data Book 1971* (Taipei, 1971).

ments and the pitfalls faced by plant builders in nonindustrialized economies, the cost superiority of the American facility derives from the more advanced technology it embodies, its scale of output, and the lower cost of engineering services. With respect to technological lag, centrifugal compressors were not employed in India or Pakistan until 1971.

Stated in the most general terms, large differences in investment cost per unit of capacity reflect the fact that the organization and construction of fertilizer plants is itself a complex production process. For developing countries there is no fixed relationship between investment expenditure and productive capacity. Rather capital formation is a production process whose real cost (time and resources) varies according to technological lag, locational circumstance (including feedstock and the presence or absence of off-site power and transport infrastructure), the quality of technical and administrative skills employed, the efficiency of the local economy in supplying inputs, and, of course, factor prices. And because capital is the dominant input, it is appropriate to assess the social profitability of the fertilizer industry in a framework which encompasses both the production of capacity and the production of final output. Having examined the former, we are now ready to consider the latter.

Given the cost of a fixed capital input, the efficiency of fertilizer manufacture is determined by the price of current inputs and the level of capacity utilization. In the case of Daudkhel, coal and gypsum are the major purchased inputs.[16] Against an estimated cost of 35 rupees per ton of coal and 7 rupees per ton of gypsum, actual prices have been 60 to 70 rupees and 10 rupees per ton, respectively; moreover, since the quality of coal was poorer than expected, twice the estimated quantity of coal is required per ton of fertilizer product. On the other hand, with the exception of one year marked by an explosion in the Iron Box, utilization rates have been close to 100 per cent of 330-day capacity. Ex-factory prices during the 1960s were 50 to 70 per cent higher than the cash cif import price.[17] In the case of Multan, input costs were in line with the revised estimates until a substantial hike in wages and the price of natural gas occurred in 1968. Both

BACKWARD LINKAGES: FERTILIZER AND FARM EQUIPMENT

Daudkhel and Multan have suffered from overstaffing. The main problem at Multan has been a utilization rate which never exceeded 78 per cent, owing to a design fault in the ammonia plant. Ex-factory prices have ranged from 40 to 100 per cent above the cif import alternative. Performance of the newer, private sector plants has been more favorable. Although less information concerning the Esso and Dawood-Hercules factories is available, they both have operated at full capacity and sold their product at ex-factory prices 20 to 40 per cent above world prices.

In the Indian case the principal impediment to efficient manufacture of chemical fertilizers has been low rates of capacity utilization. For the country as a whole, over the past two decades output has averaged about 60 per cent of designed capacity, with 67 per cent being the best performance attained in any single year. The record of individual plants is summarized in Table 8.4. As with gestation periods and investment cost per ton of capacity, the private sector has outperformed the public sector, even without allowing for the fact that Kota and Kanpur were still in their breaking-in phase. For the smaller producers of phosphate fertilizers and by-product nitrogen not shown, utilization levels have averaged about 50 per cent.

The causes for poor performance have been manifold. Among the older plants output has been hampered by design errors, capacity imbalance between processes, and defective equipment.[18] Raw material problems have been more important: at Rourkela until recently there has been coke-oven gas sufficient only for one-third capacity operation; at Sindri poor quality coal and gypsum have resulted in frequent shutdowns; recently, shortages of naphtha have affected a large number of plants. Failure of the monsoons, particularly in 1965 and 1972, have drastically reduced the supply of hydroelectric power and thereby curtailed production in at least half of the factories. Plant shutdown owing to voltage dips have been frequent occurrences at Alwaye, Nangal, Baroda, and Visakhapatnam. In the past three years labor strikes in the railways and in several plants have exacted a heavy toll in lost output. Delays in obtaining critical imported spare parts, owing to foreign exchange shortages, have been a con-

Table 8.4. Capacity utilization in the Indian fertilizer industry (Public)

Plant	Designed capacity (*thousands of tons*)	Average utilization[a] (*per cent*)	Maximum utilization (*per cent*)
(Public)			
Alwaye			
N	92	35 (1966-74)	43 (1972-73)
P_2O_5	36	32 (1966-71)	36 (1968-69)
Sindri			
N	117	61 (1966-74)	77 (1966-67)
Nangal			
N	80	84 (1966-74)	98 (1967-68)
Rourkela			
N	120	29 (1966-71)	40 (1968-69)
Trombay			
N	90	61 (1967-74)	78 (1972-73)
P_2O_5	45	39 (1966-71)	47 (1968-69)
Neyveli			
N	70	53 (1967-71)	60 (1969-70)
Gorakpur			
N	80	87 (1969-74)	91 (1972-73)
Namrup			
N	45	68 (1969-74)	80 (1973-74)
(Private)			
Ennore			
N	16		63 (1969-71)
P_2O_5	10		70 (1969-71)
Baroda			
N	230		54 (1969-71)
P_2O_5	55		46 (1969-71)
Visak			
N	85		72 (1969-71)
P_2O_5	75		79 (1969-71)
Kota			
N	120		89 (1970-71)[b]
Kanpur			
N	207		55 (1970-71)[b]

[a] With the exception of Kota and Kanpur, the first two years of operation (the break-in period of new plants) are omitted. Reported for Indian fiscal years on the basis of 330-day operation.
[b] Second year of operation.
SOURCE: Data from Economics and Statistics Division, Ministry of Petroleum and Chemicals.

BACKWARD LINKAGES: FERTILIZER AND FARM EQUIPMENT 347

tinuing problem. Also related to balance-of-payments difficulties, since 1958 the best quality coal at Sindri has been diverted to the export trade and to the steel industry, reducing the level of attainable output at that plant by some 15 per cent.[19] Finally, accidental explosions and, far more frequently, faulty maintenance of instrumentation and mechanical equipment have contributed to lost production.

Little detailed information is available for Taiwan. In recent years its average level of capacity utilization has been about 75 per cent, the principal problem being inadequate feedstock supplies. The level of ex-factory fertilizer prices in both India and Taiwan has been approximately the same as that in Pakistan.[20]

As low as it is, the level of capacity utilization in India is higher than the average for all underdeveloped countries. On the basis of data collected by TVA and FAO for some 40 low-income countries producing chemical fertilizers, average utilization in 1971-72 was 56 per cent for nitrogen plants and 52 per cent for phosphate plants.[21] As in the Indian case, a certain portion of this shortfall is attributable to new plants just coming on stream. Allowances for this might raise the figure to the mid-60 percentile range. Low levels of capacity utilization have two principal effects. They raise investment costs beyond the already high levels reported in Table 8.2, for example, operation at 60 rather than 100 per cent of capacity raises investment cost per ton by 67 per cent. For a capital-intensive industry that boasts only a modest rate of social profitability under the favorable assumptions employed by the planners, increases in the capital cost of such magnitudes inevitably transform the social rate of return from a positive to a negative number.

The second effect of underutilization is to increase the foreign exchange cost per unit of domestic production. While there are a number of items with a greater or lesser portion of foreign exchange content which do tend to vary with output rather than designed capacity—fuel, power, feedstocks, bagging—the quantitatively more important groups are those which are independent of the level of utilization. Thus a shortfall from full-capacity operation means that the foreign exchange costs associated with depreciation, interest on foreign loans, imported spare parts, catalysts, and service fees rise for every ton of fertilizer produced in proportion to the degree of underutilization. This then raises the question: does domestic fertilizer production as it is actually carried out save foreign exchange?

The calculation of the foreign exchange savings effected by producing fertilizer involves estimating the foreign currency content of domestic output and subtracting that from the cif cost of the imported alternative. The foreign exchange content of home production is made up of directly imported inputs used in fertilizer manufacture and in its supplier industries, plus the indirect opportunity costs for those inputs which might have earned or saved foreign exchange in another use (e.g., naphtha, skilled labor). Inputs which have no foreign currency opportunity cost are such items as unskilled labor, insurance, indirect taxes, and feedstocks that would not otherwise be used, for example, off-gas and flared natural gas. Such calculations have been carried out for India by I. M. D. Little and his associates at the Organisation for Economic Co-operation and Development.[22] They estimated that 64 per cent of variable inputs and 70 per cent of investment and other fixed overheads have a foreign exchange opportunity cost. In calculating the latter they employed an 80 per cent utilization rate. On the basis of the OECD calculations —and taking into account a markup for return to capital and adjusting fixed costs for the lower utilization level—at no period prior to 1972 (including 1965-66 when import prices were high) did the Indian fertilizer industry, taken as a whole, save foreign exchange. On the contrary, domestic production of a ton of nitrogen fertilizer entailed a greater sacrifice of foreign exchange than did direct importation. It is likely that the situation in Pakistan and Taiwan was similar until their low-cost natural gas-based plants came on stream in the mid-1960s, converting a foreign exchange deficit into a slight savings.

The Location of Future Capacity

On the basis of the evidence provided by our three countries, it would seem that as a general policy individual underdeveloped countries should not aim at self-sufficiency in the production of nitrogen fertilizers. This is obviously not true for countries blest with abundant natural gas, countries which for the most part are major oil producers and hence are also well stocked with investible financial reserves. But for the more typical less-developed country, possessing neither cheap hydrocarbon feedstocks or surplus investment funds, the choices are harsher. For these countries the high opportunity cost of capital, the need for a larger capital investment for a given amount of productive capacity and the greater likelihood of inefficient operation relative to producers in industrial countries combine in a powerful mixture to render fertilizer one of the least desirable candidates for import substitution.

There are, of course, risks in depending upon international trade. Against the gains in higher national income that reliance on low-cost imports brings, decision-makers must weigh the possible disruptions that are inherent in any interdependent market system. And these risks have seldom been more apparent than during 1973 and 1974 when world fertilizer prices doubled and in some cases supplies were not available at any price. Under such circumstances domestic production, even when based on coal, becomes competitive and contributes substantially to national output and to the saving of foreign exchange.

Among the more frequent causes of radical disturbance in supply and demand relationships are abrupt spurts in technological progress, strong advances (or drop-offs) in demand in a large number of countries simultaneously, the creation of cartels at one or more points in the production chain and war or political embargoes. It must be noted, however, that many of these disturbances are just as likely to increase the gain from international specialization as to nullify it. While underdeveloped countries have been suffering since 1972 with respect to fertilizer purchases, in other world markets disequilibrium raw material prices have created unprecedented windfall gains for many low-income countries specializing in primary products.

There are two separable elements in the current fertilizer crisis. One is the existing capacity of world fertilizer plants in relation to world demand. The other is the cost and availability of energy and light hydrocarbon feedstocks, that is, naphtha and natural gas. With respect to this second element, an autarkic fertilizer policy will not insulate a country from the effects of a high OPEC petroleum price (assuming the cartel remains effective). A high world price for petroleum raises the market value of domestic supplies of naphtha and natural gas in equal measure, whether they be used for fuel, for power generation, for petrochemical industries, or for export. Thus the cost of domestic nitrogen fertilizer and its foreign exchange content will rise in step with the cost of imported fertilizer. A shift to the less-efficient heavier feedstocks, such as coal, can partially free nitrogen production from the price of petroleum. For instance, India's two largest projects under construction ($200 million each), both in the public sector, will be based on coal. But this substitution entails a 50 per cent increase in capital costs (with its associated foreign exchange content) and runs the operational hazards so often encountered with coal.

This leaves a prolonged supply shortage as the only valid justification for an autarkic policy. If fertilizer prices remain at or not too far below their current levels, even inefficient producers can operate profitably without protection and their countries thereby gain. The past history of the industry offers scant support for this hypothesis: abnormally high profits have always induced new investments in those locations suited to low-cost production, so that scarcity prices have not persisted much longer than the investment gestation period. However, proponents argue that past patterns may not be repeated. They reason as follows. Fertilizer investors, who were badly burned in 1968-71, will be reluctant to commit themselves to another potential roller coaster ride; this reluctance is likely to be reinforced by the political uncertainties and consequent commercial risks attendant to investing in the oil-producing countries. Proponents of autarky also predict continued rapid growth in world fertilizer demand, placing a strain on capacity even if new investments are forthcoming.

While the above suppositions are perfectly plausible, there are many other equally plausible suppositions that imply a different re-

BACKWARD LINKAGES: FERTILIZER AND FARM EQUIPMENT 351

sult. Clearly at this juncture it is impossible to predict with a reasonable degree of confidence what the balance of supply and demand will be in five years time. In addition to decisions taken by private investors, the outcome depends critically upon such imponderables as weather conditions and actions taken in centrally directed socialist countries such as China, Russia, and Roumania. And perhaps most significant of all, are the investment decisions that may be made by OPEC governments themselves.

The circumstances that now prevail in the OPEC countries, particularly the Persian Gulf countries, provide the makings for a vigorous supply response to the current shortage. With large and rapidly accumulating financial reserves, the Iranian and Arab governments are anxious to diversify production, especially into industrial activities that are based on local raw materials. Export production of nitrogen fertilizers and petrochemicals by state corporations are, under these circumstances, the natural choice. Such projects are in fact among those now being promoted by sales representatives from Europe and Japan as these countries endeavor to exchange capital goods and industrial know-how for oil. Another factor which makes the location of future capacity in oil-producing countries not only likely but economically desirable is the fact that the hydrocarbon feedstock will in most cases be a "free" input. Of the 209 billion cubic meters of natural gas produced in OPEC countries in 1971-72, only 38 per cent was commercially utilized.[23] The 130 billion cubic meters that are currently flared would produce five times as much nitrogen fertilizer as the total 1980 consumption projected by the World Bank for all underdeveloped countries (see Table 8.1). Since the number of countries flaring gas is considerable—Venezuela, Algeria, Libya, Nigeria, Indonesia, and six Persian Gulf countries—it is quite possible that competition would result in the fertilizer importing countries eventually receiving much of the benefit from this free input.

The presence of enormous volumes of flared gas also adds to general structural elements which make price fixing by fertilizer-exporting countries highly improbable. Because natural gas supplies are more widely distributed than petroleum and because individual producers will be under strong pressures to fully utilize the new capacity which they have built at great cost, the potential for forming a cartel, as has been done for petroleum, is severely limited. The cartel potential is further diminished to the extent that there is equity participation on the part of governments of importing countries in foreign plants which supply them.

FARM EQUIPMENT

Although quantitatively less important than chemical fertilizer, the purchase of farm tools and machinery by a modernizing agricultural sector nevertheless represents a potentially sizable backward linkage to the manufacturing sector. Moreover, there are qualitative considerations which give these expenditures a significance that extends well beyond the nonfarm output and employment which they generate. With respect to the manufacturing sector, agricultural implements constitute a large segment of output of the metal-working industry in a developing country. As such, the kinds of organizational and technological developments experienced in firms making farm equipment have ramifications for the country's capacity to produce its own capital goods and to embody in these capital goods technology adapted to the economy's relative factor endowment. With respect to agricultural development, the nature of these capital inputs strongly influences productivity and farm income by virtue of their cost, the variety of tasks they perform, and the technology (design efficiency) they place at the farmer's command.

Our investigation will proceed in four stages. In the first part we will attempt to outline the broad economic forces that determine the type of implements produced, their price and quality, and the nature of the interactions between farm equipment production and the evolution of the metal-working industry. In the second part we will examine in concrete terms how farm equipment can be adapted, or fail to be adapted, to the needs of the typical farmer as agricultural

BACKWARD LINKAGES: FERTILIZER AND FARM EQUIPMENT 353

development progresses. The third part will focus on the organization of the farm equipment industry and its relationship to the light engineering sector at large. The concluding section will be devoted to an analysis of the differential impact of the farm equipment industry on output, employment, and foreign exchange requirements depending upon the agricultural strategy that is pursued.

General Determinants

We will segregate the many forces that mould the development of the farm equipment industry into two groups, those that emanate from the farmer and affect the nature of demand and those that operate directly on production and thus affect supply conditions.

The factors that operate on the demand for farm equipment are closely related to structural transformation and the cash receipts constraint. With no structural transformation there is a more or less constant demand for an unchanging set of implements. Thus, in the absence of significant alteration in operational holdings (e.g., amalgamation of smallholdings into larger units which would favor the use of tractors), there are no forces on the demand side to disturb the existing state of the farm equipment industry. This situation has characterized the Indian subcontinent for most of the twentieth century.

A second case occurs when cash sales per farm unit are gradually rising, a situation which has obtained in Taiwan. Steadily growing cash receipts tend to generate a demand for new implements (a) to ease labor bottlenecks that emerge with increased cropping intensity and use of water and new chemical inputs, (b) to upgrade energy sources, and (c) in general to reduce labor inputs and raise the speed and precision of operations. This pattern of demand calls for a continuous development of the farm equipment industry; the demand for higher performance from agricultural tools and machinery tends to promote an evolution in technical knowledge and skills employed in casting processes and materials selection, in techniques of forging and heat treating, in the machining of parts, in assembly, and in quality control.

In these two cases of a constant or gradually rising share of marketed output there is an additional factor at work. This is related to agriculture's market organization. Because farming is characterized by a very large number of producers and undifferentiated products, normal earnings beyond wages and land rent are held to a minimum by competitive forces. This in turn exercises a strict discipline on the purchasing power available for acquiring capital equipment. This pressure on the farmer to locate the cheapest implement for the job is reinforced by the extremely low utilization of many items of farm equipment, perhaps only a few weeks out of every year. The following statement by a team of agricultural engineers in Taiwan in 1953 describing animal and manually powered equipment, mostly in the $5 to $50 range, gives witness to this phenomenon:

> Farm implements in Taiwan are comparatively cheap and this is due to the farmers' low purchasing power. Manufacturers often have to sacrifice quality in order to maintain a low price. If sturdy and highly efficient farm implements were to be made, their prices will have to be raised; farmers because of their financial stringency, will not be able to buy these implements even if they are aware of their good performance. In other words, the farmers in Taiwan should be temporarily satisfied with the minimum serviceability of implements available.[24]

This pressure to locate the cheapest implement for the job is usually described in terms of the level of purchasing power. In fact, even where purchasing power is very high (e.g., the United States) as long as the farmer's product markets are competitive, his narrow profit margin above minimum cost forces him to be very price conscious about the equipment he buys. We can give a concrete illustration of this "bare essentials principle" by reference to Taiwan in 1970, by which time average farm income was approximately triple its 1953 level and labor scarcity had induced considerable mechanization. In explaining why power tillers (price $900 to $1,500) have not spread at a more rapid rate (24,640 units as of 1969) the Joint Commission on Rural Reconstruction's Farm Machinery Specialist observed:

BACKWARD LINKAGES: FERTILIZER AND FARM EQUIPMENT

In spite of the increasing demand for farm equipment by Taiwan farmers, prices of farm machines, especially power tillers, produced by local manufacturers are generally beyond the financial capacity of the average farmer. . . . It is doubly hard to market farm machinery among the farmers with their low purchasing power.[25]

A third pattern of demand is that generated by a sudden and discontinuous increase in farm cash receipts. This situation is exemplified by the Punjab region in India and Pakistan since 1967. Two preceding years of drought resulted in a 50 per cent rise in food grain prices and a high level of food imports. With the coincidental appearance of the new seed varieties the stage was set for a rapid expansion of ouput at unusually high prices and substantially reduced costs. Cash receipts rose rapidly and net farm income even more rapidly. During this disequilibrium interval, while prices that are substantially above cost obtain, the farmer makes a higher income by investing in equipment that enables rapid production increases rather than in equipment that minimizes unit cost. Augmented profits also provide enlarged purchasing power for obtaining farm equipment. The result is a shift in demand away from man and animal-powered equipment toward tractors, tractor-drawn equipment, and combine harvesters. Government lending programs unintentionally encouraged this trend. For the most part the new equipment is not produced by the same firms as before: the gap in manufacturing processes is too great. There is a sharp rise in scale of output, capital intensity, and in import content.

The principal forces working on the supply side are two in number, namely the absence of barriers to new entrants and sources of equipment design. The absence of significant economies of scale or other barriers to entry operates in the same direction as demand preferences to promote the ready supply of low-priced farm tools. The great majority of farm implements can be manufactured on a very small scale; even 14 h.p. two-wheel tractors and diesel engine pumpsets can be manufactured with a comparatively modest investment in fixed plant through the use of subcontractors and the purchase of standardized "trade" components and sub-assemblies. Most of the required metalworking skills can be learned on the job; typically only the largest firms serving the premium quality market employ craftsmen with formal technical training. The principal exception, where capital and skill barriers to entry are significant, are those complex items such as four-wheel tractors and combines which require an initial provision of technical information to the customer, extensive after-service, and the carrying of a spare parts inventory, all of which are combined in a dealership network. However, for virtually all other farm implements, as long as above normal profits are being made, the number of producers increases as experienced workers leave their employers to establish on their own. This fission process intensifies competition and leads manufacturers to seek to reduce costs.

The last and perhaps most important factor determining the nature of equipment available to the farmer is the country's capacity to borrow and adapt new prototypes and designs. Because most of the basic principles involved in the design of agricultural equipment of current interest and application in developing countries appear to have been worked out by the late nineteenth century,[26] the task of agricultural engineering research is to adapt known designs to different crop requirements, locational circumstances, and factor prices. The efficiency of the international market in farm equipment is obviously related to the extent of design transfer. Probably more important is the kind of institutional structures a country possesses for acquiring and transmitting known technical information and for carrying out adaptive research and communicating the results to farmers and manufacturers. Elements in this complex are the work of research organizations, the programming capability of government departments, the extent and quality of agricultural extension, cooperative organization among farmers and, perhaps most critical, the market environment in which the farm equipment manufacturers operate.

Farming Tasks and Farming Tools

In this section we attempt to document several of the propositions we have just put forward. Specifically, we will examine the role that

BACKWARD LINKAGES: FERTILIZER AND FARM EQUIPMENT

farm tool design plays in facilitating a pattern of evolutionary agricultural development which incorporates both new yield-increasing technical possibilities and makes full use of the farm labor force. It is this material, contrasting Taiwan with the Indian subcontinent, which provides support for our assertions about the influence of demand factors leading to stagnation, evolutionary upgrading, or abrupt shifts in the technical sophistication of farm implements.

An outstanding feature of Taiwanese agricultural implements is the degree to which each tool has been designed for its special task and specific environment. An example is the harrow, one of the eight types of tools used in secondary tillage. There were nine kinds of harrows reported in 1952, the comb harrow, three knife tooth harrows (standard, bent frame, flexible tooth), two spike harrows, the bamboo harrow, the pulverizing roller, and the stone roller.[27] Since 1952 the animal-drawn tyned tiller and the disk harrow have been introduced. A single one of these harrows, the standard knife tooth, has twelve regional variants. Width, length, material and number of teeth, shape of tooth blade, and method of affixing teeth are adapted according to local topography, field size, soil structure, and available construction materials. Similarly the basic types of hoes—earth opening, hilling, weeding—are found in six zonal varieties which differ in weight, dimensions, and angle of blade according to climate, soil conditions, and crop requirements.

A pattern of progressive agricultural modernization implies a growing inventory of farm tools. Exactly one-fourth of the 1952 stock of implements had been introduced in the preceding 30 years. Twelve of the 40 new implements performed yield-increasing tasks that were never done before, for example, the check row spacing marker and the sprayer. Sixteen new tools performed the same work as before but with far greater speed, for example, the potato-slicing machine, duster, and manure fork. The remaining items did a superior, yield-increasing job, for example, the adapted Japanese plow and the flexible knife tooth harrow, or, as in the case of the animal-drawn lister plow and tractor-powered rototiller, did both superior and faster work. Nineteen of the 40 tools were labor saving. Most of the new implements cost more than those which they displaced.

For the reasons discussed earlier, the manufacturers of this type of equipment are under strong pressure to minimize costs. Because the cost of materials is the dominant component of manufacturing costs, the price of various implements tends to vary according to weight. The modal weights for nearly two-thirds of the implements were less than 10 pounds; and the average price for half of the 160 items was under five United States dollars at 1970 prices. The majority of the animal-drawn implements fell in the 10 to 40 dollar range.

A considerable number of new and more expensive items have come into use during the decades since 1952. There has been a sharp increase in pumpsets for irrigation and drainage, the majority of which are small centrifugal pumps driven by a 5 h.p. diesel engine. These portable low-lift pumps were initially imported from Japan but are now produced by some 15 Taiwanese firms which also export them. The rapid spread of sprayers, which began in 1955, was also based initially on imports from Japan; and mist blowers and dusters were introduced from Germany in the early 1960s but are now manufactured locally. An artificial grain dryer, introduced in 1966, greatly reduces losses due to fermenting, sprouting, and moulding where harvesting must be done in the rainy season (first rice crop in the south, second crop in the north). After experimenting with American prototypes—which proved either too heavy or too costly—the Provincial Department of Agriculture and Forestry adapted a Japanese bintype design utilizing a kerosene burner and an electric blower.

Instances of partial mechanization to break emerging labor bottlenecks are numerous. The operations of threshing and winnowing have been speeded up by adding a small gasoline and electric motor to replace the foot pedal and hand crank, respectively. The efficiency of the winnower has been further improved by the addition of bearings in the revolving mechanism and an auger elevator for moving the grain into the hopper. Small electric motors have replaced the human arm as the motive power for the sweet potato slicing machine.[28]

The post-1952 development in farm equipment that has received the most attention is the power tiller. Taiwan's Joint Commission on Rural Reconstruction (JCRR) began to experiment with 2 to 10 h.p. American and Japanese two-wheel tractors in 1954, and by 1956 it was evident that the Japanese rotary-type diesel engine tiller with certain adaptations was best suited to Taiwan conditions. The spread of the power tiller has been fairly gradual and has been associated with the provision of technical know-how to the farmer and appropriate repair services. The availability of those complementary inputs along with adaptive improvements in machine design have led to a sizable increase in the efficiency and rate of utilization of tillers. The average number of hours of operation rose from less than 450 hours per year in 1960 to 828 hours in 1969; at the same time the work accomplished per hour has risen, for example, the number of hours required to prepare a hectare of paddy land was reduced from 19.4 hours in 1965 to 14.7 hours in 1969. These changes have considerably increased the social profitability of the power tiller, particularly since its importance has been expanding in a period in which Taiwanese agriculture has for the first time begun to experience a shortage of farm labor.

By contrast, in India and West Pakistan the bulk of farmers utilize a comparatively limited number of implements most of which have remained unchanged for centuries. The stick plow of antiquity, now with a metal tip, is still used as the principal instrument for plowing, harrowing, puddling, planting, and intercultivation. Other implements include the spade, hoe, leveling plank, hand sickle, ox cart, and Persian water wheel. Innovations of the twentieth century that have diffused widely are the hand-operated fodder chopper, the bullock-powered sugarcane crusher, and motorized pumpsets; this number of three compares with over 40 new items in Taiwan prior to 1952. Innovations of the last decade, confined to progressive farmers in certain regions, are the bullock-drawn disk harrow and seed drill and the motorized stationary thresher. Stimulated by high grain prices and the new seed, four-wheel tractors in significant numbers date from the mid-1960s; they have been concentrated on large farms and mainly in the wheat-growing regions. The efficient operation of tractors has been hampered by lack of trained drivers and spart parts.[29] In addition to the influence of the purchasing power constraint, the principal causes for the largely thwarted evolution of farm tools are limited engineering research, deficient extension, and oscillating government policies.

A comparison of the Indian and Pakistani Punjab, the area on the subcontinent where the seed-fertilizer revolution has progressed the furthest, reveals at a regional level the two-way interaction between the pattern of agricultural development and the capabilities of the farm equipment industry.[30] Mechanization on both sides of the border is approximately the same in terms of aggregate tractor horsepower and water pumping capacity. In the West Punjab, however, tractors and pumpsets have been concentrated on large farms (average tractor-operated farm holding 267 acres) while on the Indian side such mechanization is broadly based (average tractor-operated farm holding 35 acres). In the West, virtually all the tubewells are in the 1-2 cusec range, powered by 15-30 h.p. slow-speed diesel engines. These locally built engines, described in Chapter 3, weigh up to 2000 pounds and are permanently installed. In the East most pumps are much smaller and are powered by portable high-speed engines that can be moved from one location to another. Because the demand for these more divisible inputs in the West has been limited, Pakistani engineering firms have not yet evolved the more exacting skills to produce the vertical diesel engine. Similarly with wheat threshing and maize shelling, small-scale motorized equipment utilized by the Indian Sikh farmer is simply not available to his Pakistani counterpart. In short, a bimodal pattern of agricultural development in the West Punjab is reinforced by the limitations of the farm equipment industry, limitations in large part created by the original size distribution of farm holdings.

Structure of the Industry

Producers of farm equipment can be divided into three groups. The simple traditional farm tools are made by rural artisans, principally the carpenter and the blacksmith. Improved implements, light processing equipment, irrigation pumps and motors, and some tractor-drawn implements are fabricated by light engineering workshops which are usually located in towns near or in the farming areas. Tractors, combines, and other large items with high-performance characteristics are produced by highly modernized large-scale firms which we will label tractor manufacturers. The relative size of these three segments varies with the degree of economic development and the pattern of farm holdings. In the United States and Europe the tractor manufacturers are dominant and the artisan subsector is extremely small or nonexistent. In much of Africa, on the other hand, rural artisans produce almost all the farm equipment, except for imported items and a few implements that are turned out by stamping presses in relatively large workshops. Asia and Latin America fall in an intermediate range, where no one sector is overwhelmingly dominant.

As before, we shall confine our attention to Taiwan, West Pakistan, and India. The industry structure we shall describe for these three countries is broadly representative of other Asian economies with the obvious exception of Japan.[31]

Rural craftsmen are still the dominant sector in India and West Pakistan, while in Taiwan they appear to rank after the urban workshop sector. The village artisan and his apprentices occupy a working area adjacent to the family dwelling and employ a capital stock in the neighborhood of $50. The smithy will include a small brick forge with hand-pulled bellows, an anvil, hammer, chisels, and tongs; the carpenter will possess saws, adzes, files, hand drills, chisels, mallet, and hammer. There is no formal quality control for raw materials, forging temperatures, or product specifications; the outcome depends upon the judgment and skill of the individual. The artisan will have a few years of primary education at most and no technical training other than the traditional apprenticeship. Despite the lack of formal training and seemingly rough methods, remarkable technical results are often achieved, for example, the double-layered blade of the self-sharpening Taiwanese hoe and harvesting sickle.

The rural artisan is typically not an entrepreneur: production is on order only and the customer will pay for the materials in advance. These artisans, because of their proximity and low cost, are the principal repairers of all items of farm equipment except the tractor and power tiller. Payment, particularly for repairs, is sometimes in kind, although the trend is toward all settlements being in cash. In only two items, the Persian wheel and the improved ox cart, is there specialization by commodity; these producers are located in towns.

The segment of the industry composed of light engineering workshops differs from artisan production in a number of ways. The scale of output and employment is larger. Firm size ranges anywhere from five to over a hundred employees. There is division of labor between casting, forging, machining, and assembling. Power tools such as lathes, drill presses, and grinders are employed in addition to hand tools. Components and product specifications tend to be more uniform, although in the absence of the use of jigs, fixtures, and quality control procedures, true interchangeability of parts is not attained. Production is by batch and for sale to a general market. And finally, some of the less-expensive items are sold wholesale to distributors.

One can also point to a number of common elements between workshop and artisan production. The early urban firms are usually established by progressive blacksmiths and traders involved in selling farm tools. Although the educational levels are higher, technical training is still imparted through experience and apprenticeship. One observes a majority of entrepreneurs to have come from the journeymen ranks: in the absence of significant capital requirements, a rise in demand encourages enterprising employees to break away and establish on their own. The industry thus tends to be highly competitive and profit rates low. Finally, like the rural artisan who produces articles other than farm tools, the urban workshops are seldom wholly specialized in agricultural equipment; they manufacture such additional light engineering products as band saws, oilseed expellers, cotton gins, electric fans, textile looms, and lathes.

The third segment of the farm equipment industry is tractor manufacturers. Units in this sector, producing by far the most sophisticated

BACKWARD LINKAGES: FERTILIZER AND FARM EQUIPMENT

and exacting item of agricultural machinery that is fabricated domestically, consist of a few large firms with capitalization of a half-million dollars or more. In virtually every case these firms have as a technical collaborator and minority partner a well-known international manufacturer whose machine they are producing. The latter include such names as Massey-Ferguson, Ford, International Harvester, Yanmar, Kubota, Iseki, and Mitsubishi. The technology employed by these firms is much the same as that of the light engineering workshops; however, it is differentiated from the latter by the utilization of a number of industrial and design engineers, formally trained technicians, sophisticated testing equipment, and interchangeable parts—in short by scientific quality control at all levels. The second difference between tractor firms and the workshop sector is that the former sell their product through dealership networks and provide after-sales service. In contrast to the workshop firms which do not maintain their own sales and service facilities, such distributive arrangements contribute to a high-investment requirement. To supervise and coordinate these combined production and marketing activities calls for substantial managerial organization.

The skills, capital, and entrepreneurial organization needed for tractor manufacture provide high barriers to entrance for domestic businessmen. This potential for monopoly and consequent high-priced, poorly serviced tractors, however, has not come to fruition. Rivalry among the earlier mentioned Japanese, European, and American producers to gain a secure footing in areas with significant long-run promise—even if not initially profitable—has provided healthy competitive pressures in this third subsector. For their local partners these manufacturers have variously approached large light engineering firms already producing and selling agricultural implements, reputable merchandising concerns in the hard goods trade or, where they have already developed their own distributional network, the government.[32]

The natural division between tractor manufacturing and the engineering workshop sector is illustrated by the history of power tillers in Taiwan.[33] Local production of the simpler tractive-type two-wheel machine commenced in July 1956. By October 1959, a total of 1600 machines had been made by seven producers. Employment in these manufacturing units ranged from 25 to 147 and investment in fixed assets from $14,000 to $118,000. The principal product previously produced by each of five companies was bicycles, motor scooters, ox carts, sprayers, and diesel engines. The other two units were divisions in a well-established general engineering concern and a steel rolling mill, respectively. In the 12 months after January 1959, an additional 15 concerns began production. In the next 12 months, more quickly than it had blossomed, the industry withered as all 22 firms discontinued manufacturing the power tiller. In early 1961, the government approached Iseki and Kubota as the collaborators-to-be in two large-scale projects.

The engineering workshops failed for both technical and financial reasons.[34] The technical difficulties centered around attempts to use light-weight gasoline engines and, more generally, machine tools and quality control regimes that were incapable of the required precision. None of the manufacturers had the organization to provide after-sales service and spare parts. In terms of coping with these and lesser problems, the firms possessed insufficient capital resources and technical depth to traverse the developmental period. Currently there are five small power tiller makers who sell and service their machines within a 20-mile radius of their workshops. These power tillers are low-priced, repair-intensive copies of the Yanmar or Kubota, and are competitive only on the basis of guaranteed in-the-field servicing by the manufacturer.

The success of the farm equipment industry in providing effective inputs for agriculture is largely determined by the extent of the interconnections that exist among the three subsectors. In addition to the competitive interactions of price, quality, and service of substitutable implements in the product market, these interconnections include specialization of function in intermediate components and flow of personnel, designs, and manufacturing techniques between subsectors. The degree to which these interconnections develop depends upon the temporal continuity of the industry's growth and governmental policies. The former is related to the pattern of change of farm purchasing power, as discussed earlier, as well as to the general state of development of the light engineering sector. The policy factor encompasses procedures for licensing scarce raw materials, price control, the way in which new implements are promoted to farmers, and various tax and subsidy policies.

One of the most interesting linkages between the subsectors is the satellite or ancillary system. Although subcontracting arrangements are a notable feature of engineering, automotive, and electrical industries in developed countries, their potential for transmitting advanced technology to a large number of indigenous firms gives them a magnified significance in low-income economies. The following examples give some indication of the scope of subcontracting. The China Agricultural Machinery Company, Taiwan's largest power tiller manufacturer in which Yanmar and Iseki are the technical partners, currently purchases from 17 satellite firms components which constitute about 20 per cent of the sales price of their machine; in earlier years such purchases were as much as 40 per cent. Krishi Enterprises in Hyderabad in its second year of power tiller production had developed ancillary relations with 32 small firms. Escorts, India's largest tractor maker, subcontracts with 200 firms, of which three-quarters fall in the range of 20 to 50 workers.

Unlike specialist firms which produce standardized parts used by a large number of manufacturers, the ancillary workshop makes interchangeable components or assemblies built to the individual specifications of the contracting company. Normally the primary company supplies the ancillary with technical drawings, jigs, fixtures, and a prototype. Where the raw materials are licensed, as with steel alloys in India, these may also be provided. The primary firm will send a full-time adviser during the start-up period; afterward the ancillary has access to technical assistance through the regular visits of the quality control inspector.

The motive for initiating an ancillary system is the minimization of investment required by the primary company, both in terms of fixed capital for productive facilities and working capital for raw material stocks. Because of less-expensive labor (lower wages, more apprentices) and smaller investment and management overheads, the ancillary almost always supplies the item cheaper than the contractor can produce it internally. For his part, in addition to learning, the subcontractor is provided with those things he most sorely lacks—design, quality control, and a market outlet. While unequal bargaining power means that the ancillary is to some extent vulnerable—most frequently the abuse is delayed payment—the fact that a large portion of small metalworking firms (over half in India) choose to take up and continue such arrangements attests to the mutual benefits inherent in the system.

While virtually all Asian governments enforce schedules of diminishing import content for licensed manufacturers, only India specifies what minimum share of inputs must be supplied by ancillaries. This is of some importance since the primary firms naturally tend to reduce their use of subcontracting as accumulated earnings relieve earlier capital scarcity. They do so for reasons of flexibility—to be able to more promptly adjust production to unanticipated changes in the market situation. The higher cost of internal production is offset by the gains from smaller inventories of finished product and reduced fluctuation in the rate of return on investment. While desirable from the point of view of the primary firm, cutting back on ancillary relationships would appear to sacrifice a greater social benefit in the form of diminished transmission of technical and managerial knowhow to small firms.

In addition to imitation and learning through an ancillary relationship, a third route by which the more progressive and better-educated entrepreneurs in the workshop sector obtain new designs is from publicly supported research institutions. The firms which obtain technical drawings from the research institutes are among the largest (usually over 60 employees) and most capital-intensive firms in their subsector. Owing to little or no distribution network and a consequent inability to cover the market, these producers are unable to protect innovational returns, associated with introducing a new item, from imitators within the workshop sector. This situation has induced

BACKWARD LINKAGES: FERTILIZER AND FARM EQUIPMENT

the progressive firms to specialize in producing CKD (complete knock-down) component sets for wholesale distribution to local blacksmiths who assemble, retail, and provide after-service. An arrangement of this sort, most notable in Taiwan but gaining momentum in India, not only permits the progressive firm to better cover the market and economize on working capital, it also hastens the transfer of improved technology and design to the artisan sector.

Most of our discussion has been with reference to cultivation tools and tractors. In terms of industrial output the most important single item of farm equipment is the diesel engine. Diesel engine production in India and West Pakistan is interesting because it has grown extremely rapidly, has experienced intense competition, and has progressed further along the road to intra-industry specialization and standardization than any other branch of farm equipment manufacture.

In West Pakistan the bulk of engine production is concentrated on the slow-speed horizontal diesel used for large tubewells. The country's largest engineering firm, Batala with over 3000 workers, produces a portable air-cooled vertical engine with technical assistance from a German partner. This, however, is very expensive (the Indian Kirloskar sells at half the price) and little used in agricultural applications. The statistics below, drawn from a careful study by Edward Smith, reveal the structure of the industry in 1970.[35]

Most of the nearly 200 firms employing less than 20, accounting for 18 per cent of industry output, were established within the previous five years. It is estimated that an additional 150 firms are engaged in producing pumps and strainers. The low capital-labor ratio

Firm size by employment	Firms	Workers employed	Annual output (*engines*)	Fixed assets per man (*rupees*)	Total assets per man (*rupees*)
1–20	194	1254	1768	4257	4,393
21–100	43	1503	3082	7304	9,408
Over 100	10	9491 (5000)	4755	7916	18,058

for small producers is in part a result of the absence of foundries; these firms buy all their engine castings from Itafaq, the industry's sole possessor of an electric-arc furnace which has the capacity of producing high-quality castings from low-cost scrap charge. Most producers of all sizes buy forged crankshafts, lubrication pumps, and atomizers from specialist firms. The higher proportion of circulating capital for the large firms is related to (a) production for inventory as opposed to order and (b) the holding of large stocks of pig iron, imported under license at prices about half those paid in the market by nonprivileged firms. The disproportion between employment and output derives from the fact that engines represent only one of some 20 items for the larger producers; the figure of 5000 in parentheses is an estimate of the employment attributable to diesel engine production.

Despite the rapid growth in demand, the fission process has operated with such vigor that there is excess capacity and intense competition. Among small firms net profit is currently marginal or negative. Medium and large producers, both because they charge a higher price and have access to licensed raw materials, currently earn rates of return in the neighborhood of 30 per cent. As in other branches of the farm equipment industry, formal technical training is very rare. Only four firms employ engineers and only two employ more than one. Two firms employ formally trained technicians. Only three producers use jigs and perhaps five achieve interchangeability of parts. Nevertheless, skills developed through on-the-job training have been adequate to produce serviceable engines. Design technology has come from copying imported engines: the machine is broken down, patterns are made of each part, a duplicate machine is assembled and then adjusted until it operates satisfactorily. Minor adaptations have been made with respect to the fuel pump, the lubrication pump, the governor system, and the atomizer.

In India the production of horizontal diesel engines was initiated during the 1930s by three large Indian firms—Cooper, Oriental, and Kirloskar.[36] After the war additional large-scale units (capital greater than five million rupees) were established, frequently with a British or German technical partner. By 1956, there were 16 large-scale units employing approximately 4500 workers and some 50 smaller units engaging 1560 workers. However, the period of most rapid growth has occurred since the mid-1950s: from 13,000 units in 1956 the production of vertical and horizontal engines rose to an estimated 300,000 units by 1970. Moreover, the share contributed by medium and small scale firms rose nearly fourfold, from 15 to 55 per cent.

Technological Progress in the Capital Goods Sector

The emergence and development of small- and medium-scale light engineering firms is a critical ingredient in the process by which new technology is adapted and made widely available to producers throughout the economy. As discussed in the section on p. 50 of Chapter 2, the process is a complex one and involves changes in market structure, administrative action through cooperative organization, and the provision of public inputs in the areas of uniform standards, technical education, and adaptive research. The history of diesel engine production in India, in which small- and medium-scale firms—germinating from the original large-scale producers utilizing foreign technical know-how—emerged as the principal source for large numbers of low-cost engines, illustrates a number of the aspects of this process.

Engine production is concentrated in some eight centers in India. As the result of a careful investigation carried out by a team of researchers from the Small Industry Extension Training Institute we have a detailed history of the development of the industry in one of these centers, at Kolhapur near Bombay.[37] Responding to demand created by government takavi loans to farmers for the purchase of pumpsets, the first engine-producing firm, established by a former Kirloskar employee, started in 1952. By 1956 there were four such manufacturers, one of whom employed over 100 workers. Suspension of takavi loans in 1957-58 brought the local industry the first of its periodic depressions.

Adversity drove home the need for diversification, cost reduction, and improved quality. Several units took up ancillary relationships with large firms in Bombay; the largest firm set up 70 of its employees in business to create its own ancillaries. With the help of the Indian Institute of Standards, the Kolhapur Engineering Association persuaded the state government to establish a quality marking center in 1963. This agency assesses firms who wish to sell to takavi loan recipients, tests members' engines for issuance of quality mark seals, and checks machines being exported. In 1966, the Maharastra Engine Cooperative Society was founded by the industry association and various farm purchasing organizations. The Society buys all the components for its "Mayur" (Peacock) engine from its members, to whom it also extends technical assistance. In 1970 the Society undertook to assemble Yanmar power tillers, possibly as a first step toward their manufacture in Kolhapur.

The situation as of 1970 is shown in Table 8.5. There were 20 integrated manufacturers (units making more than 30 per cent of their components) producing 92 per cent of the industry's reported output, including the more complex, water-cooled vertical engine. Under the spur of previous recessions, 10 of these firms had built up dealer-service agencies in other states and four firms had developed export markets. Productwise these firms were diversifying into electric motors, spare parts for cars and tractors, and agricultural implements. Assemblers, typically large repair shops which make a cheaper horizontal engine, purchased virtually all of the components of their machines. The 400 small specialist and ancillary units sell almost exclusively to the 64 manufacturers and assemblers. In the peak year of 1969 total employment in the industry was around 6000. Of the 66 firms in the sample survey, only 12 engaged anyone with formal technical qualifications, usually the entrepreneur's son. With regard to investment within the industry, the larger firms made far more extensive use of working capital for the same reasons that applied in West Pakistan; the much higher capital productivity among the "manufacturers" is attributable to a rate of capacity utilization more than double that of the other categories.

The diesel engine industry in India has much in common with other segments of the country's farm equipment industry and with its

Table 8.5. Kolhapur diesel engine industry, 1970

Type of firm	Number	Total investment[a] (millions of rupees)	Sales
Manufacturers	20	27.2 (15.5)	59.4
Assemblers	45	3.8 (1.2)	2.5
Component makers	320	8.9 (2.7)	5.1
Other[b]	80	1.4 (.7)	4.9

[a] Figures in parentheses represent the working capital subcomponent.
[b] Foundry, sheet metal, painting, and packing units.
SOURCE: Data from D. Nagaiya, M. T. Zambre, and N. C. R. Guruvaiah, "The Kolhapur Diesel Engine Industry," mimeographed (Hyderabad: Small Industry Extension Training Institute, 1971).

West Pakistan counterpart, but it also exhibits signal differences. First, the process of specialization which reduces cost (Indian engines are less expensive than Pakistani) and opens the way to improved quality has proceeded much farther in India, for example, specialist production of almost all parts versus four or five items in West Pakistan. Concentration on a few components, the use of jigs and fixtures, and long runs represent the road to standard quality and cost reduction, still within the context of relatively small workshops and labor-intensive production.

The second noteworthy development in the Kolhapur experience is industry agreement to support engine performance rating and marking—important steps in reducing uncertainty about product quality. By providing the consumer with information, the progress-retarding tendency to cheapen the product by quality dilution (e.g., less-expensive casting materials, wider tolerances) is dampened so that the more skilled producers and technical innovators will have an incentive to advance the level of technical achievement. There is, of course, still much room for controlled standards of quality in the areas of castings and component manufacture. Perhaps the most urgent need with respect to the adoption of supervised specifications is in the case of spare parts for tractors; the inability of farmers to judge metallurgical standards and the extremely low price of inferior parts have discouraged efforts by reputable producers with the result that 20 to 25 per cent of the tractor population in both countries lies idle.

To what extent are the characteristics of the farm equipment subsector representative of the engineering industry at large? An exhaustive survey carried out in 1968 by the British consulting firm of O. W. Roskill makes it possible to answer this question in the case of West Pakistan. Accounting for one-sixth of manufacturing output, the engineering industry is comprised of about 1700 establishments engaging over 100,000 workers.[38] While firms producing farm equipment are more frequently among the ranks of smaller firms, the capabilities and problems exhibited in the industry at large are virtually identical to those reported for the Pakistan diesel engine industry.

The Roskill team noted that there is little specialization. Relative to India and Taiwan there are comparatively few subcontractors or manufacturers of standardized components. Over 400 firms operate their own foundries, a situation which has inhibited the development of metallurgical skills and raised the cost of castings. Owing to deficiencies in mold-making, raw material control, and foundry procedures, castings are of poor quality throughout the greater part of the industry; high rejection rates (up to 50 per cent) add to the wastage of scarce raw materials. Technical drawings, jigs, and micrometers being seldom employed, most equipment does not meet specifications and tolerances are wide. Medium and large enterprises suffer from little or no management control at the top and inadequate supervision at the foreman level. These organizational constraints on the growth of the individual firm, in conjunction with very low barriers to entry and the fission process described earlier, has produced a highly competitive industry structure. Profits are low and firm size is small except where foreign collaboration or administrative action—raw material licensing and patents—create islands of monopoly. Finally, the industry operates at a fraction of capacity—50 per cent of one-shift operation. Industries which should be major customers for standardized spare parts—cotton textile, sugar refining, paper packaging, rubber, tanning, glass, cement—have, for reasons of quality and delivery reliability, established their own foundries and machine shops.

The Roskill survey found that good engineering work is done in West Pakistan, but it is limited to 40 establishments that involve some form of foreign participation and about 20 unaided Pakistani firms. This means that quality of work comparable to international standards is achieved by only about 4 per cent of the firms in the industry.

How does the Pakistan engineering industry rank in terms of technological progressiveness? Virtually all new products and new designs originate in those firms with foreign involvement. Wholly indigenous firms have modified imported technology and have done so in economically important ways. However, these modifications almost always have been of one kind, namely diluting raw material requirements, specifications, and tolerances to a level which is appropriate to prevailing operational conditions. This kind of cost-reducing adaptation is consistent with the fiercely competitive market structure in which these units operate. The latter also explains the relative absence of higher-paid, formally trained craftsmen and technicians. For firms that have been able to break out of the low-level technology trap the initial access to more advanced technical and organizational skills has most frequently occurred when the entrepreneur is joined by one or more of his educated sons.

Better endowed with resources and facing much less severe competition, foreign subsidiaries producing a line of world-patented products generally have the earnings to finance both formal training and research on new products. The investment in training does occur, and its transmission via departing employees to technically less-advanced indigenous enterprises constitutes a principal source of technical progress for the industry as a whole. Investment in research, on the other hand, is generally related to quality control problems and minor modifications of existing products for application to local environmental conditions.[39] New tools or equipment specifically designed for the domestic market are difficult to patent and easy for competitors to copy. Without the promise of enduring profitability at accustomed levels, foreign firms have shown little inclination to undertake this type of research.

In Pakistan, as well as in India and Taiwan, the principal sources of new engineering designs specifically fitted to local circumstances have been foreign personnel working as individuals or for a minority technical partner firm in domestically controlled enterprises. Smith identified an Englishman and a Scotsman as the leading design innovators in the Pakistan farm equipment field, the former employed in a Lahore engineering firm and the latter in a jute textile mill. The English and the Germans in India and the Japanese in Taiwan have played a similar role. These individuals were well versed in underlying scientific principles and had practical experience in diverse environments; their companies, not having the alternative of an established differentiated-product monopoly, developed the prototypes in hope of initial high profits and a subsequent addition to the stock of staple production items. Apart from a longer head start, the mechanism for commercial development is essentially the same as that which applies to the first firm that purchases equipment drawings from a publicly sponsored agricultural engineering research institute, the second most frequent source of intermediate technology. Given the comparatively weak market incentives to develop such prototypes, the importance of publicly supported research in the area can hardly be overstressed.

Government Policies

We have already alluded to a number of the many government policies which bear on the development of the farm equipment industry. We will limit ourselves here to a discussion of (a) policies directed at promoting the spread of improved equipment and (b) the pricing and allocation of raw materials.

Both Taiwan and India attempt to promote the wider use of selected items of improved equipment by subsidy through bulk purchase from manufacturers for distribution to farmers. In India purchases of equipment by Block Development Officers or by the Agro-Industries Corporation for resale to farmers has been part of an integrated program of supplying the full range of improved agricultural inputs. These procurement procedures have, however, frequently been such as to minimize the benefits to manufacturers.[40] Orders are placed at infrequent intervals and with insufficient lead time for delivery; this tends to induce overexpansion and substandard output. The policy of subsidizing the price to the farmer of a particular implement for a season or two has the effect of discouraging subsequent farmer buying in the hopes that the subvention will be reinstated. Delayed payment by the purchasing agency is all too common—sometimes by as much as six months or more: this forces the manufacturer to incur interest charges that may wipe out his profit on the transaction.[41] Finally, from a structural viewpoint such arrangements inhibit contact between the manufacturer and his customers; this is detrimental to the manufacturer because it impedes both feedback for design adaptation and the development of essential marketing networks.

The area above all others where government policies have obstructed the forward movement of the farm equipment industry is the allocation of raw materials. As a result of underpricing of imports and of domestically produced metals in short supply, there is unsatisfied demand at scheduled "white" prices with the resulting emergence of resale transactions at higher, market-clearing prices, for example, pig iron and all forms of steel. Underpriced inputs coupled with the desire to prevent manufacturers from receiving windfall profits, lead to controlled prices for the finished products, for example, tractors. And so a black market appears here as well. Unlike a regime of free prices, this disequilibrium system is without self-correcting mechanisms.

We have noted at various points the misallocational consequences of these pricing policies. Because improved bullock implements are almost always produced by firms without access to allotments of high-carbon steel these firms are obliged to use lower performance and less durable mild steel for harrow disks and cultivator shovels, thus thwarting the spread of these items. Massey Ferguson in India, unable to obtain sufficient licensed materials to make price-controlled tractors at more than a small fraction of capacity, shifted its production during 1970-71 to diesel engines and tractor attachments where prices were not controlled. And, as with other industries in India and West Pakistan, the existing system gives rise to hoarding of inventories, extensive underutilization of capacity, and oligopolistic industry structures.

The Quantitative Impact

Our last task is to obtain a rough idea of the quantitative impact of different agricultural strategies upon the farm equipment industry with respect to value added, foreign exchange requirements, and employment. Because statistical coverage is very poor for the artisan and workshop sectors and because they both produce items in addition to farm equipment, it is not possible to estimate actual production. Even if we had such data, while they would give a measure of the current impact of farm equipment purchases, they would not tell us a great deal about the differential effects of various agricultural strategy choices. To resolve the data problem and obtain a sharper focus on the effects of alternative strategies we have constructed equipment packages that would be associated with three different farming regimes. These packages then yield us three alternative streams of annual equipment purchases.

The magnitude we will be calculating is an annual "equipment flow" which consists of depreciation and spare parts. This measures the variable we want, namely farm demand for manufacturing output. Equipment flow should not be confused with the capital costs of farm machinery, of which it is only a part—it excludes both interest and the labor component of repairs. We have chosen West Pakistan as the location for our calculations because the pertinent data are available, and the circumstances that prevail—the absence of iron ore and tractor assembly rather than manufacture—are more representative than those of India for the majority of developing countries.

BACKWARD LINKAGES: FERTILIZER AND FARM EQUIPMENT

The estimating procedure consists of identifying the inventory of implements found in irrigated wheat and rice farming. The cost to the farm of original equipment and lifetime spare parts for each item is ascertained from field investigations and technical sources. This cost figure is then divided by useful life and area serviced to arrive at an annual equipment flow per acre. These data are presented in Table 8.6. In Table 8.7 the individual items are aggregated into equipment packages which correspond with the three alternative farming regimes. We thus arrive at a total equipment flow per acre expressed in Pakistan rupees under fully mechanized farming with tractor and combine, an intermediate equipment set centering around the power tiller, and the improved bullock technology with stationary thresher. All packages include the tubewell powered by the still dominant diesel engine; a shift to the electric motor reduces the equipment flow by 6.5 rupees per acre and foreign exchange requirements by 0.4 rupees.

As revealed in the first column of Table 8.7, the total equipment flow, that is, the apparent demand for manufactured inputs, is highest for the power tiller package and lowest for the bullock package. Actually, because it also requires a higher fuel and labor input per acre than the tractor, the tiller is not likely to be a competitive choice under the conditions we have assumed. This leaves the improved bullock and tractor packages to be compared. However, in order to determine their relative impact upon industrial output we must deduct from the cost to the farmer import content, all forms of taxes, and distributive margins. To do this we have utilized price structure data from the Report of the West Pakistan Farm Mechanization Committee and our interviews. Situation "A" refers to the current circumstances where tractors, power tillers, and their attachments are imported partially knocked down. The figures under "B" represent the situation several years hence when all these items will be domestically produced.

The combined value of "Distribution" and "Manufacture" is obtained as the residual after "Import Content" and "Taxes" are deducted from "Total Equipment Flow." Pricing structure data are

Table 8.6. Calculation of "annual equipment flows" for farm equipment in West Pakistan
(*Irrigated wheat-rice sequence*)

Item no.	Item	Price to farmer (rupees 1970)	Spare parts (per cent)[a]	Useful life (years)	Area serviced (acres)	Annual equipment flow per acre (rupees)
1	35 h.p. diesel tractor	15,570	75	7	100	38.9
	Tractor-drawn:					
2	Cultivator (11-tynes)	1,790	40	6	100	4.2
3	Seed-fertilizer attachment	2,500	40	12	100	2.9
4	Disc plow	2,500	40	6	100	5.8
5	Sprayer (105 gallons, 21 nozzles)	4,350	40	6	100	10.2
6	Combine harvester (mounted, 5 ft cut)	17,000	45	6	100	41.1
7	Rotary tiller	5,000	40	6	200	5.8
8	Four-wheel wagon	4,000	40	12	100	4.7
9	Land plane	900	20	6	100	1.8
	Bullock-drawn:					
10	Moldboard plow	70	40	10	12	.8
11	Disc harrow	200	40	5	12	4.7
12	Comb harrow	50	40	10	12	.6
13	Seed-fertilizer drill	375	40	10	12	4.4
14	Olpad thresher	200	40	10	12	2.3
15	Leveling plank	30	20	10	12	.3
16	Cart	1,500	40	12	12	14.6
17	Harness	50	10	5	12	.9
18	Chaff cutter	140	40	10	12	1.6
19	Rotary hand weeder	30	40	5	2	4.2
	Other power-driven equipment:					
20	10 h.p. power tiller	7,000	75	6	25	81.7
21	P.T. trailer	700	40	10	25	3.9
22	Stationary thresher (8 maunds/hour)	5,500	60	4	75	29.3

23	Knapsack sprayer (hand-operated)	160	40	3	12	6.2
24	20 h.p. electric pump motor	2,500	20	20	100	1.5
25	20 h.p. diesel pump motor	6,000	60	12	100	8.0
26	Pump (6 in.)	900	50	10	100	2.9
27	Well casing (120 ft)	1,500	...	10	100	1.5
28	Strainer (100 ft)	800	...	10	100	.8
29	Valve, pulley, bolts, bearing, angle iron	750	...	10	100	.8

Foreign exchange content (*per cent*)

		Original	Spares
As imports:	Items 1-9, 20, 21	60	40
As local production:	Items 1, 20	45	30
	2-9	30	20
	10-19	20	14
	21-23	40	27
	25, 26	15	10
	24, 27, 29	50	34
	28	5	3

[a] Cost of spare parts to the farmer for the life of the item expressed as a per cent of the item's initial cost.

SOURCE: Price data from distributors and manufacturers (Rana Tractors, Itafaq, Caravan Engineering, and numerous pump-set producers), collected January 1971. Only Items 1-9 and 20-21 are sold through distributors. Items 11 and 14 interpolated from Indian data. Information on useful life, area serviced, spare parts, and import content is drawn from our interviews, the *Report of the Farm Mechanization Committee,* and Roger Lawrence's "Some Economic Aspects of Farm Mechanization in Pakistan," mimeographed (Islamabad: AID, August 1970). These estimates, particularly useful life and the weight and materials calculations relating to import content, have benefited greatly from the advice of W. J. Chancellor, Professor of Agricultural Engineering, University of California at Davis.

employed to calculate gross distributive markups, the remainder representing gross value added in manufacture. The Farm Mechanization Committee estimated that the ex-factory price of a local tractor would be 60 to 70 per cent above a comparable c & f value; we have made the assumption that cost savings from bypassing assembly (a 10 per cent reduction in the distribution margin between A and B), cheaper spares, and reduced taxes would be sufficient to offset the higher manufacturing cost, leaving the price to the farmer unchanged.

Table 8.7. Equipment flow per acre under various agricultural strategies, West Pakistan

Equipment package		Total equipment flow	Import content	Taxes	Distribution	Manufacture
			(*Rupees per acre*)			
Tractor	A	129.4	64.4	21.3	33.7	10.0
(1-9, 25-29)	B	129.4	38.7	15.5	30.3	45.2
Power tiller	A	135.1	59.8	19.7	28.2	27.4
(20-23, 25-29)	B	135.1	45.2	18.1	25.4	46.4
Bullock	B	83.9	21.9	8.8	4.2	49.0
(10-19, 22-23, 25-29)						

Explanatory Note

Numbers in parentheses refer to item numbers in Table 8.6. "A" refers to the current situation where Items 1-9 and 20-21 are imported. Under B all items are produced domestically. The import content at c & f value is calculated on the basis of percentages given in Table 8.c.

In addition to import taxes, the column marked "Taxes" included 8 per cent of c & f import content to cover license fee, clearing charges, marine insurance, and bank charges. The taxes are as follows (*per cent*):

	Tractor and implements	Pig iron	Steel billet	M.S. sheets
Custom duty, on c&f value	5	10	50	40
Sales tax, on duty-paid value	15	5	10	15
Rehabilitation tax, on duty-paid value	1	1	1	1
Defense surcharge, on sales tax	25	25	25	25

After roughly estimating the various mix of imports, a rule-of-thumb for calculating the aggregate "Taxes" was derived: .33 of import content for "A" and .40 for "B."

For items other than the tractor, power tiller, and their implements, purchases are made directly from the producer; we have, however, allowed for a 5 per cent distribution component for the bullock package for a few small hand items and spares that may be sold through distributors.

The calculations summarized in the last column of Table 8.7 point to some striking conclusions. The situation indicated by apparent demand for domestic manufacturing output when priced at farm gate is reversed and the regime utilizing bullock equipment emerges as having a slightly greater impact on industrial production than that of the tractor—an advantage that would be considerably greater if tractors were valued at the lower world prices. Thus not only does mechanized farming displace labor and make intensive use of scarce capital, it also contributes less to manufacturing output.

The factor proportions advantage of the bullock equipment package in agriculture also holds on the manufacturing side. As described earlier, tractor production is characterized by much higher capital-labor ratios and higher labor productivity than other segments of the industry. This means that for the farm equipment industry the bimodal agricultural strategy choice gives rise to lower employment of labor and higher capital requirements than under a unimodal strategy. Moreover, reflecting its intensive use of abundant domestic resources, the foreign exchange input of the bullock implement package is some 40 per cent less than that of the tractor alternative.[42]

There are, of course, considerations that run in the other direction. With the orderly development of tractor production, further reductions in the import content could be expected over a 10 to 20 year period, reducing the foreign exchange disadvantage and raising its domestic manufacture component to a level equal to or maybe even above that of bullock-drawn implements. However, this would only be achieved with a rise in the final price to the farmer, thereby further augmenting capital intensity and unit costs in agriculture. The distributive network of the tractor dealer, costly though it is, can be a significant vehicle for channelling high-payoff innovations and technical knowledge to the farmer, for example, land leveling and improved agronomic practices. On the manufacturing side there are favorable technology-diffusing effects through the training carried to less-sophisticated producers by departing employees, through ancillary arrangements, and in a number of indirect contributions to raising manufacturing standards in the engineering industry.

However, in countries in which metalworking capabilities have not yet reached a point where these externalities can take hold, such as in much of tropical Africa, the intangible as well as the resource considerations point to concentrating demand on such simple farm implements as can be produced by indigenous artisans. If emphasis on a bimodal strategy and underpricing of capital and foreign exchange encourages the concentration of the agricultural sector's demand for new farm equipment on tractor purchases, the growth prospects of even the more progressive implement manufacturers are necessarily diminished.

Our analysis so far has been with reference to existing market prices. Policy decisions should, of course, be made on the basis of social costs. The principal adjustments that must be made to private expenditure are corrections for (a) undervalued foreign exchange, (b) artificially low interest rates for loans obtained from public agencies, and (c) over-valued unskilled labor whose wage rate exceeds its marginal product in alternative employment. The effect of each of these adjustments is to further raise the cost of tractor equipment relative to the bullock package.

In West Pakistan the most important of the three adjustments is that relating to foreign exchange. Although the overevaluation of the Pakistan rupee in 1970 was generally estimated at 100 per cent, the presence of various factors for the items in question—multiple exchange rates, revenue tariffs, barter agreements, commodity loans on soft terms—counsels a more conservative figure, say 75 per cent. Applying this proportion to the import content of the tractor package "A" and "B" and the bullock package shown in Table 8.7, the equipment cost per acre rises by 48.3, 29.0, and 16.4 rupees, respectively. Ideally a sales tax equivalent to these amounts should be applied to the appropriate items in each equipment set. Since it is not administratively feasible to cover the artisan and workshop sectors, an approximate correction would be the imposition of a sales tax on tractors and their implements to adjust for the *differential* foreign exchange cost. This gives us a tax of 27.6 per cent for imported tractors and 13.0 per cent when they are manufactured locally.[43] Further corrections for low interest rates and overpriced unskilled labor might add another 7 per cent, which in round numbers gives us a sales tax of 35 and 20 per cent, respectively.

BACKWARD LINKAGES: FERTILIZER AND FARM EQUIPMENT

Given a premium in the black market for the tractor of 100 per cent or more over the controlled price we have used, such a tax currently would have little effect. The premium for tractors is a result of the temporarily widened profit margin consequent upon the sharp cost reduction brought by the high-yielding varieties. Until output expansion drives prices down to their new equilibrium level, a rational farmer with access to the necessary resources will realize a larger income by maximizing output (i.e., mechanization over an enlarged cultivated area) rather than by minimizing cost per unit of food produced. Because farming patterns established during such a disequilibrium period are likely to be difficult to reverse, there is probably a good case for an additional temporary tax on the tractor and its equipment.

Once competitive least-cost prices prevail the 20 per cent sales tax on locally produced tractors will render them unprofitable to the farmer, save where use of a tractor permits substantially greater output per acre than obtainable under an improved bullock-power regime. The principal uses where tractors are likely to have this output effect are: (a) where there are very rigid time constraints for multiple cropping which cannot be eased by crop substitution or other forms of reorganization, (b) where deep plowing in dry land areas has significant yield effects, and (c) in the use of land scrapers for leveling fields. Thus there will be limited areas and tasks in most diverse agricultural economies where the employment of tractors will be socially profitable. This means that some part of the potential external benefits from tractor distributorships and mechanical engineering spin-offs may be obtained even though a general policy of tractor mechanization is not followed.

We have now concluded our exploration of the various kinds of interaction between a growing agricultural sector and the development of manufacturing. We have seen how an agricultural strategy aimed at the progressive modernization of the bulk of a country's farmers tends to generate a pattern of demand for consumer and capital goods that is more favorable for the growth of manufacturing output and employment than is a policy aimed at a relatively small number of larger farmers. In conjunction with reliance on market-clearing prices for the allocation of scarce inputs and publicly supported research on the technological problems of small producers, the unimodal pattern of demand fosters a more competitive economy, calls forth a much broader range of entrepreneurial talent, and stimulates a wider diffusion of appropriate modern technologies. By contrast a bimodal pattern of agricultural development tends to go hand in hand with distorted factor prices, administrative rationing, and an inefficient manufacturing sector. Finally, it has been demonstrated that the mobilization of investible resources from agriculture does not require a concentration of income in one segment of the rural economy.

NOTES

1. Pumpsets used for irrigation will be treated as an item of farm equipment. Expenditures on feed and seed, although sizable, are typically intrasectoral purchases from other farm producers.
2. FAO, *Indicative World Plan* (Rome, 1969); interpolated from estimates on pp. 180 and 223.
3. This section draws heavily on International Bank for Reconstruction and Development, *Fertilizer Requirements of Developing Countries,* World Bank Group (Washington, D.C., May 1974).
4. Excluding China, North Korea, and North Vietnam. For the most part our treatment of this subject will cover up to 1971, the time at which field research was completed.
5. The following narrative on the Daudkhel project, as well as all of the statistics cited, are drawn from the Government of Pakistan, Planning Division, *Report of the Special Evaluation Team on the Pak-American Fertilizer Ltd. Daudkhel* (Islamabad, 1969).
6. The discussion of the Multan project is based on Government of Pakistan, *Report of the Special Evaluation Team on the Natural Gas Fertilizer Factory, Multan* (Islamabad, 1969).
7. Communication from the General Manager, October 11, 1971.
8. The leading equity holders in the six private sector plants are, in the order given in the table, EID-PARRY, Gujarat State Government, Chevron Chemical Company, Delhi Cloth and General Mills Company, Imperial Chemical Industries, and Sahu Chemicals and Fertilizers.
9. J. N. Bhagwati and P. Desai, *India: Planning for Industrialization* (London, 1970), p. 163. Detailed accounts of the fertilizer investment experience can be found in Stephen Merrett, "The Growth of Indian Nitrogen Fertilizer

Manufacture: Some Lessons for Industrial Planning," *Journal of Development Studies* Vol. 8, No. 4 (July 1972) and Robert Repetto, *Time in India's Development Programmes* (Cambridge, Mass., 1971), Chap. 3.

10. Merrett, "The Growth of Indian Nitrogen Fertilizer Manufacture."

11. Bhagwati and Desai, *Planning for Industrialization,* p. 81.

12. Stephen Merrett, "Snares in the Labour Productivity Measure of Efficiency: Some Examples from Indian Nitrogen Fertilizer Manufacture," *Journal of Industrial Economics* Vol. 20, No. 1 (November 1971), p. 81.

13. The principal source is M. H. Yuan, "The Fertilizer Industry of Taiwan," *Industry of Free China* Vol. 21, No. 1 (January 1964).

14. A full chronicle of this project is provided by a series of articles in *Industry of Free China* Vol. 20, No. 11 (November 1963). In 1970, in response to political pressures generated by a farm recession, the government reduced the ex-factory price of urea to $95 per ton, which was under Miaoli's cost price. Under these circumstances TFC was obliged to buy out Mobil-Allied.

15. D. R. Henderson, G. R. Perkins, and D. M. Bell, *Simulating the Fertilizer Industry: Data,* Agricultural Economics Report No. 190 (East Lansing, 1972), Tables A-1, A-8, A-30, B-2.

16. The following account of events at Daudkhel and Multan is based on the evaluation reports cited earlier; additional price data on domestic and imported fertilizers are found in a report prepared for USAID, Chemical Consultant Ltd., *Fertilizer Marketing and Distribution in West Pakistan* (Lahore, 1970).

17. As the reader might guess, 1969-71 was the period when the domestic-imported price differential was at its maximum. Here and elsewhere we refer to competitive import prices rather than the considerably higher priced fertilizers supplied under barter programs or commodity aid. Because the latter are provided on soft terms (e.g., 40-year repayment at 3 per cent interest and a grace period of 10 years) their actual cost in terms of present discounted value is about the same as commercial imports. In both Pakistan and India, fertilizer factories sell their output at individually negotiated prices to the Government Marketing Pool which in turn sells to the farmer at a uniform price.

18. Merrett reports some instances:

At FACT [Alwaye] in 1966 the third stage expansion came on-stream with no possibility of the plants attaining their design output, for whilst the end-products required 284 tons of ammonia per day, hydrogen capacity was sufficient for the production of only 244 tons of ammonia per day. At Sindri the major cause of low capacity utilization of the urea and double salt plants has been the insufficient capacity of the lean gas plant to under-fire the coke ovens, so that the hydrogen-rich gas of the ovens has had to be wastefully diverted to this end, thus directly reducing ammonia and end-product capacity. In November 1965 when Neyveli began the trial run of its ammonia plant, benzene was discovered in the gases leaving the air fractionation plant. Two purifying towers had to be transferred from one stream to the second, limiting production to that stream, thus halving design capacity. At Nangal maintenance of work in the heavy water and fertilizer plants cannot be synchronized which reduces the maximum annual output of heavy water by 14 per cent ("The Growth of Indian Nitrogen Fertilizer Manufacture," p. 404).

19. Ibid. pp. 405-6.

20. For the figures themselves, see B. F. Johnston and Peter Kilby, *Agricultural Strategies, Rural-Urban Interactions, and the Expansion of Income Opportunities,* OECD Development Centre (Paris, 1973), pp. 103-13.

21. International Bank for Reconstruction and Development, *World Bank Group Study,* preliminary report (Washington, D.C., January 1974), Annex 1, Tables 5 and 6.

22. Organisation for Economic Co-operation and Development, *Supply and Demand Prospects for Fertilizers in Developing Countries,* Development Centre (Paris, 1968), Chap. 4.

23. International Bank for Reconstruction and Development, *Fertilizer Requirements,* Annex 1, Table 9.

24. F. C. Ma, T. Takasaka, and C. W. Yang, *A Preliminary Study of Farm Implements Used in Taiwan Province,* Joint Commission on Rural Reconstruction (Taipei, 1955), p. 25.

25. T. S. Peng, "A Survey of Utilization of Power Tillers and Mist-Blowers," mimeographed (Taipei: Joint Commission on Rural Reconstruction, March 1970), pp. 3-4.

26. Exceptions to this generalization are the rotary tiller, sugarcane harvester, tree-fruit harvesters, and aerial spraying.

27. A richly detailed survey of some 160 farm implements was undertaken in 1952 by Professors Ma, Takasaka, and Yang, *Farm Implements Used in Taiwan Province.* Our treatment of post-1952 developments is based on our own field observations and various papers by a JCRR Specialist on Farm Machinery, T. S. Peng, "The Development of Mechanized Rice Culture in Taiwan," mimeographed (Taipei: Joint Commission on Rural Reconstruction, June 1969), and "Present Problems and the Future of Agricultural Mechanization in Taiwan," *Industry of Free China* Vol. 35, No. 4 (April 25, 1971).

28. This ubiquitous device is used to slice sweet potatoes which are then sun dried and used for feeding pigs and other animals.

29. The efficiency with which tractors are applied to cultivation in India and West Pakistan is considerably less than in Taiwan. Seeding, fertilizing, intercultivation, and reaping, normally carried out with the assistance of a tractor, are executed with human and animal power in most cases on the subcontinent. The other principal manifestation of underutilization is the high proportion of vehicles that are out of commission—on the order of 20 to 25 per cent at any given time. These shortfalls are due to insufficient research in adapting tractor-drawn implements to local conditions and to an underprovision of the two complementary inputs, technical knowledge for the user and the availability of repair services.

30. The material in this paragraph is drawn from Carl Gotsch, "Agriculture Mechanization in the Punjab: Some Comparative Observations from India and Pakistan," unpublished (Cambridge, Massachusetts, May 1973).

31. A brief resume of a 1969 UNIDO survey of farm equipment manufacturing for 12 Asian countries is given by A. A. Swamy-Rao, "Agricultural Machinery and Implements Industry in South East Asia," in *Agricultural Mechanization in South East Asia,* edited by Yoshisuke Kishida (Tokyo, 1971).

32. There are two exceptions to this pattern. Escorts, the largest of India's five tractor makers, originally in the import trade and a distributor of the Ferguson tractor, designed its own vehicle with the aid of a Polish tractor firm, Urus, and a British tractor design engineer; the Escorts tractor has a Kirloskar air-cooled engine and a Polish transmission. (This firm has recently gone into partnership with Ford.) The wholly Indian-owned Krishi Enterprises produces a Japanese-designed power tiller under license.

33. Howell Chou and associates, *A Survey of Power Tiller Manufacture in Taiwan,* Joint Commission on Rural Reconstruction (Taipei, 1960).

34. Tomotake Takasaka, "Multiple Characteristics of Farm Implement and Machinery Production in Taiwan, the Republic of China," in *Agricultural Mechanization,* edited by Kishida.

35. Edward H. Smith, Jr. (with the assistance of M. Tariq Durrani), "The Diesel Engine Industry of Pakistan's Punjab: Implications for Development," mimeographed (Islamabad: Agency for International Development, October 1970).

36. For a detailed account of the historical development of diesel engine production up until the late 1950s, see Government of India, Development Commissioner (Small Scale Industry), *Diesel Engines* (New Delhi, 1961).

37. D. Nagaiya, M. T. Zambre, and N. C. R. Guruvaiah, "The Kolhapur Diesel Engine Industry," mimeographed (Hyderabad: Small Industry Extension Training Institute, 1971).

38. O. W. Roskill, *Survey of Engineering Capacity in West Pakistan,* Government of West Pakistan, Planning and Development Department, Civil Secretariat, Reprint Paper No. 18 (Lahore, September 1969). The distribution by size of firm is as follows:

Number of workers	Producers of farm equipment	All establishments	All employment
1-9	510	800	5,500
10-49	125	700	18,000
50+	20	200	83,000
Total	655	1700	106,500

39. Jack Baranson, *International Transfer of Automotive Technology to Developing Countries,* U.N., Institute for Training and Research, UNITAR Research Report No. 8 (New York, 1971); and R. Hal Mason, "Technology Transfer and Adaptation of Production Processes by Foreign Agribusiness Firms in Developing Countries," mimeographed (Los Angeles: University of California, Graduate School of Business Administration, 1972).

40. The remainder of the paragraph owes much to discussions with John Balis.
41. One of the typical comments by an implement manufacturer reported in a recent Indian investigation illustrates this and other problems faced by producers:

> In spite of so many Agricultural Universities, Research Stations and other facilities available with Government, no designs or blueprints on modern implements are released for mass production. No check on the quality of goods; quality deteriorates every day due to competition. Payments from government departments are abnormally over-delayed upsetting entire working. Because of this working capital gets blocked. Banks do not advance further working capital and production cost goes high. Much energy and money are wasted in contacting government departments for getting quotas fixed for short supply items. On top of all this, the supply of material is more uncertain. Even though we have been allotted 20 tonnes of M.S. Sheets for the year 1967-68, we have, up to now, received only two tonnes against this allotment. We have also great difficulty in obtaining supply of pig iron and orders for coke take more than six months for the wagon to arrive.

See Indian Society of Agricultural Engineers, *A Committee Report on Bottlenecks in the Farm Equipment Industry* (New Delhi, 1970), p. 22.

42. We have made no allowance for multiple exchange rates (iron and steel are imported at a less favorable rate than tractors and implements) and the overvaluation of the Pakistan rupee. Adjustment for these factors (a complicated exercise because of barter agreements and commodity loans on soft terms, e.g., high-priced United States steel ingot) would increase the foreign exchange content of the tractor and would probably also slightly raise the value of its domestic component.

In India, which is exceptional in not having to import iron, steel, and some alloys, the import content of all implements is considerably less—about 25 per cent in the case of the tractor. Thus the impact upon equipment output under the bimodal strategy is more favorable than under the improved bullock technology. However, with respect to both employment effects and foreign exchange content, the bimodal approach scores lower than the unimodal approach, although not as much lower as in West Pakistan.

43. Calculated as follows: $(48.3 - 16.4)$ and $(29.0 - 16.4)$, respectively, divided by 115.4 [items 1-9 from Table 8.6].

9 The Catching-Up Process

In this chapter we attempt to bring into focus the various aspects of the development process discussed in previous chapters as they bear on the modernization of agriculture in present-day underdeveloped countries. Given the large number of factors involved, it is important that we not lose sight of the simple fact that at the heart of the process are the changes in production taking place on individual farms.

The starting point is the traditional farmer. The resources at his command are his land, the labor power of his household, and a modest range of man-made inputs. These latter "produced factors of production" encompass such land improvements, structures, tools, fertilizer, livestock, and seed as can be produced or reared on the basis of the community's accumulated practical knowledge.

A fundamental feature of the process of modernization, of achieving a progressive increase in the productivity of the farmer's land and of his labor, is a continuous decline in the importance of inputs based on the community's practical knowledge as passed down from father to son. Growth in farm output is related to increases in the quality as well as the quantity of external inputs that augment the farmer's labor and land and which replace many of the traditional internal inputs. But the growth of productivity and output also depend on two other types of changes at the farm level: advances in technical and managerial efficiency and the availability of an array of supporting services provided by increasingly efficient institutions and industries which supply technical knowledge, inputs, and credit. In brief, the rate and pattern of agricultural development in a country will depend on what new inputs (innovations) are made available, to which farmers, and on what terms.

THE CHOICE OF MEASURES FOR MODERNIZING AGRICULTURE:
AN OVERVIEW

The set of agricultural policies and programs that influence the availability of new inputs and the terms on which they are made available will determine the character of a country's agricultural expansion path. The sectorwide growth of labor productivity will, of course, depend not only on the factors influencing the rate of increase in farm output but also on the demographic and economic factors that determine the rate of increase or decrease in the size of the farm work force. Finally, new inputs that are *divisible* and lead to increases in yield per acre are, in general, more compatible with widespread increases in farm productivity than investments that affect the other component of productivity growth—increases in the acreage cultivated per worker. The basic consideration is the need to emphasize a sequence of innovations and external inputs that *complement* the internal resources of labor and land so as to achieve widespread increases in productivity and output.

The simple identity introduced in Chapter 4 emphasized that output per worker in agriculture at any point in time will be determined by the product of yield per acre and acreage farmed per worker. And because of the structural-demographic characteristics of a late-developing country, it is not feasible to increase rapidly both the acreage per worker and yield per acre on a sectorwide basis. Hence, a fundamental issue in the design of an agricultural strategy concerns the relative emphasis on acreage expansion versus yield-increasing innovations. The principal factors influencing those two components of productivity change and labor productivity generally are summarized in Figure 9.1. Some of the more important farm-level factors are identified at the top of the schematic diagram, and various

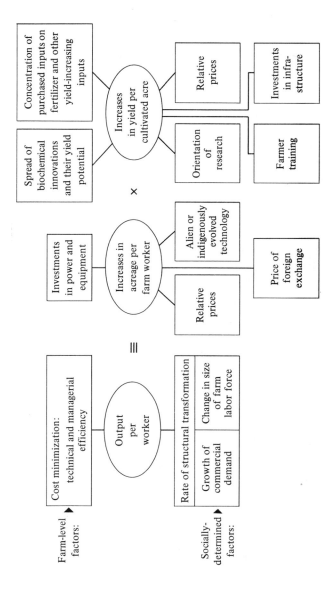

Figure 9.1 Schematic summary of the principal factors influencing changes in farm productivity.

socially determined factors are summarized in the lower part of the chart.

Relative prices are shown in the chart as exerting a significant influence on increases in both acreage cultivated per worker and in yield per acre. But because of the decisive importance of investments in farm equipment in influencing expansion of acreage per worker, the price ratio between capital and labor has special significance for this comparison. Adoption of yield-increasing innovations is sensitive to the relative price of land and land-saving inputs such as fertilizer as well as product/fertilizer response ratios and product/fertilizer price ratios. The price of foreign exchange is shown separately because of its influence on imports of farm equipment and also because it is especially likely to be affected by government action. In the prevalent case of an overvalued exchange rate with import licensing, some farm operators are able to obtain imported equipment at prices that understate the opportunity cost of foreign exchange whereas commodities that do not receive privileged treatment are not available at all or only at excessively high prices because of quantitative restrictions on imports and perhaps multiple exchange rates. The common difficulty of importing steel and other intermediate products for domestic manufacture of farm equipment is a pertinent example. As noted in Chapter 8, shortages resulting from such policies often hamper local manufacture of improved implements.

Although it is useful to stress the contrast between innovations that raise yields and investments in equipment, which mainly expand the acreage cultivated per worker, some complementary relationships between equipment and yield increases do exist. The most significant impact of tubewells and other power-driven pumps is to increase yield per acre because better water control often permits an increase in cropping intensity as well as contributing to higher yields for individual crops. There are also more subtle relationships between improvements in equipment and the yields obtained by farmers.

The marginal returns to some investments in improved equipment may, of course, equal or exceed the returns to increased outlays for current inputs—and in terms of social as well as private profitability.

Clearly, this is most likely to be true where there is only limited scope for yield-increasing innovations either because the physical environment is not favorable or because the research effort to develop biological-chemical innovations has been inadequate. Allocative efficiency requires that use of all inputs—yield-increasing, mechanical, and others—should be pushed to the point at which the ratio of their marginal value products is equal to the ratio of their prices. This standard rule offers only limited guidance, however. Difficult conceptual and measurement problems arise in attempting to compare marginal returns to unlike inputs such as fertilizers and tractors; but a more fundamental problem arises because the optimal balance between different types of inputs depends so heavily on the socially determined factors that condition the production possibilities of individual farmers. Thus, the orientation and level of reesarch activity, programs of farmer training, investments in infrastructure, and other elements of a unimodal strategy will foster a sectorwide expansion path characterized by much higher returns to yield-increasing innovations and greater use of the inputs associated with them. But the particular combination that is optimal will naturally depend on location specific factors.[1]

It will be recalled that a sequence of mechanical innovations played a highly significant role in United States agriculture during the nineteenth as well as the twentieth century. In his account of agricultural change in the northern United States, Clarence Danhof stresses a process that has been of great importance in many countries when he notes that between 1820 and 1870 "the plow was developed from a crude multipurpose instrument into a variety of special-purpose implements of superior efficiency."[2] Although biological-chemical innovations were the major forces at work in Japan and Taiwan, the complementary effects of simple but significant improvements in farm equipment were also important. As was emphasized in Chapter 8, widespread use of a range of inexpensive but well-designed implements has made a notable contribution in Taiwan in increasing the precision with which farm operations are carried out as well as in easing labor bottlenecks resulting from the adoption of more intensive techniques.

For many of today's latecomers, the role of yield-increasing innovations is likely to be even more significant than in Japan and Taiwan. Because of cumulative advances in genetic engineering, new varieties with desired attributes for various local environments can be developed a good deal more rapidly than was possible in the past. And as a result of these advances and the continuing progress in improving fertilizer manufacturing technologies, the potential for raising yield levels is also much greater. The enlarged scope for expanding output by this type of innovation can best be seen in the recent developments associated with the "Green Revolution" in India and Pakistan. Those countries have already received special attention in the examination of agriculture-industry interactions in the two preceding chapters, and their experience is also valuable in throwing light on the potential impact of new seed-fertilizer combinations in other low-income countries and in illustrating the problems to be overcome in fully exploiting the new technologies.

THE SEED-FERTILIZER REVOLUTION IN INDIA AND PAKISTAN

The abrupt change in the pace of agricultural progress in India and Pakistan between 1966 and 1970 is probably without historical precedent. The impact of the seed-fertilizer revolution has been especially great in (West) Pakistan where environmental conditions are well suited to the new semidwarf varieties of wheat and rice. Conditions are similarly favorable for wheat in northwestern India, but the diverse conditions under which rice is grown have meant slower diffusion of new varieties of rice. Partly as a result of the recent acceleration in the pace of agricultural change, both countries are at a critical juncture with respect to determining the pattern of agricultural development that they will pursue.

Their experience is of considerable interest simply because of the magnitude of the food problem in those two countries, but the opportunities and problems that have emerged also serve to illuminate a number of issues discussed in earlier chapters. First of all, this experience illustrates one of the special situations in which farm cash income can expand much more rapidly than the rate warranted by the necessarily slow growth of domestic commercial demand associated with structural transformation. In earlier chapters, considerable attention was given to circumstances in which rapid growth of agricultural exports can lead to exceptionally rapid growth of farm receipts. But in India and Pakistan it was the scope that existed for import substitution that made possible extremely rapid growth of commercial sales at essentially constant prices. A second feature that commands attention is the complementary role of increased water supplies in fostering rapid expansion of high-yielding varieties of wheat in both countries and of rice in those areas of India with controlled irrigation and throughout the rice-growing regions of Pakistan.

Developments in India and Pakistan are also of broad significance in shedding light on the response of small-scale farmers to profitable innovations and on the importance of the economies of farm size. During the first years of the seed-fertilizer revolution, it was frequently alleged that small farmers would not—or could not—take advantage of the new opportunities. The evidence is overwhelming that the view that small-scale farmers in less-developed countries are tradition bound and unresponsive is simply wrong. To be sure, larger farmers have often seized the opportunities more quickly. Moreover, the evidence suggests that the rate of adoption by farmers in the smaller size categories has been affected adversely by an understandable concern with minimizing risk and by a lack of resources that has made it difficult for them to expand rapidly their use of purchased inputs. It also seems reasonably clear that the effects of the latter disability have been accentuated by underpricing and administrative rationing of fertilizer and other scarce resources under circumstances that have often insured that large farmers with greater political power and better connections have had readier access to those inputs. The issue of economies of farm size is complex and controversial, and interpretations of the recent experience in India and Pakistan will vary. But our interpretation of the evidence, summarized in the sections that follow, is that when scale economies appear to have emerged, this has been largely a consequence of investments in tractors and related large-scale equipment that has been privately profitable but for the most part uneconomic from society's point of view. Moreover, the profitability of tractor mechanization to large farmers has been exaggerated by artificially low prices for capital and farm equipment and by the interrelated effects of other policies that have strengthened the forces tending toward a dualistic size distribution of farm operational units.

Experience in India and Pakistan also underscores the critical importance of national research efforts, to supplement and reinforce the work of international centers, and of farmer training programs in exploiting the yield potential of the new varieties. Considering the magnitude of the learning process involved in modifying farm practices to meet the needs of new crop varieties and sharply expanded use of fertilizer, it is somewhat suprising that the aggregate impact of the high-yielding varieties has been so large. But while the impact has already been substantial, it is apparent that with suitable strengthening of research and farmer training, and of programs to extend and improve water control and other types of infrastructure, the future increases in farm output will be much larger than those achieved to date. This is the first of several problem areas which bear on the design of agricultural strategies that are examined in the final section of this chapter following a brief review of recent developments which throw light on the issues that have just been enumerated.

Introduction and Spread of the High-Yielding Varieties

The changes in India's foodgrain imports during the 1960s provide a convenient summary index of a shift from a situation in which the expansion of domestic production was failing to keep pace with the growth of demand to a phase in which marketed supplies were expanding much more rapidly than the growth of domestic commercial demand. Net imports, mainly wheat, were as follows (million metric tons):[3]

Year	Imports	Year	Imports
1961	3.5	1966	10.3
1962	3.6	1967	8.7
1963	4.6	1968	5.7
1964	6.3	1969	3.8
1965	7.4	1970	3.6

The 1966/67 crop year represented an exceptionally sharp turning point because it was the second of two consecutive years of serious drought that resulted in a sharp reduction in foodgrain production on the subcontinent. The record imports of more than 10 million tons in 1966 were only about 15 per cent of India's sharply reduced production of cereals—65 million tons in 1965/66 and 67 million tons in 1966/67.[4] Yet these imported supplies may have represented as much as 40 per cent of foodgrain purchases by India's urban population, implying that imports were about two-thirds as large as domestic sales. In any event it is clear that through 1966 expanding imports were satisfying a substantial fraction of the growing commercial demand whereas in recent years increased domestic sales have expanded so rapidly that they have satisfied not only the growth of demand associated with the increase in food purchases but have also largely replaced imports. The substitution amounted to nearly 7 million tons if 1970 imports are compared with the peak level in 1966; and additions to government stocks amounted to 2.1 million tons in 1968 and 1.2 million in 1970.

A dramatic increase in domestic wheat production from 9.1 million tons in 1966 to 17.7 million tons in 1970 accounted for more than half of the 14 million ton increase in foodgrain production between 1966 and 1970. For the reasons just noted, the rate of expansion of commercial sales of wheat was unquestionably a good deal higher than the rate of increase in total output. Although the effect of the new varieties on rice production has been relatively limited to date, the evidence seems clear that in the long run improved seed-fertilizer combinations and associated changes in farming practices will have an even greater impact on India's food economy than the semidwarf varieties of wheat. Even with the dramatic increases in wheat production that have taken place, the rice crop is still nearly twice as large as the output of wheat. Because rice is so widely distributed in India, innovations must be evolved for a great variety of environmental conditions.

For Pakistan it is possible to make a direct comparison between the expansion of wheat production, the country's major food crop, and the increase in marketable surplus. Between 1965/66 and 1969/70 total wheat production in Pakistan increased from approximately 3.9 to 7.1 million tons. According to estimates for the 21 districts which account for nearly all of the commercialized production, the marketable surplus rose from 274,000 in 1965/66 to 968,000 tons in 1968/69, a 250 per cent increase in three years compared to the 80 per cent increase in output over a four-year period.[5] In Pakistan as in India, the extremely rapid increase in domestic production of wheat has been associated with rapid import substitution. Estimates of the increase in commercial sales of rice are not available, but there is no doubt that the rate of increase has been even more rapid than the growth of output. Rice, produced and consumed in much lower quantities than wheat in Pakistan, is grown almost entirely under conditions of controlled irrigation well suited to IR-8 and other IRRI varieties. Its increase in output from 1.3 million tons in 1965/66 to 2.3 million tons in 1969/70, was even more rapid than the growth of wheat production.

During 1971 and 1972 production of cereal crops in India and Pakistan experienced setbacks. In Pakistan especially, political tensions and disruptions associated with the India-Pakistan conflict over Bangladesh were contributing factors, and in both countries erratic monsoon rains in 1972 created drought and flood problems that had serious adverse effects. India's wheat crop was the only major cereal crop on the subcontinent that continued to record impressive increases in production during those years. But in spite of the recent setbacks, it seems probable that India and Pakistan are both near the end of the import substitution phase that has permitted exceptionally rapid growth of farm cash receipts because expanded domestic sales have substituted for imports with little adverse effect on grain prices received by farmers. And government price support programs have helped to maintain prices at or near the high levels reached during the period of acute grain shortage in the mid-1960s.

During the 1974/75 crop year, India is once again facing grain shortages and rising food prices. Bad weather and fertilizer shortages have played a principal role. This turn of events, which is causing

THE CATCHING-UP PROCESS

great hardship in India and a number of other developing countries, provides compelling evidence of the necessity to expand world fertilizer manufacturing capacity rapidly enough to keep pace with the growth of demand. Indeed, this will probably be the most important single factor in determining the success of efforts to expand per capita food production. The task that we have set ourselves in this chapter is to review the Indian and Pakistan experience during the first five years of the seed-fertilizer revolution and to consider the implications of that experience as it bears on the choice of strategies for fostering agricultural development. The extent to which the *potential* for supplying abundant and relatively low-cost fertilizers is in fact realized in the years ahead will clearly have a major impact—favorable or unfavorable—on the success of efforts to expand farm output, irrespective of the agricultural strategy that is pursued.

The acceleration in the rate of increase of farm cash incomes in the years since 1968 was especially sharp because there was so much scope for replacing large P.L. 480 shipments and other imports.[6] As noted above, in the early and mid-1960s imported supplies were satisfying a substantial fraction of the commercial demand for cereals. And this large potential for import substitution was highly significant because in both countries commercial demand for agricultural products is small relative to the size of the agricultural sector and total domestic production.

For India, the census data show a slight increase in agriculture's share of the total labor force from 72 to 73 per cent between 1951 and 1961. In Pakistan (formerly West Pakistan), where most of the industrial and urban growth took place, the share of agriculture declined from 65 to 59 per cent between 1951 and 1961. In Bangladesh (East Pakistan), the farm labor force actually increased from 83 to 85 per cent of the total according to the census estimates. (See Appendix Table V.)

Information about changes in nonfarm employment in the period since 1961 is limited. But the evidence that is available suggests that in India there has been little acceleration in the growth of nonfarm employment and that the rapid growth of nonfarm employment in Pakistan between 1951 and 1961 has not been maintained. Given the structural-demographic situation in the two countries, it is certain that their farm labor force has continued to increase in absolute size—and probably at a rate not much below the growth rate of their total population of working age.

Although there has been a marked acceleration in the increase in foodgrain output since 1966/67, the recent changes have, of course, been influenced in important ways by developments that preceded the rapid spread of the new varieties. It is estimated that distribution of nitrogen fertilizer in India increased from 108,000 metric tons in 1955/56 to 547,000 metric tons in 1965/66. Between 1965/66 and 1969/70 the increase was from 575,000 tons to 1.4 million tons in terms of estimated consumption. The annual rate of increase was 17.6 per cent (from a very low base) in the earlier period and continued at an average rate of 25 per cent between 1965/66 and 1969/70. The increases prior to 1966/67 are to be attributed mainly to more favorable grain/fertilizer price ratios, increased supplies of fertilizer at the farm level, and the spread of knowledge concerning fertilizer use. In subsequent years the rapid spread of fertilizer-responsive varieties of wheat and rice has obviously been a major factor in the continued rapid increase in fertilizer use.

The other noteworthy change that was initiated prior to 1966 was substantial extension of irrigation. This has increased the level and reliability of returns to the new inputs of seed and fertilizers and made possible a considerable increase in multiple cropping. In both countries this was related particularly to a rapid increase in the number of tubewells which are very effective in supplementing water from the canal systems. Virtually all of the total of nearly 76,000 private tubewells in operation in Pakistan by late 1968 were installed in the 1960s with a concentration during the years 1965-68.[7] In addition some 8000 public tubewells, which have a considerably larger capacity and command area than the private tubewells, had been installed by mid-1968, primarily for the purpose of reclaiming saline and waterlogged lands.

The rapid increase in tubewells and other types of pumpsets began somewhat later in India, partly because of regulations which had restricted the installation of tubewells in areas commanded by canal irrigation. There were only 80,000 tubewells in India in the beginning of 1966, but between 1966 and 1969 an additional 175,000 tubewells were installed. A great variety of low-lift pumps and filter points, as well as tubewells, have been installed in India, sometimes to supplement water supplies from canals but often as the only source of water for irrigation. The total number of energized pumpsets, including tubewells, increased from a little less than 200,000 in 1961 to approximately 1.3 million by March of 1970.[8] Electric motors and diesel engines are both important, and a great variety of types and sizes are used. In contrast with Pakistan, where nearly all of the diesel-powered tubewells use heavy, stationary engines which drive pumps of about 1 cusec capacity, many of the pumps in India are of only about 0.5 cusec capacity and are driven by light, vertical engines that are moved from field to field. As a result of the greater number and mobility of pumpsets in the Indian Punjab, the sale of water by farmers with tubewells appears to be more widespread and at more competitive prices.

The spread of high-yielding varieties in India and Pakistan demonstrates that where environmental and other conditions are favorable, farmers adopt the new varieties with remarkable alacrity. It has often been claimed that only the larger farmers are able to make the cash outlays required for efficient utilization of the package of high-yielding seeds, fertilizer, and other inputs needed to realize the yield potential of the new varieties. It is a fact that the larger farmers were usually the first to plant the high-yielding varieties. That is hardly surprising since they can more easily assume the risks of innovations; and most of the initial trials were on the fields of some of the larger and more progressive farmers. However, large numbers of small and medium farmers have followed the lead of the larger farmers. Reports from both Pakistan and India have indicated that farmers of all size groups generally committed only a small fraction of their wheat area to a new variety in the first year of adoption, enlarged the percentage in the second year, and then committed most of their wheat acreage to the new varieties in the third year. As this process has gone forward there has been a gradual narrowing of the differential between large and small farmers in the extent of adoption.

A study by Max K. Lowdermilk of 353 farmers in Multan District in Pakistan provides especially useful documentation of the earlier adoption of high-yielding varieties by large farmers and the subsequent narrowing of the differentials in adoption rate by size group. For farmers in the smallest size category (2.5 to 7.5 acres), the percentage planting 50 per cent or more of their wheat acreage to the new varieties rose from 5 per cent in 1966/67 to 69 per cent in 1969/70. This was considerably less than the figures of 81 and 90 per cent for the two largest size categories. But the rapid increase among the smallest farmers is especially noteworthy considering their limited contact with field assistants and other extension staff. Only 11 per cent in the small farmer group reported such contact in

Table 9.1. Alternative projections of gross output of foodgrains in West Pakistan
(*Million long tons; rice figures are for clean rice*)

Years	With rapid spread of yield-increasing innovations				In absence of yield-increasing innovations	
	Mainly bullock power		With rapid tractor mechanization			
	Wheat	Rice	Wheat	Rice	Wheat	Rice
1964/65	4.2	1.3	4.2	1.3	4.2	1.3
1969/70	7.1	2.3	7.1	2.3	4.4	1.4
1974/75	11.2	4.2	11.6	4.3	4.6	1.5
1979/80	14.3	5.5	15.1	5.8	4.9	1.7
1984/85	18.2	7.3	19.7	8.0	5.1	1.8

SOURCE: See text for a summary explanation. The projection model is described in detail in John Cownie, Bruce F. Johnston, and Bart Duff, "The Quantitative Impact of the Seed-Fertilizer Revolution in West Pakistan: An Exploratory Study," *Food Research Institute Studies,* Vol. 9, No. 1 (1970).

1970 compared with 35 and 64 per cent, respectively, for those with farms of 25 to 50 or over 50 acres.[9]

The projections reproduced in Table 9.1 summarize a rough attempt to quantify the potential impact of the spread of the new varieties and expanding use of fertilizers on the production of wheat and rice in Pakistan, a region where the environmental conditions are highly favorable to their introduction. The projected increases in output between the mid-1960s and 1985, based on the spread of the semidwarf high-yielding varieties, are more than three times as large as the increases shown in the last two columns which attempt to depict the situation that would have confronted Pakistan in the absence of the seed-fertilizer revolution. Because of the much greater responsiveness of the new varieties to high levels of fertilizer application, the expansion paths that reflect the spread of the new varieties assume a much greater increase in the use of chemical fertilizers. Those expansion paths also assume more rapid improvements in irrigation, facilitated by the spread of energized pumpsets and improved water management at the farm level. For reasons that are discussed in detail elsewhere, the differences in the assumed rates of increase in the planting of high-yielding varieties and in the growth of output between the primarily bullock-powered expansion path and the expansion path that assumes rapid tractor mechanization are not very large.[10]

These projections were merely intended to indicate the order of magnitude of the increases in wheat and rice output that would be possible given the yield potential of the new varieties, and to emphasize the contrast with the limited potential for expansion if the yield-increasing innovations had not become available to Pakistan farmers. The actual growth of output will obviously depend on a host of factors that influence the spread of the new varieties and the extent to which Pakistan farmers have the ability and incentive to fully exploit their genetic potential. By coincidence, Pakistan's estimated production of 7.1 million tons of wheat and 2.3 million tons of rice in 1969/70 are identical with the projections for that year. Those figures represent increases of about 55 per cent and nearly 75 per cent, respectively, as compared to the 1964/65 harvests, which were record crops for the period prior to the spread of the new varieties. If assumptions of the projection model were to be fulfilled, wheat production would register a further increase of more than 150 per cent by 1984/85 and rice production in that year would be more than three times the level of 1969/70. But such an outcome is doubtful. The fact that projected and actual output in 1969/70 were the same is to be explained by compensating errors: expansion in acreage planted to the new varieties was more rapid than projected whereas the gap between the potential and the average yields actually realized was greater than had been assumed.

Future expansion of output at the rates projected in Table 9.1 seems most unlikely because of the probable effect of demand conditions on cost-price relationships as well as factors affecting production. The projected output of wheat would exceed domestic demand by some 8 million tons in 1984/85 and the implied exportable surplus of rice would be about 5 million tons. Increases of output of that magnitude seem unlikely because of the difficulties of rapidly expanding grain exports quite apart from the numerous problems on the production side that make it difficult to realize the yield potential of the new varieties. As noted above, the current shortages and high prices of fertilizer obviously represent a severe problem affecting the expansion of output.

Annual surveys carried out by the Programme Evaluation Organisation of India's Planning Commission also reveal a general tendency for the differential between large and small farmers in the rate of adoption of new varieties to narrow over time, but there is considerable variation from state to state.[11] In Punjab State, the differential for wheat had virtually disappeared in 1969/70 by which time the rate of adoption exceeded 95 per cent in even the smallest size category. For rice during the *rabi* season (the relatively dry winter months in contrast with the *kharif* season which coincides with the monsoon rains), the percentage of adoption among holdings in the largest category was more than three times as large as for the smallest size group in 1967/68; but in 1969/70 the differential had narrowed

THE CATCHING-UP PROCESS

to about 2 to 1. There are, however, instances in which the differential between size groups in the rate of adoption of rice has increased. And the average rate of adoption for rice has remained considerably below the adoption rates for wheat in India and below those for both wheat and rice in Pakistan.[12] This is probably to be attributed primarily to the great diversity of environmental conditions under which rice is grown in India and to the fact that many rice-growing areas do not have the controlled irrigation that is needed to obtain really high and reliable yields with the dwarf varieties. There is also greater need to modify traditional agronomic practices in order to realize the yield potential of the dwarf varieties of rice. The dwarf wheats incorporate resistance to rust, the principal disease affecting wheat. Although there are now disturbing signs of a partial breakdown of rust resistance in the major wheat variety, the disease and pest problems affecting rice have been more serious and have usually required chemical control measures.

Although the seed-fertilizer revolution has already resulted in notable increases in wheat and rice production in India and Pakistan, only a fraction of the potential has been realized to date. There is large scope for expansion in the acreage planted to the new varieties and for narrowing the large differential between the yields that are possible and the yields actually obtained. The average yields of wheat, a crop that is grown under fairly similar conditions in the two countries, seems to have increased from a level of 700 to 800 pounds per acre in the period prior to the drought years of the mid-1960s to close to 1100 pounds in 1969/70. Although an increase in national average yield of somewhere between 35 and 60 per cent is no mean achievement, it is only a fraction of the increase that can be realistically expected with further spread of the new varieties and progressive improvement in farming practices. Even though roughly half of the wheat acreage in India and Pakistan is planted to high-yielding varieties, most farmers are still growing the new varieties with essentially traditional practices. Some progressive farmers, both small and large, are obtaining per-acre yields of close to 5000 pounds, but the average yield for the new varieties is only about 2500 pounds in India and less than 2000 pounds per acre in Pakistan.[13] Not only is there large variation among farmers in the yields obtained, but it also appears that the variation in the production costs is very large—significantly larger for the new varieties than for local varieties.[14]

Failure to apply economically optimal rates of fertilizer is clearly a major factor responsible for the gap between potential yield levels and yields being achieved by farmers. Most farmers are applying considerably more nitrogen to the dwarf varieties than the local varieties, but the levels are considerably below those required for maximum profitability. On the basis of a survey of wheat farmers in Pakistan, for example, Jerry Eckert found that an average of about 50 pounds of nitrogen per acre was being applied to dwarf varieties compared to 37 pounds on the local varieties.[15] According to Eckert's production function analysis, farmers were applying fertilizer to local varieties up to the point where the value of its marginal product was approximately equal to the price farmers had to pay for fertilizer. But because of the greater response to fertilizer (an average response ratio of 17 pounds of grain per pound of nitrogen compared to a grain/nitrogen response ratio of just over 8 to 1 for local varieties), the economically optimal level of application for the dwarf varieties would have been approximately twice the 50 pounds of nitrogen that was being applied. Estimates of the application of nitrogen to dwarf varieties of wheat in India suggest a similar margin between actual and optimal use.[16]

Failure to apply an adequate amount of phosphate fertilizer—or any at all—represents an increasingly important factor limiting wheat yields in both India and Pakistan. According to a 1970 government survey carried out in three districts of the Pakistani Punjab, only a quarter of the farmers were applying phosphate and half of the farmers interviewed had not even heard of it.[17] The effects of failure to apply phosphate fertilizer are undoubtedly becoming increasingly serious because the heavier yields of recent years are depleting soil reserves of phosphates. Hence, deficiency of this nutrient is limiting plant growth directly and also reducing the effectiveness of nitrogen applications.[18] It is also reported that shortages of potash are becoming a limiting factor in some areas. In addition, agronomic research in India indicates that deficiencies of zinc or other micronutrients are affecting yields adversely in particular areas.[19]

Inasmuch as a major learning process involving millions of farmers is a necessary condition for realizing the potential of the new crop varieties, this is inevitably a time-consuming process. There is considerable evidence which suggests that differentials between large and small farmers in the use of proper amounts of fertilizers is greater than the differentials related to rates of adoption of new varieties. This may be partly a result of a tendency for small farmers to apply a larger risk discount in determining the use of purchased inputs, but the principal factors are probably related to their unequal access to technical knowledge and credit. In Pakistan, for example, larger farmers have found it relatively easy to obtain loans at subsidized interest rates of 8 or 9 per cent from the Agricultural Development Bank to finance the purchase of tubewells and tractors, but smaller farmers have had to rely on their own resources or on the informal credit market, where interest rates are much higher, for financing purchases of fertilizer and other current inputs.

In view of the recent spread of the new varieties in India and Pakistan, it is not surprising to find that larger farmers with their more favorable access to credit and other production requisites have increased their production expenses per acre more rapidly than small farmers. The figures shown in the following tabulation based on a 1967 survey of 120 progressive farmers in Uttar Pradesh undoubtedly give an exaggerated impression of the contrast because they relate to such an early period in the spread of the new varieties. The data are presented here as cash expenditures per acre in United States dollars; all consumption in-kind and family-supplied labor are excluded.[20] It is of interest to contrast these figures with the average cash expenditures by farmers in Taiwan summarized in Table 2.6 (Chapter 2). First, production expenses for the farmers in Taiwan, with a mean farm size of 2.5 acres, amounted to $234 per acre compared to an average of $68 for the progressive farmers in Uttar Pra-

Item	Farm size (*acres*)		
	Under 10	10-30	Over 30
Production expenses	31.50	53.90	71.96
Fertilizer	1.96	7.28	9.80
Seed	2.80	2.24	3.50
Livestock[a]	18.48	8.26	7.14
Irrigation[a]	7.84	25.34	16.38
Machinery and equipment[a]	.42	10.78	35.14
Wages	17.22	14.70	15.26
Consumption	34.02	49.14	34.86

[a] Including net investment.

desh. Second, the share of expenses going to the yield-increasing inputs of fertilizer and agricultural chemicals was far greater in Taiwan. And third, there is a notable contrast in the relation between production expenses and size of operational holding. Whereas cash outlays per acre were more than twice as high for large progressive farmers in Uttar Pradesh as compared to farmers with less than 10 acres, in Taiwan both expenditure and output per acre diminished with every increase in farm size.

There are reasons to believe that the situation revealed by the 1967 survey for Uttar Pradesh is transitory, and that the economic forces operating at the farm level will tend to induce greater per-acre use of nonland inputs on small than on large farms. Numerous studies based on farm management data for various states indicate that in India as in Taiwan there is generally a negative relationship between output per acre and farm size. Although some of these studies seem to suggest decreasing returns to scale, the more usual situation appears to be one of constant returns to scale but higher output per acre on small farms because of the inverse relation between farm size and per-acre application of inputs[21] For India, this inverse relation seems to apply most clearly to the use of labor. It thus tends to confirm the expectation that the imputed price of labor on a family-based small farm is lower than the cost of labor on large farms with a consequent tendency for small farms to use more labor and therefore produce more output per acre. Use of nonland inputs other than labor may be restricted on small farms by lack of technical knowledge or by nonprice rationing of credit that gives large farmers preferential access. Apart from those handicaps, however, small farmers in India and Pakistan can be expected to gradually increase their intensity of cultivation, including expanded use of fertilizer and other land-saving inputs.[22] The speed and extent of such changes will be determined in large measure, however, by the type of agricultural strategies that are pursued.

The Seed-Fertilizer Revolution and the Elements of an Agricultural Strategy

Given the rapidity of the changes that have resulted from the seed-fertilizer revolution in India and Pakistan, it is not surprising that it has given rise to problems and a number of controversial issues of agricultural policy. In a single year—1967/68 to 1968/69—wheat production in the Punjab State of India recorded a phenomenal 50 per cent increase, and commercial sales in the postharvest period increased by an incredible 150 per cent.[23] In Pakistan, the processing problems to be overcome are complicated by the need to produce milled rice of qualities that will be able to compete successfully in export markets. These problems are important and difficult, but they are the sort of disequilibria that represent an important dynamic force in economic growth because they give rise to new opportunities for profitable investment.

Far more important are the social tensions and policy issues that have emerged as a result of the widening of interfarm and interregional disparities in income. Discussion of these issues in India has to a considerable extent polarized on the basis of a misleading dichotomy between "efficiency" and "equity" objectives. On one hand there is a tendency to condemn the seed-fertilizer revolution, and more particularly the so-called New Agricultural Strategy with which it has been associated, because it has accentuated income disparities and social tensions in the countryside. The other dominant tendency is a vigorous defense of the new agricultural strategy, emphasizing the vital importance to the economy of the accelerated rate of increase in agricultural output that has been achieved. This second viewpoint has been the dominant theme in government policy, although government statements certainly do not overlook the fact that rural poverty is a serious problem. Alleviation of poverty is regarded, however, as distinct from the goal of increasing output. Thus the Fourth Five Year Plan sets as its "first objective" providing the conditions necessary to sustain a 5 per cent annual increase in farm output. Alongside the programs aimed at maximizing production, attention is being given to a second category of programs "which aim at remedying imbalance" in pursuit of the "second objective" of the government's agricultural programs which "is to enable as large a section of the rural population as possible, including the small cultivator and the farmer in dry areas, to participate in development and share its benefits."[24] To further this second objective a Small Farmers' Development Agency has been set up to provide various types of assistance to small farmers in 45 selected districts.

A central thesis of this book is that an agricultural strategy can and should be designed to promote simultaneously rapid increases in farm output at low cost and the three objectives that were considered in Chapter 4: overall economic growth and structural transformation, widespread improvement in the welfare of the farm population, and changes in attitudes and behavior which promote social modernization. The fundamental requirement lies in a choice and time sequence of innovations adapted to the country's factor proportions and capable of being adopted by a growing fraction of the nation's farm households. But even though policies are well designed to foster such progressive modernization of the agricultural sector, a considerable widening of regional and interfarm inequalities is probably an inevitable concomitant of growth. Even apart from differences among farmers in the resources that they command and in their entrepreneurial ability and drive, technical progress and other changes that create new opportunities are never uniform in their impact. M. L. Dantwala has put the issue clearly. After noting that "no innovation, however benevolent, can all at once become universally applicable," he suggests that even though the forward thrust of the seed-fertilizer revolution has widened disparities, it has brought gains to "millions of big as well as medium and small farmers and even tenants who, but for the HYV [high-yielding varieties], would have remained poor for a long time . . . and must be preferred to a more egalitarian stagnation."[25] He also emphasizes that cheaper food is a highly important "egalitarian device" that benefits millions of consumers—and in rural areas as well as in the towns and cities.

The technical considerations that lead to interregional disparities in technical progress are likely to be reinforced by shortages of funds and trained personnel which make it necessary to concentrate initially on areas in which known technologies can be expected to yield the highest returns. But this type of concentration differs from the concentration of resources under a bimodal strategy in two fundamental respects. First of all, the focus is on improved technologies, notably yield-increasing innovations which are neutral to scale, that are of such a nature that they can be progressively extended throughout a large part of the agricultural sector. Second, concurrent attention is given, through research, farmer training, and promotion of investments in key elements of the infrastructure, to enlarging the area in which it is possible and profitable to apply yield-increasing innovations.

It was emphasized in Chapter 4 that the design of an agricultural strategy should be based on intimate knowledge of the specific problems and potentialities of a particular country and its agricultural regions. Because we lack that intimate knowledge, it would be inappropriate to undertake a detailed consideration of the policies and programs that should be included in strategies for agricultural development in India or Pakistan. It may be useful, however, to put forth some observations concerning measures which appear to be particularly pertinent to exploiting the potential benefits of the seed-fertilizer revolution in ways that will foster rapid and widespread increases in agricultural output and also promote overall economic growth and structural transformation. The programs and policies that seem to merit particular attention fall into four categories:

1. improved agronomic practices and supporting services to achieve the yield potential of the new varieties;
2. investments in irrigation, institutional innovations, and farm level changes in water management;
3. the role of mechanical innovations;
4. policies affecting the size distribution of operational units and the mobilization of resources for development.

We leave aside public health and nutrition programs and family planning activities, although we recognize the importance of direct action in those areas in order to raise rural welfare more rapidly than will occur simply as a result of rising per capita incomes. (It may be noted in passing that qualitative deficiencies in protein may well have been accentuated by the seed-fertilizer revolution. Production of grain legumes and certain other important protein sources has been affected adversely as a result of the sharp increase in the relative profitability of wheat production which has not been matched by productivity advance applicable to the grain legumes or the other crops that are particularly good sources of high quality protein.) We will, however, be noting some of the significant interrelations among the four categories.

Improving agronomic practices and supporting services to achieve the yield potential of the new varieties. Even in this summary treatment, it is necessary to note a number of factors that exert a significant influence on realizing the genetic potential of the high-yielding varieties now available—and the succession of new varieties that will become available as research programs achieve success in incorporating additional attributes to meet the needs of a variety of local environments. The following six categories are obviously of crucial importance:

1. larger and more balanced application of fertilizers, including attention to the placement and timing of fertilizer applications;
2. plant protection measures (especially for the new varieties of rice);
3. improvements in the quantity and timing of water applications

and provision for drainage, particularly as required for multiple cropping;

4. better preparation of seedbeds and more accurate planting in terms of depth and plant population;

5. more effective weed control; and

6. improved availability of credit and farm inputs.

The critical role of larger and more efficient use of fertilizers has already been discussed. It is to be emphasized that progress in that area, as with the other agronomic practices, will depend on well-conceived programs of applied research as well as action to extend technical knowledge through farmer training programs. There appears to be a particular need for fertilizer trials and demonstrations, using a simple experimental design so that they can be carried out with sufficient accuracy on farmers' fields. A major effort of that nature is needed to provide a basis for elaborating more accurate and more highly differentiated recommendations with respect to the quantity and timing of fertilizer applications. Particular attention should be given to determining the amounts of phosphate, potash, and (where appropriate) micronutrients to be applied under various soil conditions and to demonstrating to farmers the payoff to applying economically optimal amounts of all nutrients. Distribution of compound fertilizers suitable for sizable areas can simplify the problems faced by farmers in applying an appropriate balance of nutrients although in particular areas the standard mixture would obviously have to be supplemented to take account, for example, of a localized deficiency of zinc. Analysis of soil samples and of the correlations between soil types and the results of yield trials can facilitate the task of adapting recommendations to local conditions.

The ability of farmers to provide controlled irrigation is usually dependent upon publicly financed irrigation systems and their management, the availability of energized pumpsets, or both. It is convenient to consider the need for improvements in water management at the farm level along with the requirements for investments in infrastructure and institutional innovations to improve water control. Action to improve the quality of seedbed preparation, planting practices, and weed control obviously can be facilitated by the use of improved items of farm equipment, to be considered shortly, as well as by better understanding on the part of farmers of the interactions between those practices and crop yields.

The requirements for improving supporting services, such as the availability of credit and the distribution of farm inputs, are both complex and controversial. We have noted earlier that measures aimed at cheapening artificially the price of capital creates excess demand for the supplies of loanable funds available from institutional sources. And the fragmentation of capital markets and administrative rationing, which are a consequence of those policies, exacerbates the problems which the great majority of farmers face in obtaining credit. Given the high returns obtainable with proper use of fertilizer and other yield-increasing inputs, it appears to be more important to stress expanded and timely availability of those inputs rather than the subsidies which have often been provided even under conditions of excess demand when farmers who lack the power and status to secure favored treatment have often had to pay black market prices. The development of effective programs for seed multiplication and for promoting regular replacement of seed to maintain its purity is a phase of input distribution for which government encouragement and supervision appears to be essential. It also seems likely that government should play an active role in promoting distribution of new and unfamiliar inputs such as insecticides. But burdening an inadequately staffed agricultural extension organization with this essentially commercial task is probably not an optimal solution.

Investments in irrigation, institutional innovations, and farm level changes in water management. It is generally recognized that the impact on output of the new varieties is restricted by the extent and quality of irrigation facilities available. This limiting factor is of decisive importance in India where only about 20 per cent of the total cultivated area has controlled irrigation. In Pakistan and in the Indian Punjab, where semiarid conditions limit the scope for rainfed agriculture, the comparable figure is 60 per cent. But it is not so widely recognized that there are also highly significant possibilities for improving water management at the farm level.

There are in fact important trade-offs between alternative investments to increase the available supply of water for irrigation and measures to promote improved use of water at the farm level.[26] The alternatives for augmenting water supplies available include major and minor irrigation projects, tubewells or low-lift pumps, and combinations of public and private investment in which pumpsets enable farmers to supplement supplies available from a canal system. The possibilities for increasing the efficiency of water use at the farm level include measures to reduce losses in handling water, improving the timeliness of delivery of water to fields, and fixing prices on water that discourage wasteful use. Deficiencies in water management at the farm level are often compounded by inadequate leveling of fields and lack of drainage. The use of tractor-drawn soil scrapers for land leveling appears to be one of the uses of mechanical power in which the social returns are likely to exceed the social costs. Even in rainfed regions there are a number of noteworthy opportunities for more efficient utilization of the moisture available, for example, by terracing or other measures to facilitate infiltration of rainfall.

There appears to be a serious lack of information concerning the technical, economic, and institutional questions involved in choosing among alternatives and fixing priorities for expanding the availability of irrigation water and improving the efficiency of its use. Under present systems of management, the lack of predictability, certainty, and control that characterize the distribution of water to farmers in India and Pakistan is very great indeed. Those deficiencies stem largely from the fact that the present canal systems and management practices were designed for the purpose of preventing famine. Emphasis has therefore been placed on spreading the water thinly according to a rigid and automatic procedure to provide a measure of famine insurance with little regard for the efficient use of this scarce resource. The inability of farmers to control the timing of water delivery and the lack of advance knowledge about its availability means that decisions with respect to time of planting cannot be made so as to maximize yields within the limits of the water that the system can deliver.[27]

The potential returns to be realized from research, irrigation investments, and institutional innovations that permit more efficient use of water resources are greatly increased by the availability of the high-yielding varieties. The interactions between water management and the use of fertilizer are highly significant. According to a 1970 survey of Pakistani farmers, those who did not have access to water from a tubewell used less than half as much nitrogen per acre as farmers able to buy tubewell water. Farmers who owned their own tubewell, and therefore had maximum control over their water supply, used close to three times as much nitrogen as farmers who had to rely entirely on canal water.[28] According to another survey of Pakistani farmers, an average of 7.5 irrigations were applied to dwarf wheat compared to an average of 6.5 for local varieties.[29] The differential might well have been larger if there had been greater understanding on the part of farmers of the particularly adverse effects on the new varieties of water stress at the time crown roots are developing and at flowering—and if canal or tubewell water had been available for additional irrigations.

The shorter maturity period that characterizes many of the new varieties also enhances possibilities for increased multiple cropping provided that irrigation and drainage facilities are adequate. Investments to augment the capacity for generating power and distributing it in rural areas appear to promise an especially high payoff. Electric motors have a cost advantage compared to diesel engines. The differential is, however, exaggerated by the underpricing of electricity.[30] In addition, problems arise in years of low rainfall; inadequate water supplies in the dams on which hydroelectric plants depend cause power shortages which seriously interrupt irrigation. The availability of electricity in rural areas can also be expected to facilitate the development of agricultural processing and other local industries utilizing electric power. Tubewells and other types of pumpsets provide a water source that farmers can control with relative ease. Moreover, water provided by pumpsets can be highly efficient in supplementing canal irrigation. There is an acute need, however, for more information about the adequacy of groundwater reserves in various localities and the possibilities of making water available more economically by the construction or redesign of canal systems, including modified systems of management as well as the redesign of canals and laterals.

The role of mechanical innovations. Questions related to agricultural mechanization call for a somewhat more extended treatment. Mechanization policy has been the subject of sharp controversy in both India and Pakistan, and the problems raised have considerable relevance to other latecomers. It is on this issue of mechanization that there has been the greatest tendency for discussion in India to become polarized on the basis of the misleading dichotomy between efficiency and equity. The issue is complex, but much confusion can be avoided by making a clear distinction between the mechanization of field operations and mechanized pumping of water for irrigation. The former is almost entirely labor displacing whereas the latter tends to increase labor requirements per acre and leads to a considerably less drastic reduction in labor requirements per unit of output.

The mechanization represented by rapid introduction of diesel- and electric-powered pumpsets has in fact been a great deal more extensive than the substitution of tractors for bullock power in field operations. It is estimated that in 1972 India's agricultural economy was able to draw upon some 62 million horsepower provided by the following animate and inanimate sources of energy:[31]

Power source (*million units*)		Horsepower (*million*)
126	cultivators	8.44
85	draft animals	34.00
1.26	electric motors	11.34
1.0	diesel engines	5.00
.13	tractors	2.86
	Total	61.64

According to these estimates, electric motors and diesel engines provide about five times the horsepower available from tractors.[32] Their predominant use by far is in driving tubewells and low-lift pumps, but they are also widely used to power stationary threshers and, to a lesser extent, sugarcane crushers and chaff cutters.

The main effect of the greatly expanded use of power-driven pumps has been a tremendous increase in the use of groundwater for irrigation. Although performing the same function as a Persian wheel and other traditional devices, the difference in efficiency and capacity of the new techniques is so decisive that for all practical purposes they are new processes. It is estimated, for example, that an irrigation pump powered by a 7.5 h.p. electric motor takes five hours and one man to irrigate an acre of wheat compared to 60 bullock hours and 60 man-hours with a Persian wheel.[33] The spread of power-driven pumps has meant a large net increase in the irrigation water available, an increase that raises productive capacity of the agricultural sector and the demand for labor. Although controlled irrigation is not an absolute requirement, it is certainly highly complementary to the new varieties and heavy application of fertilizer.

The proposition that mechanization is a technical complement to the new varieties is often extended to apply to the substitution of tractors for bullocks in performing tillage operations. A common argument is that tractors, pumpsets, and various other items of equipment, with the list often including combine harvesters, are required to break the "vicious circle" that otherwise prevents intensification of farming and rapid increases in production. In addition to noting the advantages of carrying out farming operations in a timely manner, it is also stressed that tractors release land from crop production by reducing the need to produce fodder for draft animals.

Proponents of rapid expansion of tractor cultivation even contend that "mechanization increases employment." This argument is related mainly to the fact that mechanical power may ease labor bottlenecks and thus facilitate the increase in multiple cropping. It is also argued, however, that the growth of off-farm employment resulting from increased production of tractors and tractor-drawn equipment and the manpower requirements for distributing and servicing farm equipment will go far toward offsetting any possible reduction in on-farm labor requirements.

Several factors probably account for the intense controversy over tractor mechanization. In part it reflects recognition of the fact that in the economically advanced countries where agriculture is highly mechanized, tractors are of dominant importance, accounting for about half of the total investment in mechanization on an average farm.[34] Indeed for many people they are the symbol of a modern, highly productive agriculture. More directly relevant to the situation in India and Pakistan, however, is the rapidity with which tractor numbers have increased in recent years. Although on an all India basis there are still only about 2.5 tractors per thousand holdings, the number of tractors has increased sharply from only 54,000 in 1966 to approximately 120,000 in 1970. And they are heavily concentrated in northwestern India where irrigated commercial production is most advanced. In Ludhiana District, in the vanguard of the seed-fertilizer revolution in Punjab State, the number of tractors reached 100 per thousand farms in 1970, a threefold increase in only four years. It is also pertinent that there are five firms in India that produced more than 75,000 tractors in the past 10 years, and they have a strong interest in further expansion.

Finally, it should be emphasized that tractors have been a highly profitable investment for the farmers who have been able to purchase them; and their political influence is considerable in spite of the small numbers involved. The purchase of a tractor has enabled many large farmers to adopt the new varieties and intensify their production with great rapidity and thus reap the profits of innovation. The supranormal profits earned by many of the early adopters have been large by any standard, and this has provided a strong incentive to acquire tractors and related equipment and a large cash flow to finance such purchases. These forces have been strengthened by the effects of the price distortions that have made capital and foreign exchange artificially cheap together with the circumstances that have maintained prices—especially wheat prices—at a high level.

Underpricing of tractors is especially obvious in Pakistan where most of them have been imported at a greatly overvalued exchange rate and purchased on credit at subsidized interest rates of only about 8 per cent in nominal terms (and even less in real terms). In India there is also a considerable subsidy element in tractor prices because of the preferential access of large manufacturers to capital and to scarce materials (domestic and imported) at prices well below those paid by the small- and medium-size firms manufacturing equipment for small farms that continue to rely on bullock power. Moreover, the two governments have not been much deterred by concern about the foreign exchange costs associated with importing tractors because these imports have been financed primarily under foreign aid or barter arrangements. It has been estimated that tractor loans from the International Development Association of the World Bank covered about two-thirds of the foreign exchange cost of Pakistan's tractor imports.[35] If foreign loans for tractor imports are easy to negotiate, there may be a tendency for officials to regard them as a net addition to investable resources even though the repayment obligations reduce the availability of foreign exchange in future years.

For a variety of reasons the net social benefits from investments in tractor mechanization are much less than the net private benefits. It is obvious that farmers are basing their decisions on prices of capital and of foreign exchange that understate the social opportunity cost of those scarce resources. It is also obvious that individual farm operators cannot be expected to take account of the social costs that result from premature mechanization which exacerbates problems of under- and unemployment.

Probably of even greater importance, however, is the fact that many policy-makers and research workers as well are failing to analyze these problems in the context of an overall agricultural strategy. As a result, two fundamental considerations are often neglected. First, insufficient attention is given to the significance of the tradeoffs between investments in tractors and other measures to promote increased agricultural production, notably action to foster the spread of the new varieties and widespread increases in yields by attention to applied research, improvements in agronomic practices, and better water control as discussed in the two preceding sections.[36] Much attention has been given to comparing the "efficiency" of tractors and bullocks, neglecting the basic difference between external and internal inputs that derives from the purchasing power constraint that characterizes the agricultural sector in a late-developing country. Because the land and labor required for the rearing and maintenance of bullocks are internal, farm-supplied resources, their social opportunity cost is much less than the private cost to an individual farmer. This proposition, which is by no means obvious, derives from the structural-demographic features and the effective demand constraint that characterize a late-developing country and which were examined at some length in earlier chapters. In terms of the efficiency of an overall agricultural strategy, a much more relevant comparison is between the returns that can be obtained from investments in tractors compared to the social returns to expanded outlays for fertilizer, for pumpsets and other means of spreading and improving irrigation, and a host of other output-increasing investments. Among the alternatives are less costly improvements in farm equipment, and these will be discussed shortly. In brief, the basic issue concerns the balance to be struck between investments in large-scale farm equipment, as epitomized by tractors and combine harvesters, versus expanded investment to increase the capacity of millions of small-scale, labor-intensive units to take advantage of the seed-fertilizer revolution.

It also tends to be overlooked that the "need" for farm equipment to overcome labor bottlenecks is largely a function of the size distribution of operational units. For those cultivating large holdings, investments in labor-saving equipment that facilitate intensive production even on these large units are indeed complementary to maximum exploitation of the new varieties, including increased multiple cropping. It is thus obvious that the private profitability of investments in labor-saving equipment such as tractors will be much greater on large than small operational units.[37] It is less obvious but even more important to emphasize that in terms of social profitability an expansion path related to a unimodal size distribution of operational units represents a more efficient alternative than a bimodal growth path for the reasons set forth in Chapter 4.

The success achieved in Japan and Taiwan in obtaining high yields based on human and animal draft power should make one suspicious of the argument that tractor cultivation is a necessary condition for realizing the yield potential of the new varieties. Although casual comparisons may suggest a correlation between use of tractors and crop yields, this is usually a consequence of the fact that large farmers using tractors are also likely to be the first to adopt high-yielding varieties and to increase substantially their use of fertilizers.

Studies that have compared yields obtained on tractor and bullock farms that were reasonably comparable except for the type of draft power, do not provide evidence of any significant yield differential.[38] One exception should be noted. In rainfed areas, tractor cultivation may increase yields considerably because of permitting more efficient utilization of the limited rainfall: cultivation during the dry season increases percolation and water retention and timely planting improves germination.

The argument that mechanization enables farmers to increase cropping intensity is more persuasive, especially when the emphasis is on power-driven pumpsets. As already noted, when an electric- or diesel-powered pumpset provides the controlled irrigation that is a necessary condition for multiple cropping the argument is clearly valid, although it may be pushed too far. The greater speed of land preparation with tractors is commonly stressed, but the use of stationary threshers to ease the labor bottleneck during the period of harvesting and threshing appears to have been a more important factor in facilitating the recent increases in multiple cropping in Pakistan and northern India.

The tremendous increase in wheat yields and output has stimulated a very rapid expansion in the manufacture and use of relatively simple and inexpensive stationary threshers. It is estimated that by 1971 there were some 200,000 of these threshers in operation in India, more than half of them located in the Punjab. The number of farms served by these threshers has naturally been much larger because most of them are used for custom work as well as threshing the owner's own wheat.

It will be recalled that a stationary thresher was only one of a number of items included in the "bullock package" of improved equipment that was examined in Chapter 7. Other items that offer considerable promise of easing labor bottlenecks and permitting greater precision in carrying out such operations as seeding and fertilizer placement include: moldboard plows, disk harrows, seed-fertilizer drills, carts, improved harnesses, knapsack sprayers, and of course electric- and diesel-powered pumpsets. These items vary considerably in their cost and "lumpiness," but all of them are much better adapted to widespread use on small, labor-intensive farm units than tractor-based technologies.

It is only during the past 15 to 20 years that reasonably well-designed seed-fertilizer drills and cultivators, especially the bullock-drawn disk harrow, have become available. Sales of these items began to accelerate in the late 1960s in the Punjab and other areas where the dwarf wheat varieties were being adopted. The increase in farm cash receipts was obviously a major factor, but the spread of the seed-fertilizer drills was also influenced by the sensitivity of the new varieties to depth of planting and a steep rise in the price of seed in 1967 which encouraged the use of seed-economizing drills. Seed-fertilizer drills, patterned after Indian prototypes, are also being manufactured and sold in Pakistan, but the bullock-drawn disk harrow has apparently not been introduced.

A number of economic, technical, and institutional factors seem to account for the very limited spread of improved equipment in India and Pakistan as compared to the universal use of a considerable range of simple but well-designed and adapted implements by farmers in Taiwan. The slow growth of farm cash income and consequent lack of purchasing power have undoubtedly been the main impediment, but various technical considerations also appear to have been important. Being a specialized implement, the moldboard plow cannot be used for harrowing and intercultivation. Many farmers who have bought a moldboard have not acquired the knowledge, technical skill, and associated implements to use it effectively. In fact, they have not infrequently employed it as a wedge in the manner of a local (*desi*) plow. In some areas the techniques used to control bullocks are not very satisfactory so that plowing is not done in a straight line with parallel rows, and the adjustments of the moldboard to reap its benefit are not carried out properly if at all. There is even a question whether a full inversion plow is well suited to conditions in the greater part of India and Pakistan. In such areas as Maharashtra, where clay soils and severe weed problems exist, the inverting action of a moldboard plow has important advantages and they have been adopted relatively widely. But in areas where turning under trash is not required and the need to conserve moisture is paramount, a semi-inversion plow, similar to the Japanese spade plow, may well be more satisfactory, especially in view of the limited draft power provided by the small, poorly fed bullocks that are often used.

Perhaps the most basic technical limitation, and one that is reinforced by the purchasing power constraint, stems from the need to simultaneously adopt better implements for secondary as well as primary tillage. There is also a technical linkage between the adoption of an improved plow and harrow and the use of a seed-fertilizer drill. When all three implements are used, only about half as much time is required for land preparation and planting; and with more accurate placement of seed and fertilizer, there is a considerable increase in yield.

It is also significant that the recent acceleration of technical progress and growth of farm cash income has been rapid in the areas that have been able to take advantage of the new varieties and the scope for import substitution. As already noted, the profits of innovation were so great that many farmers had the incentive and capacity to shift directly to tractor cultivation. And that tendency was reinforced by some technical and institutional considerations as well as the price distortions mentioned earlier. Because imported tractors embody a huge investment in R&D, they are technically far superior to the indigenously evolved equipment available. Moreover, as described in the previous chapter, the use of locally manufactured bullock equipment is often impeded owing to the lack of hard (alloy) steel and to defective procedures for encouraging farmers to buy such equipment. Finally, demonstrations of the use of improved bullock equipment tend to be poor as compared to the skillful demonstrations carried out by tractor distributors. Extension workers are given little practical training; and it is reported that they are often averse to getting into the field to carry out demonstrations which are performed by lower-caste assistants who have little knowledge of what they are demonstrating.

The slogan that "mechanization increases employment" has received surprisingly wide acceptance considering the weight of the evidence which indicates that mechanization of field operations will have adverse effects on opportunities for productive employment in agriculture. This can probably be explained in part by the fact that rapid spread of mechanization in the Punjab in recent years has been associated with increased use of labor and some increase in real wages. When consideration is given to three special circumstances that have affected the relationship between mechanization and the demand for labor in that region, however, it becomes apparent that there is no justification for generalizing from that experience. First, as stressed earlier, the spectacular increases in output that have taken place in the Punjab could not possibly be achieved sectorwide because of the effective demand constraint on the growth of aggregate output. As a result of substantial expansion of acreage and a rapid rise in yields, production of wheat, the dominant crop in Punjab State, registered phenomenal *annual* increases of about 35 per cent in 1967/68 and again in 1968/69 and has continued to expand at a high rate in subsequent years. Substantial increases were registered for other crops as well. In addition, the considerable expansion of canal irrigation and the huge increase in the number of tubewells have fostered a large increase in multiple cropping and created a demand for labor for land shaping and other investments in land improvement. Inasmuch as those demands for labor were superimposed upon requirements associated with rapid expansion of production, it is apparent that labor input requirements per unit of output must have been reduced substantially.

Second, it should be stressed that the effect of tractor mechanization on the demand for labor that has already taken place is probably only a fraction of the future labor displacement that is to be expected as a result of the rapid expansion in tractor numbers that has already occurred. Farmers and tractor drivers have not yet learned how to take full advantage of their tractors, and the inevitable shortcomings resulting from the time required to acquire operating skills have been accentuated by serious problems of maintenance and spare parts. Moreover, most farmers have only acquired a nine-tyne cultivator for field operations which many of them are using as an all-purpose implement, a sort of mechanized and multiplied *desi* plow.

Perhaps most important of all, time is required for the reorganization of production into large, mechanized operational units and to reach a new equilibrium. In considering the "catching-up" process that characterized agricultural mechanization in the American South, it was noted that the initial introduction of tractors in the Mississippi Delta led to a rapid switch from share tenancy to reliance on hired labor and a marked change in the seasonal pattern of labor use; but for a time the total demand for labor was not reduced appreciably. Richard Day's analysis that was summarized in Chapter 5 emphasized that it was only in the "third stage" that followed the initial introduction of tractors that Delta agriculture was fully mechanized and cropping patterns altered so that the requirement for labor was reduced drastically. In a subsequent study, Carl Gotsch has argued that the really sharp reduction in the demand for labor seems to have been precipitated by the events of the "Freedom Summer" of 1964 which led to a breakdown of the traditional paternalism of the planter class which had previously slowed the pace of labor-displacing mechanization so that it did not exceed an "acceptable" level of social dislocation. However it is to be explained, there is clear evidence that the fairly moderate decline in employment in the 1960-63 period was followed by remarkably rapid reduction during the next four years.[39]

The third and last consideration relates to the expectation that growth of nonfarm employment, including workers engaged in manufacturing and servicing tractors and tractor-drawn equipment, will be a major offset to any displacement of farm labor that might result from mechanization. The evidence presented in Chapter 5 concerning the growth of "indirect" labor inputs embodied in the manufactured inputs used in farming suggest strongly that this increase in demand for labor is trivial compared to the parallel reduction in "direct" labor input requirements in farming. More directly relevant to the evidence from the Indian Punjab, however, is the fact that the rate of growth of nonfarm employment in that region has been unusually high for two reasons. The exceptionally rapid expansion of farm output and cash receipts has provided a powerful stimulus for expanded production of goods and services by the nonfarm sectors in that vanguard region. The brisk demand for farm inputs such as electric motors, diesel engines, pumpsets, stationary threshers, and implements for both bullocks and tractors has represented only a part of the enlarged demand resulting from the rise in farm receipts. In addition, there has been rapid expansion in the production of textiles and a variety of other products; and to a much greater extent than in other states industrial expansion in the Punjab has taken place in decentralized and fairly labor-intensive workshops and factories.

Policies affecting the size distribution of operational units and the mobilization of resources for development. Two propositions that have been emphasized in earlier chapters are that the size distribution of farm operational units is one of the most basic factors determining a country's pattern of agricultural development and that success in mobilizing resources to finance investments in infrastructure and industrial expansion is a necessary condition for transforming the agrarian structure of a late-developing country. Each of those variables is influenced by a great many factors, including policies that give rise to price distortions and monetary and financial policies that discourage healthy growth of financial intermediaries. Those more general influences have been examined in earlier chapters. Here we concentrate on some issues related to land tenure and agricultural taxation that appear to be having especially significant effects on both the size distribution of operational units and on resource mobilization in India and Pakistan.

Official policy in India as set forth in the Fourth Five Year Plan continues to place major emphasis on "fixation of fair rent and assurance of security of tenure" as "crucial to the hole scheme of land reforms."[40] A searching re-examination of that tenet of land tenure policy appears to be needed for several reasons.

Until very recently, the government's announced intention to fill gaps in land reform legislation and to achieve more effective implementation was concentrated on attempting to legislate "equitable" rents rather than on redistribution of ownership rights. Although legal ceilings on rental rates are commonly regarded as a politically feasible "second best" solution, the analysis presented in Chapter 4 indicates that they are not a satisfactory substitute for acreage ceilings and land redistribution. If it is politically feasible to carry out a redistributive land reform, the resulting change in the distribution of ownership of this key asset will not only reduce income inequalities but will also favor a more unimodal size distribution of operational units. Although rental ceilings may be easier to legislate, they are in practice almost invariably unenforceable because, as Doreen Warriner puts it, "tenants will connive with landowners in evading the laws for fear of being evicted from their holdings."[41] In fact the potential nuisance value of such legislation has probably been a factor in the widespread eviction of tenants. Fortunately, recent reports indicate that the major emphasis is now being placed on enforcing acreage ceilings and redistribution of land in excess of an authorized maximum ownership unit. In most states the legal maximum is 18 acres of perennially irrigated or double-cropped land, with considerably larger ceilings for arable land without irrigation and for land suitable only for grazing.[42]

Whatever degree of success may be achieved in carrying out the redistribution of ownership rights in land, the renting-in of land represents an important possibility for some small farmers to enlarge their operational units by renting land from large landlords or from households whose holdings are very small and inefficient. Even a pair of bullocks and family labor are likely to be seriously underutilized in India on farm units below, say, two or three irrigated acres or five or six unirrigated acres; and the option of hiring out labor may be more rewarding than operating such an "uneconomic" holding. And finally, a more realistic view of land rent payments being determined by bargaining between landlords and tenants, in a situation in which the bargaining power of tenants is extremely weak because of the lack of alternative sources of income, may encourage increased attention to the importance of substantially increasing the rate of taxation on agricultural land.

It is generally recognized that agriculture's contribution to tax revenue in both India and Pakistan is very small, mainly because inflation has so drastically eroded the real value of land revenue taxes fixed in monetary terms.[43] It is estimated that in 1966/67 land revenue in India amounted to only .8 per cent of gross value added in agriculture, and the rapid growth of farm output in recent years has further reduced the tax burden on agriculture.[44] For (West) Pakistan it is reported that an increase in agricultural income from 7.7 billion rupees in 1959/60 to 15.5 billion rupees in 1969/70 was associated with an increase in agricultural taxes of only 11 million rupees, and agricultural taxes declined from 2.2 to only 1.2 per cent of agricultural income.[45]

It is a misleading simplification to speak of a tax burden on "agriculture."[46] In India especially there are great interregional as well as interfarm variations in agricultural income and in taxable capacity. In principle, agricultural incomes should be subject to the same progressive income tax that applies to wage and salary incomes; but there are obviously severe administrative problems in assessing and collecting income tax from farm households. For economic reasons as well as those related to tax administration, there are noteworthy advantages in relying heavily on the taxation of agricultural land; but for historical and constitutional reasons it is exceptionally difficult to raise substantially the level of taxation on agricultural land in India.[47]

If land taxes based on periodic reassessment of land values or "potential income" could extract a substantial part of the economic rent accruing to land, as was the case in Japan and Taiwan, this would provide a very effective means of reducing the interregional disparities in agricultural income that have increased so much because of the uneven impact of the seed-fertilizer revolution. Such a tax policy would also have some deterrent effect on landowners establishing large operational units and instead encourage the renting of land to smallholders prepared to cultivate the land more intensively. It appears, however, that at least in Pakistan the present system of assessing land revenue and the water rate have the opposite effect. Because these assessments are based on the cropped area rather than the total cultivated area, the tax burden per acre is heavier for small farmers who cultivate their land intensively than it is for large farmers who cultivate a smaller percentage of their holding and practice multiple cropping to a lesser degree.[48] It has often been argued that a land tax should have a progressive rate structure in order to make the tax burden more equitable. The problems of administering a graduated land tax appear to be so severe, however, that it is probably advisable to rely on alternative techniques for introducing an element of progressiveness into the agricultural tax system. M. Ghaffar Chaudhry has argued that a tax on marketed produce merits attention in this regard. Although such a tax tends to have an adverse effect on marketed output, the deterrent effect is not likely to be significant if the rate is low and if it is associated with a fairly heavy land tax; and a tax on marketed output has the further advantage of being income and price elastic. Another alternative that has been advocated is a simplified agricultural income tax, based on an assessment of "standard income" per acre related to the productivity of the land.[49]

A particularly cogent case can be made for levying a heavy excise tax on tractors, combine harvesters, and perhaps other types of labor-displacing farm equipment. Our calculations in Chapter 8 indicated that a sales tax on tractors in Pakistan of 20 to 35 per cent was

THE CATCHING-UP PROCESS

needed to correct for the underpricing of scarce inputs used in their manufacture. Additional taxation on the tractor to reflect the social cost of the unemployment it creates would in many cases be advisable. Magnitudes of 50 to 75 per cent have been suggested.[50] As a policy instrument such a tax would have the effect of encouraging large landowners to rent their land to be farmed in smaller, more labor-intensive units. Once a large farming operation has been established and a lumpy investment in a tractor has been made, there are powerful forces that induce the operator to progressively reduce his dependence on hired labor.

Finally, it is important to emphasize that increasing the total tax take from agriculture represents the only feasible means of enlarging the resources available to foster the progressive modernization of agriculture. Strengthening agricultural research and farmer training, extending and improving the agricultural infrastructure, and other measures to spread and increase the impact of the new varieties all involve substantial capital outlays and recurrent expenditure. And because of the capital requirements for industrial expansion and other components of the structural transformation process, a net transfer of resources into agriculture would be detrimental to overall economic growth and to long-run progress in improving rural welfare. As was emphasized in Chapter 7, this does not mean that there should be a net outflow from agriculture regardless of the comparative returns to investments in agriculture and other sectors. But given the potential for achieving a "sufficient" expansion of agricultural output by exploiting the potential for increasing farm productivity and output by relatively low-cost methods together with the more rapid growth of demand for nonfarm goods and services, the presumption is strong that the total net flow should be in that direction.

NOTES

1. As noted in Chapter 4, this is not an optimization problem in a formal sense but rather an attempt at the best approximation of an "optimal" combination of policies and programs in a situation of incomplete and uncertain knowledge.

2. Clarence H. Danhof, *Change in Agriculture: The Northern United States, 1820-1870* (Cambridge, Massachusetts, 1969), p. 182.
3. Data from Government of India, Directorate of Economics and Statistics, Ministry of Agriculture, *Bulletin of Food Statistics* (New Delhi, 1971), p. 162.
4. According to the terminology used in India, production of "foodgrains" was about 10 million tons higher because grams and other pulses as well as cereals are included in that category.
5. *Development Statistics of West Pakistan* Vol. 2, No. 4 (October 1970).
6. We eschew any attempt to assess the advantages and disadvantages of the considerable reliance by India and Pakistan on aid in the form of P.L. 480 shipments. It is apparent, however, that the sharp increase and then decline in P.L. 480 aid contributed to the stagnation of farm cash income prior to 1966/67 and the exceptionally rapid growth of receipts since that time. There were also important effects on the government budget. Especially in Pakistan, government receipts from the sale of P.L. 480 grain represented a significant source of funds for financing development projects, and difficult budget problems arose when those funds were reduced with the sharp cutback in P.L. 480 shipments.
7. *Development Statistics*, p. 22.
8. M. L. Dantwala, "From Stagnation to Growth: Relative Roles of Technology, Economic Policy and Agrarian Institutions" (Presidential Address prepared for the Fifty-Third Annual Conference of the Indian Economic Association, Gauhati, December 1970), p. 15.
9. Max K. Lowdermilk, "Diffusion of Dwarf Wheat Production Technology in Pakistan's Punjab" (Ph.D. dissertation, Cornell University, 1972), pp. 134, 245.
10. Bruce F. Johnston and John Cownie, "The Seed-Fertilizer Revolution and Labor Force Absorption," *American Economic Review* Vol. 59, No. 4 (September 1969); John Cownie, Bruce F. Johnston, and Bart Duff, "The Quantitative Impact of the Seed-Fertilizer Revolution in West Pakistan: An Exploratory Study," *Food Research Institute Studies* Vol. 9, No. 1 (1970).
11. See P. K. Mukherjee and Brian B. Lockwood, "High Yielding Varieties Programme in India: Assessment" (Paper prepared for the 28th International Congress of Orientalists, Canberra, Australia, January 6-12, 1971); and Brian B. Lockwood, P. K. Mukherjee, and R. T. Shand, *The High Yielding Varieties Programme in India: Part I,* Government of India, Planning Commission, Programme Evaluation Organisation and Australian National University, Department of Economics (Canberra, 1971).
12. On the basis of the Programme Evaluation Organisation's surveys, it is estimated that the adoption rates for *kharif* and *rabi* rice were 28 and 39 per cent, respectively, whereas *rabi* wheat had reached 69 per cent, somewhat higher than the estimate for the Pakistani Punjab. But the figures for India overestimate the percentage of adoption on an All-India basis because the surveys cover localities where conditions are reasonably favorable for adoption of the new varieties.
13. U.S. Department of Agriculture, *Agricultural Situation in the Far East*

and Oceania: Review of 1971 and Outlook for 1972, Economic Research Service, ERS-Foreign 337 (Washington, D.C., 1972), Appendix Table 4; idem, *Pakistan's Agricultural Development and Trade,* Economic Research Service, ERS-Foreign 347 (Washington, D.C., 1973), p. 5.

14. Jerry B. Eckert, "The Impact of Dwarf Wheat on Resource Productivity in West Pakistan's Punjab" (Ph.D. dissertation, Michigan State University, 1970).

15. Ibid.; idem, "The Economics of Fertilizing Dwarf Wheats in Pakistan's Punjab," mimeographed (Lahore: July 1971). See also Government of Punjab (Pakistan), Planning and Development Department, Bureau of Statistics, *Fertilizer and Mexican Wheat Survey Report 1970,* Survey Unit, Fourth Plan Economic Research Project (Lahore, 1971).

16. William E. Hendrix, "The Green Revolution in India: Achievements and Fourth Plan Prospects and Problems," mimeographed (New Delhi: U.S./AID, Agricultural Economics Division, August 12, 1970).

17. Government of the Punjab (Pakistan), *Fertilizer and Mexican Wheat Survey.*

18. There is evidence that many farmers in Pakistan have begun to witness a decline in yield with the new varieties, and the senior wheat breeder reports that this is to be attributed mainly to the reduced availability of phosphate since farmers applying large amounts of phosphate are continuing to obtain very high yields. S. A. Quereshi 1971: personal communication.

19. According to a recent report from IRRI, it has been found that zinc deficiency accounts for the fact that only 10 per cent of 120,000 hectares of potential rice land in the central plain of Agusan in the Philipipnes is planted to rice. In some locations zinc made the difference between no yield at all, with or without conventional fertilizers, and a high yield. For one set of trials, applying 1 kg of zinc oxide per hectare (at a cost of between $1.00 and $2.00), meant a yield of 4.2 tons compared to zero on the control plots; application of zinc along with a complete fertilizer (N, P, and K) gave a yield of 4.9 tons per hectare, International Rice Research Institute, *The IRRI Reporter* 1 (Manila, 1973).

20. S. L. Shah and R. C. Agrawal, "Impact of New Technology on the Level of Income, Patterns of Income Distribution and Savings of Farmers in Central Uttar Pradesh," *Indian Journal of Agricultural Economics* Vol. 25, No. 3 (July-September 1970), pp. 111-14.

21. The latest contribution is an article by P. K. Bardhan based on individual farm-level data for approximately 1000 Indian farms ("Size, Productivity, and Returns to Scale: An Analysis of Farm-Level Data in Indian Agriculture," *Journal of Political Economy* Vol. 81, No. 6 [November/December 1973]). This article, which includes references to the more important studies of farm size, output, and use of inputs in Indian agriculture, contains an interesting analysis of the reasons for the inverse relation between farm size and use of non-land inputs.

22. In Japan, as in Taiwan, the inverse relationship between the per-acre use of purchased inputs and farm size is nearly as pronounced as for labor inputs.

According to the Economic Survey of Farm Households for 1964, farms in the .5 to 1.0 hectare size class reported use of about 500 hours per .1 hectare compared to not quite 220 hours for "large" farms of 2.5-3.0 hectares. Expenditures per hectare for other nonland inputs were slightly over twice as high in the smaller size class, and in both cases this inverse relationship is evident for each of the intermediate size categories. Kazushi Ohkawa, *Differential Structure and Agriculture: Essays on Dualistic Growth* (Tokyo, 1972).

23. K. S. Gill, *Wheat Market Behaviour in Punjab Post-Harvest Period 1968-69*, Punjab Agricultural University, Department of Agricultural Economics and Sociology (Ludhiana, 1969?), p. 54.

24. Government of India, Planning Commission, *Fourth Five Year Plan 1969-74: Draft* (Delhi, 1969), p. 112.

25. Dantwala, "From Stagnation to Growth," pp. 17-18.

26. Gilbert Levine, "The Water Environment and Crop Production," in *Some Issues Emerging from Recent Breakthroughs in Food Production*, edited by Kenneth L. Turk (Binghamton, New York, 1971), pp. 385-92.

27. These characteristics and their historical origins are emphasized by W. Eric Gustafson and Richard B. Reidinger, "Delivery of Canal Water in North India and West Pakistan," *Economic and Political Weekly* Vol. 6 No. 52 (December 25, 1971). They suggest that making it legal for farmers to sell or trade water to one another would be an important means by which increased controllability could be achieved, an arrangement that is common in some countries and one which would be facilitated by some form of water users' association.

28. Government of the Punjab (Pakistan), *Fertilizer and Mexican Wheat Survey*.

29. Eckert, "Impact of Dwarf Wheat," p. 53.

30. In fact, according to a 1969 study by C. E. Finney, in terms of "social prices" the annual profit per tubewell was a little higher for diesel- than electric-powered wells. See his study on "The Economics of Farm Power in the Indus Plains of West Pakistan" (Master of Philosophy Thesis, University of Reading, 1972), p. 224.

31. Gajendra Singh, "Energy Inputs and Agricultural Production Under Various Regimes of Mechanization in Northern India" (Ph.D. dissertation, University of California, Davis, 1973).

32. Another source reports that these stationary power units provide three times the farm power represented by tractor purchases but at only twice the investment; Roy E. Harrington et al., *Agricultural Mechanization in India*, The Ford Foundation (New Delhi, October 1972), p. 21.

33. Singh, "Energy Inputs and Agricultural Production."

34. Harrington et al., *Agricultural Mechanization*, p. 22.

35. Carl H. Gotsch, "Tractor Mechanisation and Rural Development in Pakistan," *International Labour Review* Vol. 107, No. 2 (February 1973), p. 141.

36. This point is also stressed by Amartya Sen in his monograph on "Employment Policy and Technological Choice," mimeographed (Geneva: Inter-

national Labour Office, World Employment Programme, 1973), p. 205.

37. This is indicated very clearly by Finney's linear programming analysis of the social and private returns from alternative packages of investment in mechanical equipment on operational units of 12.5, 50, and 150 acres ("Economics of Farm Power," Chaps. 11-13).

38. A recent paper by Gajendra Singh and William Chancellor provides a very useful summary of evidence available from experimental trials and farm surveys ("Relations Between Farm Mechanization and Crop Yield for a Farming District in India" [Paper prepared for the 1973 Annual Meeting of the American Society of Agricultural Engineers, Lexington, Kentucky, June 17-20, 1973]). See also Finney's summary of the literature pertaining to the yield effects of mechanization in Pakistan in "Economics of Farm Power," Chap. 2. A 1970 study in (West) Pakistan contains a rather extreme example of exaggerating the effect of mechanization on yields. In this study it was assumed that tractor cultivation would result in a yield increase of 400 to 500 pounds of wheat per acre. See Roger Lawrence, "Some Economic Aspects of Farm Mechanization in Pakistan," mimeographed (Islamabad: AID, August 1970). It turns out that this estimate was based on a single trial of the effects of chisel plowing to a depth of 9 inches carried out by the AID mechanization specialist on the farm of a former minister of agriculture, Malik Khuda Bakhsh Bucha, who reports that the practice was never repeated even on his own farm.

39. The Farm Placement Department of the Mississippi Employment Security Commission has estimated that agricultural employment in the Delta still amounted to 1.1 million man-days in 1963 but dropped sharply to only 221,000 man-days in 1966. Both figures are the sum of spring and fall employment of seasonal and nonseasonal workers, but the decline was concentrated in the seasonal category. See Carl Gotsch, "Utilization of Human Resources in the Mississippi Delta: Some Preliminary Results," mimeographed (Cambridge, Massachusetts: Harvard University, 1970?).

40. Government of India, *Fourth Five Year Plan*, p. 133.

41. Doreen Warriner, "Results of Land Reform in Asian and Latin American Countries," *Food Research Institute Studies* Vol. 12, No. 2 (1973), p. 128.

42. C. H. Hanumantha Rao, 1973: personal communication.

43. V. P. Gandhi, *Tax Burden on Indian Agriculture*, Harvard Law School, International Tax Program (Cambridge, Massachusetts, 1966); and S. S. Johl, "Agricultural Taxation in a Developing Economy: A Case of India," *Indian Journal of Agricultural Economics* Vol. 27, No. 3 (July-September 1972).

44. Emmerich M. Schebeck, "An Analysis of Capital Flows Between the Agricultural and Non-agricultural Sectors of India," International Bank for Reconstruction and Development, Economics Department Working Paper No. 42 (Washington, D.C., June 6, 1969), pp. 14, 18n.

45. Javid Hamid, "Suggested Approach to Agricultural Taxation Policy in West Pakistan," *Pakistan Development Review* Vol. 10, No. 4 (Winter 1970), pp. 442.

46. Raj Krishna, "Intersectoral Equity and Agricultural Taxation in India"

(Paper prepared for the Food Research Institute Conference on Strategies for Agricultural Development in the 1970s, Stanford University, Stanford, California, December 13-16, 1971).

47. As a result of an early example of an inappropriate transfer of economic doctrines, Ricardo's concept of differential rent was used to justify very heavy reliance on a land tax in India during the nineteenth century. Because farm cash incomes were so exceedingly limited, the tax worked a great hardship on Indian cultivators and it seems that a land tax is still tainted by its role during the colonial period. The constitutional problem arises because land tax is under the control of the state legislatures. See William Barber, "James Mill and the Theory of Economic Policy in India," *History of Political Economy* Vol. 1, No. 1 (Spring 1969).

48. M. Ghaffar Chaudhry, "The Problem of Agricultural Taxation in West Pakistan and an Alternative Solution," *Pakistan Development Review* Vol. 12, No. 3 (Summer 1973), pp. 106-10.

49. Ibid.; Krishna, "Agricultural Taxation in India"; and Johl, "Agricultural Taxation."

50. Ralph W. Cummings and Robert W. Herdt, "The Future of India's Agriculture: Implications of the Green Revolution," book manuscript (April 1971), p. 830; Finney, "Economics of Farm Power," pp. 238-39.

10 | Intercountry Variations and the Choice of Strategy

A major theme running through this book is the proposition that the structural-demographic characteristics of late-developing countries and broad similarities in their relative factor prices provide certain guidelines concerning the types of policies that should be pursued. However, since agricultural development depends so heavily on technical innovations and on institutional arrangements, the exact design of an agricultural strategy must be location specific.

ELEMENTS OF DIVERSITY

The most promising means of increasing farm productivity and output in a particular country will depend on (a) its resource endowment and land/man ratio, (b) the technologies available and in prospect, (c) its infrastructure, (d) factors influencing the readiness and ability of farmers to adopt innovations, and (e) existing institutions and administrative capabilities. Differences in those parameters are obviously a crucial consideration in the formulation of the specific programs and projects that translate a strategy into action at the regional, district, and, ultimately, the farm level.

Physical environment, technologies available, and infrastructure requirements

It is apparent that in Japan and Taiwan the emphasis on measures to increase crop yields and the extent of multiple cropping was influenced by the limited scope that existed for enlarging the cultivated area. The economic and social advantages of a unimodal strategy are no doubt especially great when the density of population in rural areas is high. And it is sometimes argued that the existence of large areas of unused land, as in much of Africa and Latin America, means that the encouragement of large, capital-intensive, holdings is appropriate. There is also a tendency to question the relevance of seed-fertilizer combinations as a major output-increasing innovation in countries where irrigation is of slight importance and crop production depends on rainfall that is often unreliable in amount and in its seasonal distribution.

It is true, of course, that where there is abundant land to be brought into cultivation, there is greater likelihood that it will be advantageous to increase farm output by expansion on the "extensive margin" as well as the "intensive margin." In fact, much of the expansion of agricultural output in such regions has been of the "vent-for-surplus" type analyzed by Hla Myint. The establishment of trade links with overseas markets provided the "vent" that made it possible and profitable to introduce new high-value "cash crops" based on an essentially "horizontal expansion" of the cultivated area and fuller utilization of the available stock of farm labor. This type of expansion has been especially characteristic of much of tropical Africa during the past 50 to 75 years.[1] It is significant that in Africa the term "cash crops" has been virtually synonymous with export crops which have in fact been the main source of increased farm cash income. At the low levels of income that prevail, cash receipts tend to be used primarily to purchase consumer goods to augment subsistence production; and it has been difficult for African farmers to enlarge their use of external inputs—even divisible inputs such as fertilizers. Hence, the paramount importance of expanding the cultivated area by fuller utilization of available resources of labor and land.

Although the scope for enlarging the cultivated area in Africa and Latin America is clearly larger than in Asia, prevailing views tend to exaggerate the abundance of land that can be brought into cultivation economically. On the basis of a careful review of the literature, William Hance has concluded that nearly 40 per cent of the land area in sub-Saharan Africa was already experiencing "land pressure" in the late 1960s, in part as a result of the acceleration in population growth since the 1940s. (For northern Africa the corresponding figure is over 70 per cent of the land area.) On the basis of this study, Hance concludes that "despite the difficulties of increasing output on existing lands, it is probably much more important in meeting population pressure than extension to new lands. . . ."[2] There is, of course, great variation within individual countries as well as among countries in the scope that exists for enlarging the cultivated area at costs which compare favorably with expanding output by raising crop yields on land already under cultivation.

Differences in the availability of land for expanding the cultivated area will also exert a strong influence on the profitability of investments in irrigation. In those regions in Latin America and tropical Africa where there are possibilities for enlarging the cultivated area, as well as raising crop yields, investments in irrigation facilities will rarely be the low-cost alternative for fostering increased production. But differences in infrastructure needs will also be a function of past investments. Some countries, for example, have already made large investments in their transport networks. Elsewhere this is a critical problem because of past neglect—or a tendency to concentrate too exclusively on main routes linking ports and urban areas—leaving much of the countryside remote from low cost modes of transportation.

Many of the savanna regions of Africa also have considerable untapped potential for expanding the area under cultivation by the use of animal draft power. In a number of areas there has been considerable use of oxen for plowing, but Mazabuka District in Zambia is one of the few areas where African farmers are making effective use of a full range of ox-drawn equipment, including cultivators, harrows, planters, and carts.[3] As emphasized earlier, use of ox-drawn equipment has significant advantages because it minimizes the cash requirements for external inputs; such equipment also represents a purchased input that can provide a valuable stimulus to the development of indigenous metal-working capabilities. The prospects for raising farm productivity through arrangements for contract tractor plowing seems particularly good in rainfed areas, although the social returns to use of mechanical power would perhaps be greatest if tractors were used primarily for the difficult operations, such as opening up new land or land regenerated under a bush fallow. Tractors also have a useful role to play in establishing bench terraces, which reduce erosion and improve infiltration and storage of water in the soil.

One of the most ubiquitous problems in raising yields in rainfed agriculture is related to the uncertainty of returns to the use of improved seed and fertilizers that result from variability in rainfall. Nonetheless, highly significant opportunities exist for raising yields above the low levels that now prevail. Indeed, by promoting vigorous early growth of roots, fertilizers often lessen the adverse effects of below average rainfall.

Limited success in raising crop yields in rainfed regions in less developed countries is to a large extent a consequence of the meager resources that have been devoted to research on yield-increasing technologies applicable to the tropics and subtropics. Even in Argentina, with a long history of commercial development of agriculture and a temperate climate that lessens the problems of technological transfer, there has been gross neglect of those possibilities. Alain de Janvry, in an excellent study that deals explicitly with the problems of risk, emphasizes the seriousness of the loss to the Argentine economy because of "the *real unavailability of the fertilizer technology to farmers* in the sense that technical and economic information on its use are almost totally nonexistent."[4] In addition to the failure to develop fertilizer-responsive varieties and the neglect of research on fertilizer use under various soil and rainfall conditions, fertilizer use has been discouraged by unnecessarily high fertilizer prices. The price that farmers must pay for fertilizers could be reduced either by relying on imports or on local production in plants of the efficient size that would be justified if fertilizer use was not being discouraged by high prices and lack of technical and economic information.

In many of the developing countries the neglect of research, particularly research on food crops, has been much greater than in Argentina. Moreover, the restricted cash income has meant that the demand for fertilizer and other technical inputs has been insufficient to stimulate the establishment of efficient systems of distribution. In addition to the problems of low volume and lack of competition among suppliers, poor road networks may raise transport costs to such an extent that product/input price ratios are unfavorable. The interrelatedness of this whole set of constraints obviously increases the difficulty of achieving a breakthrough.

In an early article on the impact of the seed-fertilizer revolution, it was noted that until the late 1960s the possibility of developing and applying agricultural strategies based on divisible, yield-increasing innovations "rested very much on an article of faith; it seemed reasonable to infer that the cumulative progress in agricultural science and in research techniques in the developed countries could generate technical innovations adapted to the physical, economic, and sociocultural conditions of other countries."[5] With respect to dryland farming, there is still only limited evidence from which inferences can be made. As noted in Chapter 6, experience with the Puebla Project in Mexico has been somewhat disappointing, at least in relation to the initial expectations. The reasons for an apparent leveling off in the rate of spread of the new practices do not seem to be well understood. The principal hypothesis seems to be that risk aversion is a major factor, but lack of relevant technical knowledge may also be significant.

Experience in other areas is mixed. There has been an impressive spread of high-yielding hybrid and synthetic varieties of maize, together with greatly increased use of fertilizer, in parts of Zambia, Kenya, and a number of other countries.[6] It is probably significant that the local varieties being grown in Kenya and Zambia were ill-adapted to the local ecology so that the package represented by the new varieties in combination with fertilizer had a large impact on yield; in the Puebla area, on the other hand, the local varieties have a high yield potential provided that the rate of fertilizer use and other agronomic practices are modified. Inter- and intra-seasonal variations in rainfall can be critical and crop failures are not uncommon. Timely planting has an important influence on maize yields, and the successful introduction of the high-yielding varieties in Zambia's Mazabuka District was probably facilitated by the fact that farmers in that area make use of a considerable range of ox-drawn equipment, including planters, cultivators, harrows, and carts in addition to a plow of good design. Also, the district is near the "line of rail" to Lusaka and the copper mines and accounts for a considerable fraction of commercial maize production in Zambia. Even the smallest and least progressive group of farmers had average cash receipts of about £18 from maize sales at the time of the Anthony-Uchendu survey in 1967. Farmers in a particularly fertile locality (Magoye) had average cash receipts for maize of about £45 even though their holdings averaged only 6.6 acres (with 4.4 acres in maize). A high percentage of farmers in this area were planting hybrid maize, and their mean yield with hybrid seed, always planted with fertilizer, was nearly 3300 pounds. In contrast, a local variety gave an average yield of only 1800 pounds with fertilizer and 1400 without.

A recent account of the introduction of Mexican wheats in Tunisia provides interesting information on their performance under dryland conditions with sparse and variable rainfall.[7] Although the new varieties have given average yields double the average obtained with local varieties, this comparison is misleading because the dwarf varieties are grown on a relatively small area and under much more favorable conditions. The high yield potential of the new varieties is mainly a consequence of their greater responsiveness to "control variables"—relatively high doses of fertilizer and attention to seedbed preparation, seeding rates, date of planting, and weed control. Under comparable conditions the new varieties typically have a yield advantage of only about one-third; the margin of superiority is greater when the environment permits high yields whereas the yield advantage is considerably less than a third under adverse conditions. It is reported that adequate control of the factors essential for high yields has only been achieved so far on large, modern, mechanized farms. Because of superior management and the availability of mechanical power, these units are able to insure that cultivation operations are carried out in a proper and timely fashion. The mechanized sector uses wheeled and caterpillar tractors and combine harvesters, which are costly and impose heavy foreign exchange requirements. The significant observation is made that "technology for achieving control without the use of mechanical power has not yet been developed in Tunisia."[8]

The words "not yet" raise some challenging questions. In fact, Randolph Barker and Don Winkelmann assert that "the major challenge now facing many countries in the developing world is that of achieving agricultural growth in unirrigated or poorly irrigated areas." It is their considered judgment that "it will be possible to obtain varieties with good yield potential and reasonable yield stability."[9] It is an encouraging development that the international research institutes for rice and for maize and wheat, IRRI and CIMMYT, are now devoting enlarged resources to research directed at increasing yield potential and yield stability under the less favorable environmental conditions which account for such a large part of the farming area in developing countries. It is also encouraging that new international research institutes, notably the International Institute of Tropical Agriculture (IITA) in Nigeria and the International Crop Research Institute for the Semi-Arid Tropics (ICRISAT) in India, are launching major research programs focused on tropical root crops, grain legumes, and millets and sorghums, crops which have received comparatively little attention although they are of widespread importance in developing countries.

It needs to be stressed, however, that even the most outstanding international research institute will have little or no impact unless individual countries strengthen their national research programs. Plant material and scientific and technical knowledge developed at international or regional institutes can contribute to the effectiveness of national programs, but testing, selection, and adaptation to specific local conditions remains indispensable. Some of the most serious deficiencies in past research programs have been in the agronomic research required to translate knowledge of new technical possibilities into recommended practices that are feasible and profitable under the conditions faced by farmers in a particular district.

Because of their training and orientation, agricultural scientists have an understandable tendency to emphasize technical rather than economic efficiency and to neglect especially the considerations relevant to a country's sectorwide expansion path. Unless a conscious effort is made to counter that tendency, there is a danger that both the international institutes and national research programs will emphasize new farming systems which, because of their complexity and requirements for drastic change and sharply increased cash outlays, will not be adapted to the needs of the small units that predominate in a late-developing country. Failure to develop technologies adapted to smallholder conditions, as reported above for Tunisia, will obviously have the effect of polarizing the agricultural sector. Although timeliness is a crucial factor in semiarid regions, small operational units using animal draft power, may be able to avoid delays entailing any sizable reduction in yield, especially if they are equipped with a satisfactory range of tillage implements. On the other hand, it is possible that under these circumstances there are significant net social as well as private returns to tractor cultivation because of the impact of timeliness on the profitability of using new varieties and fertilizer and on the resulting yields. In that event, contract plowing, as an institutional arrangement to make tractor services divisible, is likely to have both economic and social advantages. When tractor services are hired by farmers operating small units, they are more likely to use mechanical power as a complement to the relatively abundant family labor available rather than as a first step toward sharply reducing labor inputs.

The institutional environment, the readiness of rural communities and farmers to accept change, and administrative capacity

In addition to the differences in physical environment, availability of profitable technical innovations, and adequacy of infrastructure,

INTERCOUNTRY VARIATIONS AND THE CHOICE OF STRATEGY 445

there are also large intercountry differences in the performance of institutions for agricultural extension, farmer training, and other agricultural support activities. Sometimes this is mainly a consequence of giving low priority to agriculture, but frequently it is part of a general scarcity of experienced and competent administrators.

The choice of measures also needs to take account of certain characteristics of the rural social structure and dissimilarities in the level of social, economic, and attitudinal development of rural communities and farm households. Different rural communities, and individual farm households within particular communities, are at different points on a continuum that extends from situations that still have a strong subsistence orientation to those where producers are already well integrated in an exchange economy. Their position on this continuum is conditioned by past social and economic change—changes both within the local farming community (affecting social values, attitudes, and technical knowledge), and changes in the external environment (availability of services, marketing and other institutions, and roads, irrigation works, or other infrastructure).[10]

The nature of the existing social structure at the local level will clearly have an important influence on the functioning of agricultural cooperatives as well as supporting institutions such as the extension service. Many traditional societies have a strongly hierarchical type of social organization; and under those conditions cooperatives are apt to strengthen the existing social stratification and be controlled so that the services they provide reinforce inequality in the distribution of wealth, income, and power. As emphasized in earlier chapters, these problems are accentuated when credit and inputs are made available at artificially low prices, thus creating an excess demand situation which makes it necessary to resort to some form of administrative rationing. There is an almost universal need to encourage the creation of local organizations of farmers—to facilitate the dissemination of technical information, to reduce the administrative costs of distributing credit to small farmers, to manage the distribution of irrigation water, and various other activities that may require group action. But the instrument of choice will depend on local circumstances. A full-fledged multipurpose cooperative organized according to Rochdale principles and with a hierarchical structure of unions and federations built on top of primary societies is only one of many ways of organizing farmers into cooperatives, "pre-cooperatives," or associations, and one that is often inappropriate in an early phase of development.

Developing countries also differ markedly in their ability to design an efficient agricultural strategy and to formulate the policies and programs required to achieve development objectives. The contrasts in their ability to implement programs at the local level is perhaps even greater. Although the availability of competent staff is clearly a key factor, performance is also influenced greatly by the nature of a country's administrative structure and the extent to which programs are adapted to administrative capabilities and are concentrated on objectives that merit priority attention. Although leadership and control at the national level are essential, a common shortcoming is the failure to provide for a suitable balance between planning and policy formulation by the central government and the devolution of authority to administrative bodies at the local level. Because of the great diversity that characterizes a country's agricultural regions and rural communities, it is virtually impossible to adapt programs to local circumstances without considerable decentralization of decision making and the allocation of funds.

FINAL REFLECTIONS ON THE CHOICE OF STRATEGY

Considerable attention was given in Chapter 4 to the governmental decision-making process that determines a country's agricultural strategy. It was emphasized there that it is an oversimplification to assume that a government "opts" for a unimodal or bimodal strategy. It can be misleading to view the activities of the various organizations and individuals that comprise a government as though the process were analogous to purposive decision making by an individual human being. Graham Allison's analysis, to which we referred, emphasizes the need to supplement the "rational actor model" with an "organizational process model" and a "governmental politics model."[11] The former focuses on the role of specific organizations and parochial interests, organizational routines, and standing operating procedures. The latter model directs attention to the roles of individual participants who influence the outcome because of their position in the action channels pertaining to agricultural policy and agricultural programs.

The organizational structure and processes and the power of various individuals and groups to influence decisions will obviously be specific to an individual country—and to a considerable extent to a particular point in time. Hence, any serious evaluation of the administrative and political feasibility of alternative measures to promote agricultural development needs to be based on very specific knowledge of the administrative structure and the political and personal factors. A related implication is that attention to the decisions that determine a policy objective or preferred solution is only a first step: program implementation as affected by these same organizational and political influences may have a greater impact on shaping the final outcome than does the formal policy objective itself.

There is a growing awareness that problems of implementation are of crucial importance and considerable agreement that the performance of government field staff at the local level is often particularly unsatisfactory. Remarkably little attention has been given, however, to careful diagnosis of the reasons for this poor performance. A common response of the World Bank and other donor agencies has been to rely on administrative arrangements aimed at by-passing the problem. Thus, the implementation of aid-financed projects frequently involves the creation of a semiautonomous organization, usually with a considerable complement of foreign experts, rather than relying on existing field organizations. In brief, the emphasis has been on the direct management of projects rather than raising indigenous managerial capacity by training and by devising better procedures for implementing rural development programs and for monitoring and evaluating performance.

It is plausible to argue, however, that agricultural development objectives could be advanced much more effectively by measures to raise the level of performance of the existing organizations and field staff. Given the large resources in the form of trained personnel and recurrent expenditures already committed to these organizations, it is obvious that the potential return from obtaining a higher level of performance is very great. It is by no means obvious, however, that such improvement in performance is a realistic expectation. On the basis of their intensive study of agricultural administration in Kenya, Deryke Belshaw and Robert Chambers are persuaded that much better performance can be achieved by improving the formulation and implementation of agricultural programs. In particular they argue that it is feasible to devise and introduce management systems which make it easier to optimize the allocation of resources, particularly of staff time, between activities and which both encourage and require a higher standard of performance by field staff. They contend that these goals can be achieved by the use of suitable procedures for 1. translating plans into program targets, 2. involving field staff in the formulation of detailed work programs, 3. closer monitoring of the performance of field staff, and 4. reviewing the progress achieved in implementation as an input to the formulation of plans in subsequent periods.[12] A rural management system based on those principles is currently in use in Kenya on a pilot basis, but it is too early to judge its effectiveness. It is clear, however, that the success of programs to expand and improve the rural infrastructure and to promote farmer training and the diffusion of technical knowledge will depend to a large extent on action to strengthen program implementation under diverse environmental and institutional conditions.

Given the great diversity in development situations, what scope remains for general conclusions about the design and implementation of agricultural strategies? The possibilities for government action in any country will depend very much on views concerning priorities because these largely determine the "agenda" of problems and activities that will receive serious attention. In practice, experience that is fresh in the minds of policy-makers and the latest crisis are likely to dominate the agenda. For example, it is clear from a recent analysis of rice policy in Indonesia that awareness of the disastrous effects of soaring food prices has led to a dominant concern with price policy. Great sensitivity to the reactions of urban consumers and historical factors have created a bias in favor of direct action to control prices and the supply of rice rather than reliance on measures to improve the production possibilities available to farmers and on their response to prices that provide an adequate incentive to increased productivity and output.[13]

In view of the pressures on policy-makers to respond to immediate problems, it is especially important to identify those priorities that are of crucial importance in relation to the objectives of increasing farm productivity and output and promoting a pattern of agricultural development that will simultaneously enhance rural welfare and facilitate structural transformation. From that perspective, a list of priorities confined to the rural sector could be boiled down to a half dozen items[14]:

1. strengthening the research base;

2. influencing the size distribution of farm operational units to curb tendencies toward a dualistic size structure with subsectors using drastically different technologies;

3. expanding and improving the agricultural infrastructure;

4. promoting the diffusion of technical knowledge and wide access to external inputs;

5. improving systems of agricultural taxation; and

6. Undertaking certain direct measures to enhance rural welfare, for example, public health and nutrition programs, together with policies and programs that will accelerate the lowering of birthrates to levels compatible with sharply reduced death rates.

Merely to itemize priorities in this way is, however, only a beginning. Recognition of the need to translate those general priorities into concrete programs and to devise suitable institutional arrangements for implementation is obviously an important further step. We suspect, however, that the most critical aspect of the problem is to achieve a sufficient consensus among decision makers at various levels concerning the fundamental features of an agricultural strategy.

Achieving the minimum consensus required for decisions and action that will constitute an efficient unimodal strategy is extremely difficult. It is obvious that strong political forces will frequently limit the options that are feasible. However, the complexity of the issues involved represents an obstacle to reaching agreement that is additional to the difficulties that arise because of political constraints. The three conditioning factors that were outlined in the Prologue and examined in detail in subsequent chapters appear to be particularly germane to the task of forging the minimum consensus that is required.

The fact of being late and the magnitude of the technological backlog means that policy-makers in underdeveloped countries and in aid-giving agencies must be sensitive to the demanding task of drawing maximum advantage from the store of accumulated knowledge and techniques while minimizing the adverse effects of borrowing technologies that are ill-suited to their resource endowment. An especially difficult task, because of the vested interests that have been created among administrators as well as favored enterprises, is to eliminate or reduce the price distortions that encourage the direct transfer of inappropriately capital-intensive equipment and processes.

The effects of factor and product price distortions are not narrowly limited to the choice of production techniques for a given commodity; they extend to the composition of output itself. As frequently noted in earlier chapters, restrictions on imports for the purpose of curbing balance-of-payments deficits have been applied differentially. Since consumer goods are typically judged less essential to development than investment goods, foreign exchange rationing during the early stages of import substitution is greatest for the former. The relative scarcity (and hence profitability) of these consumer goods attracts the first wave of import-replacing industrial investments. To encourage the new infant industries, tariff duties on intermediate products and capital equipment that must be purchased abroad are fixed at low levels. The effects of these complementary foreign exchange and tariff policies are (a) to raise the average ratio of domestic industrial prices to world prices to above unity and (b) within the

INTERCOUNTRY VARIATIONS AND THE CHOICE OF STRATEGY 451

manufactured products category, to raise the ratio more for consumption goods than for capital equipment and raw materials. The resultant growth-inhibiting distortions divert resources from agriculture to industry and, within industry, lead to a concentration of investment in consumer goods irrespective of relative comparative advantage considerations. High-cost home industry combined with low duties on imported inputs means that further deepening of the industrial structure via backward linkages is very difficult. Since the new supplier industries themselves require protection, costs in the purchasing industries rise and the markets of all firms are contracted.

The importance of market-clearing pricing policies has been noted for the interdependence between agricultural development and the expansion of manufacturing and other nonfarm sectors. Here the most frequent impediment is rationing policies which deny scarce inputs to small-scale producers of farm equipment and inexpensive consumer goods which have the greatest potential for reaching the bulk of the farm population. Because of its impact on rural demand, a unimodal strategy re-enforces the output and income-distribution gains to be had by abandoning government-administered licensing schemes for market-clearing prices.

It has been emphasized repeatedly that the dominant position of the farm sector in these late-developing countries and their rapid rates of growth of population and labor force have strong implications for the design of an agricultural strategy. A direct consequence is the fact that the *average* farm unit is inevitably *small* and subject to a severe purchasing power constraint. Although the possibility of rapidly expanding agricultural exports modifies that constraint to some extent, especially in small countries, the fact remains that the volume of intersectoral commodity flows is constrained by the small size of the nonfarm sectors. Our stress on the effects of the size distribution of farm operational units and on the nature of the technological innovations that are made available as the third conditioning factor derives from those structural-demographic features. So also does the stress on expanding the agricultural infrastructure and ensuring wide diffusion of knowledge and inputs. And the emphasis on improving agricultural tax systems is related not only to increasing their effectiveness in mobilizing resources but also because of their potentially powerful influence on the size distribution of operational units and on rural income distribution.

Clearly these various considerations do not apply with equal force to all countries that might be classed as late developing. In countries such as Mexico or Brazil where considerable structural change has taken place the net advantages would no doubt be less than in countries at an earlier stage of structural transformation. A considerable development of agriculture based on a dualistic size structure has already taken place, and the costs of a drastic reorientation of policy at this stage might be substantial. However, even in the Brazilian case, high birth rates concomittant with the risks of subsistence farming and acute rural poverty remain endemic to the Northeast. It is difficult to envisage a solution to these two problems in the absence of measures that permit the mass of small cultivators in the region to partake in rising productivity and income. A similar situation, plus the need to expand more rapidly total agricultural output, obtains in most of Asia and Africa, and in much of Latin America. In these latter economies a dualistic farm structure has not yet taken root: elements of both the unimodal and the bimodal pattern are present. For these countries a unimodal agricultural development strategy promises a more rapid advance in per capita output as well as social and demographic advantages.

NOTES

1. Hla Myint, "The 'Classical Theory' of International Trade and the Underdeveloped Countries," *Economic Journal* Vol. 68, No. 270 (June 1958); and Bruce F. Johnston, "Changes in Agricultural Productivity," in *Economic Transition in Africa,* edited by Melville J. Herskovits and Mitchell Harwitz (Evanston, 1964).
2. William A. Hance, *Population, Migration, and Urbanization in Africa* (New York, 1970), pp. 421, 426.
3. Kenneth R. M. Anthony and Victor C. Uchendu, "Agricultural Change in Mazabuka District, Zambia," *Food Research Institute Studies* Vol. 9, No. 3 (1970).

4. Alain de Janvry, "Optimal Levels of Fertilization Under Risk: The Potential for Corn and Wheat Fertilization Under Alternative Price Policies in Argentina," *American Journal of Agricultural Economics* Vol. 54, No. 1 (February 1972), p. 10. Emphasis in original.
5. Bruce F. Johnston and John Cownie, "The Seed-Fertilizer Revolution and Labor Force Absorption," *American Economic Review* Vol. 59, No. 4 (September 1969), p. 570.
6. See Anthony and Uchendu, "Agricultural Change: Mazabuka," and Festus Ogada, "Maize in Kenya," in *Some Issues Emerging From Breakthroughs in Food Production,* edited by K. L. Turk (Binghamton, New York, 1971). It is estimated that between 1954 and 1971 the acreage planted to hybrid maize in Kenya increased from 30,000 to about 500,000 acres. Small farms, with some 344,000 acres planted to hybrids in 1971 compared to only 1750 acres in 1964, accounted for most of the increase. Carroll P. Streeter, *Reaching the Developing World's Small Farmers,* The Rockefeller Foundation (New York, 1973?), p. 48.
7. Malcolm J. Purvis, "The New Varieties under Dryland Conditions: Mexican Wheats in Tunisia," *American Journal of Agricultural Economics* Vol. 55, No. 1 (February 1973).
8. Ibid. p. 56. The correlation between mechanization and success in growing the new varieties may not have the causal significance suggested by Purvis. The new technology currently available is a spring wheat technology. And the valleys in which spring wheat is grown in Tunisia are occupied predominantly by large, mechanized farms. Progress is now being made in developing a new technology for durum wheat, the type that is grown by most small farmers; and their response may be quite different once an adapted technology is available. Don Winkelmann, personal communication, August 1973.
9. Randolph Barker and Don Winkelmann, "Cereal Grains, Future Directions for Technological Change" (Paper prepared for the Conference of the International Economics Association, Bad Godesberg, Germany, August 26-September 4, 1972), p. 10. The authors are the senior economists at the International Rice Research Institute (Barker) and the International Maize and Wheat Improvement Center (Winkelmann).
10. Guy Hunter, "Towards Criteria for Administrative & Institutional Choices, Related to the Continuum of Change," Reading University, Overseas Development Institute Joint Programme on Agricultural Development Overseas, Working Paper (London, 1971); idem, "Agricultural Administration and Institutions," *Food Research Institute Studies* Vol. 12, No. 3 (1973).
11. Graham T. Allison, *Essence of Decision: Explaining the Cuban Missile Crisis* (Boston, 1971).
12. See Deryke Belshaw and Robert Chambers, "A Management Systems Approach to Rural Development," University of Nairobi, Institute for Development Studies Discussion Paper No. 161 (Nairobi, January 1973). Their approach also has pitfalls. There is a danger that inappropriately complex and burdensome management systems will be imposed and that much staff time will be devoted to setting and reporting on targets that are not meaningful.

See Guy Hunter, *The Administration of Agricultural Development* (London, 1970), particularly pp. 62-64 and 97-99.

13. C. Peter Timmer, "Objectives and Constraints in the Formation of Indonesian Rice Policy: A Proto-Type Essay," Food Research Institute, Stanford Rice Project Working Paper No. 2 (Stanford, California, September 1973).

14. Perhaps the most conspicuous omission from this short list concerns policies related to the marketing of farm products. A fundamental feature of structural transformation is, of course, the need to progressively increase marketing efficiency and governments clearly have an important role to play in attaining that objective. In addition, there are often cogent reasons for a government buffer stock operation to moderate the seasonal rise in the price of a major staple food crop such as rice, wheat, or maize. There is, however, virtually no evidence to support the claims that are frequently made concerning the scope that is alleged to exist for substantially increasing farm prices while simultaneously reducing prices to consumers. Such allegations are based on false premises concerning the "inefficiency" of existing marketing systems that can be eliminated by creating a government organization charged with responsibility for "orderly" marketing. In fact, food marketing margins in developing countries tend to be low and the *average* seasonal price increase is generally in line with storage costs. It is weather-related fluctuations in output and the uncertainty to which they give rise that account for the large year-to-year variations in the magnitude of the seasonal price rise; and a government marketing operation cannot eliminate those fluctuations in output. Timely action to arrange for food imports and a well-managed storage program can reduce the magnitude of the variations in supplies available to meet market demand. Yet it must be stressed that the potential for mismanagement of a buffer stock program is considerable. Even if well managed, the financial and manpower requirements for such a program are substantial, as are the claims on the time of top policy-makers who must be involved in a number of difficult decisions, for example, the prices at which supplies will be purchased or sold, and the timing and volume of imports to augment releases from stocks.

Appendices

Appendix Table I. United States: *Growth of Total Agricultural and Nonagricultural Labor Force and Coefficient of Differential Growth, 1820-1960**

Year	Agricultural labor force as per cent of total (1)	Labor force (*thousand persons*)				Annual growth rate (*per cent*) [a]				Coefficient of differential growth (7)-(6) [b] (9)
		Total (2)	Agricultural (3)	Nonagricultural		Total (6)	Nonagricultural		Manufacturing (8)	
				Total (4)	Manufacturing (5)		Total (7)	Manufacturing (8)		

Lebergott's Estimates: Persons Aged 10 and Over

1820	78.8	3,135	2,470	665	...	...	...	...	...
1830	70.6	4,200	2,965	1,235	...	2.97	6.38	...	3.41
1840	63.1	5,660	3,570	2,090	500	3.04	5.40	...	2.36
1850	54.8	8,250	4,520	3,730	1,200	3.84	5.96	9.15	2.12
1860	52.9	11,110	5,880	5,230	1,530	3.02	3.44	2.46	.42
1870	52.5	12,930	6,790	6,140	2,470	1.53	1.62	4.91	.09
1880	51.3	17,390	8,920	8,470	3,290	3.01	3.27	2.91	.26
1890	42.7	23,320	9,960	13,360	4,390	2.98	4.66	2.92	1.68
1900	40.2	29,070	11,680	17,390	5,895	2.23	2.67	2.99	.44
1910	31.4	37,480	11,770	25,710	8,332	2.59	3.98	3.52	1.39
1920	25.9	41,610	10,790	30,820	11,190	1.05	1.83	2.99	.78
1930	21.6	48,830	10,560	38,270	9,884	1.61	2.19	-1.23	.58
1940	17.0	56,290	9,575	46,715	11,309	1.43	2.01	1.35	.58
1950	12.0	65,470	7,870	57,600	15,648	1.52	2.11	3.30	.59

1960	7.6	72,142	5,458	66,684	16,796	...	...	...
1969	4.3	84,239	3,606	80,633	20,121	1.74	2.14	2.03	.40

* The estimates for 1820 through 1960 are Lebergott's careful adjustments of available figures resulting in comparable data for this period. Military forces and unemployed persons are included in the nonagricultural figures. Data are from Stanley Lebergott, "Labor Force and Employment, 1880-1960," pp. 117-210 in National Bureau of Economic Research, Conference on Research in Income and Wealth, Vol. 30, *Output, Employment, and Productivity in the United States after 1800* (New York, 1966).

The alternative figures for 1960 shown as Current Estimates are included to permit comparison with 1969. These figures, which relate to the work force over 16 instead of 10, also include military forces and unemployed persons in the nonagricultural component. The included figures are as follows:

	1960	1969
Military forces	2514	3506
Unemployed	3852	2831

Data are from U.S. Bureau of the Census, *Statistical Abstract of the United States, 1970* (Washington, 1970), pp. 213, 218.
^a Annual percentage rate of increase (compound) from the preceding period.
^b Indicates the rate at which the percentage share of the nonagricultural labor force will increase.

Appendix Table II. Japan: *Growth of Total Agricultural and Nonagricultural Labor Force and Coefficient of Differential Growth, 1883-1968**

Year	Agricultural labor force as per cent of total (1)	Labor force (*thousand persons*)				Annual growth rate (*per cent*) [a]			Coefficient of differential growth (7)÷(6) [b] (9)
		Total (2)	Agricultural (3)	Nonagricultural		Total (6)	Nonagricultural		
				Total (4)	Manufacturing (5)		Total (7)	Manufacturing (8)	
1883-87	76.2	20,360	15,511	4,849	1,524	...	...	...	...
1893-97	69.2	22,258	15,397	6,861	2,393	.90	3.53	4.48	2.63
1903-07	62.6	24,252	15,184	9,068	3,263	.86	2.83	3.28	1.97
1913-17	56.3	25,967	14,613	11,354	4,131	.68	2.28	2.39	1.60
1920	52.4	27,263	14,287	12,976	4,357	...	...	...	...
1930	47.7	29,619	14,131	15,488	4,891	.83	1.78	1.16	.95
1940	42.3	32,478	13,842	18,636	7,160	.93	1.87	3.88	.94
1955	38.9	41,190	16,040	25,150	7,560	...	...	...	...
1964	25.6	46,730	11,970	34,760	11,370	1.41	3.66	4.65	2.25
1968	18.7	50,020	9,340	40,680	13,050	1.72	4.00	3.50	2.28

* Reproduced from B. F. Johnston, "Agriculture and Economic Development: The Relevance of the Japanese Experience," *Food Research Institute Studies*, Vol. VI, No. 3, 1966, p. 308. Data for 1968 from Japan, Office of the Prime Minister, Bureau of Statistics, *Monthly Statistics of Japan*, January 1971, p. 8.

Data from 1955-68 are for the employed labor force 15 years old and over; earlier data are for the gainfully employed. Agriculture includes workers in forestry; their number increased from about 200,000 to a peak of 520,000 in the mid-1950's.
[a] Annual percentage rate of increase (compound) from the preceding period. Growth rates were not computed for the periods ending 1920 and 1955 on account of statistical incomparability with the preceding period.
[b] Indicates the rate at which the percentage share of the nonagricultural labor force will increase.

Appendix Table III. Taiwan: *Growth of Total Agricultural and Nonagricultural Labor Force and Coefficient of Differential Growth, 1905-1966**

Year	Agricultural labor force as per cent of total (1)	Labor force (*thousand persons*)				Annual growth rate (*per cent*) [a]				Coefficient of differential growth (7)-(6) [b] (9)
		Total (2)	Agri-cultural (3)	Nonagricultural		Total (6)	Nonagricultural			
				Total (4)	Manu-facturing (5)		Total (7)	Manu-facturing (8)		
1905[c]	70.7	1404	993	411	80	...	...	...	...
1915[c]	70.9	1643	1165	478	132	1.58	1.52	5.13	−.08
1920[c]	69.5	1637	1137	500	146	−.07	.90	2.03	.97
1930[c]	67.7	1790	1212	578	152	.90	1.46	.40	.56
1940[c]	62.4	2244	1400	844	221	2.29	3.87	3.81	1.58
1952	61.0	2936	1792	1144	272	...	...	...	...
1956	59.9	3015	1806	1209	298	.66	1.40	2.31	.74
1960	56.1	3344	1877	1467	377	2.62	4.96	6.05	2.34
1964	54.2	3710	2010	1700	439	2.63	3.76	3.88	1.13
1966	53.0	3870	2050	1820	477	2.13	3.47	4.24	1.34

* Data for 1905 through 1930 from Taiwan, Govt. Stat. Bureau, *Statistical Summary of Taiwan in Past 51 Years* [translated title] (Taiwan, 1946), Table 59, pp. 130-31; for 1940 from Taiwan, Bureau of Accounting and Statistics, *Results of the Seventh Population Census of Taiwan, 1940* (Taiwan, 1953), Table 15, p. 60; data for 1952-66 from *Taiwan Statistical Data Book 1970*, p. 7, for persons aged 12 and over.

[a] Annual percentage rate of increase (compound) from the preceding period.
[b] Indicates the rate at which the percentage share of the nonagricultural labor force will increase.
[c] The labor force estimates for 1940 and earlier years are to be treated with caution. Changes in definition that affect the inclusion of women in the labor force are especially important in impairing the comparability of the figures for different years.

Appendix Table IV. Mexico: *Growth of Total Agricultural and Nonagricultural Labor Force and Coefficients of Differential Growth, 1895-1960**

	Agricultural labor force as per cent of total (1)	Labor force (*thousand persons*)				Annual growth rate (*per cent*)[a]			Coefficient of differential growth (7)-(6)[b] (9)
		Total (2)	Agri-cultural (3)	Nonagricultural		Total (6)	Nonagricultural		
				Total (4)	Manu-facturing (5)		Total (7)	Manu-facturing (8)	
Year									
1895	66.5	4,446	2957	1489	512	...	...	...	...
1930	68.6	5,352	3674	1678	531	.53	.34	.11	−.19
1940	65.4	5,858	3831	2027	567[c]	.91	1.91	.66	1.00
1950	58.3	8,272	4823	3449	1044	3.51	5.46	6.29	1.95
1960	54.2	11,332	6144	5188	1572[c]	3.20	4.17	4.12	.97

* Data for 1895, 1930, and 1950 as adjusted from the censuses by Donald R. Keesing, "Structural Change Early in Development: Mexico's Changing Industrial and Occupational Structure from 1895 to 1950," *Journal of Economic History*, December 1969, p. 724; data for 1940 and 1960 from International Labour Office, *Year Book of Labour Statistics, 1949-50*, p. 13 and *ibid.*, 1968, p. 77.
[a] Annual percentage rate of increase (compound) from the preceding period.
[b] Indicates the rate at which the percentage share of the nonagricultural labor force will increase.
[c] As reported plus one-fifth of those "insufficiently specified" (the adjustment for manufacturing specified by Keesing for both 1930 and 1950).

Appendix Table V. India and Pakistan: *Total Agricultural and Nonagricultural Labor Force**

	Agricultural labor force as per cent of total (1)	Labor force (*thousand persons*)			
				Nonagricultural	
Year		Total (2)	Agricultural (3)	Total (4)	Manufacturing (5)
Prepartition India					
1931	67.2	148,817	100,037	48,780	...
Indian Union					
1951	71.7	142,337	102,118	40,218	...
1961	72.9	188,675	137,546	51,129	17,906
Pakistan					
1951	75.5	22,393	16,903	5,490	1,420
1961	74.3	30,206	22,412	7,764	2,454[a]
East Pakistan (Bangledesh)					
1951	83.2	12,887	10,716	2,171	499
1961	85.3	17,443	14,872	2,571	...
West Pakistan					
1951	65.1	9,506	6,187	3,319	921
1961	59.3	12,763	7,570	5,193	...

* Data for Prepartition India and the Indian Union, 1961 are from the 1953 and 1968 issues of the International Labour Office (ILO) *Year Book of Labour Statistics*. The agricultural figures include forestry and fishing.
  Indian Union figures for 1951 for "self-supporting persons and earning dependents" are from India, Central Statistical Organization, *Statistical Hand Book of the Indian Union 1948-1957*, pp. 4-5. The agriculture figures may not include forestry and fishing.
  Data for Pakistan are from Pakistan, Central Statistical Office, *Pakistan Statistical Yearbook 1968*, Tables 9 and 11. The 1951 figures are for those aged 12 and over, the 1961 figures are for 10 and over; both years include those seeking work. The agricultural figures exclude forestry and fishing which, in 1951, amounted to 201,000 in East Pakistan and 22,000 in West Pakistan.
  Rates of change are not shown on this table because of the effects of changes in definition and territorial changes that impair the comparability of the figures for different years.
[a] Supplied from the ILO source cited above.

Subject Index

Administrative capacity, 444, 446
Agricultural strategy: bimodal, 32, 127-29, 132, 133, 139, 140, 151, 152, 156, 158, 162, 178, 179, 241, 257, 261-63, 265, 274, 275, 277, 281, 300, 302, 304, 305, 310, 360, 381, 382, 411, 422, 441, 443, 446, 449; choice of, 121, 130, 299, 437-52; competitiveness and complementarity among the objectives of, 128, 139, 140; design of, 65, 78, 127-81; economic constraints in the choice of means of an, 128, 132, 140-61; elements of an, 128-33, 409-31; objectives of an, 130, 132-40, 285; political constraints on the governmental decision-making process, 128, 153-61; unimodal, 17, 32, 127-29, 132, 133, 137, 139, 140, 142, 148, 151, 152, 156, 159, 160, 162, 166, 168, 171, 173, 178, 203, 232, 243, 244, 253, 255, 257, 274, 290, 302, 304, 305, 325, 381, 393, 422, 428, 446, 450, 451
Agricultural sector, contributions to economic development, 133, 134, 187, 212, 213, 243, 256, 257, 270, 276, 284-88, 321, 323
Agriculture: associations, 250, 434; commercialization of American, 198-201; cooperatives, 445; development, factors determining the pattern, 64, 74, 133, 161, 173; labor force ratio, *see* Farm labor force ratio; methods, 22-25, 57, 149; research, 72, 92-95, 129, 132, 141, 147, 161, 207-12, 224, 230-32, 250-52, 257-61, 274, 287, 288, 316, 393, 407, 411-13, 416, 421, 431; zones, 19-22
Agriculture-industry interactions, 134, 212, 299-324
Agronomic practices, improvement of, 405, 412-14, 421
Algeria, 351
Argentina, 6, 114, 440
Asparagus, 254, 323
Attitudes and behavior in rural communities, changes in, 128, 133, 136-39, 290, 410
Australia, 78

Bangladesh, 136, 175, 179, 290, 399
Barbados, 248
Belgium, 336
Bimodal, farm size structure, 17, 18, 175, 452; *see also* Agricultural strategy, bimodal
Birthrate, 78, 80-83, 85, 86, 139, 242, 449
Brazil, 17, 75, 80, 152, 170, 175, 177, 178, 452

Canada, 270
Capital formation, 43, 119, 178, 216, 252, 264, 302, 325, 344
Capital intensity, 88, 89, 91, 109, 110, 119, 220, 311, 313, 325
Capital-labor ratio, 91, 107, 111, 114-16, 119, 307, 311, 313, 315, 381

Capital markets, *see* Financial intermediation
Catching-up process, 294, 389-431
Ceylon, 78, 80, 84
Change: readiness of rural communities and farmers to accept, 437, 444-46; sequences of, and their cumulative effect on rural progress, 169-73
Chile, 6, 8, 11, 37, 78, 80, 99, 100
China, 157, 158, 276, 332, 351, 384
Climate, 19-22
Coffee, 270
Collectivization of Soviet agriculture, 277-88
Colombia, 15, 17, 18, 120, 126, 127
Commodity markets, 41, 42, 43, 327
Comparative advantage, 299, 302
Costa Rica, 324
Cotton, 177, 205, 260, 265, 266, 270

Death rate, 78, 80-82, 139, 240, 242, 449
Demographic revolution, *see* Population growth
Denmark, 35, 234
Despecialization, 107, 113
Differentiation, 34, 42, 52
Division of labor, 25-27, 30, 34, 41, 49, 52
Dualistic pattern of agricultural development, *see* Bimodal, farm size structure

Economies of scale, 37, 49, 51, 58, 105, 120, 152, 164, 204, 355
Egypt, 84
Employment expansion, *see* Labor absorption
England, 4, 19, 50, 76, 77, 113, 182, 183-90, 195, 207, 240, 372, 374
Equipment, *see* Farm equipment
Ethiopia, 72, 73, 75, 174, 302
Exports, the role of, 299, 321-24

Factor productivity, total, 187, 196, 221, 222, 258, 262, 287-89, 298
Factor proportions: fixed, 87, 115; problem, 87-121, 299
Family planning, 138, 139, 175, 412
Farms: cash disbursement pattern, 68, 69, 72, 132, 315, 407; cash income, 64, 65, 67, 69, 72, 75, 134, 141, 142, 149, 199, 200, 215, 219, 243, 257, 319, 321, 355, 394, 398, 399, 423, 424, 427, 432, 438, 441, 442; demand, aggregate level, 302; demand, pattern of, 134, 299, 302-7, 319; equipment, 299, 303, 311, 317, 328, 352-84, 392, 393, 414, 430, 439, 442, 444; (*see also* Farm mechanization); labor force, 60, 64, 188, 193, 194, 195, 204, 214, 223, 227, 235, 238, 243, 246, 253, 254, 272, 274, 282, 291, 294, 296, 399, 400; labor force ratio, 4, 8, 76, 84, 86, 188, 194, 196, 243, 272, 282, 291, 294, 399; labor productivity, 142-48, 214, 244, 246, 288, 289, 381, 390; mechanization, 78, 201-7, 209, 224, 232, 236, 241, 260, 265, 266, 280-82, 287, 396, 403, 417-27, 431, 443 (*see also* Farm equipment); population, welfare of, 128, 133, 135, 136, 290, 410, 412, 449; productivity, 183, 190, 191, 246, 320, 431, 437, 440, 449; purchasing power constraint, 65, 128, 141, 147, 152, 300, 317, 323, 353, 360, 421, 424, 451; size, economics of, 262-67; wages, 230, 232, 233, 243, 274
Fertilizer: demand for and consumption of, 223, 227, 246, 253, 259, 282, 289, 291, 319, 329, 330, 400, 403, 406; developments in the world fertilizer market, 329-33, 399; factory, location of, 348-52; input to agriculture, 3, 44, 54, 64, 68, 92, 149, 151, 168, 172, 191, 205, 208, 209, 227, 260, 273, 303, 328, 352, 412, 416, 423, 424, 438; investment cost, 73, 169, 254, 257, 399, 401, 407; new varieties, 93, 95, 224, 295, 414, 418, 422, 433, 440, 442; organic, 165, 237, 389; prices, 92, 95, 97, 98, 230, 233, 237, 239, 331, 332, 392, 440; technology, 77, 95, 97, 98-103, 227, 230, 299, 310, 311, 329, 333-48
Financial intermediation, 43-45, 48, 244, 258

INDEX

Foreign exchange constraint in manufacturing, 300, 302, 323
France, 337

Genetic engineering, *see* Plant breeding
Germany, 100, 187, 235, 358, 367, 374
Ghana, 19, 26, 65, 323, 324
Government decision-making models; government politics, 177, 447; induced development, 154, 227, 232; organizational process, 177, 447; rational actor, 153, 446
Government policies, *see* Monetary policy; Pricing policies; Taxation policies
Green revolution, 93, 120, 394; *see also* Seed-fertilizer revolution

Haiti, 86
Highland zones, 32
Holland, 9
Hong Kong, 109

Import: control, 116, 117, 325, 392; substitution, 37, 67, 77, 78, 115-17, 146, 265, 267, 275, 301, 308, 399, 424
Income distribution, 17, 18, 72, 86, 111, 119, 135, 139, 140, 147, 159-61, 162, 169, 171, 177, 180, 244, 264, 272, 304, 305, 312, 316, 409, 410, 428, 445, 451
Income elasticity of demand: food, 65, 67, 146, 215, 301, 304, 325; manufacturing, 39, 301, 325; personal services, 75
India, 13, 18, 23, 37, 67, 76, 80, 86, 93, 108, 112-14, 120, 124, 126, 149, 161, 167, 168, 173, 175, 236, 259, 299, 305, 311, 324, 334, 339-44, 345-48, 355, 357, 359-61, 366-71, 372, 374-76, 385, 386-88, 394-411, 423, 425, 429, 432, 443
Indonesia, 12, 84, 175, 248, 289, 290, 298, 329, 351
Infrastructure investments, 252, 258-61, 316, 393, 411, 413, 427, 431, 449

Innovations: divisible and complementary, 148-53; sequence of, 142-48
Institutional: environment, 444-46; innovation, theory of, 154-56
Intermediate technology, 105-14, 120, 301
Intersectoral: commodity flows, 285; resource flows, 244, 256, 257, 270, 271, 285, 292, 299, 301, 302, 315-21, 431, 451
Iran, 351
Irrigation, 328, 329, 384, 412, 414-18, 421, 422, 425, 434, 438, 439, 445
Italy, 113, 123
Ivory Coast, 324

Japan, 9, 13, 17, 50, 69, 76, 77, 84, 93, 108, 113, 123, 124, 127, 134, 143, 154, 173, 182, 183, 187, 190-96, 203, 207-33, 240, 242, 246, 248, 250, 254, 259, 289, 290, 313, 321, 332, 333, 351, 358, 361, 363, 374, 387, 393, 394, 422, 430

Kenya, 113, 114, 138, 175, 214, 237, 324, 384
Korea, 113, 114, 138, 175, 214, 237, 324, 384

Labor: absorption, 61-63, 139, 160, 198, 272; addition, 107, 113, 114; market, 42, 43, 57; productivity, 61, 62, 317; productivity, aggregate, 226, 227; slack, 150, 151, 243, 274; surplus, 149
Labor force, distribution of, 58-64
Labor intensity, 108-10, 118, 119, 315
Land: ownership, distribution of, 160, 162, 165, 168, 171, 179, 249, 428; productivity, 244, 291; rental payments, legal ceilings on, 163, 164, 165, 428; tenure arrangements, 17, 55, 72, 162-69, 178; tenure policies, 129, 147, 428
Land reform, 156, 158, 162, 163, 165-71, 218, 244, 249, 250, 255, 256, 262-67, 271, 293, 428
Libya, 9, 11, 37, 123, 351

Livestock, 277, 278, 280, 389
Lorenz curves, 15, 17
Maize, 136, 223, 233, 260, 267-70, 272, 274, 275, 287, 295, 441-43, 453, 454
Malaysia, 12, 78
Malnutrition, 6, 7, 290
Manufacturing productivity, 226, 227
Markets, government influence on, 45-47
Meat, 270
Medical technology, 77, 78-87, 412, 449
Mexico, 77, 80, 84, 86, 93, 114, 126, 127, 134, 143, 145, 175, 233, 240-42, 250, 257-76, 290, 295, 441, 442, 452
Mobilization of resources for development, 148; *see also* Intersectoral resource transfers
Monetary policy, 78, 117, 428
Mushrooms, 254, 323

Natural resources, 8-13
New Zealand, 35, 78, 121
Nigeria, 25, 26, 29, 30, 109, 111, 112, 120, 126, 329, 351, 443
Norway, 100
Nutrition, 3, 6, 7, 55, 412, 449

Off-farm income, 219, 220, 243
Operational units, size distribution of, 13, 15, 18, 72, 147, 148, 160, 162-69, 396, 412, 421, 427-31, 449, 451

Pakistan, 18, 67, 112, 114, 119, 149, 168, 175, 180, 236, 259, 299, 305, 308-11, 313, 315, 334, 342-45, 347, 348, 355, 359-61, 367, 368, 371-74, 376, 377-81, 385, 386, 388, 394-409, 420, 423, 425, 429, 431-33
Peru, 11, 99, 120, 126
Philippines, 75, 93, 167, 433
Physical environment, 437-44
Plant: breeding, 92-95, 136, 224, 233; protection measures, 405, 412, 414

Population growth, 64, 77, 87, 115, 187, 195, 240, 242, 267, 289, 290, 317, 400, 439
Potatoes, 260, 288
Poverty, 156, 157, 171, 178, 290, 410
Price distortions, 162, 230, 267, 311-15, 396, 414, 419, 420, 424, 428, 445, 450, 451. *See also* Pricing policies
Pricing policies, 114-21, 129, 147, 168, 214, 219, 220, 266, 267, 282, 324, 375, 382, 449, 454
Process simplification, 111, 112, 115, 120
Production function, 49, 88, 91, 93, 233, 304, 406
Productivity: differentials, intersectoral, 62; growth, 47-51; *see also* Factor productivity, total
Product variation, 109, 111, 115, 307
Project evaluation, 130, 174
Public health technology, *see* Medical technology

Rain forest zone, 20
Rationing of scarce inputs, 46, 168, 217, 218, 267, 301, 375, 445; *see also* Pricing policies
Rice, 92-95, 123, 203, 210, 214, 219, 220, 247, 248, 251, 254-57, 305, 394, 397, 398, 400, 409, 443, 454
Riverine areas of alluvial zones, 21
Roumania, 351
Rural works programs, 136, 140, 160, 175

Savanna zone, 19, 20, 439
Sector models, construction of, 130
Seed-fertilizer revolution, 67, 95, 112, 148, 161, 167, 207, 233, 268, 305, 316, 360, 394-412, 441
Senegal, 13, 18, 29
Share tenancy, 168, 169, 179, 205, 254, 426
Silk industry in Japan, 210, 211
Social change, elements of, 51-58
Soviet experience, relevance of, 288-90
Soviet Union, 158, 240-42, 276-90, 332, 351; state farms, 277-88

INDEX

Specialization, 34, 41-49, 52, 54, 57, 64, 65, 73, 79, 134, 200, 210, 283, 301-3, 320
Strawberries, 270
Structural change, patterns of, 35-40
Structural transformation, 4, 34-77, 84, 86, 90, 115, 121, 128, 133, 134, 135, 152, 153, 182, 187, 214, 218, 240, 242, 244, 290, 299, 319, 321, 323, 353, 395, 410, 411, 449, 454; rate of, 132, 135, 161; turning point, 142, 194, 196, 218-21, 243
Substitution: capital for labor, 118; labor for capital, 106, 107, 303
Sugarcane, 251, 256, 270, 319, 418
Sweden, 4, 26
Sweet potatoes, 255

Taiwan, 15, 17, 72, 73, 75, 77, 78, 80, 84-86, 93, 113, 114, 127, 134, 138, 143, 145, 151, 173, 175, 214, 233, 237, 240-50, 270, 289, 290, 299, 302, 303, 308, 311, 313-15, 317-21, 323, 324, 333, 334, 340, 347, 348, 353, 354, 357-59, 361, 363-65, 367, 372, 374, 386, 393, 394, 407, 408, 422, 430, 437
Tanzania, 80
Target setting for agricultural commodities, 129, 130, 173
Taxation policies, 46, 55, 72, 129, 139, 147, 213, 230, 236, 249, 257, 280, 316, 427-31, 449, 452
Technology: adoption, 299; backlog, 76-121, 182, 206; choice of, 87-92, 98, 110; transfer of, 90, 105
Terms of trade, 66-68, 117, 146, 211, 275, 316, 317, 320, 323, 324
Togo, 8, 37
Tomatoes, 270
Tunisia, 442-44, 453

Unimodal, *see* Agricultural strategy, unimodal
United States, 4, 35, 50, 69, 72, 73, 75, 77, 78, 84, 93, 98-100, 113, 114, 124, 143, 154, 182, 183, 187, 189-209, 221-33, 240, 259, 265, 266, 270, 275, 302, 303, 313, 332, 341, 354, 358, 361, 363, 393
Urban sector, 29-31

Venezuela, 329, 351
Vent-for-surplus economies, 438
Vietnam, 384
Wheat, 77, 92-95, 123, 259, 260, 265-70, 275, 280, 281, 283, 286, 288, 305, 394, 396-400, 403-6, 409, 412, 419, 422, 423, 425, 433, 443, 453, 459

Zaire, 11
Zambia, 439, 441, 442

Name Index

Adams, D. W., 170, 178, 180
Agrawala, R. C., 433
Allied Chemical, 334
Allison, G. T., 153, 177, 446, 453
Almeida, A. L. O. de, 75
Anthony, K. R. M., 33, 442, 452, 453
Arthur, H. B., 74
Athwal, D. S., 123, 124
Ayer, H. W., 177

Bakewell, R., 184
Baldwin, K. D. S., 33
Balis, J., 388
Banerji, R., 144
Baranson, J., 387
Barber, W. J., 176, 436
Barclay, G. W., 292
Bardhan, P. K., 179, 433
Barker, R., 443, 453
Beckett, W. H., 26, 33
Bell, D. M., 102, 124, 343, 385
Belshaw, D., 448, 453
Bennett, R. L., 292
Berg, A., 174
Bergson, A., 285
Bhagwati, J. N., 177, 384, 385
Bird, K. M., 74
Bosch, C., 101
Boulding, K. E., 174
Brazil, Instituto Brasileiro de Estatística, 14, 16
Breeze, S., 235
Brewster, J. M., 33, 178, 181, 255, 292
British Sulphur Corporation, 331

Brothers, D. S., 292
Butler, G., 144

Caird, J., 189, 234, 235
Cano, J., 273, 274, 295
Chambers, J. D., 234, 235
Chambers, R., 448, 453
Chancellor, W., 379, 435
Chao-chen, C., 292
Chaudhry, M. Ghaffar, 430, 436
Chemical Consultant Ltd., 385
Chen, Y. E., 176
Chenery, H. B., 39
Cheung, S. N. S., 168, 179
Chiang, General Kai-shek, 255
Chilalo Agricultural Development Unit, 174
China, Republic of, Commission of I.C.C.T., 310
China, Republic of, Council for International Economic Cooperation and Development, 85, 292, 343
Ching, Adrienne, 292
Chou, Howell, 387
Christensen, R. P., 291
Clark, C., 5, 7, 32
Coke, T., 186
Collings, G. H., 124
Cownie, J., 122, 123, 402, 432, 453
Crisostomo, C. M., 245
Cummings, R. W., 436
Curtler, W. H. R., 234

Dalrymple, D. G., 269, 295
Dalton, G., 181
Dandekar, V. M., 173

Danhof, C. H., 191, 199, 200, 201, 235, 236, 393, 432
Dantwala, M. L., 410, 432, 434
Dapice, B., 175
David, P., 236
Davis, L. E., 154, 155, 156, 177
Day, R. H., 204, 205, 236, 426
Desai, P., 177, 384, 385
Dina, I. O., 33
Dobb, M., 284, 297
Dovring, F., 84, 122, 226, 239, 265, 294, 296
Duff, B., 402, 432
Duignan, P. J., 126
Duloy, J. H., 295
Durrani, M. T., 387

Eckert, J. B., 406, 433, 434
Ernle, Lord R. E. P., 183, 184, 234, 235
Ethiopia, Central Statistical Office, 71

Falcon, W. P., 136, 175
Ferree, P., 32
Fertilizer Association of India, 343
Fertilizer Corporation of India (FCI), 332, 339, 340
Fertilizers and Chemicals (FACT), 339, 340, 385
Fesca, M., 207
Festinger, L., 181
Finney, C. E., 434, 435, 436
Fishel, W. L., 176
Fishlow, A., 178
Fliginger, C. J., 293
Flores, E., 263, 294
Ford Foundation, 81
Frank, A. G., 298
Frankel, F. R., 167, 179
Freebairn, D. K., 75, 179, 261, 293
Freithaler, W. O., 293, 294, 295
French, J. T., 166, 179
Friedland, W. H., 75
Fung, K. K., 326

Galletti, R., 33
Gallman, R., 199
Gandhi, V. P., 435

Gann, L. H., 126
Gardner, R., 121
Gatovski, Lev Markovich, 297
Geertz, C., 289, 298
General Agreement on Tariff and Trade, Contracting Parties to the (GATT), 322
Gibb, Sir Alexander, 14
Gibb, Arthur, 75
Gilbert, Sir Joseph Henry, 186, 234
Gill, K. S., 434
Gittinger, J. P., 173
Goldberg, R. A., 74
Goreux, L. M., 296
Gossling, W. F., 226, 229
Gotsch, C. H., 180, 236, 386, 426, 434, 435
Gourou, P., 21, 32
Guha, S., 175
Gurivaiah, N. C. R., 370, 387
Gustafson, W. E., 434

Haber, F., 100
Halcrow, Harold G., 235
Hall, Sir A. D., 186
Hamid, J., 435
Hance, W. A., 439, 452
Hansen, R. D., 16
Hardt, J. P., 296
Harrington, R. E., 434
Harwitz, M., 452
Haswell, M., 5, 7, 32
Hayami, Y., 121, 144, 154, 177, 192, 193, 220, 221, 225, 230, 232, 234, 235, 237, 238, 239
Heady, E. O., 141, 173, 176
Helmer, O., 174
Hemmi, K., 237
Henderson, D. R., 102, 124, 343, 385
Hendrix, W. E., 433
Herdt, R. W., 93, 94, 123, 436
Herskovits, M. J., 452
Hertford, R., 293
Hicks, W. W., 293
Hirschman, A. O., 155, 169, 171, 177, 180, 181
Ho, S. P. S., 292
Hopkins, R. F., 177
Horcasitas, V., 292

INDEX

Hoselitz, B. F., 75
Hsieh, S. C., 291
Hsing, Mo-Huan, 291, 314
Hufbauer, G. C., 313, 325
Hunter, G., 29, 33, 453

Ilchman, W. F., 177
India, Government of, Cabinet Secretariat, 14, 16
India, Government of, Development Commissioner, 125, 387
India, Government of, Ministry of Agriculture, Directorate of Economics and Statistics, 432
India, Government of, Planning Commission, 434, 435
Indian Society of Agricultural Engineers, 388
International Bank for Reconstruction and Development (IBRD), 10, 14, 36, 66, 74, 330, 384, 386
International Center for Tropical Agriculture (CIAT), 126
International Crop Research Institute for the Semi-Arid Tropics (ICRISAT), 126, 443
International Federation of Planned Parenthood, 81
International Institute for Tropical Agriculture (IITA), 126, 443
International Labour Office (ILO), 14, 85
International Maize and Wheat Improvement Center (CIMMYT), 120, 126, 259, 443, 453
International Potato Center (IPC), 126
International Rice Research Institute (IRRI), 120, 121, 126, 251, 398, 433, 443, 453
Inukai, I., 231, 239
Islam, N., 178, 308, 309, 325

Jackson, W. A. D., 296, 297
Jacobs, K. D., 124
Janvry, Alain de, 440, 452
Jasny, N., 284, 297
Jiménez Sánchez, L., 295
Johl, S. S., 435, 436

Johnson, D. G., 179, 281, 287, 296, 298
Johnston, B. F., 33, 123, 176, 177, 178, 234, 237, 238, 239, 386, 402, 432, 452, 453
Joint Commission on Rural Reconstruction (JCRR), 71, 292, 352
Jones, E. L., 186, 187, 189, 234, 235
Jones, W. I., 269, 295
Jones, W. O., 74, 176
Joy, L., 177

Kamarck, A. M., 22, 32
Kaneda, H., 237, 238
Kaohsiung Ammonium Sulphate Corporation (KASC), 334, 340
Karcz, J. F., 284, 287, 296, 297, 298
Katō, Y., 237
Katz, E., 181
Kautsky, Karl, 297
Kawano, S., 220, 238
Keesing, D. B., 294
Khan, A. Rahman, 311, 312, 313, 325
Kilby, P., 124, 125, 126, 386
King, T., 295
Kishida, Y., 387
Klein, J. L. V., 202, 235
Kocher, J. E., 175
Krause, K. R., 236
Krishna, R., 435, 436
Kuroda, Y., 229, 239
Kuznets, S., 40, 48, 58, 59, 60, 61, 74, 75
Kyle, L. R., 236

Landes, D. S., 190, 235
Latham, M. C., 175
Lawes, Sir J. B., 98, 99, 185, 186, 234
Lawrence, R., 379, 435
Lebergott, S., 197, 226, 234, 235, 239
Lee, T. H., 176, 245, 256, 291, 292, 317, 318, 320, 326
Leff, N., 83, 122
Leites, N., 177
Lele, U. J., 305, 307, 325
Lenin, V. I., 277, 297
Levine, G., 434

Lewin, M., 284, 297
Lewis, J. P., 151, 176
Lewis, S. R., 313, 325, 326
Leys, C., 156, 157, 158, 167, 177, 179, 180
Liebig, Baron Justus von, 98, 186, 191, 207
Lim, Y., 327
Little, I., 125, 126, 326, 327, 348
Lockwood, B. B., 432
Lockwood, W. W., 217, 238
Lorimer, F., 290, 296
Lowdermilk, M. K., 402, 432
Lyman, P. N., 166, 179
Lysenko, T. D., 287

Ma, F. C., 386
MacArthur, General Douglas, 256
Malthus, Thomas R., 290
Manne, A. S., 296
Mao Tse-tung, 157, 277
Marx, Karl, 155, 297
Mason, R. H., 387
Matsukata, M., 230
Mellor, J. W., 93, 94, 123, 176, 305, 307, 325
Merrett, S., 339, 384, 385
Mexico, Direccion General de Estadistica, 14
Mill, J. S., 137, 175, 186
Millar, J. R., 285, 298
Minami, R., 238
Mingay, G. E., 234, 235
Mobil Oil Company, 334
Moore, W. E., 75
Morse, C., 75
Mosher, A. T., 181
Mueller, E., 122, 138, 175
Mukherjee, P. K., 432
Musgrave, R. A., 139, 175
Myers, R. H., 292
Myint, H., 438, 452
Myren, D. T., 261, 267, 273, 274, 293, 294, 295

Nagaiya, D., 370, 387
Nakajima, C., 176
National Bureau of Economic Research, 234, 235
National Institute of Agricultural Research (INIA), 259

National Productivity Council, 32
Nedelin, S., 283
Nelson, R. R., 174, 178
Neva, 298
Newbery, D., 179
Nicholls, W. H., 152, 176
North, D. C., 154, 155, 156, 177
Norton, R. D., 295
Nove, A., 282, 296, 297
Nunn, C., 297

Obolenski, K. P., 283, 297
Ogada, F., 453
Ogura, T., 237
Ohkawa, K., 123, 192, 216, 220, 229, 237, 238, 434
Olson, M., 179
Organisation for Economic Co-Operation and Development (OECD), 348, 386
Organization of Petroleum Exporting Countries (OPEC), 333, 350, 351
Owen, W. F., 153, 176, 177

Pack, H., 106, 124
Page, J. M., Jr., 177
Pakistan, Government of, Planning Division, 384
Papi, U., 297
Parker, W. N., 181, 202, 206, 208, 235, 236
Patten, R., 175
Peña, F. de la, 265
Peng, T. S., 386
Perkins, G. R., 102, 124, 343, 385
Pillet, B., 292, 294
Poleman, T. T., 75, 179
Popkin, B. M., 175
Population Council, 81
Population Reference Bureau, 122
Preiser, E., 178, 180
Punjab, Government of the, Planning and Development Department, Bureau of Statistics, 314, 433, 434
Purvis, M. J., 453

Quereshi, S. A., 433

Ranis, G., 113, 125, 292
Rao, C. H. H., 180, 435

INDEX

Raup, P. M., 178, 236, 296, 297, 298
Raynaud, E., 176
Reidinger, R. B., 434
Reisegg, F., 173
Repetto, R., 385
Rescher, N., 174
Reyes Osorio, S., 265, 271, 294, 295
Reynolds, C. W., 263, 264, 271, 292, 294, 295
Reynolds, L. G., 179
Rockefeller Foundation, 259
Rodman, W. L., 295
Roemer, M., 12, 32
Roskill, O. W., 372, 373, 387
Rosovsky, H., 216, 236, 238
Rothschild, K. W., 178
Ruttan, V. W., 121, 144, 154, 177, 192, 193, 221, 225, 230, 232, 234, 237, 238, 239

Sahota, G. S., 97, 124
Sansom, G. B., 239
Sargen, N. P., 236
Scalapino, R. A., 238
Schebeck, E. M., 435
Schuh, G. E., 435
Schultz, T. P., 177
Schultz, T. W., 122, 174, 178
Scitovsky, T., 125, 126, 326, 327
Scott, M., 125, 126, 326, 327
Seers, D., 177
Sen, A. K., 174, 176, 434
Shah, S. L., 433
Shand, R. T., 432
Shen, T. H., 292
Shinohara, M., 192, 229
Simantov, A., 69, 75
Singarimbun, M., 298
Singh, G., 434, 435
Sisler, D. G., 75, 322, 323, 326
Slack, S. V., 124
Slighton, R. L., 174, 178
Smelser, N. J., 75
Smith, E. H., Jr., 125, 374, 387
Smith, T. C., 179, 212, 237
Solís, L., 264, 265, 292, 293, 294
Southworth, H. M., 33, 176, 178, 181
Srinivasan, T. N., 179
Stalin, Joseph, 277, 278, 285
Stavenhagen, R., 265
Stewart, F., 110, 125

Streeter, C. P., 295, 453
Stringer, H., 294
Suachelli, V., 124
Swamy-Rao, A. A., 387

Taiwan Fertilizer Corporation (TFC), 333, 334, 340, 385
Takasaka, T., 386, 387
Tang, A. M., 297
Taylor, L., 39
Teketel Haile-Mariam, 71
Thomas, B., 235
Thorbecke, E., 123, 130, 174, 296
Timmer, C. P., 324, 453
Townshend, Charles Townshend, 2nd Viscount, 184, 186
Treml, V. G., 296
Tsuchiya, K., 238
Tull, J., 184, 186
Turk, K. L., 434, 453
Turner, F. J., 197
Turnham, D. J., 291
Tussing, A. R., 231, 239

Uchendu, V. C., 442, 452, 453
Umemura, M., 192, 229, 235
United Nations, 79, 125, 291, 343
United Nations, Food and Agriculture Organization (FAO), 5, 10, 14, 15, 16, 32, 36, 66, 85, 330, 384
United Nations, Industrial Development Organization (UNIDO), 124
United States, Agency for International Development, 322
United States, Agency for International Development, Office of Capital Development, 343
United States, Department of Agriculture, 71, 96, 229, 432, 433
United States, Department of Commerce, Bureau of the Census, 74, 235
United States, Public Health Service, 80
Uphoff, N. T., 177

Venn, J. A., 234

Wädekin, K. E., 296
Walker, H. O., 32
Warr, P., 177

Warriner, D., 167, 178, 179, 234, 428, 435
Waterston, A., 174
West Pakistan Industrial Development Corporation (WPIDC), 336, 337
Wharton, C. R., Jr., 176, 267, 294
White House, The, 105
Wilczynski, J., 297
Williams, W. A., 235
Williamson, H. F., 235
Winkelmann, D., 176, 273, 274, 295, 443, 453
Winston, G., 119, 125, 126
Wittfogel, K. A., 297
Wolf, C., Jr., 177

World Health Organization (WHO), 22, 80
Wortman, S., 294
Wriggins, W. H., 177

Yamada, S., 144, 235, 237
Yang, C. W., 386
Yokoi, T., 209
Young, A., 183
Yuan, M. H., 385
Yudelman, M., 144

Zaman, M. Raquibuz, 180
Zambre, M. T., 370, 387
Zarembka, P., 176